Corpus Christi

A History

Corpus Christi

A History

Murphy Givens

and

Jim Moloney

Nueces Press

Published by Nueces Press, Corpus Christi, Texas.

Cover design by Jeff Chilcoat

Library of Congress Cataloging-in-Publication Data   2011925015

Givens, Murphy

Corpus Christi – A History / Murphy Givens and Jim Moloney.

ISBN   978-0-9832565-0-2

www.nuecespress.com

Alan —

Your 50th is a date in history —

We thought this history of where you are from should be on your coffee table — Robert & Linda

2011

We dedicate *Corpus Christi–A History* to our wives
Karen W. Givens and Candace Moloney.

PUBLISHER'S REMARKS

After the publication of *1919-The Storm*, Murphy Givens and I were frequently asked if and when there would be a future compilation of Murphy's columns from the *Caller Times*. We both agreed that such a book would be difficult to publish due to the brevity of each column and the change of subjects each week. We noted that there had not been a new history of Corpus Christi published since the Walraven book of the early 1980s and decided that a history of Corpus Christi based upon Murphy's extensive notes and references and written in his style would be in order.

This book, *Corpus Christi – A History,* is the result of our discussions. Murphy Givens has captured much of the colorful history of our city, including stories of its citizens and trends through time. My role in this publication was that of a sounding board; offering comments on the writing, asking questions, watching for the occasional error or typo and arranging the book for publication. It was a team effort, but Murphy Givens led the team.

While most of the plates illustrating our book come from our personal collections of Corpus Christi ephemera, we are grateful to several institutions for giving permission to use their material. They are Corpus Christi Museum of Science and History, Corpus Christi Public Library, Brownsville Historical Association, Institute of Texan Cultures, Museum of the Confederacy, *Texas Highways*, Texas Capital Archives, Texas A&M University – Corpus Christi Library Special Collections. Special thanks are offered to the Corpus Christi Public Library for use of the Local History Archives, where much of the basic research was done.

We owe a debt of gratitude to Mary Jo O'Rear and Fr. Michael Howell for reviewing the manuscript and offering constructive comments before publication. Many thanks to Sylvia Ronan who provided critical help in formatting the book for publication. And a final thank you to Michelle Haas for her work on a final edit and sending the manuscript off to the printer. All errors and omissions are our responsibility.

Jim Moloney
Nueces Press

FOREWORD

This book started as an idea discussed by Jim Moloney and me. The original plan was to do a compilation of my historical columns published in the *Caller-Times* from 1998 through 2009, but that fell through and we decided that a history of Corpus Christi, based on my research done in preparation for the history columns, might be worthwhile. Most of the information in this book has been published here and there over a period of years. What we have done is to collect, organize and put together the various strands in the city's and region's history in what we hope will be a useful whole. We have relied heavily, and owe a debt of gratitude, to historians and writers of history who have written about the city, including Mary Sutherland, Coleman McCampbell, Eugenia Reynolds Briscoe, Bill Walraven, among many others. We have also relied heavily on newspaper stories, which have rightly been called the first draft of history.

For the main part, this history begins with the founding of Corpus Christi in 1839 and carries on through Hurricane Celia in 1970. After that there is an epilogue that covers some of the high points of the decades that followed Celia. The cutoff point for the main narrative was purely arbitrary; it could have been the 1980s or 1990s or beyond. But getting too close to our own time would cloud our historical judgment and, from a practical standpoint, every book has only so much space; trying to cram in the events of more recent years would reduce the space available for the long-ago past which, we believe, has a greater interest. You would like to have some closure, some neat date when the narrative can end with an emphatic period that has some symbolic meaning. But this cannot be since the history we're attempting to cover is still happening today and tomorrow. Time marches on and the conclusion is not in sight.

There are so many stories connected to the history of Corpus Christi that no single book can help but leave some out. Some are given short shrift and some are given no shrift at all. You could fill a book, for instance, with the history of the city's struggles to find an adequate source of water; in fact, Atlee Cunningham wrote such a book. Tom Lea filled two thick volumes telling the story of the King Ranch. So to cover the city's history, from 1839 to 1970, requires some abbreviation, some condensation, and some choices of what to put in and what to leave out. In the end, the choices fell entirely to me. That's what writing is all about. Other writers would no doubt make different choices. A substantial amount of space is devoted to events that fall well outside the city proper. But if Corpus Christi is to be understood, one must also try to understand the larger territory around it. In the early years, when the city was small, the region around it was more dominant. In the 20th Century, after the port was built, the city became more dominant. This history reflects that shift.

The logic behind the divisions of the chapters should be explained. Big events, war and peace, for instance, can be said to begin and end periods in history. But at other times, historical periods overlap, with no clear beginning or ending. The rise of the cattle and sheep industry spread across three decades. Reconstruction straddled the latter part of the 1860s and first part of the 1870s. Except for the end of the Civil War and the end of World War II, which ended definite periods of history, the chapter divisions were arbitrary, made for convenience.

We can call this a history. And it is, I suppose. But I like to think of it as a story—the story of a city, of a region, of a people, of events that have shaped our lives more than we probably know. If this book creates a desire to learn more about the city's rich and colorful history, then it will have served its purpose. We can claim no higher function than that.

Murphy Givens

TABLE OF CONTENTS

CHAPTER 1   1

Old Indian trading grounds
The cannibals of the coast
Early times at Kinney's Rancho
"Robber Texians"
Comanche raid and discovery of the reef road
Kinney in the Texas Senate

CHAPTER 2   13

Zachary Taylor's troops land on North Beach
"Fort Marcy"
Steamer Dayton explodes
Training for war with Mexico
U.S. Grant in Corpus Christi
Leaving for the Rio Grande

CHAPTER 3   25

Corpus Christi's "lost years"
Mustang Gray's Rangers
"Buffalo Hunters"
The "Great Chihuahua Train"
Going to California in the Gold Rush
The scalping of Charles Bryant
Tragedy at Doyle's Watering Hole
The first census
Henry Kinney's Lone Star Fair
The Army returns and the Fandango Riot

CHAPTER 4   39

Richard King and King Ranch
The slaying of "Legs" Lewis
Henry Kinney's immigrants
Yellow fever epidemic

CHAPTER 5   49

Runaway slaves
Secession and Civil War
Blockade and the Cotton Road
The bombardment of Corpus Christi
Yankee commander is captured at Flour Bluff
War brings hard times

CHAPTER 6   61
  Union troops capture Fort Semmes
  Gen. Bee retreats
  The trial and hanging of Chipita Rodriguez
  A terrible drought
  The killing of Mat Nolan
  The bloodiest war in the nation's history comes to a merciful end

PLATES   *Chapters 1 to 6*   73

CHAPTER 7   89
  County is reorganized after the war
  Union troops occupy city
  Jim Garner hanged
  Yellow fever outbreak ravages city
  Corpus Christi judge becomes hated governor
  Trail drives begin to Kansas
  Market Hall opens

CHAPTER 8   103
  Birthplace of the cattle industry
  Cattle kings and sheepherders of the Nueces Valley
  Corpus Christi, a leading great wool market
  Lawless times follow the Civil War
  Dredging of ship channel across the bay

CHAPTER 9   119
  Skinning War of South Texas leaves a trail of violence
  Beef packing houses slaughter cattle for hides and tallow
  1874 hurricane floods downtown
  Nuecestown Raid scares Corpus Christi
  The Mercer logs

CHAPTER 10   135
  Schools and education
  Train to Laredo
  Wool trade ends
  Richard King dies
  Shooting clouds
  Fire burns a block of Chaparral
  The Ropes boom
  Fitzsimmons on North Beach
  The boys of '98
  Blizzard of '99

CHAPTER 11   151
  Anderson windmill torn down
  City lands Epworth revival
  Former McNelly Ranger goes on trial
  Ranch lands turned into farm plots
  City copes with first automobiles
  President Taft comes to visit
  Streets paved and bluff balustrade built
  1916 hurricane
  Soldiers trained at Camp Scurry
  City stricken in Spanish flu epidemic

PLATES   *Chapters 7 to 11*   170

CHAPTER 12   189
  1919 storm
  "Temporary" causeway to Portland
  Streetcars reach the end of the line
  Electric light plant burns
  Sheriff tried for murder
  Four men killed in brothel shootout
  Pleasure Pier lives up to its name
  City celebrates port opening
  "Skyscrapers" built on the bluff

CHAPTER 13   205
  Causeway opens Pat Dunn's Island
  Ben Garza heads LULAC
  Wall Street crash ushers in Great Depression
  Dance marathon on North Beach
  Oil found in Saxet Field
  La Fruta Dam collapses
  "Old Ironsides" visits port
  City gains its first chemical plant
  President Roosevelt lands a tarpon
  Seawall gives city a new look

CHAPTER 14   223
> *War in Europe affects port business*
> *Flour Bluff chosen for Navy base*
> *City experiences growing pains*
> *Driscoll Hotel built on the bluff*
> *Pearl Harbor attack stuns city*
> *U-boat threat leads to blackouts*
> *People learn to cope with war rationing*
> *President Roosevelt visits NAS*
> *Escaped POWs caught on North Beach*
> *Roosevelt dies*
> *War ends*

CHAPTER 15   235
> *Postwar Corpus Christi*
> *Causeway to Padre Island opens*
> *Marine reservists leave for Korea*
> *Refineries, chemical plants build on salt flats around the port*
> *The great legacies of Clara Driscoll and Ada Wilson*
> *Schools and education*
> *Harbor Bridge replaces the bascule bridge over Hall's Bayou*
> *North Beach falls on hard times*

CHAPTER 16   255
> *City builds new airport near Clarkwood*
> *Carla a near miss for Corpus Christi*
> *O&R reopens as Army Depot*
> *NASA tracking station monitors early space flights*
> *City annexes Flour Bluff, but not without a fight*
> *Three fishermen slain in a bizarre crime*
> *Dr. Hector P. Garcia leads fight for equal rights for Mexican-Americans*
> *Religion got a slow start in Corpus Christi*
> *A storm named Celia wreaks havoc*

EPILOGUE   271

PLATES   *Chapters 12 to 16*   275

MAPS   300

APPENDIX   309

ENDNOTES   311

PLATES LISTING

1.1   Henry L. Kinney
1.2   Zachary Taylor
1.3   Army Encampment
1.4   U. S. Grant
1.5   Lone Star Fair Prizes
1.6   1850 Texas Census
1.7   Flinthoff Painting
1.8   Richard King
1.9   Land Promotion
1.10   Ranchero Special Edition
1.11   Union Exploits
1.12   Attack on Corpus Christi
1.13   Major Mat Nolan
1.14   Corpus Christi Men on the Border
1.15   Thomas J. Noakes

2.1   Merriman Grave
2.2   Governor Davis
2.3   Oxcart
2.4   Market Hall
2.5   Stock Brands
2.6   Mifflin Kenedy
2.7   Grocery Receipt
2.8   Aransas
2.9   Bird's Eye View
2.10   Bar Signals
2.11   Mercer House
2.12   Uriah Lott
2.13   Ocean Park
2.14   Alta Vista
2.15   Anderson Windmill
2.16   Epworth-by-the-Sea
2.17   George H. Paul Co.
2.18   Land Excursion
2.19   Land Clearing
2.20   Road Building in St. Paul
2.21   Country Road
2.22   Taft's Visit
2.23   Welcoming Outfit
2.24   1916 Hurricane
2.25   Camp Scurry

PLATES LISTING - Continued

3.1	1919 Hurricane
3.2	Causeway
3.3	C. C. Street & Interurban Ry. Co.
3.4	Bayfront Pier
3.5	Port of Corpus Christi
3.6	Nixon Building
3.7	The Exposition
3.8	Nueces Coffee Company
3.9	Ranch House
3.10	Driftwood Corral
3.11	Ben Garza
3.12	Saxet Field
3.13	North Beach
3.14	Dam Collapse
3.15	Frigate's Arrival
3.16	The U.S.S. Constitution
3.17	Southern Alkali
3.18	Fishing Trip
3.19	Bayfront Work In-Progress
3.20	Step by Step
3.21	Amphitheater on the Bay
3.22	Building the NAS
3.23	Naval Air Station
3.24	Flight Times
3.25	Driscoll Hotel
3.26	U-Boats in the Gulf
3.27	Christmas 1945
3.28	ASARCO
3.29	Clara Driscoll
3.30	Sam and Ada Wilson
3.31	Incarnate Word
3.32	High School
3.33	New High School
3.34	Old and New Bridges
3.35	Carla
3.36	Dr. Hector P. Garcia
3.37	Pres. Lyndon and Lady Bird Johnson
3.38	Celia

CHAPTER 1

Old Indian trading grounds - The cannibals of the coast - Early times at Kinney's Rancho - "Robber Texians" - Comanche raid and discovery of the reef road - Kinney in the Texas Senate

Before it was called Kinney's Rancho, before it was Corpus Christi, the place along the curve of the bay was known as the old Indian trading grounds. It was a place where traders landed contraband goods, like bales of leaf tobacco, to avoid paying customs duties to the government of Mexico, far from the prying eyes of customs officials. They could land goods on the beach and then load them on pack trains to carry into Mexico. A more fitting name of the place could have been the smugglers' trading grounds. That was the place that came to be called Kinney's Rancho and then the frontier settlement of Corpus Christi.

Trader John J. Linn[*] in 1829 landed a cargo of tobacco at the site, planning to meet a man named Wright with a mule train to haul the tobacco to Camargo in Mexico. Linn found no settlement at the place that became Corpus Christi.[1] Another trader, H.A. Gilpin, landed that same year with goods for sale in Mexico. Like Linn, he saw no signs of civilization.[#2]

The written record citing Corpus Christi for this time is scant. A high government official, Gen. Manuel de Mier y Teran, made a tour of the Mexican state of Texas in 1828. Teran noted that some officials favored Corpus Christi for a port, referring only to a place on the bay since there was no settlement called Corpus Christi.[3] Gen. Juan Nepomuceno Almonte mentioned Corpus Christi as a port in 1834 and Col. Enrique de la Pena, with the retreating Mexican army after San Jacinto, datelined the stop of June 2,

---

[*] John Joseph Linn had a mercantile business in Victoria. He was a quartermaster for the Texas Army during the Revolution and later founded the town of Linnville on Matagorda Bay. He wrote his autobiography called *Reminiscences of Fifty Years in Texas*. Linn died in Victoria in 1885 (*Handbook of Texas*).

[#] Henry Alfred Gilpin, a native of Halifax, Nova Scotia, was in business in Matamoros, where he met Frederick Belden. He became a business partner of Belden's and moved to Corpus Christi in the 1840s. He held various offices in Nueces County, including that of chief justice.

1836 as "Corpus Christi."[4] Like Teran, the colonel was probably referring to the vicinity of the bay. As for Almonte mentioning it as a port, he probably meant that it was a place where shallow-draft vessels could unload goods, not that there was a settlement at the place.

Surveyors in 1838 camped where the city would be built. "We saw no indication of any former settlement at this place," wrote the Rev. Z. N. Morrell, "but were informed by an Irishman accompanying the surveyors that this was the point at which the colony of San Patricio procured its supplies."[5]

The old Indian trading grounds were still being used as a place to land goods. While traders and surveyors found no village here, author Mary Sutherland wrote that a shipwreck survivor in 1824 found villagers living where Corpus Christi is today. She believed the villagers were killed in an Indian attack and the survivors carried into captivity.[6] There is some evidence to support this story, though the time and details vary. In 1902, 18 human skeletons were dug up on the grounds of the Nueces County Courthouse on Mesquite Street. An oral history account attributed the remains to a raid by Lipan Apaches in 1835. Those killed were said to be employees of a ranchero, Alejandro Garcia, whose ranch was west of where the city was later built. When the Indians attacked, Garcia and his ranch workers fled. The Lipans gave chase and caught them at the present site of Corpus Christi where they were all killed. After the massacre, Mexican soldiers and rancheros from San Antonio arrived and buried the victims.[7] As far as the written record goes, these were times of misty pre-history. Time exists only where there is someone or something to mark its passage.

That misty pre-history along the Texas coast belonged to the Karankawas and their tribal relatives. They occupied the coast from Galveston Island to Corpus Christi, drifting in and out of their favorite haunts. The men were tall, over six feet, and carried bows of red cedar as tall as they were. They could use those bows with great accuracy. They smeared their almost naked bodies with alligator grease. The men's hair was braided with rattlesnake rattles tied at the end; they made a rustling sound when they walked. They poled their dugout canoes on the lagoons and bays and ate great quantities of shellfish. Their guttural language, consisting of whistles, grunts and sighs, was like nothing ever heard.* They were said to be, and probably were, cannibals.[8] In their defense, W.W. Newcomb, Jr. and others have noted that the cannibalism they practiced was distinct from that of eating human flesh for food, that they ate pieces of the dead to gain an enemy's courage and strength. It has also been noted, in a favorable reassessment of the Karankawas, that they may have been "the most maligned and misunderstood Native American peoples who once inhabited Texas."[9]

---

* Alice Bridges, the daughter of a settler on the shores of Matagorda Bay, learned as a child to speak the language. In later years, she relayed what she could remember of the Karankawan language to Albert S. Gatschet, a linguistic scholar studying the Indian languages of Texas.

Cabeza de Vaca was shipwrecked somewhere on the Texas coast in 1528. When he encountered Karankawas, the curious Indians reached out to touch his face, which Cabeza took to be a gesture of shared human identity.[10] Two decades later, 300 survivors of a shipwrecked Spanish fleet washed ashore on Padre Island. It was summer, when Karankawas camped on the island. The Indians gave food to the survivors, but the Spanish noted that, for friends, they had many arrows. They soon put them to use, slaying the Spanish as they tried to flee in the sand dunes. All but two of the 300 were slain.[11] In 1684, Sieur de la Salle's French colonists built Fort St. Louis on Garcitas Creek off Matagorda Bay. The Karankawas attacked the fort, killing all the colonists but five children, whom they took away. A Spanish expedition later recovered the five children. One of them told how he went hungry for three days during a cannibal feast. And he told how the Karankawas cried when the French youngsters were taken away.[12]

French seaman Jean Beranger, who explored the coast in 1720, landed on Harbor Island where he watched Karankawas whip the water to attract fish, then shoot them with their arrows.[13] Fray Gaspar Jose de Solis in 1767 recorded a Karankawan celebration in which a victim was tied by a fire while the Indians with sharp knives would dance up to the victim and slice off a bit, roast it in the fire, and eat it before the victim. But de Solis didn't see this himself; he got it secondhand. He said Father Joseph Escovar of the San Rosario Mission near Goliad found the Karankawas to be "barbarous and lazy." Escovar's low opinion was shaped by the fact that the Indians preferred their liberty as cannibals rather than living as converted Christians by the mission.[14] About 1818, Jean Laffite's pirates on Galveston Island kidnapped a Karankawa girl. In retaliation, the Indians captured and ate two of Lafitte's men. This led to a battle in which 30 warriors were killed. They left Galveston Island to the pirates.[15] In the 1820s, Stephen F. Austin's colonists signed a treaty with the Karankawas, but killings on both sides continued. Austin wrote that the cannibals were "universal enemies to man" and that the approach of civilization "will be the signal for their extermination."[16]

Mexican Gen. Manuel de Mier y Teran, on an inspection tour of Texas, wrote in admiration that Austin's colonists knew how to deal with the Karankawas. "If the Indians kill a settler, a large party of settlers would set out to hunt down and kill 10 of the tribe, of any age or sex." By such decimation, he wrote, the Karankawas had become almost extinct.[17] Noah Smithwick said the Karankawas lived on fish and alligators "with a man for fête days when they can catch one."[18] Wilbarger said they were "the Ishmaelites of Texas, for their hands were against every man, and every man's hand was against them."[19]

J.H. Kuykendall tells this story. In 1834, before the Texas Revolution, people in Victoria—Martin de Leon's town—persuaded Tonkawas in the area to wipe out some troublesome Karankawas. The Tonkawas visited the

3

Karankawas and took a small boy with them. The boy was a able to cut all the bowstrings of the Karankawas, after which the Tonkawas attacked, killing 20 Karankawan warriors, all but two or three of that tribe.[20]

This wasn't the first time they tried to wipe out the Karankawas. Kuykendall said the de Leons were beset by Comanches stealing their horses and Karankawas killing and eating their cattle. The Karankawas were accused of eating more than cattle. Martin de Leon, said Smithwick, organized his men to attack the Karankawan camp. He mounted a four-pounder cannon on a jackass and planned to wipe out the tribe. He ran the Karankawas to cover, brought his cannon to bear, and touched it off. But he did not take the precaution of bracing up the jackass and the cannon's recoil turned the jackass into a flying somersault, landing him on top of the gun with his feet in the air. The Karankawas fled.[21]

One of the de Leons in Victoria came up with another plan to kill off this tribe. He bought arsenic and dumped it into a pot of boiled hominy corn, which was given to the Karankawas. To his surprise, the Karankawas came back the next day asking for another pot of corn. The store owner had substituted cream of tartar for arsenic.[22] The arsenic didn't work, but the future of the Karankawas was annihilated all the same. Over time, they may have been decimated, as many Indians were, by measles, smallpox, tuberculosis. However it happened, they were doomed. In 1844, a few ragged Karankawan survivors were killed in a battle south of Corpus Christi by a ranging company from Mexico under the command of Capt. Rafael Aldrete.[23] The last of the Karankawa, reduced to a dozen families or so, were living in abject poverty in Tamaulipas.[24] Almost nothing about the Karankawas remains, not the place names of their stomping grounds, only a few shell middens and burial grounds. With history being written or distorted by the winners, the Karankawa story from their point of view will never be told. They were hunted down, pushed off their land, reduced to misery itself. Their world collapsed.

Were they the savage man-eaters depicted by their enemies? As Newcomb pointed out in *The Indians of Texas*, there is nothing in De Vaca's account to suggest that the Karankawan tribes he lived among practiced cannibalism. The accounts of the Spanish priests De Solis and Fray Morfi were based on hearsay; they did not see the cannibalistic rites themselves. But A.J. Sowell, an early Texas pioneer, has a damning account of a Karankawa raid on a Texas settlement on the Lower Brazos. In the raid, the Karankawa warriors killed several persons and carried off a little girl: "After going some distance, they camped, killed the child, and proceeded to eat her, first splitting open the body, then quartering it, and placing the parts on sharp sticks and cooking them." The settlers surprised the Indians during the feast and killed all the men; a woman and two children escaped. Later, the settlers found the woman and two children and killed them.[25] Austin, who led expeditions against the Karankawas, wrote in his diary for Sept. 5 and 6,

4

1824 that they found a deserted Karankawa encampment with the bones of two men who had been cut up and boiled. They called the site Cannibal Creek.[26] Naturalist Roy Bedichek in *Karankaway Country* related the story of an Indian warrior mesmerized by watching the sun go down. "Early explorers report a curious habit of the Karankawan warrior. At times he was fascinated by the sight of the sun submerging itself in the sea. The wonder of sunset over water was too much for the mind of this simple savage. He became still as a statue, oblivious to his surroundings, gazing spellbound at the point on the horizon where the waters had closed over and quenched this great ball of fire. Finally, in the deepening dusk, he stirs. The fire has gone out. The sea is gray again. The rattles awaken as he moves away toward his camp behind the dunes."[27]

"The Karankawa are gone," writes Bedichek. "Only bitter memories of them remain. In the minds of our people they are eternally damned, largely because they refused a culture we offered, resisting our proffered blessings to the last . . ."[28]

The retreating Mexican army, after their defeat at San Jacinto, crossed the Nueces River at the Santa Margarita crossing, an old ford that had been used since the time when Spain ruled Texas; it was just south of the village of San Patricio. The retreating Mexican army came by under the command of the Italian-born Gen. Vicente Filisola. One tale repeated for many years is that Filisola ordered Fort Lipantitlan destroyed and two cannon, a two-pounder and a four-pounder, dumped into a mud slough by the river. That tale is not substantiated in any known records of the time.[29] The old fort of Lipantitlan was established in 1830 on the recommendation of Manuel de Mier y Teran; the name refers to Lipan land.[30] The fort ostensibly was constructed to guard the Santa Margarita crossing, but mainly to discourage immigration. The commander of the fort in 1831 was Capt. Enrique Villarreal, a famous Indian fighter. One Texan described the fort as more pig-pen than fort.[31] Three years later, the federalist army under Gen. Antonio Canales used the old fort as a staging ground for the coming campaign in Mexico. This was during the federalist-centralist civil war when the northern states of Mexico were trying to secede from the central government at Mexico City. This conflict began before the Texas Revolution and resumed afterwards. The federalist army at Lipantitlan, with the support of Texas, hoped to establish a Republic of the Rio Grande.[32]

In September of 1839, Henry Kinney, a 25-year-old merchant from Pennsylvania via Illinois, moved from Live Oak Point* to the old Indian trading grounds that later became the site of Corpus Christi and built a trading

---

* Henry Kinney and partner William Aubrey opened a store in James Power's town of Aransas City on Live Oak Peninsula near the old Spanish fort of Aranzazu. It was at the south end of where Copano Bay Causeway is today.

5

post on the bluff with a view of the bay. Corpus Christi has been a settlement in continuous use since that fall day in 1839. Kinney's customers were the remnants of the federalist army camped at Fort Lipantitlan*# biding their time and preparing for another campaign in northern Mexico. A number of Texans, under the leadership of Reuben Ross and S.W. Jordan, signed on to the federalist cause. The Texas volunteers were promised $25 a month, half a league of land, and whatever plunder they could carry off.[33] After the defeat of Gen. Antonio Canales at Monterrey, the Texans crossed the Rio Grande and returned to Texas. Gen. Canales built up his forces again, to about 700 men, and was again defeated, bringing an end to the Republic of the Rio Grande and the federalist-centralist struggle in Mexico.

While the federalist forces were camped at Lipantitlan, Kinney sold them supplies.[34] The old Indian trading grounds at the mouth of the Nueces was a good location that put him closer to the old Spanish fort than other traders up the coast, and he may have been freighting supplies up the river; the Nueces was navigable then. Kinney called his store and the settlement taking shape around it Kinney's Rancho, but by 1841 in letters to Mirabeau B. Lamar, president of the Republic of Texas, he was calling it Corpus Christi, after the bay.[35]*#

Between its founding in 1839 and Texas becoming one of the United States in 1846, Corpus Christi was at the limits of the frontier. It was essentially the capital of no man's land, which for decades to come would be a favorite venue for lawbreakers on both sides of the border. During the time of the Republic, both Texas and Mexico claimed the territory between the Nueces River and the Rio Grande, the area known as the Nueces Strip and the Wild Horse Desert. But neither country held possession of this sparsely settled region. In past years, before the Republic of Texas was established, possession of the region had been more Indian than Spanish, more Spanish than Mexican, and more Mexican than Texican.

With Mexico and the Republic of Texas claiming this no man's land, Kinney played it safe. He kept friendly contacts with both sides. He was going to be on whichever side prevailed. On one day, Kinney would write Mirabeau Lamar, president of the Republic of Texas, then he would write Gen. Mariano Arista, his influential friend in Matamoros.[36] A British consul

---

* Lipantitlan was so named because it was a camping place, a convention site, of the Lipans on the west bank of the Nueces, just below the later town of San Patricio. Until the 1840s, it was said, large herds of buffalo roamed the area around the site.
*#John P. Kelsey, who had a store on Water Street, claimed credit for first calling the village Corpus Christi. The first known reference to Corpus Christi is on Diego Ortiz Parrilla's map of 1766. Parrilla led an expedition in search of English intruders rumored to be on Padre Island. His map shows two tents with the notation *"Campamento en la playa Corpus Christi"* (Encampment on Corpus Christi Beach). Another issue of energetic pedantry for more than a century is whether Alonso Alvarez de Piñeda, sailing around the Gulf looking for a passage to the East Indies, named the bay Corpus Christi when he passed by, supposedly, on the Feast of Corpus Christi, 1519.

at Galveston, William Kennedy, wrote a dispatch saying that Corpus Christi was important as a Texas trading post, "which Mexican contrabandists resort to for the purpose of smuggling goods across the Rio Grande."[37]

In May, 1841, Philip Dimmitt, a hero of the Texas Revolution, set up a trading post on the Laguna Madre at Flour Bluff* for the purpose of selling or smuggling goods across the Rio Grande. His partners in the venture were James Gourley Jr. and John Sutherland. Dimmitt was preparing to compete with Kinney for a share of the Mexican trade. A unit of Mexican cavalry under Gen. Pedro Ampudia, another friend of Kinney's, raided Dimmitt's store. The Mexican soldiers carried away merchandise and seized Dimmitt and two other men. The Mexican force spent the night near Kinney's Rancho, but Kinney's place was not molested.[38] It looked peculiar, as if Dimmitt's place had been intentionally targeted for the raid. Dimmitt apparently committed suicide while he was under arrest in Mexico.

Kinney and his partner William Aubrey were suspected of having a hand in the affair, perhaps even of instigating the attack to get rid of a competitor. They were tried in Victoria before Judge A. Hutchinson on charges of treason and, after a hurried trial, were found not guilty. But the suspicion that they were somehow behind Dimmitt's capture and death never went away. Kinney's influential friend, President Lamar, may have played a role that resulted in the speedy trial and the acquittal. If Lamar intervened behind the scenes, the reason, other than his friendship for Kinney, was explained in a sworn statement to the court by Kinney and Aubrey: "We have lived on the extreme frontier nearly two years, unprotected by our government. Our object has been the Mexican trade, to do which we have necessarily been at great expense, having had for three months some 30 to 50 men in our employ for no other purpose but protection; we have purchased arms and ammunition, we have made a stockade, mounting a 12-pounder and two small pieces, and when at home we are ready to receive our friends or enemies."[39]

During the early years of Corpus Christi's history, before statehood, Mexican cavalry patrolled parts of the region, perhaps as a way to assert Mexico's claim to the land between the rivers. The Republic of Texas was broke; it didn't have much of an army. It tried to enforce its claim to the disputed land by authorizing volunteer "spy" companies to patrol the region and keep an eye on the activities of Mexican forces. Some of these spy companies, who were not paid, took their authority as a license to plunder, to continue the war by attacking peaceful traders from Mexico. The loot was rich and protection weak. Several massacres were perpetrated against peaceful merchants. Mexico retaliated by sending cavalry patrols into the Nueces Strip to hunt down and punish the rogue spy companies. The time between the Revolution and the Mexican War a decade later was in many

---

* It may have been on Ward Island, though the exact location has never been pinpointed.

ways a continuation of war by other means.[*40]

One spy company of 40 men under John Yerby operated out of Corpus Christi.[41] Kinney in a letter to Lamar called Yerby's men "robber Texians" and urged the president to take steps to stop them from preying on peaceful traders. "Having arrived home two days back," Kinney wrote Lamar on Aug. 15, 1841, "we find as expected a gang of desperadoes on our frontier perfectly regardless of the rights of anyone, robbing indiscriminately . . . if this state of things continue, we shall be compelled to give all up for lost at this place."[42]

In one attack, eight merchants from Mexico were killed for their goods and in an argument over dividing the spoils Yerby's band split up, with most of the men leaving with James Ornsby (also spelled Ormsby). A force of 200 Mexicans (Kinney called them "rancheros") ambushed the remnant of Yerby's company south of Corpus Christi at La Parra and nine of the band, including Yerby, were killed. The men who went with Ornsby disbanded and some were hired as gunmen by Kinney.[43] Another renegade spy company riding out of San Patricio was led by W. J. Cairns (also spelled Karnes). This outfit attacked a caravan of Mexican traders that left Kinney's Rancho on Christmas Day, 1841. A Mexican patrol caught up with Cairns, killing him and four others in his band.[44]

Between the Texas Revolution and Texas statehood, the Wild Horse Desert was a place of roaming bands, with Texas volunteer companies operating on both sides of the law and with Mexican military units and volunteer "rancheros" sent into the region to punish the renegade Texians. There were outlaws, army deserters, bandits, and hostile Indians. In the final years of the Republic, it truly was no man's land and Corpus Christi, with a population of fewer than 100 people, was its capital.

Early in 1842, war clouds loomed over Texas and Mexico. Periodic and sporadic raids into South Texas from Mexico became more militarized and organized expeditions. On March 5, sizable Mexican forces crossed the Rio Grande and captured Refugio, Victoria and San Antonio, and held them briefly, before returning to Mexico. This looked to be a renewal of a state of war between Texas and Mexico, now that the federalist-centralist civil conflict in Mexico had ended.[45] Back in office, President Sam Houston, with limited resources at his command, called out the Galveston Coast Guards, called the "Sea Fencibles," and ordered them to Corpus Christi on board the steamer *Lafitte* and the sloop *Washington*.[46] Houston also appealed for volunteers from the United States. The volunteers who arrived in Texas were directed to Corpus Christi. By June of 1842, U.S. volunteers, comprising six companies of 266 men, were at Corpus Christi. They were described as a drunken, unruly body of men not inclined to follow orders.[47] The volunteers would not accept the commanders appointed by Houston, insisting they had

---

[*] South Texas, as part of a contested border, was always a point of friction between Texans and Mexicans.

8

the right to elect their own officers, and then turned to robbing and plundering outlying houses.[48]

Texas Adjutant General James Davis arrived to take command. He was ordered to move the unruly troops to Fort Lipantitlan up the Nueces River, away from Corpus Christi.[49] Many of the volunteers deserted and drifted away.[50] Davis also had spy companies and rangers join his forces. Aware of the concentration of Texas and U.S. volunteers at Lipantitlan, Mexico sent a force of some 700 poorly armed militiamen and ranchero volunteers under the command of two colonels, Antonio Canales and Cayetano Montero.[51] Canales knew the area well from his time at Lipantitlan as commander of the federalist army.[52]

They attacked the Texas volunteers at Lipantitlan early on July 7, 1842. The Texans and their volunteers fell back to a gully near where the old fort had been. One account of the battle, reported by the *Houston Telegraph and Texas Register*, said the Texans were amused at the way the Mexican soldiers fired their weapons in all directions, blazing away at nothing: "The Mexicans, when in the act of firing their guns did not take aim, but pointed the guns towards us and just as they were about to fire turned their faces away, as if they were afraid to look in the direction they wished to shoot."[53]

One ranger in Ewen Cameron's spy company, Nathan Boone Burkett, said the Mexicans had one cannon "which played over us with grape and canister shot" but did no damage. He said after the battle that five Mexican soldiers were killed, "that we know of."[54] Col. Canales' account of the half-hour battle is considerably different. At the first sound of firing, Canales said, the Texans ran, not stopping until they were "inside their burrow." He said the concentrated fire of his infantry forced the Texans to "turn in flight again into the densest part of the forest." Col. Montero wanted to enter the thicket and "kill all the cowardly Texans," but it was deemed inadvisable to subject his soldiers to such danger.[55] Canales reported that 22 Texans were killed in the battle while he lost four men, with two others badly wounded.[56] Canales' force returned to Mexico.

The next incursion came in September when Gen. Adrian Woll seized San Antonio and fought an encounter against the Texans at Salado Creek. The Texas and American volunteers who fought at Lipantitlan, still under the command of James Davis, withdrew to the town of Lamar on the Lamar peninsula.[57] The Congress of the Texas Republic, on July 15, passed a resolution thanking the American volunteers who came to aid the Texans "in their present critical emergency."[58]

In Corpus Christi, Henry Kinney faced his own emergency. The land he had leased from Dr. Levi Jones, a Galveston lawyer and land speculator, on which Kinney's trading post and his ranch were located, was apparently owned by Capt. Enrique Villarreal,* who had been granted grazing rights on

---

* Capt. Enrique Villarreal was in command of Mexican forces at Lipantitlan when the army of

9

the ten leagues of land called the Rincon del Oso by the governor of Tamaulipas in 1831, when the land was indisputably part of Mexico. (A league in distance was 2.43 miles; a square league was 4,428 acres.) That Oso tract included the site of today's Corpus Christi.

Villarreal showed up with a small army to reclaim his 590 square miles of land on the shores of Corpus Christi Bay. Kinney convinced Villarreal that he had booby-trapped the place with secret bombs, which could be detonated.[59] Kinney also agreed to pay Villarreal $4,000 (10 cents an acre). Kinney bought the Rincon del Oso grant from Villarreal on July 16, 1843. It took Kinney seven years to finish paying for the land.[60]

During this time, Indian depredations were made against the settlement of Corpus Christi. Most of the attacks in the Corpus Christi area were mounted by Comanches from central Texas and by Lipan Apaches raiding up from Mexico. The Karankawas were becoming scarce.

On May 27, 1844, a raiding party of 25 Comanches attacked the settlement and, in a brief fight, a man named Louis Cooke was shot in the temple, costing him an eye. The Indians escaped, taking horses and mules with them. Three days later, the Comanches returned, but the residents of Corpus Christi were expecting them and forted-up behind Kinney's stockade. After an exchange of fire, the Indians left, taking many horses with them. They were chased by Kinney and 11 other men, who caught them 10 miles west of the settlement.

Both sides dismounted for the battle. After firing at each other for some minutes, the Indian chief rode to the front, holding up his shield of tough buffalo hide, and yelling insults at the Texans. The Texans fired repeatedly at him, but their bullets were stopped by the rawhide shield, said to be as tough as iron. The chief's taunting antics were meant to draw the fire of the Texans and then, before they could reload, the warriors would charge. The Indians rushed Kinney's men, attacking with spears and tomahawks. When the man-to-man fighting was over, a man named George Gleason had been killed, along with two unidentified Hispanics. Kinney, H.W. Berry, and Francisco Silva were wounded.[61] After this attack, Kinney appealed to Austin for help. On Dec. 14, 1844, he was authorized to raise a company of 40 men for the protection of Corpus Christi.[62]

One day near sundown a Comanche raiding party hit Corpus Christi on a horse-stealing foray. By coincidence, a Ranger company was in town. As darkness fell, the Rangers chased the Comanches to a spit of land on the north end of North Beach. The Rangers had them cornered. They decided to keep them pinned up there, with no escape, and attack them at sunrise in full light and at their leisure. At daybreak, to their surprise, there were no Comanches. They had vanished. Their pony tracks led straight into the bay.

Gen. Martin Perfecto de Cos landed at Copano on Sept. 20, 1835 to begin the campaign against the Texas colonists.

10

The Rangers solved the mystery. There was a raised oyster reef between the two bays. By keeping on the reef, the Indians had walked their horses across in the darkness in water no more than three feet deep.[63] That's how Corpus Christi discovered the natural oyster shell ridge between Nueces and Corpus Christi bays that became known as the reef road. One of the first acts of the Nueces County Commissioners Court was to order stakes erected to mark the way on this underwater road.*

In 1844, Kinney was elected to the Senate of the Ninth Congress of the Republic. He represented San Patricio, Goliad and Refugio counties. He attended sessions in the old town of Washington-on-the-Brazos, the capital of Texas for a short time after Sam Houston moved it from Austin. Kinney helped ratify the terms of annexation to the United States and took part in writing a new constitution. Two incidents during the constitutional convention show Kinney's best side. A proposal was expected to pass stipulating that those who left Texas for the purpose of avoiding taking part in the revolution of 1835 would forfeit all rights of citizenship, including their land. This was a punitive measure aimed at Texans of Mexican descent. Kinney argued that it would deprive loyal citizens of their homes and land. It was finally agreed that all property would remain as it was during the Republic. Kinney on another occasion argued that using the word "white" in fixing representation to the Legislature could discriminate against the state's Mexican-Americans, and he won that argument.[64]

---

* The reef road was used by travelers on horseback and wagon to cross Nueces Bay from the 1840s when the reef was discovered until the first Nueces Bay Causeway was completed in 1915.

CHAPTER 2

Zachary Taylor's troops land on North Beach - "Fort Marcy" - Steamer Dayton explodes - Training for war with Mexico - U.S. Grant in Corpus Christi - Leaving for the Rio Grande

As the United States prepared to welcome the Republic of Texas into the Union, war with Mexico loomed. Mexico had warned that any attempt to annex Texas, which Mexico considered a breakaway province, would mean war. But Texas was independent and wanted to join the United States. If Texas was in danger, it would have to be defended, especially the contested area of South Texas between the Nueces and the Rio Grande. In June 1845, a month before Texas ratified annexation, the U.S. army command under Gen. Zachary Taylor was ordered to move his forces into the contested territory of South Texas. The site was up to the general.[1]

As the army was being assembled south of Natchitoches, La., at Fort Jesup, Taylor received letters from superiors in the War Department passing on a recommendation from Henry Kinney, founder of Corpus Christi, that his trading outpost would make a good staging area for the army. Kinney understood the likely ramifications of Texas statehood. He had friends in Mexico and realized that Texas joining the United States would likely mean war, and war would mean armies and armies would mean supplies. The secretary of war, William Marcy, instructed Gen. Taylor to keep in touch with the U.S. envoy to Texas, Andrew Donelson.

Kinney anticipated events. He had already been in touch with Donelson, advising him that the border should be fixed at the Rio Grande, not the Nueces, and that Corpus Christi would be an ideal place for a base of operations for Taylor's army if and when it should be moved to Texas.[2] Kinney's words had their intended effect. Donelson wrote Taylor and informed him that, "Corpus Christi would be a likely point at which to establish a base of operations against Mexico, as it is the most westerly point now occupied in Texas." The argument that Kinney used was that Corpus

Christi was roughly equidistant from any point on the border, from Laredo to the west or Matamoros to the south. That argument would be repeated by Taylor to justify his selection of Corpus Christi as the place to concentrate the army. But that decision had not been made when the army left Louisiana for Texas. Taylor was ordered to move the army from Fort Jesup to a point on or near the Rio Grande and Taylor, following Donelson's suggestion, would eventually choose Corpus Christi. Without Kinney's settlement at Corpus Christi, Texas' claim to the territory below the Nueces would have been considered weak.

As the troops prepared to leave New Orleans, the destination was reported to be Corpus Christi. *The Daily Picayune* reported, on Saturday morning, July 19, 1845, that "The ships *Queen Victoria* and *Suviah*, and the steamship *Alabama*, have been chartered to convey the U.S. troops now in this city to Corpus Christi. We learn they are to sail on Monday." Three days later, the *Picayune* reported that the 2nd Dragoons at Fort Jesup "are prepared to take up the line of march overland for Corpus Christi . . ."

The advance units of Taylor's troops embarked from the New Orleans levee in front of the Lower Cotton Press on a hot day, July 22, 1845. The first aboard the steamer *Alabama* was the 3rd Infantry under the command of Lt. Col. Ethan Allen Hitchcock. Gen. Taylor was also on board.[3] Three days later, the *Alabama* arrived at the Aransas Pass channel. Lt. D.T. Chandler, quartermaster of the 3rd Infantry, was the first man ashore on St. Joseph's Island, across the pass from today's Port Aransas, on Saturday, July 26, 1845. Chandler raised the Stars and Stripes over the sand dunes of St. Joseph's, the first American flag to fly over Texas soil, and companies of the 3rd Infantry were quickly ferried ashore. Officers and men stretched their legs on St. Joseph's; some of the soldiers played in the surf like children. Hitchcock went ashore with the last of the men. The companies were strung out along three miles of the island. "We have found good water," Hitchcock wrote in his diary, "and had fish and oysters for breakfast. There are two or three families living on shore."[4] A letter from Capt. Grice of the *Undine* to the *Daily Picayune* reported that his ship was carrying troops from the *Undine* to the shore. "There are now 500 men encamped here, and the scene is full of interest. The other vessels with troops are not expected to arrive for several days."[5]

Despite Kinney's letters promoting Corpus Christi as a site for the army encampment, Taylor was not completely committed to Corpus Christi as the place on the Texas coast to concentrate his army. In letters to Washington, he wrote that eight companies of the 3rd Army were temporarily camped on St. Joseph's Island. He was trying to decide between Corpus Christi or the area between where Rockport is today and Live Oak Point.

Taylor went to Live Oak Point, where he was invited to dinner at the home of the great Irish empresario, Col. James Power.[6] Taylor also sent a scouting party to Corpus Christi before deciding that this site near the mouth of the Nueces River had certain advantages. One advantage, according to his scouting report, was a large tableland behind the bluff, a perfect parade ground where troops could be drilled. One disadvantage was a lack of a good water supply. Another disadvantage was that Corpus Christi was on the backside of a shallow, troublesome bay, clogged by shoals and mudflats.

The mudflats in the bay made it difficult to get the army and its supplies from St. Joseph's Island to Corpus Christi. The shallow-draft lighter *Undine* drew four feet, but there were only three feet of water over the mudflats that blocked Corpus Christi Bay. Hitchcock advised Taylor to keep the army on St. Joseph's until a strong southwest wind would give them higher water over the shoals.[7] The commanding general, however, was impatient to get the troops on the mainland. This was one of the first of many disagreements between Hitchcock and Taylor. It is made clear in Hitchcock's papers that he and the general did not see eye to eye on hardly anything. Hitchcock, a West Pointer and stickler for details and Army procedures, had little respect for Taylor, the Louisiana plantation owner who dressed like a farmer, sometimes rode his horse "Old Whitey" side-saddle, and cared little for the customs and traditions of the regular Army.[8]

Taylor ordered companies K and G to sail across the bay on the *Undine.* The vessel soon ran aground and remained stuck in the mud for two days. Seven local fishing boats were hired to ferry the soldiers to Corpus Christi in a peevish sea worked up by a strong breeze. The soldiers had a rough time, tossed and buffeted about in the fishing boats. The men from companies K and G of the 3rd Infantry landed, tired, hungry and wet, on North Beach.[*] They landed at sundown on Aug. 1, 1845. The waves were too high to land their supplies. They ate hard ship's biscuits for supper and stretched out on the sand, with no tents or blankets, and slept under a canopy of stars. Next morning, the bay was still whipped to a froth by strong winds. They were able, with much difficulty, to land their supplies. They put up tents and looked for water. They learned to step carefully. Big rattlesnakes by the hundreds buzzed angrily at the intruders in the high grass on North Beach. Lt. Napoleon Jackson Tecumseh Dana in a letter to his wife wrote that rattlesnakes were their bedfellows. "Yesterday morning Whiting (Daniel P., his brother-in-law) found a huge rattlesnake coiled up at the foot of his bed. A lieutenant Smith had one crawl over his bare legs; he laid still until His Snakeship crawled off."[9] Besides the snakes, clouds of mosquitoes and horseflies "big enough to put a saddle on" kept them engaged.

Within days, military order began to emerge with tents, squared in military fashion, stretching along the shoreline across the mud slough toward the small village of Corpus Christi.[10]

A letter to the *Daily Picayune* from Corpus Christi, dated Aug. 30, said, "The position taken by Gen. Taylor is one of extreme beauty; and when the

---

[*] Believed to be about where the Texas State Aquarium is today.

15

eye first rests upon his Camp, clustered with a thousand spotless white tents, along the shelly margin of the shore of Corpus Christi Bay, irresistible bursts of admiration follow. It is a position of security, as well as beauty."[11]

In coming months, Corpus Christi became a major military outpost with the concentration of half the U.S. Army in Taylor's command. It was a small trading post of some 100 souls when Taylor's army pitched tents on North Beach. It became a boomtown of 4,000 soldiers and perhaps as many as 2,000 citizens, most of them camp followers, grog shop proprietors, gamblers and prostitutes. Some soldiers were not impressed by Corpus Christi. Lt. Richard H. Wilson called it, "The most murderous, thieving, gambling, God-forsaken hole in the Lone Star State, or out of it." The soldiers thought of it as a border town and some, including Lt. U.S. Grant, thought of it as a "Mexican hamlet." Lt. Abner Doubleday[**] wrote that Corpus Christi "must have been a charming place for people who dislike the restraints of civilization." Another wrote that "all the people here are rascals; there is not a man among them who is not a renegade from justice."[12]

A few officers were invited to dine at the home of merchant Frederick Belden and his wife Mauricia (Arocha). Capt. W. S. Henry said they were given a dish he called "*themales*." "It is made of corn meal, chopped meat, and cayenne pepper wrapped in a piece of corn husk, and boiled. I know of nothing more palatable." The officers explored their environment, at the edge of a great sweep of bay with few inhabitants. Henry said they found many "Mexican families" living on the bluff. "Their residences are made of crooked mesquite wood, and their roofs thatched with long grass which grows in the marshes, called '*tula*.' "[13]

Two weeks after the first troops landed, in the middle of August, Gen. Taylor and staff arrived. Taylor issued his first order from Corpus Christi and the heading shows he was no longer calling it the "Army of Observation" but the "Army of Occupation."[14] The shallow-draft lighter *Undine*, which wasn't shallow enough to cross over the mudflats, was replaced by a small, miserable pig boat, a coastal steamer hired in Galveston, the *Dayton*. It was used to ferry men and supplies from the transport ships riding at anchor off the pass separating St. Joseph's and Mustang Island.[15] Other units of the Army continued to arrive. In an apple-polishing letter to Washington, Taylor called the encampment "Fort Marcy," named for Secretary of War William L. Marcy. Although it was called a fort by Taylor, it really was a large encampment.[16] Col. Hitchcock, commander of the 3rd Infantry, had embankments thrown up as a line of defense. Since no artillery had arrived, Hitchcock borrowed two old cannons from Kinney.[*] Capt. W.S. Henry thought the borrowed guns "were more dangerous to ourselves than to

---

[**] The man wrongly reputed to have invented baseball.
[*] Kinney referred to the guns in his sworn statement in the Dimmitt affair, saying he built a stockade and mounted a 12-pounder and two small pieces to protect his trading post.

any enemy."[17] It was just as well that they never had to put them to the test.

The army fell into a routine. Troops were kept busy with drills, marching, wheeling, counter-marching, and target practice. George G. Meade complained that camp life consisted of "nothing but drills and parades, and your ears are filled all day with drumming and fifeing."[18] Lt. Doubleday wrote that, "The Mexican Army being largely composed of cavalry, and a collision being more than probable, our infantry were constantly drilled in forming square to resist cavalry."[19] Sgt. George K. Donnelly in a letter to a friend wrote that, "We have been firing ball cartridges at targets. And in almost every instance, at a hundred paces, the targets fall shattered to the ground."[20] A group of officers on a three-day hunting trip to the Nueces River bottoms killed deer, geese, and a seven-foot panther that sprang at a Lt. Dobbins. The panther missed, and when he tried again, Dobbins shot him in the head. "No one but the most irreclaimable cynic," said Henry, "could have ridden over this beautiful country, in the vicinity of the Nueces, without being enchanted with its beauty."[21]

The soldiers were put to work digging wells, including one at what would be called Artesian Park, but the water was brackish, with an unpleasant taste and smell. For drinking and cooking, they relied on water hauled in wooden casks from the Nueces River 12 miles away. Basic military procedures for setting up a campsite (used by armies since the days of Roman legions) were ignored. Army training called for choosing a campsite on high ground, with good drainage, with sanitation trenches dug on lower ground below, and the camp within easy reach of wood, for campfires, and water. Yet "Fort Marcy" violated all the standard rules covering water, wood, sanitation and drainage. "Our water is poor," wrote one officer, "and we are made sick by its use."[22]

In the third week of August, 1845, Henry Kinney returned from Austin, escorted by two Lipan Apache Indians, one known as Chief Castro.* Kinney used the Lipans for protection on the long trips to the capitol. Shortly after they arrived, one dark night, Chief Castro was shot from ambush. Suspicion fell on a man named Louis P. Cooke, who had lost an eye to an Indian arrow in the attack on Corpus Christi the year before and was known to be an implacable enemy of all Indians, regardless of tribe. (Cooke, who had been secretary of the Navy for a year under President Lamar, was indicted for murder in a shooting scrape in Austin; he escaped and relocated to Corpus Christi, working as a bricklayer with John A.F. Gravis.)[23] With Corpus Christi effectively under martial law, Gen. Taylor questioned Cooke about the shooting, but Cooke denied he shot the Indian chief and there was no evidence to charge him. Though he received what normally would have been

---

* Lipan Chief Culegas de Castro fought with Texans against Comanches. J.W. Moses saw Chief Castro in Laredo in 1850. He said he was dressed as a military officer from the waist up and as a Lipan Apache with leggings from the waist down. He said Chief Castro was one of the most handsome men of the West.

17

fatal gunshot wounds, in the head and chest, Chief Castro survived the attack.[24]

While the army settled in, traders arrived from Mexico, bringing horses, mules, Mexican blankets and crude silver bars molded in sand. Gen. Taylor relied on traders and Kinney's spy, Chipito Sandoval,* for intelligence of army movements in Mexico. Taylor and Hitchcock met Sandoval on a social call to Kinney's house.[25]

On Aug. 24, the camp was hit by a violent thunderstorm and a lightning bolt hit a tent center pole, killing a slave owned by Lt. Braxton Bragg, and injuring another slave in the same tent. During the storm, a baby was born to a woman laundress. Capt. W.S. Henry thought the baby should have been named "Thunder." From a distance, the rumbling echo of the thunder was at such regularly spaced intervals that it sounded like gun-fire from field guns. The dragoons (cavalry trained to dismount and fight like infantry) were camped at the village of San Patricio up the Nueces River. The dragoons were trying to get their baggage across the river on rafts when they heard what they thought was an artillery bombardment. They thought Taylor's army was under attack by hostile forces and they galloped toward Corpus Christi in relief. They were met on the way by Gen. Taylor, who had been riding to visit the dragoons. Taylor presented quite an appearance on horseback, riding side-saddle like an old woman. They all had a good laugh at the thunderstorm that had the dragoons riding to the rescue.[26]

One reason Taylor stationed the dragoons at San Patricio, up the river from Corpus Christi, may have been to furnish protection for the ranch of John Howland Wood, who had signed a contract to supply the army with beef providing the army could protect him from marauding Indians.[27]

The day after the thunderstorm, the steamship *Alabama* arrived with soldiers in the 7th Infantry. As troops and supplies were being offloaded to a lighter, Lt. Ulysses S. Grant somehow fell head-first into the bay. Men lining the rail were laughing as he was hauled back on deck, like a wet parcel.[28]

Three weeks later, on Sept. 12, two boilers on the *Dayton* exploded near McGloin's Bluff.* Those on the boiler deck were thrown into eight feet of water. A Lt. Higgins was killed by a piece of iron striking him in the head. Those badly injured clung to the boat's wreckage until they were rescued. A scalded Lt. Graham arrived at Corpus Christi with news of the accident. The wounded and dead were brought to Corpus Christi. Col. Hitchcock picked a burial site on a hillside overlooking the army encampment, which would later be called Bayview Cemetery. The dead were buried at sundown with the Fourth Regiment band playing Handel's "Dead March in Saul." "May the God of Battles receive and cherish them," Capt. Henry wrote. The toll from the *Dayton* explosion was 17 wounded and 10 killed.[29] An unnamed

_____

* Kinney named a street on the bluff "Chipito" for his friend and favorite spy.
* Near today's Ingleside.

officer in the 7th Infantry wrote in a private letter printed by the *Daily Picayune* that, "Gloom like a pall hangs over our whole camp . . . The explosion took place at half-past 12 o'clock, in day time, and Dr. Crittenden, who was on board (slightly injured) informs me that she sunk in 15 minutes after and as she went down (covered by the water) another boiler exploded, with a most terrific report."[30]

The cemetery would be needed, as more men died from dysentery and other causes linked to bad water, poor sanitation and a cold winter with four thousand men living in tents.

The army cleared an area west of the camp for drills and on Nov. 1 Gen. Taylor reviewed the First Brigade.[31] About this time, a contingent of Texas Rangers under the command of John Coffee Hays arrived. The Rangers made it a point of honor to slouch about and look as unmilitary as possible, as a demonstration of their special status. They also had a reputation to uphold, as being undisciplined when not in a fight. As a way to insult the regular soldiers of the U.S. Army, the Rangers, with an easy-going irony, said they had been sent in the event of any hostile moves from Mexico in order to protect the U.S. Army. While John Coffee Hays was respected by the army officers for his reputation as a fearless Indian fighter and leader of men, the officers didn't think much of his Rangers. Lt. Dana wrote his wife that "the best of them look like they would steal sheep."[32]

Soldiers found that wild mustangs could be bought cheap. Lt. Grant, a fine rider who loved horses, soon had four mustang ponies. A free black man named Valere, whom Grant hired to prepare his meals and keep his tent clean, was taking Grant's horses to water and they got away. Capt. W.W. "Perfect" Bliss, Gen. Taylor's adjutant, joked about the young lieutenant's loss. "I heard that Grant lost five or six dollars worth of horses the other day." That was a slander, said Grant; the horses were worth $20.[33]

The men spent a lot of time buying and selling horses or racing horses. One soldier in a letter home wrote, "I bought a good pony for one dollar-fifty and saw another swapped for an old pair of soldier's trousers." Capt. W.S. Henry wrote that almost every day for a month some kind of race was held. He described one race, for 300 yards, between two mustang ponies. "One pony bolted, and, not at all alarmed by the crowd, cleared two or three piles of rubbish, knocked one man down, threw his rider, then ran about 50 yards and stopped, turned around, and snorted, as much as if to say, 'Beat that if you can.' "[34]

Bored with camp life, Lt. Grant and other officers volunteered to escort a wagon train to San Antonio. Grant wrote that wild game abounded, but, as for people, it was unlived-in land. They found no inhabitants until they approached San Antonio. Three weeks later, afraid they would be late and listed as absent without leave, Grant and another officer started back by themselves, ahead of the army wagon train. One night, they heard an unearthly howling of wolves; Grant figured there were at least 20 or more in the pack. But when they got close enough to see them, there were only two. Grant said he often thought of that when he heard the howling of politicians. "There are always more of them before they are counted."[35]

That winter, a theater was built and planning began to stage Shakespeare's *Othello*. There was no trouble casting men for the parts, but there was no one to play Brabantio's daughter Desdemona. James Longstreet was too big for the costume. Grant, whom the officers called "Beauty," was persuaded to try out for the role. Grant was effeminate, almost pretty, and had a girlish figure; the costume fit him perfectly. But the officer playing the Moor couldn't look at Grant without laughing and they decided to send to New Orleans for a professional actress (Gertrude Hart) to relieve Grant and play the part of Desdemona. Grant later grew his famous beard, with enough whiskers to stuff a pillowcase, so that he would never be considered "pretty" again.[36]

At the end of November, Lt. Jeremiah Scarritt and a party of soldiers were put to work cutting through the reef that divided Nueces and Corpus Christi Bays (the reef road).[37] This cut in the reef on the Corpus Christi side would allow small boats to pass up the Nueces River to ferry supplies to the dragoon camp at the settlement of San Patricio.* On Dec. 3, the camp was hit by a vicious norther that came, as Henry described it, like a thief in the night and next morning every tent had a covering of ice . . . "the cracking of the canvas sounded like anything but music." The temperature dropped to 23 degrees, stunning fish and turtles in the bays. Cartloads of fish and green sea turtles were gathered along the shore. Soldiers surrounded their camps with chaparral brush to deflect the bitterly cold wind. Henry thought the brush made the camp look like it was set in the middle of an orange grove.[38]

Since the first companies of Taylor's army had arrived, on Aug. 1, 1845, the village of Corpus Christi, with less than 100 in population before the army came, grew to something like 2,000, most of them camp followers, people who stirred about at night and slept in the daytime. These were lounging gunfighters, adventurers, gamblers, saloon-keepers, prostitutes, all looking to make a profit from the 4,000-odd troops encamped. One soldier said that there was Sodom and Gomorrah and Corpus Christi. W.S. Henry wrote that "houses appear to have grown in a night. There are all sorts, from a frame covered with common domestic (cloth), to a tolerably respectable one, clapboarded and shingled."

Josiah Turner arrived from New Orleans and stayed at a hotel on Chaparral, a one-story frame building run by a man named Moore. "There were a good many temporary houses being constructed with frame walls and covered with domestic sheeting, for saloons and different purposes; some for drinking, some for gambling to win the soldiers' money, and others for

---

* For years afterwards, the cut in the reef meant that horses had to swim across that small opening on the south end, the Corpus Christi side, of the reef road.

restaurants." Turner found work as a carpenter. "When we came here," Sgt. George Donnelly wrote home, "the celebrated city of Corpus Christi consisted of about two good frame houses, seven or eight miserable huts, all of which were grog shops or gamblers' dens. Now it has 60 or 70 good houses, about 1,400 inhabitants, but I am sorry to say that more than two-thirds are of the lowest class of villains, men who are reckless of character and human life." Lt. R.E. Cochrane, of the 4th Regiment of Infantry, had written his parents glowing accounts of Texas when he first arrived. But after he spent a cold Christmas in his tent, with chills and fever, he wrote home that "Uncle Sam made a mighty poor bargain when he got Texas, even though he did get it for nothing."[39]

Gen. Taylor celebrated New Year's Day, 1846, by inviting his officers to share a glass of eggnog at his headquarters.[40*] The Jan. 1 edition of Corpus Christi's new paper, the *Gazette,* reported that a play called "The Wife" would open at the Army Theater. This building had recently been constructed by army officers, led by Capt. John B. Magruder of the 1st Artillery. The Union Theater, at Lawrence and Chaparral, was built by a transplanted architect from Maine, Charles J. Bryant. The Union Theater that New Year's was featuring performances of "La Polka" and "The Ambassador's Ball." Besides plays at the two theaters, Howes and Maybie's circus from New Orleans arrived to entertain the troops.[41]

On Feb. 19, Texas officially joined the Union. While President Polk signed the act that merged Texas with the United States on Dec. 29, 1845, the Lone Star flag didn't come down and the U.S. flag take its place until Feb. 19, 1846. Three days before, on Feb. 16, an "Annexation Ball" was held at the Union Theater, with music provided by five army bands. Among the tunes played by the bands was one created for the occasion, called "General Taylor's Encampment Quick Step." The town's leading citizens and army officers attended the ball. The citizens listed as sponsors included Charles Bryant, J.P. Kelsey, William Mann, William Aubrey, and Jose de Alba.[42]

Not long after the Annexation Ball, Gen. Taylor was a dinner guest at the home of merchant Frederick Belden. Belden's wife Mauricia, a native of Mexico, asked the general about the prospects for a war. Taylor said if war did break out, his intention was to march on and capture Mexico City. Mrs. Belden bet him that he would never get there. (Even though Taylor didn't personally get to Mexico City, Gen. Winfield Scott's army did; Taylor sent Mrs. Belden a silk dress from Mexico.)[43]

The rest of February was spent with intense activity in preparation for the army's departure to the Rio Grande, closer to the prospect of war. Taylor had the Army quartermasters scouring the area buying horses, mules, oxen, and wagons to carry the army's supplies and equipment. Capt. W.S. Henry wrote

---

* The building on Water Street was later known as the Byington house. It was torn down in 1910. A bank parking garage is on the site today.

that during the winter months, "The most active means were used by the quartermaster's department to collect transportation. We were miserably deficient; wild mules were purchased and broken; and everything, you may say, had to be created out of nothing."[44]

Taylor also sent reconnaissance patrols to look for a suitable route of march. One party of officers traveled down the middle of Padre Island, where they found the bones of shipwreck victims attached to ship hatch covers. Another scouting party followed the old Matamoros Road, an old trail long followed by smugglers and traders. Because of a shortage of forage for horses and draft animals, not to mention the difficulty of marching through the sand of Padre Island, Taylor chose the inland route. They were fortunate that it had been a dry and not a wet February, or the march across the "hogwallow prairie" would have been more difficult than it proved to be.[45]

Gen. Taylor issued the army's marching orders, which were published in the *Corpus Christi Gazette*: "The Army of Occupation is about to take up a position on the left bank of the Rio Grande. As the army marches south, the commanding general wishes it distinctly understood that no person not properly attached to it will be permitted to accompany the troops." Despite orders, grog shop purveyors packed up—lock, stock, and barrels of whisky —and followed the army. On the way, at Santa Gertrudis Creek, some were sent back in irons and their liquor poured out, but other whisky drummers, gamblers and prostitutes traveled south, like troopers themselves.[46] There was no reason for them to stay in Corpus Christi, without 4,000 soldiers getting regular wages to spend on whisky and other vices. They followed the money. A celebrated prostitute known as "The Great Western," was allowed to follow the army; ostensibly, she was a laundress and married to an enlisted man. The Great Western, it was said, was anxious to see "her boys" whip the Mexicans.[47]

The soldiers were more than ready to leave. The seven months spent at Corpus Christi had no doubt helped to meld various units into a real army. But lack of good water, bad sanitation, prevalent sickness, and inadequate tents that were often water-logged and offered little protection against fierce northers made them eager to leave. And they were ready for a fight. Their fighting abilities would soon be tested at places like Palo Alto and Resaca de la Palma, as well as famous battles to come in Mexico. "We are delighted at the prospects of the march," Henry wrote, "having become restless and anxious for a change; we anticipate no little fun, and all sorts of adventure, upon the route."[48]

Sgt. Charles Masland of the 3rd Infantry (he would be killed at the battle of Resaca de la Palma) wrote his brother: "Packing up was the order of the day. Here and there might be seen groups of Mexicans bargaining with our men for wearing apparel, and giving cash for what they might have had for nothing in a few days, for we could not carry half our 'plunder.' "

On March 8, 1846, the 2nd Dragoons and a company of artillery, the first to leave, marched out of Corpus Christi. The 1st Brigade left on the 9th. Elements of the 3rd Infantry, which had been the first to arrive on Aug. 1, 1845, were the last to leave. As they marched away, army drummers beat out the traditional marching-away tune, "The Girl I Left Behind Me." Henry was one of the last to leave. He took note of the prodigious contrast. He looked back at the site where Taylor's army had camped for the past seven months, seeing the bay and the strand of sand looking peaceful while who knew what they were heading into. "The fields of white canvas were no longer visible," Henry wrote, "and the campground looked like desolation itself. But the bright waters of the bay looked as sweet as ever." The thousands of white tents were gone. Some 4,000 soldiers were gone. Nearly 2,000 of the town's transient inhabitants were gone. The Army and the Union theaters, so recently filled to capacity, sat empty. Corpus Christi was all but deserted.[49]

The *Niles National Register*, a popular magazine headquartered in Baltimore, printed the route Taylor's army took when it left Corpus Christi. The army crossed over "hogwallow prairies" and the desert country called the Big Sands, glistening with salt deposits. Streams the army forded were the Santa Gertrudis, Bobedo, Olmos, and Arroyo Colorado. The route Taylor's army followed was the same that shattered remnants of Gen. Filisola's army took after the Mexican army's defeat at San Jacinto 10 years before.[50] Along the way, Grant would ride out to high ground to see the vast herds of mustangs that covered the horizon, too many, he estimated, to be corralled in the state of Rhode Island. It was rough marching country through the region known as the Big Sands and the Desert of the Dead. Lt. Grant wrote a friend that ponds of drinkable water were sometimes a day's march apart. The sand belt, 65 miles wide and a 100 miles long, had to be crossed in traveling from Corpus Christi to the lower Rio Grande. It was said that on entering the Big Sands, you felt a blast of hot air and your first temptation was to turn back. After a mile or so, you became nauseated from the hot sun and your lips cracked, your throat parched. As the army marched through this "Desert of the Dead," Grant admired the endurance of the enlisted men.[51]

The march from Corpus Christi to the Rio Grande stretched for 196 miles, "through deep, sandy plains, here glistening with salt, and there varied with briny marshes or sticky black dirt. In some places, Mexicans had burned the herbage; and the light ashes, raised by the tramp of many feet, settled on the soldiers' faces till they could scarcely recognize one another. Tortured with thirst, they would occasionally break ranks pell-mell at the sight of water; but as a rule they found it brackish."[52]

A funny thing happened on the march. A soldier fired at a longhorn bull. The feisty little bull charged and the soldier ran into the column of troops for the protection of numbers, but the bull didn't pull up, charging into their midst, waving his horns from side to side and scattering several regiments.

He finally emerged on the other side of the column unhurt, "having demoralized and put to flight an army which a few days after covered itself with glory by victoriously encountering five times its numbers of human enemies."[53]

Among those officers marching south from Corpus Christi were many who would become famous generals in years to come: Ulysses S. Grant, James Longstreet, George Gordon Meade, George H. Thomas, George A. McCall, Braxton Bragg, E. Kirby Smith, John B. Magruder. Robert E. Lee was not at the encampment at Corpus Christi, but he joined Zachary Taylor's army at Monterrey. The concentration of the army at Corpus Christi and the battles of Mexico provided the training ground for a generation of young officers for the coming Civil War.

CHAPTER 3

Corpus Christi's "lost years" - Mustang Gray's Rangers - "Buffalo Hunters" - The "Great Chihuahua Train" - Going to California in the Gold Rush - The scalping of Charles Bryant - Tragedy at Doyle's Watering Hole - The first census - Henry Kinney's Lone Star Fair - The Army returns and the Fandango Riot

The departure of Zachary Taylor's army led to the "lost years" of Corpus Christi, which lasted from 1846, when the army left, until 1848, when the war with Mexico ended. In those two years the town was nearly deserted; it almost ceased to exist when most of the men left to follow the army or, really, to follow the excitement. A Houston newspaper, *The Telegraph*, noted the town's sudden downfall. "Since the removal of the U.S. Army from Corpus Christi, the town has fallen almost as rapidly as it rose. The population has dwindled from nearly 2,000 souls to a few hundred. The 200 grog shops that were the glory of the citizens a few weeks since, the faro banks, the roulette tables . . . have disappeared. A few stores . . . are about all that is left of the late flourishing town of Corpus Christi."[1]

Even the town's founder, Kinney, left with the army. He was appointed to the staff of Texas Gov. J. Pinckney Henderson, in command of Texas troops.[2] Kinney's partner, William Aubrey, also went south with a wagonload of Dicky Jones brandy, Madeira wine, and Monongahela whisky.[3] When Taylor occupied Matamoros, grog shop owners who had been at Corpus Christi were in business again. A young soldier, William McClintock, passed through Corpus Christi on his way to join the army in Mexico. He thought it was a town living on borrowed time. In a letter he wrote, "The town is situated on a low beach containing some 30 houses, and on the hill are 15 or 20 Mexican huts now deserted . . . Corpus Christi was a poor insignificant place until the army took up its quarters there. I think its existence will be an ephemeral one."[4]

The month after the army left, in April, 1846, Nueces County was created. The county was immense, larger than some states, stretching from Corpus Christi west to Laredo and then southeast from Laredo to this side of Matamoros (there was no Brownsville then). The county's first voting

25

precincts were No. 1, at Corpus Christi, a village of less than 200 souls, No. 2 at Point Isabel, No. 3 at Santa Rita, No. 4 at Rio Grande City and No. 5 at Laredo.[5]*

The first act of Nueces County was to establish ferry tolls on the Nueces River and on the Rio Grande: 25 cents for each pair of oxen, 25 cents for a man and horse, 25 cents for every wheel on a wagon, 10 cents for each loose horse, 6 cents for each head of meat cattle, three cents for each head of sheep, goats or hogs.[6] The main ferry on the lower Nueces was at the Santa Margarita crossing, below the Irish settlement of San Patricio.

Samuel Bangs, editor of *The Corpus Christi Gazette*, joined the exodus. He packed up his type trays to get closer to the "seat of conflict." He was soon printing *The American Flag* in Matamoros, but he kept up with the news from Corpus Christi. On July 17, 1846, *The Flag* printed a report from a correspondent (most likely Kinney, who was able to visit the town regularly while he was with the army). "According to promise," the correspondent wrote, "I write you what information I have been able to gather since my return to Corpus Christi. I found the old inhabitants of the place, almost to a man, had departed for the Rio Grande, and not only the men, but the women too. Corpus Christi is indeed deserted. But think not that those who have departed, under excitement, will have left us forever. When they have 'seen the elephant' and find that his haunts afford no resting place so lovely and calmly beautiful as this delightful village, they will return . . ."[7]

The American Flag reported a rumor that a Comanche raiding party had attacked Corpus Christi and forced the citizens to "retire for safety to St. Joseph's Island." The paper said the rumor was unfounded, but noted that the town was badly exposed. "Nearly all the male population of the place are now in Matamoros or upon the Rio Grande and there are no ranging companies nearer than San Antonio."[8] Rumors of the attack led to orders returning a company of Texas volunteers from Corpus Christi to be sent back to protect the town.[9] This company, under M.B. "Mustang" Gray, spent several months at Corpus Christi in late 1846 then in early 1847 they were ordered back to Camargo to protect Taylor's supply lines.**

When the U.S. and Mexico signed the treaty of Guadalupe Hidalgo on Feb. 2, 1848, ending the Mexican War, Henry Kinney returned to Corpus Christi to find his town almost deserted. It had languished after Zachary

---

* The county was whittled down over the years: Webb, Starr, Cameron, Hidalgo, Zapata, Live Oak, McMullen, Duval, Jim Wells, Jim Hogg, Kenedy, Brooks, Kleberg, Willacy, were all carved, in whole or in part, from Nueces County of 1846.

** A year later, "Mustang" Gray died, perhaps of cholera, and was buried in an unmarked grave near Rio Grande City. Gray's last words (according to A.J. Sowell) were, "Boys, when I am dead, bury me in Texas soil, on the banks of the Rio Grande." *The American Flag* obituary said, "The name Mustang Gray was a terror to Mexican marauders . . . A gallant soldier is dead. Peace to his ashes." John J. Linn called him a moral monstrosity and cold-blooded killer. John B. Dunn said Mustang Gray owned a ranch on the Oso called Grulla Motts, which was later sold to George Pettigrew.

Taylor's army left two years before. Kinney set about using his talents as a promoter and salesman to improve the town's fortunes, and his own.[10] In the next two years, many soldiers who had "seen the elephant" were ready to settle down in Corpus Christi. They included men who would become prominent names in the growth and progress of the city: Norwick Gussett, Forbes Britton, Cornelius Cahill, and Matthew Dunn, among others. The correspondent for the *American Flag* was right: The town did not stay deserted for long. Corpus Christi after the war became a settlement of Mexican War veterans, who became the influential leaders in the town for many years to come.[11]

A strange news item in the *Corpus Christi Star* on Sept. 19, 1848, reported that a party of 190 buffalo hunters departed St. Joseph's Island. The men left on a schooner with the man in charge, Capt. L.A. Besancon, bound for New Orleans. The remaining buffalo hunters left for places along the Mexican border.

But where were the buffalo? Nowhere in the Corpus Christi area had buffalo been seen or hunted in many, many years. These men, however, were after different game. They were filibusters, not hunters. These veterans of the Mexican War planned to invade Mexico to establish a Republic of the Sierra Madre. There was strong sentiment among veterans and super patriots after the war that the U.S. in the Treaty of Guadalupe Hidalgo gave away too much by establishing the Rio Grande as the eastern-most boundary, that the U.S. should have claimed even more of Mexico's territory. "Our government committed a great error in accepting the Rio Grande as the boundary line," wrote the *New Orleans Delta*. "We should never have stopped this side of the great natural boundary, the Sierra Madre range." The *Corpus Christi Star* noted the spirit of independence prevailing in the northern states of Tamaulipas, Nuevo Leon, and Coahuila and said, "It is no wonder, then, that many of our soldiers returned to their homes impressed with the belief that, to the end in question, an effort would soon be made."

In August, 1848, a large party of Mexican War veterans, the so-called "buffalo hunters," were brought by schooner from New Orleans to St. Joseph's Island. They camped on the island and whiled away their days, preparing for and waiting for an armed incursion into Mexico to start a war and foment a revolution. They expected that the people of northern Mexico, with their encouraging nudge, would rise and establish their own republic free of the dominant hand of Mexico City. The *New Orleans Delta* reported that, "The buffalo hunters are mustering strongly; many of them have started for the hunting grounds; more are preparing to follow . . ." A Houston newspaper, *the Democratic Telegraph and Texas Register*, reported, "There were about 3,000 wagons at Corpus Christi belonging to Col. Kinney, and it was supposed they were intended for the Sierra Madre expedition. About 200 Sierra Madre volunteers arrived at St. Joseph's Island . . . And another large detachment was expected in a few days. Our informant did not learn their destination."[12]

J. Williamson Moses, a sergeant in J. S. Sutton's company of Texas Rangers, who were stationed at San Patricio, wrote that the buffalo hunters camped on the island, with beef and supplies being sent over by Kinney and other merchants. In time, these filibusters grew restive with the tedium of waiting and they came up with a scheme to rob Kinney. They had heard he had a vast amount of gold at his home on the bluff. Kinney got wind of the plan and sent word to Capt. Sutton, camped with his Rangers at San Patricio. When the buffalo hunters arrived at Kinney's house, they were confronted by a determined squad of Rangers, armed and ready. Faced with the prospect of a fight with Texas Rangers, who were not known for backing down, the buffalo hunters were convinced to leave peacefully. Kinney provided them with the means to leave the country.[13]

On Oct. 13, 1848, the *Galveston Weekly News* reported that Capt. Besancon and his buffalo hunters returned to New Orleans. Besancon wrote to the *Democratic Telegraph and Texas Register* in Houston apologizing to Kinney, writing that he regretted "having brought down men for the purpose of engaging in what has been called the Sierra Madre expedition. Had I been aware of your (meaning Kinney's) own opinion, and not relied upon Madame Rumor, I should have saved the expense of subsistence and transportation of a large body of men." The buffalo hunt, said the *Star*, turned into a wild goose chase. Kinney, in a letter to the *Star* that was reprinted in several Texas papers, disclaimed any connection with the affair, pointing out that the United States was at peace with Mexico and "it would certainly be a breach of neutrality to organize a force in our limits to invade any portion of her territory, and I certainly would not, with my consent, lend my name for such a purpose . . . I will say that I am not nor have I been connected with the movement in question, and my friends will much oblige me by disabusing the public mind on the subject."[14]

Corpus Christi began to prosper again. Kinney, a tireless promoter, pushed several ventures, all pointing west. He tried to establish trade with the Chihuahua region of Mexico. He lobbied the Army to lay out a road from Corpus Christi to the upper Rio Grande. Kinney had purchased hundreds of wagons and mules, war surplus, and joined a partnership with Gen. William Cazneau, who had been quartermaster general for the Texas army during the Revolution, and William Mann. Kinney and partners planned to open a trade route to Chihuahua; Kinney put up $10,000 for the venture.[15]

Gen. Cazneau began to assemble a train of wagons filled with goods destined for the Chihuahua market. Kinney sought to supplant the old trade route, which ran from Independence, Mo., via Santa Fe to the Chihuahua region of northern Mexico, hence the Chihuahua trade. Corpus Christi streets were filled with wagons and ox carts as the "Great Chihuahua Train" began to take shape. Kinney and his partners hoped to make a profit from the sale of goods in Chihuahua, and they hoped to establish regular trade traffic with northern Mexico. They also hoped to demonstrate the need for a road, protected by the Army, from Corpus Christi to the upper Rio Grande.

The huge caravan of 50 wagons and ox carts departed in March 1849 for Casa Blanca, the old Spanish ranch house built of white caliche blocks on the cliffs of Pinetas Creek near where it joins the Nueces River (between today's Orange Grove and Sandia). It was chosen because there was plenty of grass and water for the teams, and because William Mann, one of the partners, had recently bought the Casa Blanca land grant. As the wagons left for Casa Blanca, the *Corpus Christi Star* reported: "It is General Cazneau's intention to form two trading posts on this side of the Rio Grande, one at Presidio del Norte and one at El Paso, where the traders will buy goods and themselves convey them into Mexico."

The trip was important for another reason. Kinney had urged the Army to open roads to the West from Corpus Christi. The Army had the same interests. With the war's end, the U.S. acquired a vast territory open to settlement and expansion. Forts would have to be built and supplied. Much of this territory was unmapped and unexplored, and this would be a task for the Army.[16] Kinney's lobbying efforts with his Army contacts about the need for a road from Corpus Christi to West Texas paid off.

The Army ordered Lt. Nathaniel Michler of the Topographical Engineers to accompany the Great Chihuahua Train and explore the country between Corpus Christi and Fort Inge on the Leona River (in Uvalde County). Michler was ordered to determine if a road (more a route than a road) could be opened between the two places.[17] Lt. Michler made his report on July 31, 1849. He found the region abounded with wild game; he described the terrain near the Frio and Leona rivers; and reported that the region offered "every facility for opening a good road." The only difficulty was that there were no settlements along the way to purchase supplies; there was nothing between Corpus Christi and Fort Inge but Indians and rattlesnakes.

Through Kinney's efforts, Corpus Christi's prospects improved. Congress designated Corpus Christi as a port, with its own customs inspector. Kinney bought a steam dredging machine to deepen a channel through the shallow mudflats of the bay. A local shipyard built its first ship, the schooner *Ranchero,* made of mesquite.[18]

The week before the Treaty of Guadalupe Hidalgo was signed, gold was discovered on the American River at Sutter's Mill in California. Kinney understood what that meant. He ran ads in eastern newspapers claiming that the best route to the California goldfields started at Corpus Christi. There was no easy way to get there. The main route was overland, starting at Independence, Mo. Another was 18,000 seasick miles around the storm-tossed Horn and a third was by ship to Chagres, Panama, across the narrow isthmus by pack mule, and then book passage on another ship on the Pacific side. The wet-dry route promoted by Kinney was by ship or packet boat to Corpus Christi, then overland across Texas and the Mexican states of

Chihuahua and Sonora to southern California, then a march up California to the goldfields.

Corpus Christi was convulsed with gold fever. The town's new newspaper, the *Corpus Christi Star*, was filled with gold news from California, news that described the geography of the gold fields, the techniques of extracting gold, and how to get there. There was a spoof ad for Gold Grease: "The operator is to grease himself, lay down on top of a hill, and roll to the bottom; gold and nothing else will stick to him." Price, $94 a box.

Gold seekers began arriving in Corpus Christi in January 1849. The miners were brought in by the *Neptune*, a fast-sailing packet boat plying between Galveston and Corpus Christi, or the *Fanny*, a packet steamship. The town filled with emigrants going west. Steamers and packet boats brought in more each week. The emigrants needed everything a town could supply. Gunsmiths, blacksmiths, coopers set up shop, along with cobblers, barbers and chandlers. The first group of 49'ers arrived on Jan. 20, 1849. The town began to stir with the kind of economic activity it hadn't seen since Taylor's army left in March 1846. Edward Ohler, a merchant who moved to Corpus Christi in 1848,[19] built a wharf from the end of Peoples Street into the bay where goods could be unloaded.[*] The old Kinney House was reopened as the Corpus Christi Hotel (at Chaparral and William), advertising rates of $30 a month, "the same for man or horse." The wagons, horses and mules that were sold dirt cheap as army surplus after the Mexican War were in demand at high prices. Mustangs were caught and tamed for sale to emigrants.

Corpus Christi was a coming town again. The stream of gold-seekers traveling to the California goldfields brought a surge of energy and prosperity to Corpus Christi. The *Corpus Christi Star* advised the arriving emigrants to learn Spanish "or they will be puzzled when they get into Mexican country, where even the mules understand no other language." The groups of California emigrants, when they arrived, were organized into companies with bylaws, judicial tribunals, and elected officers. Among the groups arriving to begin their overland trek were the Mazatlan Rangers, the Essex Mining Company of Boston, the Carson Association of New York, the Kinney Rangers (named in honor of Henry Kinney), and the Holmes County (Miss.) Mining Company.[20]

The companies picked up a few Texans for the trip. For months, the editor of the *Corpus Christi Star*, John H. Peoples, for whom Peoples Street was named, had filled his paper with news about the gold rush. He came down with the fever himself. He turned over his press to Charles Callahan and joined the Mazatlan Rangers, under the command of Col. E.W. Abbott.

---

[*] Ohler's store, with living quarters upstairs, was at the corner of Peoples and Water. In 1867, this two-story shellcrete building and the lot it stood on were sold to Helen Chapman and Charles Stillman for $55.

Peoples knew him from the Mexican War, where Abbott led a Massachusetts regiment and Peoples was a war correspondent, one of the nation's first war correspondents. Peoples listed the 43 members of Abbott's company and wrote, ". . . the company is made up of orderly and respectable persons, and although the majority of them may not be familiar with the rough life they will have to lead between here and the Pacific, we believe they will readily accustom themselves to it."[21]

Charles Callahan, who took over the *Star* from Peoples, would also leave for California later in the summer. James R. Barnard continued to publish the *Star* until another paper appeared, *The Nueces Valley*.[22]

Peoples and the Mazatlan Rangers stepped off for California in the first week of February, 1849. As the *Star* described it, they took up a line of march for the Rio Grande in the Laredo area. They struck out from their encampment at Twelve-Mile Motts (later Nuecestown). The trip across Texas took 33 days, far longer than it should have taken. Pack-mule trains carrying trade goods from Corpus Christi routinely made the trip in nine or 10 days. Peoples wrote a letter to the *Star* from the Presidio Rio Grande that was scathing in his criticism of some of his fellow travelers.[23] Peoples said some of the Mazatlan Rangers had paid their $150 fee to join the company at New Orleans and expected that nothing more was required of them. He said some of them deemed it below their station to do any physical labor. He said their wagons, when they left Twelve-Mile Motts, were weighed down with all kinds of useless, unnecessary personal possessions. Many of the wagons were pulled by oxen and mules in poor condition. On many of the days when they should have been traveling, Peoples wrote, some of the indolent men refused to stir and they were required to rest and take their leisure.

"A large number of the men were unfit to go to California by any route," Peoples wrote, "and will be unfit to stay there if they ever arrive, unless they get a situation in the shade next to a cologne lake."[24]

The Mazatlan Rangers, feuding between those who pulled their weight and those who didn't, broke up before they started across the arid regions of northern Mexico. The main group, with Peoples, continued across Chihuahua and Sonora. They ran out of water and suffered dysentery. Their most difficult undertaking was to cross raging rivers. They would caulk the cracks of the wagon beds and turn them into rafts. Peoples didn't make it to the California goldfields. He was drowned crossing the Gulf of California on the way to San Diego.[25] The word quickly spread that the route from Corpus Christi across Chihuahua and Sonora was difficult and dangerous. The argonauts fell back on more established routes, traveling to Chagres and across the isthmus, or going overland and over the mountains. For Corpus Christi, the gold rush was over by the summer of 1849.

Charles Bryant, from Maine, was killed and scalped by Indians at Chocolate Bayou, north of St. Mary's,* in 1850. His was a lonely death far from his native home. Bryant, a talented architect in Bangor, Maine, designed some of that city's most famous buildings. In 1837, he became involved as a leader in a rebellion in Canada against British power. He was captured and sentenced to be hanged. The night before the scheduled execution, friends helped him escape from prison and he slipped across the border into the United States. The British authorities posted a reward for him, dead or alive.[26]

Bryant decided he needed a change of scenery. He sailed for Galveston with his oldest son. They arrived in 1839. At Galveston, Bryant designed St. Mary's Cathedral, which still stands. When Zachary Taylor's army concentrated at Corpus Christi in 1845, Bryant moved to Corpus Christi and built the Union Theater to cater to the troops. After Taylor's army marched to the Rio Grande, Bryant moved his family to Corpus Christi. In 1849, Bryant began work to restore the Union Theater and operate it as a hotel. He also joined the Texas Rangers and was appointed mustering officer for three Ranger companies.[27]

He was summoned to Austin in January, 1850. On his way near Goliad, at John H. Wood's ranch on the Chocolate Bayou, Bryant was killed by a band of Lipan Apaches. As people from Wood's ranch watched (too few to go to his rescue), the Indians scalped Bryant. Later, Capt. John Grumbles' company of Rangers buried the body and took a lock of what was remaining of Bryant's hair. They chased the Indians for 300 miles, but couldn't catch them; the Indians had captured fresh horses and could change mounts.[28]

Bryant left a widow and six children with an estate of $1,500, town lots in Corpus Christi worth $1,100 and a case of architect's tools worth $5. His family received 640 acres of land in recognition of his services to the state of Texas.[29]

There was another killing that same month of January, 1850, that aroused Corpus Christi. A boy named James Doyle was given a gun for his 16th birthday. He and a friend crossed over the reef to go hunting on the north side of the Nueces Bay at a popular hunting spot at Gum Hollow. At a spring, they were supposedly surprised by Indians. Doyle dropped his gun and ran, the story went, while the friend hid in some bushes. The Indians picked up Doyle's gun and shot him to death.[30] Legendary Ranger "Rip" Ford was in Corpus Christi that day with a squad of Rangers. They crossed over the reef and made an effort to follow the Indians, but, Ford said, laconically, there was just no trail to follow. Ford said that if young Doyle was killed by Indians, they were on foot and left no tracks.[31] The spring became known as Doyle's Watering Hole.

---

* The present day Bayside is two miles from St. Mary's, which was once the largest lumber port in the western part of the Gulf. A road connected Corpus Christi to St. Mary's. The town and port went into decline with the growth of Rockport.

In February, 1850, two companies of the 1st U.S. Infantry, under the command of Capt. S.M. Plummer, moved up the Nueces River, 50 miles northwest of Corpus Christi, and built Fort Merrill overlooking the river and the Corpus Christi-San Antonio stage road. The soldiers built the fort from pine logs.[32] Soon after the fort was built, a company of Rangers under the command of "Rip" Ford camped nearby. They built a fire and boiled water to make mesquite tea.[33] That night, a Comanche raiding party tried to steal the Rangers' horses. There was a shootout before the Indians escaped. After the fight, Ford sent word to the officer in charge at the fort, telling him what happened. The officer was astounded that hostile Indians were so bold as to come up within shadows of the fort. The officer told Ford he believed the gunfire came from Texans fighting among themselves. A soldier from the fort cut off the head of a slain Comanche warrior, which caused harsh words between the Rangers and the soldiers.[34] One of Ford's Rangers was a young Irish orphan, Mat Nolan, who would later be elected sheriff of Nueces County.[*35]

The Fort Merrill incident demonstrated that a fort built to protect the stage road and surrounding countryside, which couldn't protect its own environs, was useless. Within five years, Fort Merrill was closed; the army realized that forts manned by largely foot-bound soldiers or (at best) inept riders were no match for Comanche warriors, the greatest fighters on horseback since the Mongols of Genghis Khan. Texas already knew the answer: a few fast-moving and hard-riding Ranger companies, living in the saddle and off the land, were far more effective than any number of forts, which one critic described as being the equivalent of sawmills on the ocean, in other words, useless and out of place.[36] A Texas newspaper declared, "The idea of repelling mounted Indians, the most expert horsemen in the world, with a force of foot soldiers, is ridiculous."[37]

At the beginning of the 1850s, Corpus Christi underwent its first census. It wasn't part of the United States in the previous census of 1840. The 1850 census showed Nueces County (mostly Corpus Christi) had 689 free citizens, 47 slaves, and 112 soldiers stationed in the city in an army attachment. The population was one-fourth what it had been (estimated) at its peak during the Taylor encampment in 1845-46. The town in 1850 had nine merchants; one of the richest was William Mann, a former customs inspector at Aransas City, with property worth $50,000, but Henry Kinney, the town's founder, had property worth $300,000. There was one hotel owner, one saddle-maker, one doctor. The census-taker, A.W. Hicks, had trouble with Spanish names; Garcia was spelled "Gorsea," Manuel as "Manwell" and Guadalupe was turned into "Warloope." J.W. Moses in that census is identified as a "herdsman." Moses at that time was a captain of an outfit that captured wild

---

[*] Nolan defeated Samuel R. Miller, county commissioner and ferry operator on the Nueces River, in the 1858 election.

mustangs for sale, called mustangers. Many of the Hispanics in that first census of the county are also listed as herdsman, probably meaning they were also mustangers, in Spanish *"mesteneros."*[38]

That first census shows the cosmopolitan makeup of Corpus Christi. Sixteen residents listed Pennsylvania as their home state, 15 came from Alabama, 51 emigrated from Germany, 32 came from Ireland. Many of those of Mexican descent (about half the total of the census for Nueces County) came from Mexico, although many of them may have been born in Texas while it was part of Mexico.[39] The census also listed 14 slave-owners in the county, including H.L. Kinney, who owned 10 slaves, and J.A. Baskin, who owned eight. There were 47 slaves in the county in 1850.[*40]

Two years later, on Sept. 9, 1852, Corpus Christi's first city government was chartered, the first council elected, and the first mayor took office, Benjamin F. Neal, a lawyer and newspaper publisher who came to Corpus Christi in 1844.[41] The first ordinance passed regulated dances and fandangos. It levied a $10 fine for holding any "fandango, dance or ball" without getting a $1 license from the mayor. The ordinance spelled out that fandangos had to end by 3 a.m. and it levied a $5 fine for anyone carrying a weapon at such an entertainment.[42#]

As the country began to expand into new territory acquired from Mexico, Kinney's bid to revive the town's fortunes achieved mixed results. The effort to establish a trade corridor to Chihuahua fizzled; Kinney and his partners lost money on the trade trip and the traffic of gold-seekers ceased. But Kinney's effort to get the Army to establish a route west from Corpus Christi paid off.[43] Gen. Persifor Smith, commander of the Eighth Military District, moved his headquarters from San Antonio to Corpus Christi, where he liked the breeze from the bay. In 1854, Smith married Ann (Millard) Armstrong, the sister of Forbes Britton's wife, Rebecca Millard. Military supplies were shipped to Corpus Christi and hauled by wagon trains to the new forts, like Fort Inge, being manned on the frontier. Once again, Corpus Christi was drawing its wealth and importance not from trade, but from the military.[44]

A big success story of 1851 was the Great Exhibition in London. Some six million people visited the fair held in a prefabricated glass-and-iron building at Hyde Park covering 19 acres, Paxton's Crystal Palace.[*] The Great Exhibition, the first world's fair, may have prompted Henry Kinney to hold

---

[*] Eight complete South Texas counties and parts of seven others were formed from the original Nueces County. Before it was carved up, the county stretched up the Nueces River to a point near Three Rivers, went west to Laredo and then down the Rio Grande to the Gulf of Mexico.

[#] Violence and the potential for violence at dances was a staple of conversation in the 19th century. J.B. "Red" Dunn wrote of attending a dance at San Patricio, where most of the men were carrying pistols. One man gave his girl a hard swing and his pistol got a hard jolt. He pulled his gun to assess the damage, the dancing stopped, he cocked it a time or two and decided it was all right, and the dancing resumed.

[*] The full title was the Great Exhibition of the Works of Industry of All Nations. American exhibits included the sewing machine and the Colt revolver.

his own fair—the Lone Star Fair in Corpus Christi. Kinney was looking for a way out of debt. His idea was to attract thousands of people to the fair, hoping some would settle here and buy some of the thousands of acres he had to sell. To promote the fair, Kinney sent out handbills throughout the U.S. and Europe. He expected 20,000 visitors and he borrowed $45,000 to cover expenses.[45]

As the day for the fair drew near, a New Orleans newspaper reported that "every movement in and around Corpus Christi seems to have some connection with the Great Fair." Kinney brought in a steamboat to ferry visitors from ships anchoring off the bar at Aransas Pass. Maria von Blucher wrote that the town was filling up with circus riders and sluttish "German girls of low morals."[46] Exhibits included Mexican blankets, saddles, bridles, spurs, farm products. Silver cups were awarded for the best flock of sheep, the best herd of brood mares. Gail Borden (of canned milk fame) won a prize for his canned meat biscuit.[47]

There were cockfights, riding contests, and lectures on philosophy and literature. One featured performance was that of Mexico City bullfighter Don Camerena. There were livestock auctions in the mornings, horse races in the afternoon, circus acts in the evening. Tents with ices and refreshments were dotted throughout the town. Maltby's Circus erected its big top on the beach.* The town was filled with Comanche and Lipan Indians, mustangers, U.S. soldiers, sheepherders, gunfighters.[48] Some visitors would later become famous, including steamboat captain Richard King. Ranger 'Rip' Ford attended and got his first glimpse of the pistolero Sally Skull.

Sally Skull (Sarah Jane Newman) defied the conventions of her time. She cursed like a muleskinner, rode like a man; she could rope like a vaquero and pick flowers with her black-handled bullwhip. She was deadly accurate, with right or left hand, with the two six-shooters she wore. She owned a horse ranch at Banquete. She took the name Skull from her first husband, George H. Scull. He disappeared and when asked what happened to him, Sally would say, "He's dead," with a look that terminated the conversation. But she kept the name Skull. She hired vaqueros and made horse-buying trips to Mexico; some said she got the horses by other than legal means, but they didn't say it in her hearing. One man learned that lesson. Sally had heard that a man made uncomplimentary remarks about her. When she ran into him, she whipped out one of her guns. "Been talking about me, huh? Well, dance, you son of a bitch, dance!" shooting at his feet while he did a frantic two-step.[49]

Rip Ford came across Sally at the Lone Star Fair as he was leaving town. He heard a pistol shot and, raising his eyes, saw a man fall to the ground and a woman in the act of lowering her six-shooter. "She was a noted character named Sally Skull," Ford wrote. "She was famed as a rough fighter, and

---

* About where Peoples and Water streets intersect, on the water side.

prudent men did not willingly provoke her in a row."[50]

For Henry Kinney, as it turned out, the Lone Star Fair was no Great Exhibition. Kinney had hoped to attract 20,000 visitors, but no more than 2,000 attended, and after the fair his creditors closed in.[51] Despite his financial difficulties, Kinney donated a block of land that surrounded Zachary Taylor's artesian well for a public park.[*52]

That summer, following the great fair, the town was filled once more with teamsters and wagons. The army came to the town's rescue once again. Supplies for army forts came in by sea and were hauled by wagon trains to the frontier garrisons. When Gen. Smith, commander of the Eighth Military District, prepared to move his headquarters to Corpus Christi, he sent Maj. William Chapman, the quartermaster at Fort Brown, to prepare the way.[53] Chapman arrived in August, 1852. He knew the town well; he had been here in 1845 with Zachary Taylor. He found a small village of 700 people by a bay with houses on a high bluff. He found the prevailing sea breeze a refreshing change from Brownsville, where it was sultry, hot and humid.[54]

Chapman, like other officers of the time, augmented his salary with various enterprises on the side. He brought in a flock of sheep and later became a partner in Richard King's ranch on the Santa Gertrudis. Chapman rented houses on the bluff for Gen. Smith and his officers. He rented a complex of buildings on the bayfront to house the quartermaster and commissary operations. The army established storerooms, saddler's shops, wheelwright and blacksmith shops, a huge wagon yard, and quarters for a company of soldiers and transient wagon masters and muleskinners.

Soldiers had hardly arrived before there was a riot. From its very beginning, more than a decade before, Corpus Christi was socially and ethnically a segregated city, with Hispanics occupying "jacals" on the back side of the bluff, an area called "Little Mexico." A New Year's fandango (a dance) was held at the home of Blas Falcon in the Hispanic community on the Hill. A fight broke out between the inhabitants and the soldiers. One soldier was stabbed to death and four others wounded. Next day, angry soldiers set fire to jacals in Little Mexico and the inhabitants fled into the brush west of town.[55] The fandango riot of January, 1854, led county commissioners to authorize a police patrol to prevent "disturbances, riots," in the city.[56]

During those years, Corpus Christi became a transit point for officers stationed at Texas forts. Lt. Phil Sheridan stopped here on his way to Fort Duncan. Lydia Spencer Lane, the new bride of a lieutenant, wrote about their arrival in 1854. They stayed in tents on North Beach. Mrs. Lane wrote that a spacious wall tent had been floored for her and her husband, as newlyweds, but an unmarried officer of higher rank, with an eye to his own comfort,

---

[*] Half of Kinney's donated block is today's Artesian Park. At some point, the other half of the block passed into private hands.

pulled rank and claimed it. "We only saw the outside of it," she lamented.[57]

Even with the presence of the army, there were sporadic Indian attacks around Corpus Christi. In 1854, a wagon train carrying army supplies was attacked by Lipan Apache warriors. Patrols were dispatched from every fort in the region, including Fort Merrill on the Nueces. At a place called Lake Trinidad, described as a pond in a wet year, south of Ben Bolt, the patrol ran into a party of Indians who had just killed three mustangers. Lt. Blake Cosby, in command of the dragoons (infantry trained to ride) from Fort Merrill, ordered his men to charge. The Indians fled into a skirt of mesquite timber and then turned to fire on the soldiers who came in pursuit. When the soldiers ran out of ammunition, the fight became hand-to-hand. Three soldiers were killed and five wounded, including Lt. Cosby, who was wounded in his sword arm. Cosby led his detachment back to Corpus Christi; the wounded men were treated at the army's military hospital. The fight at Lake Trinidad was covered in a report by the Secretary of War to Congress; it led Gen. Winfield Scott to order soldiers at army forts in Texas to be armed with Colt six-shooters and Sharp's rifles.[58]

CHAPTER 4

Richard King and King Ranch - The slaying of "Legs" Lewis - Henry Kinney's immigrants - Yellow fever epidemic

Richard King became an orphan when his parents, Irish immigrants, died when he was five. His aunt apprenticed him to a jeweler in New York. He ran away to sea when he was 10. After four days at sea as a stowaway, the boy was found and taken to the captain of the *Desdemona*. King told the captain he ran away because he didn't like having to look after the jeweler's kids. The captain made him his cabin boy to earn his passage.[1]

When the ship docked at Mobile, the captain found King a job on an Alabama steamboat. A few years later, the steamboat captain sent King to school in Connecticut, but he left school and returned to the riverboat life, this time in Florida, where he met Mifflin Kenedy, captain of the steamboat *Champion*. Kenedy took the *Champion* to New Orleans and then up the Mississippi. He had been hired to select boats for Zachary Taylor's campaign in Mexico. Kenedy wrote his friend King, urging him to join him on the Rio Grande. King arrived in 1847 and became the pilot on the *Corvette*.[2] King and Kenedy spent the war ferrying supplies up the Rio Grande. After the war ended in 1848, the two formed a partnership with Charles Stillman and bought three surplus army steamboats.[3] On July 10, 1850, King celebrated his 26th birthday at Miller's Hotel in Brownsville.[4]

In late April or early May of 1852, King and fellow travelers rode out of Brownsville to travel to Corpus Christi to visit the Lone Star Fair. King and the party probably followed the same route used in 1846 by Zachary Taylor's army when it left Corpus Christi and marched to the Rio Grande. King's party would have passed the sandy alkali flats around the salt lakes known as *El Desierto de los Muertos*, Desert of the Dead, before reaching the coastal prairies.[5] There had been isolated ranches in the region; Gen. Manuel de Mier y Teran, on his inspection tour of Texas in 1834, noted that the ranches belonged to residents of Camargo and they had suffered from Indian attacks.[6] The land that Richard King and his party rode through opened into a level prairie covered with stirrup-high grass, often described as a wide expanse or sea of grass. There were a few motts of trees on the horizon. King would have seen huge herds of mustangs which gave this area its name, the Wild Horse Desert. We can speculate that this is when King got the idea of starting a ranch, or perhaps he already had the idea and the trip served as a chance to look over the land.[7]

King may have stopped to visit Manuel Ramirez (Elizondo) at the Bobedo Ranch, which straddled the main route from Corpus Christi to Brownsville, northwest of Baffin Bay.[*8] While visiting the Bobedo Ranch, King asked about land for sale. This story was told by King Ranch vaquero Francisco Alvarado. Alvarado said King asked Ramirez about land suitable for ranching that could be bought. Ramirez told him about the Santa Gertrudis grant 12 miles to the north. Praxides Uribe of Matamoros claimed title to the grant.[9]

The party camped on a slight rise about three-fourths of the way from Brownsville (125 miles north). It was here that King apparently saw a pattern of the future. The party camped by a small stream called Santa Gertrudis, named by Blas Maria de la Garza Falcon, who had his own ranch in the area almost 100 years before. The party's campsite was a half mile below Rip Ford's old Ranger camp from 1849 and 1850.[10]

King went on to Corpus Christi to see the sights of the Lone Star Fair.[11] Back in Brownsville, King acted on his idea, talking it over with his friend, Capt. Robert E. Lee, who told him it wasn't Virginia, but it was a country with a future.[12] In July 1853, King bought 15,500 acres, part of the Santa Gertrudis grant, from the heirs of Juan Mendiola. He paid two cents an acre. He signed on a partner, G.K. "Legs" Lewis, a Ranger captain in Corpus Christi who could provide protection for the enterprise. Felix Blucher surveyed the land with King serving as chain carrier. The deed was filed in Corpus Christi on Nov. 14, 1853. This was the beginning of King Ranch[13] and the genesis of the cattle industry of South Texas. Its importance to Corpus Christi and South Texas would become clear in a few years.

Richard King the riverboatman knew nothing about ranching. But he knew enough to get expert help. He hired all the vaqueros (and their families) from a village in Tamaulipas, perhaps named Cruillas.[14] The ranch's first vaqueros were named Patino, Alvarado, Flores, Chapa, Ortiz, Villarreal, Cabazos, Villa, Ebano, and Cantu. They were called King's Men, "*Kinenos.*" King bought cattle in Mexico at $5 a head, cheap because it was a drought year.[15]

In Brownsville, Richard King met Henrietta Chamberlain, daughter of a Presbyterian preacher, who ran a girl's school, the Rio Grande Female Institute. She broke an engagement with another man and in 1854 married King. Mifflin Kenedy was best man at the wedding. King called his bride

---

* The name Bobedo is a corruption of the Spanish grant name, *Rincon de la Boveda.*

Etta; she called him Captain. They spent their honeymoon on the new ranch. The ranch account book tells of preparing for of the event in an oblique entry for Nov. 28, 1854: "One large closed carriage (a stagecoach) and harness now in Corpus Christi $400."

The trip from Brownsville in this stagecoach took Richard King and his new bride four days.[16] Years later, Henrietta King wrote of her first days at the ranch: "When I came here as a bride in 1854, the little ranch home then—a mere jacal as Mexicans would call it—was our abode for many months until our main ranch dwelling was completed. But I doubt if it falls to the lot of any bride to have had so happy a honeymoon. On horseback we roamed the broad prairies. When I grew tired, my husband would spread a Mexican blanket for me and then I would take my siesta under the shade of a mesquite tree . . ."[17]

King's ranching partner, Gideon K. "Legs" Lewis, was born in Ohio in 1823 and grew up in New Orleans, where he worked as a printer's devil (apprentice). He moved to Texas when he was 18. He worked as a reporter in Galveston until 1842 when he joined a punitive raid into Mexico.[18] At Mier, "Bigfoot" Wallace teased the young Lewis—"You better run, or the Mexicans will get you sure."[19] Lewis didn't run fast enough. He was captured at Mier, along with legendary Texans Ewen Cameron and Bigfoot Wallace himself. Perhaps it was on the long march into Mexico that Lewis gained his nickname of "Legs" for his long, purposeful stride.

Lewis and the other Mier captives were taken to Perote Castle, on the road to Vera Cruz, and locked in a dungeon. Santa Anna wanted to execute all the captives, but decided that one in 10 would be shot, a decimation, with the men to be chosen by lot. They were ordered to take a bean from a clay jar filled with 159 white beans and 17 black ones. The jar was held up so they couldn't pick and choose. A white bean meant life, a black bean death, and Lewis drew a white bean.[20]

After 17 of those who drew black were executed, Lewis and the surviving captives were freed. Lewis returned to Galveston and worked as a reporter until 1846. As war with Mexico was brewing, he took off for the Rio Grande and joined Samuel Bangs, who had been editor of the *Corpus Christi Gazette*, in starting a newspaper called *The Reveille*. But Lewis soon left it to Bangs and joined the Rangers assigned to Zachary Taylor's army. He fought in Mexico for the next two years and was cited for bravery in carrying dispatches.[21]

"Legs" Lewis stayed with the Rangers after the war. By 1852, he was in Corpus Christi, helping Kinney put on the Lone Star Fair. Lewis was sent to New Orleans to buy the silver cups that were awarded as prizes.[22] During this time, he bought two waterfront lots in Corpus Christi for $100 and $150 and Kinney's interest in the *Nueces Valley* newspaper; he served for a time as editor and publisher.[23] That September, Lewis was made a captain of a Ranger company stationed in Corpus Christi.[24]

41

Lewis joined Richard King in starting a ranching operation in 1853. King needed Lewis and his Rangers for protection. Lewis gave King $2,000 for a half interest in the ranch. An accounting note in 1854 in King's hand says: "Capt. G.K. Lewis, one pair boots, $5.50." Lewis was running the ranch while King ran his steamboats on the Rio Grande, but it was King who was paying the bills.[25]

The King-Lewis partnership was short-lived. Lewis was famous as a handsome, pleasure-loving, ladies' man; one account said that wherever he went, his gifts with the opposite sex did not go unappreciated. In 1855, he was accused of having an affair with the wife of Dr. J.T. Yarrington of Corpus Christi. The doctor, known as a wife-beater, found love letters between Lewis and his wife. Lewis was making his second run for Congress (he ran and lost in 1852) and he wanted the letters back. He showed up in Yarrington's office and demanded the doctor return them. Yarrington refused and warned Lewis not to come back. But Lewis returned and on April 14, 1855, Yarrington shot him with a double-barreled shotgun.[26]

The slaying of "Legs"—the boy captive of Mier—was big news in Texas papers. The *San Antonio Herald* wrote, "Few braver men could be found, where all were daring, than G.K. Lewis." The *Galveston Weekly News* wrote: "We learn that Capt. G.K. Lewis was shot on Saturday last, the 14th inst., at Corpus Christi by J.T. Yarrington. The particulars of this catastrophe, so far as we have ascertained, were that Mrs. Yarrington had sued her husband for a divorce, in which object she was aided by Lewis. Lewis went to Yarrington's house to demand some papers having reference to the matter, when Yarrington, who was armed with a double-barreled gun, shot him down. Lewis reeled, and fell against the house. He died soon after without speaking a word. Yarrington, in default of bail, was ordered to be committed to jail, and was brought to this city this morning by the sheriff of Nueces County for safe confinement, there being no secure prison in Corpus Christi. Whatever causes may have been at the bottom of this tragical affair, we cannot but regret the death of Capt. Lewis. He had his failings it is true, as who of us have not?, but there were many excellent traits in his character. He was generous and open-hearted; firm and devoted to his friendships, and guile and malice were not nursed in his heart. He was fearless among dangers and served his country in the field on many occasions. He drew a white bean at Mier, when a mere boy, and could point to many honorable scars received in the public service."[27]

Yarrington wrote a letter from Indianola that was printed in the *Gonzales Inquirer* and reprinted in the *Texas State Gazette*: "Dear Sir—I drop you a line hastily to inform you that I had the misfortune to kill Capt. G.K. Lewis, at Corpus Christi, on the 14th inst. The reason was, he seduced Mrs. Yarrington from me and my children, and then added insult to injury by continually coming to my house, and also trying to steal my children from me, and for trying to force from my possession certain letters, which I intercepted, addressed to my wife . . . I am in charge of the Sheriff, Mr. Graham, we are bound to Galveston."[28] He was taken to Galveston by the sheriff, but was never tried for the shooting.[*]

Lewis' death complicated King's affairs. Lewis left no heirs; his undivided half-interest in the ranch was put up in auction. King asked Maj. W. W. Chapman to bid for the property for him by proxy. Maj. Chapman was in charge of disposing of surplus army property at the end of the Mexican War. He sold army steamboats on the Rio Grande to King and Kenedy. Chapman bought Lewis's half interest, which later became the subject of a bitter lawsuit (*Helen B. Chapman vs. Richard King*).[29]

The failure of Henry Kinney's Lone Star Fair in 1852 added $50,000 to his load of debt. Gen. Hugh McLeod foreclosed on Kinney's Mustang Island ranch, which Kinney purchased in 1848, and Forbes Britton sued Kinney for repayment of a debt of $1,000 in gold. Kinney, it turned out, had mortgaged some property several times, leading to multiple claims.[30] Kinney's other ranches were the Oso, the Alazan near Baffin Bay and Barranco Blanco on the Nueces. In the months before and after the fair, Kinney borrowed more than $40,000 from his friend John Peter Schatzell, the former American consul at Vera Cruz who retired to Corpus Christi.[31]

To try to recoup his losses, Kinney stepped up his land promotions. He sent an agent to London, John Holbein, and distributed 20,000 handbills in England, Scotland and Ireland. His handbills under the heading of "Nueces Valley Land & Emigration" praised the moderate climate and unlimited opportunities in the Corpus Christi region. Kinney's offer was 100 acres of land at six shillings (about one dollar) an acre. With the purchase of 100 acres, he would provide the buyer with a yoke of oxen, one horse, 10 cows, and one lot in Nuecestown. The pamphlet read, in part: "To any family of good repute for honesty, industry and perseverance, he will let them have 10 cows on shares; he will sell them one hundred acres of land at six shillings per acre; also one yoke of oxen, and one horse; two shillings per acre to be paid to the agents in London, on execution of the contract—and the balance for the land and stock to be paid in ten years, with interest annually; he will also give to each family one building lot in the town of Nueces . . . The soil and climate of this region is unsurpassed—two full crops of corn and other cereals in perfection, are secured annually. Irish and sweet potatoes, with all other roots and vegetables, make huge returns; the peach, the vine, and other fruit trees thrive luxuriantly . . . Corpus Christi, situated in the vicinity of this property, is a town of considerable commercial activity, and being the chief mart for merchandize for the western districts of Texas and the Rio Grande country, is fast rising in importance . . ."[32]

Kinney's efforts to sell his land by distributing handbills produced a flow

---

[*] Jacob Yarrington and wife divorced. He moved to Oakland, Calif., where he died in 1894. Mrs. Yarrington, Anna Maria Perlee, moved to Shubuta, Miss., where she taught school.

of immigrants who, in time, would have a great impact on Corpus Christi and the Nueces Valley disproportionate to their numbers. Why did they come? Why did they decide to leave behind families and associations of a lifetime? They came because land in Texas was cheap, because those who worked hard were better rewarded, because there was the prospect of a future without poverty and a chance that their children would have better lives than they had inherited. This was a powerful lure. They came from England, Scotland, and Ireland. Thomas Dunn and his wife Catherine bought 100 acres from Kinney. They left Ireland and arrived in Corpus Christi in 1849. So did master mason James Ranahan and his wife; they left Belfast that same year. Ranahan bought a lot from Kinney for $150 and set up brick kilns below the bluff. James and Agnes Rankin read Kinney's advertising and migrated, with their five children, to Corpus Christi from Glasgow, Scotland in 1852.[33]

In England, Scotland and Ireland, where land fetched exorbitant prices, Kinney's offer looked to be a real bargain. Many were taken in by the handbills. One of those was Joseph Almond of Newcastle-on-Tyne. Another was John Wade of Yorkshire, and Robert Adams. Each put up money to buy Kinney land. In October of 1852, they brought their families to Liverpool and boarded a sailing ship, the *Essex*. When they stepped on the gangplank, they were leaving behind family ties for an uncertain future.[34]

The Adams family, the Almonds, and the Wades were cabin passengers on the voyage across the Atlantic. The hold was filled with German immigrants. William and Robert Adams, who were four and five at the time, would later recall that the captain gave them raisins when they took their dose of castor oil. After eight weeks at sea, they landed in New Orleans and took an old side-wheeler, the *Mexico,* to Galveston, where they boarded a smaller ship for Indianola and then the mailboat for Corpus Christi. They landed at Ohler's Wharf, at the foot of Peoples Street, and were met by Reuben Holbein, son of John Holbein, Kinney's London agent.[35]

Kinney's handbills described Corpus Christi as "a city of considerable commercial activity, being the mercantile center of South Texas." In reality, it was a semi-hamlet rather than a city. The place had only three small stores and a few dozen houses. Robert Adams remembered that the stores were Mrs. Elizabeth Hart's on the beach, Noessel's on Chaparral, and Norris's on the bluff. It didn't look like the center of anything. It could hardly be called a town.[36]

It had to be a bitter disappointment when the immigrants located their parcels of land. They had staked all on glowing promises made in the Kinney handbills. It was not the land they expected. The handbills described the land as rich farmland, "the fairest region of America." The land had never been broken to the plow. Even if they worked the land, there was no ready market within reach for what they could produce. Despite the pamphlet claims, there was no market for there was no population of any size in the region and no easy way to transport their produce to population centers. There were no buyers waiting for what they could produce, if they could have produced it. They turned to other occupations.

Robert Adams, Sr. had been a railway inspector in England. He wanted to be a farmer, but he was disgusted with prospects in Texas. He had made a payment on 100 acres of Kinney's land, but it was not farmland as advertised, nor was Nuecestown the thriving settlement of 1,000 people the handbills described; less than half a dozen families lived there, struggling to make a living. Even if Adams could farm, there was no market for the produce. He didn't take up the land, so he lost his down payment. Adams wanted to return to England, but he was persuaded to stay. He moved the family to a farm near Nueces Bay, working as a hired hand.[37]

But despite their disappointment, the Adams, Wades, Wrights, Reynolds, Almonds and other immigrants attracted on the basis of Kinney's land promotions, fraudulent or not, made the most of what they found and created their own future. They got jobs as teamsters and muleskinners for the army and, in time, many of them became wealthy sheep and cattle ranchers in the Nueces Valley. Their success, along with the ranchers like Richard King, became the foundation of wealth in Corpus Christi which, after the army departed, became the regional headquarters of the sheep and cattle industry.[38]

Many of Kinney's immigrants reached Corpus Christi at a bad time in its history. The town in 1854 suffered a yellow fever outbreak, called "vomito" in Mexico, that was brief, but lethal. Yellow fever was a viral, often fatal, disease that caused vomiting and jaundice and destroyed the liver. People thought it came from swamp vapors because it afflicted low, tropical areas. No one knows how it spread to Corpus Christi, but the popular version was that a Mexican ship loaded with fresh fruit docked at the wharf. The vessel's arrival broke the monotony of life in a small town. The ship stayed a week; many of the people of the town went down to the wharf to buy lemons, limes, bananas and pineapples; fresh fruit was a rare treat. The ship was afterwards blamed for bringing the yellow fever. The entire town became a fever ward. Those stricken were easy to spot. They had red eyes, yellow skin, they coughed and retched a lot, and their vomit was black. Smoke hung over the city; clothes and bedding of those who died were burned and smoldering tar buckets, thought to prevent the spread of the disease, sat on doorsteps and hung in front of homes. But nothing worked. The fever claimed victims in every home, families were wiped out and children left with their parents dead.[39]

A new army bride and her soldier husband on their way to Fort Inge arrived at Corpus Christi at the height of the epidemic. Lydia Spencer Lane wrote that they heard, even before they landed, that people were sick from yellow fever. "It was dreadful news to us, as there was no escape, no running away from it, nothing to do but land, take the risk, and trust in Providence.

45

However, I had 'gone for a soldier,' and a soldier I determined to be."[40]

More bad news was on its way. When the Eighth Army Headquarters moved to Corpus Christi, and with army supplies moving through, the town looked sure to grow and prosper. Gen. Persifor Smith and his superior, Gen. William S. Harney, bought thousands of acres of land south of town.* The town was encouraged by rumors that the army would move its huge depot from San Antonio to Corpus Christi. But those hopes were dashed by a report by Lt. Col. W. G. Freeman, who said Corpus Christi was unsuitable due to the same problems that plagued Zachary Taylor's army—a lack of fresh water and the difficulty of bringing in supplies because of the shallow mudflats choking the bay and channels to the Gulf. Freeman recommended the army move its supplies through the port of Indianola and from there by wagon train to San Antonio.[41]

This was a severe blow to Corpus Christi. Henry Kinney, the town's founder, didn't think the decision would stand. He was off on his Nicaraguan expedition, but he wrote to friends back home: "Our government is all right. The depot will be removed from Indianola to Corpus Christi and other things done to the great advantage of Corpus Christi."[42]

In 1856, the army began to move the headquarters back to San Antonio. The army's shops, forges and stables were closed. Wagon drivers, many of them immigrants, were out of work. Corpus Christi's army paycheck-based economy was gone, once again. The move was completed in the spring of 1857. Once again, Corpus Christi was in a bad way. William Headen, a future mayor of Corpus Christi, later wrote that the city relied too much on government contracts, that it was all but helpless when the army relocated the Eighth Military District headquarters. Those who depended on the $15 a month army paychecks, Headen wrote, were forced to find a new livelihood in the country. Many of them were immigrants attracted to South Texas by Kinney's land promotions. "Some became farmers, others became stockmen, and not a few turned their attention to sheep-raising."[43] The shift to stockraising in the region, both cattle and sheep, would become a major driving force behind the growth and future prosperity of the town.

Maj. Chapman, the army quartermaster who bought "Legs" Lewis's share of King Ranch, brought in merino sheep from Pennsylvania to breed with hardy Mexican sheep. Chapman's flock grazed near Richard King's new ranch headquarters. This marked the beginning of the sheep era, which in time contributed enormously to Corpus Christi's prosperity. The city eventually became one of the world's great wool markets and a leading wool exporting port, shipping out millions of pounds of wool each year. The cattle kingdom of Texas began at about the same time, in almost the same location, along Santa Gertrudis Creek and on the fertile grazing lands of the Nueces Valley. Corpus Christi's coming prosperity was tied to Chapman's merino

---

* Much of the Ocean Drive property was once part of the Harney tract.

46

crossbreed sheep and longhorn cattle. Corpus Christi's position, for decades to come, as the trading center for sheepmen and cattle ranchers, allowed it to regain some of its lost importance and prosperity.[44]

When the army headquarters were removed to San Antonio, Henry Kinney was gone. After Kinney lost upwards of $50,000 on the Lone Star Fair and other ventures in 1852, he was broke and decided to recoup his fortune by setting up his own empire in Nicaragua, living up to his reputation as a man of low inclinations and high aspirations. He borrowed money on his land. He left for New York in September 1854 to finalize his filibuster plans. He was jailed briefly on charges of violating the neutrality act but, finally, he set sail with 100 followers on the *Emma* on June 6, 1855. In a letter to a friend, he wrote, "I expect to make a million dollars."[45]

The schooner hit a reef and floundered off the Mosquito Coast. Kinney helped to rescue people on the ship and save the provisions. It was a bad start for his venture, but Kinney was an optimist. He wrote again, saying, "I am at last on Central American soil with 100 men . . . This is a beautiful place and is to be the principal of the world. My force will be augmented in the course of three weeks to 2,000 men, when I shall move up country. I have a larger space to act in than I had in Corpus Christi and the result of my undertakings in Central America can hardly be imagined."[46] Kinney, the central character in his own drama, was elected military governor by his followers, members of a cabinet were named, and a new flag raised. But Kinney's filibustering venture failed. His funds dwindled and his supporters deserted him in favor of another Yankee empire-builder, William Walker of Tennessee.[47]

Kinney, a broken man, made his way back to Corpus Christi in 1858. He was greeted with a bill of divorce from Mary B. Herbert. They were married in 1850, but she left him and moved to Galveston two years later. About the time of their breakup, Kinney was having an affair with Matilda Ohler, wife of merchant Edward Ohler, which was the talk of the town.[48] The divorce was granted in 1858.[49] Kinney, who had been gone four years, was hailed as a hero when he returned at the end of June, 1858, despite bad debts he left behind and the absolute failure of his Mosquito Coast filibuster. The newspaper said there was "heartfelt rejoicing" on his return to the city he founded. His invitation to a public dinner was signed by the town's leading citizens. It said, in part, "We feel great pleasure in extending to you an invitation to meet your friends here at a public dinner, or barbecue, at such time as may suit your convenience (it was held on July 19). This invitation is extended as a mark of respect and attachment to you personally, and as evidence of our gratitude to one who has stood by us for so many years in the counsels of the state, and at home, as the prompt and fearless asserter of the rights of this neglected frontier."[50]

The summer of Kinney's return to the "neglected frontier" was also the summer of the Laguna Madre monster. There were reports of a "great serpent" in the laguna that had killed and eaten full-grown cows and was a danger to any unwary traveler. An expedition was organized to capture the monster. It failed when the ship ran aground near Flour Bluff, "resulting in the loss of rudder and boom, and compelling the return to town of the disappointed party." Talk of the Laguna Madre monster died down.[51]

CHAPTER 5

Runaway slaves - Secession and Civil War - Blockade and the Cotton Road - The bombardment of Corpus Christi - Yankee commander is captured at Flour Bluff - War brings hard times

T here were slaves in Corpus Christi in the 1850s, but they were not a sizable percentage of the population. Many were brought to Corpus Christi as personal servants of Southern officers in Zachary Taylor's army. Taylor himself freed his valet, "Little Bob" Thompson, who settled down to raise a family in the Juan Saenz community west of Corpus Christi.[*][1] The 1850 census showed the city with 47 slaves, 20 male and 27 female, in a population of 651.[2] By 1860, there were 135 slaves, valued at $91,050.[3]

Beyond the town, slavery was not prevalent in the ranch country south of the Nueces. Field hands were not in demand because not much cotton was grown on coastal prairies more suited to grazing than growing. Labor from Mexico was cheap, and the nearness of the border made it too easy for slaves to escape. Mexico provided a sanctuary for runaways; slavery was illegal (prohibited by the Constitution of 1823) and the sentiments in Mexico favored the slaves instead of the slave-owners. Under the heading of "Runaway Negroes," the *Nueces Valley* reported: "Yesterday we learned that three negroes belonging to the estate of James H. Durst, left for the Rio Grande, for Mexico . . . Yesterday, those negroes were worth four thousand dollars; today they are worth nothing."[4] One slaveholder chasing a runaway slave said: "We caught him once, but he got away. I had my six-shooter handy; every barrel missed fire. Shot at him three times with rifles, but he'd got too far off. Got into them bayous and kept swimming from one side to the other. If he's got across the river, the Mexicans will take care of him."[5]

---

[*] The community took its name from an employee of Henry Kinney, Juan Saenz Garcia, who owned property seven miles west of the town on Up River Road at the (later) intersection with Clarkwood Road. In the 1875 Nuecestown Raid, bandits plundered George Frank's store in the Juan Saenz community

Catching runaway slaves was a lucrative business on the border. Bounty hunters worked for the rewards posted on runaways; since slaves were considered valuable property, rewards could run into the hundreds of dollars. Slaveholder Maj. Stephen Peters had persistent problems with a slave family that kept trying to escape. The family, a man, woman, and two children, were caught once near the border by bounty hunters and returned to the owner. They escaped again. Peters offered a $250 reward for their recapture. They were again caught near the border and returned to Peters at his place on Padre Island.[6] They ran a third time. The Corpus Christi newspaper, rooting for the slave-owner, said, "It is supposed they are making their way toward Mexico. Boys on the Rio Grande, times are hard, now you have a chance to get a large reward. Look out for them."[7]

Andrew Anderson, the son of a pioneer ship captain who lived on Water Street, as a boy saw his neighbor Edward Ohler buy two slaves from Matagorda. Anderson said he paid $300 for a 16-year-old boy and $100 for an 18-year-old girl. He recalled another story involving one of Ohler's slaves. A slave named Rachel was accused by Mrs. Ohler of stealing silver, which was found under her mattress. A constable took her to the jail where there was a whipping post. Andrew and several other boys peeked through the cracks and watched as the constable tied her to the post and lashed her with a rawhide whip until the blood ran. She got 25 lashes. "With each blow of the whip, she would give a big jerk."[8]

The fact that slavery was not an important part of the local economy did not prevent Corpus Christi from siding with the state and the South when secession came to a vote. Speeches for and against secession were made at the Nueces County Courthouse. Pro-secession speeches were made by A.A. DeAvalon, J.B. Conley, Simon Jones, George Pfeuffer and Jacob Ziegler. Some prominent citizens opposed Texas seceding from the Union, including state Sen. Forbes Britton, a West Point-trained veteran of the Mexican War. Before he died in February, Sen. Britton spoke against seceding. Britton's fiery son-in-law, Judge Edmund J. Davis, also spoke out against secession, but his view did not prevail.[9] In a referendum on Feb. 23, 1861, the citizens voted 164 to 42 to support secession and leave the Union.[10] It was reported that some men who voted for secession broke down and cried, as they bade farewell to the flag they were born under and for which the Mexican War veterans had fought. The *Ranchero* editor was very critical of the pro-Unionists in the town, saying: "Let them seek some spot where in seclusion they can spend their days and await death at the end of their mental sufferings."

When the war began after Confederate forces bombarded Fort Sumter, Abraham Lincoln ordered a blockade of Southern ports.[11] The analogy used by Lincoln's generals was that a blockade of Southern ports would strangle the Confederacy like an anaconda. As the blockade took hold in the Gulf, it strangled Corpus Christi, one of the few Texas cities to suffer during the

Civil War. Grim times were ahead, as the city's newspaper, *The Ranchero*, warned: "We are in danger, and we should be prepared for any emergency. Corpus Christi, with her 2,000 inhabitants, lives at the mercy of any gunboat that chooses to steer over Aransas Bar up to our city."[12]

But the outbreak of war was a festive occasion. The first troop of Confederate soldiers organized wore handsome red sashes presented to them by their wives and sweethearts. In a ceremony on the courthouse steps, Capt. William B. Wrather, organizer of the company, accepted a Confederate flag from Mary Woessner. After this ceremony was over, the captain and Miss Woessner were married.[13] Within days after the war began, Corpus Christi formed a Committee of Public Safety, with Benjamin F. Neal as chairman.[14] Five units of home guards were formed, with each man responsible for bringing his own weapon. The muster rolls indicate the types of weapons the enlistees brought, everything from pistols to shotguns and hunting rifles, many of them ancient.[15]

As the blockade anaconda tightened, goods became scarce and commerce all but dried up. The newspaper couldn't get its newsprint from Galveston. Editor Henry Maltby (a native of Ohio, but a fierce Confederate) wrote, "This is the first time we have missed an issue. We trust the (devil) will lay violent hands on Old Abe and anchor him in the middle of a lake of fire and brimstone." As the blockade of the coast began, Maltby warned, "The enemy is now at our very doors . . . We are in danger and should be prepared for an emergency." The paper advised, under the heading, Defense of Aransas Pass: "Aransas Pass (the channel) can be effectively defended by a mounted battery for 10 guns and one company of artillery, near the lighthouse. This position commands the channel of three miles long between the bar and the bay. . ."[16]

The blockading forces turned their attention to the South Texas coast between Corpus Christi and the Rio Grande.[17] The blockade forced cotton, the lifeblood of the Confederacy, to be transported overland on what became known as the Cotton Road. The major stops on the road were at Banquete and King Ranch.[18] Many thousands of bales of white, fluffy cotton were hauled by wagon, oxcart and mule cart down the Cotton Road.[19] In Nueces County, the road followed the old Matamoros Road, the same route followed by Zachary Taylor's army when it marched from Corpus Christi to the border in March 1846.[20] In time, boys too young and men too old to fight were conscripted to drive cotton wagons to Brownsville. Robert Adams and his brother William, 15 and 16 years old, took two loads down the Cotton Road. Each had a wagon to drive, pulled by oxen. They had a horse to use to hunt up the oxen, which were turned loose at night to graze. At night, the men would gather around their campfires to cook their meals of bacon and burnt-okra coffee. On the way south, the "road" was decorated with tufts of cotton that got caught in the brush.[21]

John Warren Hunter was 16 when he helped haul cotton down the Cotton

Road. He traveled from Hopkins County to Brownsville. He described the crowded scene at the Santa Margarita crossing on the Nueces River, northwest of Corpus Christi, with long caravans of wagons waiting on either bank to cross.* Santa Margarita, on the west bank of the Nueces, was at a place where a shallow gravel bottom made an ideal ford. As they passed through the little village of San Patricio, Hunter wrote, they saw few people, but when they approached the river, a busy scene came into view, where there were several wagon trains loaded with cotton going to Brownsville. On the opposite bank were trains and pack mules returning from the Rio Grande loaded with guns and ammunition.[22]

South from Santa Margarita on the river, the next major stop was Banquete, west of Corpus Christi, where long trains of wagons and oxcarts passed day and night, some going south loaded with cotton, others going north loaded with war materiel. A company of Confederate troops under the command of James A. Ware (later Matt Nolan) camped on the San Fernando Creek to guard the Cotton Road. Banquete was a busy, clamorous place, with the Byington Hotel, saloon, stables, and supply stores all on the south side of Banquete Creek.[23]

Sally Skull, a pistolero who had made her living buying horses in Mexico and selling them in East Texas, was a regular traveler on the Cotton Road. She bought cotton in East Texas for pennies a pound and sold it in Matamoros for up to a dollar a pound. She had her own fleet of wagons driven by Mexican vaqueros. John Warren Hunter ran across her on the Cotton Road; he said she was wearing a black dress and sunbonnet, with a six-shooter hanging at her belt, and was sitting on her black horse as fine and erect as a cavalry officer on parade.[24]

From Banquete, the next major stop was King Ranch headquarters on the Santa Gertrudis. The ranch was a receiving depot for the Confederate government. The teamsters could load up with fresh water before they hit the Big Sands, and they could buy supplies at the ranch commissary. Richard King was one of the organizers behind the Cotton Road. King, from a vantage point at the top of the ranch watchtower, on any day could see hundreds of cotton wagons slowly moving south, the long trains stretching to the horizon and kicking up a tan ribbon of dust.[25]

From King Ranch, the Cotton Road went due south to the Rio Grande near Brownsville (the route shifted west after Brownsville was captured by Union forces). Some Cotton Road teamsters were from Corpus Christi, and they weren't volunteers. Rosalie Bridget Hart Priour, a schoolteacher who lived by the Salt Lake near the town, wrote in her memoirs that her son-in-law, James Hatch, had pneumonia, but he was forced to go to Brownsville with a load of cotton for the government. When he returned, he

---

* Santa Margarita had long been used as a fording place where the Camino Real from the Rio Grande to Goliad crossed the Nueces River. It was south of San Patricio near the present day community of Bluntzer. James H. Durst's ranch, Diezmero, was there.

was still sick but he had another load to take. Mrs. Priour asked the provost marshal in Corpus Christi to let her oldest son Julian go in James' place. He refused because he knew Julian soon would be 18, making him old enough to be conscripted into the army.[26] The conscription law took effect in April, 1862, and all of Texas was placed under martial law, with the rights of *habeas corpus* suspended. If Julian was allowed to go to the border with a load of cotton, he might take the opportunity to cross into Mexico to avoid conscription, which so many Union sympathizers in Texas were doing. Confederates called them "renegados."[27] Julian was not allowed to go; he was conscripted into a local unit of the Home Guards.[28]

At the Rio Grande, cotton was loaded on steamboats owned by Richard King and Mifflin Kenedy (operating safely under Mexican registry) and taken downriver to be sold for gold. These boom times on the border were known as "Los Algodones", cotton times. Matamoros was full of Union and Confederate agents, cotton brokers, soldiers of fortune, renegados, the flotsam and jetsam of war. From Matamoros, the cotton was hauled 25 miles east to the Mexican fishing village of Bagdad, on the southern bank at the mouth of the Rio Grande, a place originally called Boca del Rio. Bagdad in the Civil War was a shanty boomtown filled with tent hotels and tarpaulin restaurants, with cotton piled everywhere in sight, waiting to be lightered to hundreds of ships waiting outside the bar. Lt. Col. James Arthur Lyon Fremantle, a British military attaché, landed at the village of Bagdad on his way to join Robert E. Lee's Army of Northern Virginia as an observer. For an immense distance, Fremantle wrote, you could see endless bales of cotton.[29]

Throughout the war, a stream of wagons loaded with cotton traveled down the Cotton Road to be sold in Mexico for gold, which in turn was used to buy medical and military supplies for the Confederacy. Goods that crossed the river, under the eyes of Mexican authorities, were labeled, with a knowing wink, Hollow Ware (rifles), Bean Flour (gunpowder) and Canned Goods (percussion caps). The Cotton Road that passed to the west of Corpus Christi was the back door of the Confederacy.[30]

At the start of the war, Henry Kinney, bankrupt and in bad health after his filibustering effort in Nicaragua, wrote Abraham Lincoln offering his services as a foreign minister to Mexico. Lincoln didn't respond so Kinney, who could switch from one side to the other with equal facility, made the same offer to Jefferson Davis, who also turned him down. In 1862, Corpus Christi's founder, Henry Kinney, was shot to death in Matamoros. Kinney had had a longtime affair with a woman in Matamoros, Genoveva Perez, with whom he had a daughter named Adelina. Early one morning in March, Kinney was killed. Reports said he was shot in the chest during a civil disturbance between rival factions, the Crinolinos and Rojos, in Matamoros, but that skirmish happened weeks after Kinney was slain. The real story was that he was shot at the door of his old flame Genoveva by her jealous husband, Cesario Falcon. Julius Henry was there. He said he lifted Kinney up after he was shot, assisted by Martin Hinojosa, and removed his pistol.[31] Of Kinney, a complex man, no good things were remembered, except that he founded Kinney's Rancho, the settlement that became the town, and did his utmost to promote its welfare.

There was news about the formation of the Mounted Coast Guard to defend the city and the construction of a gunpowder mill in Corpus Christi. George Pfeuffer signed a contract to furnish 20,000 pounds of powder to the Texas Military Board. Pfeuffer was given 150 bales of cotton to sell in Matamoros to buy the raw materials, sulfur and saltpeter, but no gunpowder was ever produced in Pfeuffer's mill; the enterprise was abandoned in 1863.[32] The blockade of the Texas coast near Corpus Christi was commanded by Lt. J.W. Kittredge, described as a bold, daring man. Before the war, Kittredge had been captain of a steamer sailing between Galveston and the Rio Grande; he was familiar with the passes and bays of the Texas coast. Kittredge, not satisfied with tacking back and forth in boring blockade duty, led forays ashore and tried cutting-out attacks in the inner bays.[33]

In January of 1862, he captured a blockade-running ship, the *J.J. McNeil*, loaded with tobacco and coffee, near Pass Cavallo. In February, he captured the *Bellefont*, loaded with cotton, at the Aransas Pass. He landed 50 Marines on Mustang Island and they burned the homes of bar pilots Thomas Clubb and Robert Mercer. They crossed over to St. Joseph's Island and burned homes and warehouses. Kittredge captured a sloop loaded with medical supplies bound for Corpus Christi and, in general, kept the Texas coast in an uproar of fear and uncertainty. His most daring move was an attack on Corpus Christi.[34]

When news reached Corpus Christi that Kittredge had captured the shallow-draft vessels he needed to enter Corpus Christi Bay, Col. Charles Lovenskiold, Corpus Christi's provost marshal, had three old ships loaded with concrete rubble and scuttled in Corpus Christi Bayou* to block navigation; any vessel going to Corpus Christi had to use the bayou.[35] But Kittredge's gunboat *Sachem* tied on to the sunken ships and towed them out of the way with no trouble.[36]

On Aug. 12, 1862, five Union warships anchored off Ohler's Wharf.** Town residents that night could see the lights shining on Kittredge's ships. Next morning, a captain's gig pulled away from the *Corypheus* and Kittredge, flying a white flag, stepped onto Ohler's Wharf. He was met by Chief Justice (County Judge in today's terms) H.A. Gilpin and Col. Alfred M. Hobby, from Refugio, a 26-year-old Confederate officer in charge of coastal defenses. Kittredge, known as an arrogant man, said he intended to inspect U.S. government property in the town. Hobby informed him the U.S.

---

* Corpus Christi Bayou was located where the Aransas Pass causeway is now.
** Ohler's Wharf was just south of where the Peoples Street T-Head roadway is today; the Ladies Pavilion was later built at this location.

government had no property in Corpus Christi, that whatever it had at one time was the property of the Confederate government. Kittredge said he would land "under the national ensign" whenever and wherever he chose. He politely gave them 48 hours to get the civilians out of the way, provided that the time would not be used to build up defenses; the truce could only be used for the removal of non-combatants.[37]

People buried valuables and began to stream out of town, flushed from their habitat like startled quail. Rosalie B. Hart Priour wrote that "every wagon, cart, carriage, and ambulance (buggy) that could be found was pressed into service; even wheelbarrows were in use to carry articles of household furniture to a place of safety. You could see in every direction women and children running to the country loaded with chickens, wash tubs, pots, kettles . . . " Mrs. Priour said her husband laughed aloud at the sight of one girl carrying a wash tub who, after going a short distance, called back, "Mama, don't forget the looking glass."[38]

The John Anderson family went to Flour Bluff.[39] Maria von Blucher took her children to Nuecestown, 12 miles away.[40] Malvina (Britton) Moore, a slave, took her daughter Anna to Judge Matthew Cody's place at Nuecestown. That night, Anna said, people slept in the judge's yard, wherever they could; a few had blankets spread on the ground. They were given cornbread, buttermilk and black coffee; it was the first time the six-year-old Anna tasted coffee.[41]

Others camped on the prairie three miles west of town. Some used umbrellas and others set up quilts on sticks to escape the broiling sun. One 10-year-old boy, James Ranahan, slipped back into town to see what would happen. When the guns began to fire, he ran all the way back to the camp west of town.[*][42] The evacuees listened to the bombardment, no doubt wondering if their homes were safe. Maj. Hobby would allow no defensive preparations that would violate the truce. When the truce period was over, three guns, an 18-pounder and two 12-pounders, were placed behind old fortifications that had been put up by Zachary Taylor's army in 1845.[43]

At dawn on Friday, Aug. 15, 1862, Felix von Blucher, a Confederate major, sighted the 18-pounder, taking aim at the *Corypheus,* and said, "I believe I'll take a pop at it." He fired and the shell hit short of the ship. He fired another shot, which passed through the mainsail of the *Corypheus*. A third shot went through the side of the *Sachem*. The ships returned fire, with the shells landing on the earthwork fortifications, throwing up sand.[44]

Firing from the ships and the shore battery continued for two days, then fell silent on Sunday. On Monday morning, Kittredge sent the *Belle Italia* close to shore and landed 30 men with a 12-pounder howitzer on North Beach, to take the battery from the rear. Hobby led a cavalry charge on the 30 men with the howitzer and they were forced back to their launches,

---

[*] About where the Corpus Christi Country Club is today.

dropping rat-tail files in the sand. The files were intended to be used to spike the Confederate guns. One Confederate, Pvt. Henry Mote, was killed, shot in the head during the charge. After the shore landing was repulsed by the Confederate cavalry charge, Kittredge moved his ships out of range of the shore battery and began shelling the city. On Tuesday morning, Kittredge's ships sailed back to their blockade station in the Gulf. The battle of Corpus Christi was over.[45]

The evacuees returned home. Many houses were damaged. A hole three feet across had to be repaired on one house on Chaparral. A corner was shot off a house on Tancahua. A cannonball smashed a clock brought from Germany by Mrs. John Ernest Petzel. One cannonball whizzed along the shelf in a saloon, breaking all the whisky bottles. Family lore said a shell fragment took off the ear of the Anderson children's gray cat. Later, it was told that some of the cannonballs, which the residents called "Kittredges," were filled with whisky. The story told was that Capt. Kittredge's supply of whisky was stolen by his sailors and hid in cannonballs, after the powder was removed. On night watches, they could uncap a cannonball and take a few sips. During the bombardment, they forgot which of the cannonballs were filled with whisky and which with powder. That was the popular story circulated after the bombardment. Some of the spent cannonballs were used in homes as doorstops, with people pointing out their "Kittredges," no doubt proud of the stout resistance Col. Hobby's Confederates put up in defense of their town.[46]

The Ranchero called it "the Vicksburg of Texas." It aroused the anger of the town's Confederate loyalists. As the vote in favor of secession showed (164 to 42), Corpus Christi was split between Confederate loyalists and Union supporters. Some prominent citizens were pro-Unionists, including Judge Edmund J. Davis, the son-in-law of Sen. Forbes Britton; the Swiss baker, Conrad Meuly; Henry W. Berry, a builder and the county's first sheriff; Charles Weidenmueller and Edward Ohler, merchants; Joseph Fitzsimmons, city secretary; John Anderson, bay pilot; and John Dix, a retired ship captain. There was an uneasy truce during the first year of the war, but as the blockade tightened, as the war caused hardships at home and families received news of casualties from the great battlefields in the East, the uneasy truce turned into open hostility. That intensified after the bombardment. The Confederates, provoked by the attack, began to take revenge by plundering the homes and property of known Union supporters. The suspicion that some people in the town were secretly delighted with the Union attack was resented with especial bitterness by the Confederates.[47]

That fall, the threats and dark scowls became more serious. Two New York boys were captured and brought to town. The New Yorkers, who had been too outspoken in expressing their sentiments against the Confederacy, were taken past the end of Mesquite Street to a slight rise above the arroyo and summarily hanged. The Confederate officer in charge was Capt. John

Ireland. Some of the town's pro-Unionists were marched at gunpoint to see the bodies. The bodies were decorated with placards that read "Traitors Take Warning" and "Union Men Beware."[48] John Anderson, the Swedish ship captain who had built a home on Water Street, received a warning from his friend Bill Tinney. Tinney overheard Confederates planning to "string up old man Anderson." Anderson took his family to Flour Bluff in an ox-drawn wagon. They lived in an old house that had been used to store salt.[49] Edward Ohler, one of the city's most prominent merchants since he arrived in 1848, was imprisoned as a Yankee spy. John Dix, a native of Michigan, was accused of hanging a lantern from his home on Water Street to signal Union ships in the bay. Conrad Meuly, who owned a bakery, was threatened in the street.[50]

After that, the pro-Unionists began to leave town. Meuly took his family to his Palo Alto ranch on the Agua Dulce, 22 miles west of Corpus Christi. Meuly's ranch became a way station for those trying to evade Confederate conscription laws by escaping to Mexico. Fitzsimmons went to Matamoros, along with Henry Berry, the former sheriff. There were other Corpus Christi Unionists in Matamoros, most notably Judge E.J. Davis, who commanded a federal cavalry regiment on the border.[51]

Confederate loyalists also began to leave. After the bombardment, John Moore's family moved to Goliad, along with the Manns. The Noessels went to Matamoros. W.S. Rankin's family drove a horse and a mule to Brownsville; it took them a week to get there. John B. Dunn's family moved to Gonzalez for the duration of the war.[52]

Flour Bluff (the Rincon de Grulla) became known as a center for federal sympathizers. Perhaps it was this collection of Union supporters, "renegados," that enticed Lt. Kittredge to come ashore. One month after the bombardment, Kittredge and seven men landed at Flour Bluff, ostensibly to get fresh eggs and buttermilk, but perhaps to get information. The Confederates were tipped off and lay in wait. They captured Kittredge and his crew. The captives were marched through Corpus Christi, and people came out to see what the devil looked like. Kittredge was taken to San Antonio and given his parole.[53] He was court-martialed a year later for pistol-whipping a seaman and discharged from the Navy.[54]

On Dec. 5, 1862, Confederate Capt. H. Willke and Capt. John Ireland (later governor of Texas) took the sloop *Queen of the Bay* to sound the depth of water at Corpus Christi Pass. They took seven soldiers from Ireland's infantry company, a captain of the sloop, Jack Sands, and three sailors. They measured the depth on the bar on the Gulf side of the pass (where Packery Channel is today) at 5½ feet and on the bay side at 3½ feet. Due to contrary winds, they spent the next two days in the pass.[55]

On Dec. 7, they were chased by two launches manned by 22 sailors from the Union blockade ship, the bark *Arthur*. The *Queen of the Bay* tried to escape, with the launches in pursuit, using sails and oars. The Confederates ran their ship ashore on Padre Island. The men of Ireland's company, crack shots from Seguin, clambered to the top of sand hills and opened fire on the Union men in open boats. The Union sailors tried to escape by beaching their boats on Mustang Island, across the pass, and running for cover into the dunes. They fired back at the Confederates, who returned fire, killing one of the sailors.[56]

As shots were fired, the wind blew the launches away from shore. Capt. Ireland secured one of the abandoned launches, in which he found a dead man, another wounded man, heavy coats, arms and ammunition. The other launch, drifting toward the Gulf, was secured by the captain of the *Queen of the Bay*, Jack Sands.[57]

On Mustang Island, the man in charge of the two launches, Acting Ensign Alfred Reynolds, had been shot twice. Reynolds and another wounded sailor began the slow march up Mustang Island to rejoin the federal fleet lying off the Aransas Pass.[58] The Confederates recovered the body of the man killed in the dunes. Capt. Willke's command returned to Corpus Christi without the loss of a man. One wounded man they brought back had been helping guide the Union launches. He was a civilian from Corpus Christi, named Peter Baxter, an immigrant from Scotland.[59]

Andrew Anderson, whose family was known to be Union supporters, was a teenager then. He had a different spin on the story. He said the Union launches arrived at Corpus Christi Pass by mistake, that after the shooting started they tried to surrender. "As the launches entered the pass," Anderson said, "the Confederates on the big hill some 40 or 50 feet high could look down into the boats and shoot the soldiers. There must have been much bitterness by the Confederates because the federals were helpless and made every effort to make them understand that they would surrender; but little attention was given this and a number of federals were killed and the others captured." Anderson remembered that the wounded civilian, Peter Baxter, had a great ring on his finger. "He said they had wanted to surrender but were not allowed to; he died from his wounds and was buried somewhere in Corpus Christi, probably in Bayview." The launches full of bullet holes lay on the beach near the Anderson home on Water Street.[60]

Maria von Blucher, whose husband Felix, a Confederate officer, was in charge of coastal defenses at Corpus Christi and Saluria, wrote her parents about the skirmish. "The other day eight of our soldiers took two boats from the Yankees in Corpus Christi Bay and killed three Yankees, who were buried here. Captain Ireland and Captain Willke were our leaders. They were in a small boat reconnoitering Corpus Christi Pass. Realizing they were being pursued by two launches (the Yankee blockade bark was near the mouth of the pass), they landed and lay in ambush until the 25 Yankees were near. Then they fired, killed three, wounded the officer, put the soldiers to flight, and returned to Corpus Christi, safe and sound, with the Yankee boats, three dead, and a great number of excellent arms and provisions."[61]

By the end of 1862, the newspaper complained that "Corpus Christi is provision-less, subsistence-less, less of everything calculated to nourish the inner man, than at any former period. We ask the interior producer, Have you any conscience? If yea, bring us something to put down our throats . . . but don't sell it to the speculators."[62] Maria von Blucher wrote her parents that it was not the shortage of food that made things so expensive, "but the speculation of the greedy money-grubbers." She identified Matilda Ohler (Kinney's paramour) as one of the worst of the war-time speculators.[63]

While commerce was at a standstill, the Corpus Christi area had one precious commodity, salt. As a medium of exchange, salt was almost as good as gold and much better than Confederate currency. Around the Laguna Madre and the Salt Lagoon (Baffin Bay), salt was scraped up to be traded for corn, bacon, and foodstuffs that were in short supply around Corpus Christi.[64] In inland Texas, salt was so scarce people would dig up smokehouse floors to strain the dirt for leftover traces. The demand for salt gave South Texas a strategic importance because this area was rich in saline deposits. Beds of tide salt were scattered along the shores of the Laguna Madre and Baffin Bay. The salt was collected and hauled away on oxcarts or loaded on flat-bottomed scows, with armed guards riding atop the cargo, and taken to Corpus Christi. From there it was shipped inland, where it sold for up to $8 a bushel or was traded for flour, cornmeal, sugar, hams and other foodstuffs.[65] The story was told that a man in central Texas told his wife, "Sarah, let's live it up; put a little salt in the cornbread today."[66]

Libby Shoemaker, who lived on Mustang Island as a child, said the salt was scraped up and shoveled into large sacks. It was piled on canvas, such as an old sail, and hoisted by the four corners, then water was poured over it to strain off the impurities. The debris would sink to the bottom and after it was left in the sun, shining white salt could be recovered.[67] One man who worked as a salt laborer, Robert Adams, said gathering salt was quite an industry. "When the water came in high, it filled the shallow lakes; when the water receded, the salt could be gathered. It was in small grains, the size of peas, and you had to rake it out of the water. We would pile the salt on the bank and let it drain, then put it in sacks and buckets. Wagons used for hauling the salt were pulled by six yoke of oxen. I used to carry salt on my back to the wagons. The salt was wet and the brine ran down my back. I guess I got pickled in those days."[68] After Union troops occupied Mustang Island at the end of 1863, they spent much of their time trying to disrupt the salt traffic. They would use launches to try to capture the salt barges on the Laguna Madre. Men with rifles sat on the barges prepared to shoot the Union soldiers who tried to capture their cargoes. Union soldiers were under orders to "dissolve the cargo if you cannot capture it."[69]

The blockade cut off commerce. Trade through Corpus Christi came to a standstill. It was all but impossible to get manufactured goods; stores closed and the economy collapsed. Texas was overrun with longhorns, so it had plenty of leather, but no shoe manufacturers. It was a cotton state, but it had no cotton mills. All the factory products and tools used for making things came from the North or Europe. Now these were unavailable. People were forced by circumstance to relearn old skills. Women learned to weave cloth for homespun clothes; it was said that one could not approach a house without hearing the sound of a loom.[70] The cloth woven on homemade looms inspired songs about "homespun dresses, like Southern ladies wear." "We wash, iron, dye, make soap, and make indigo from a shrub (which is a curious procedure)," Maria von Blucher wrote. The procedure included packing wild indigo plants into a barrel, letting them steep in water for several days, after which the plants and water were poured off, leaving a cake of dark blue dye at the bottom.[71]

As food became scarce and prices rose, the value of Confederate currency declined. Six Confederate dollars were worth about $1 U.S. in purchasing power. By the end of the war, the value fell to a nickel on the dollar. In reality, the money-based economy was gone, replaced by a more primitive system of barter. In the last two years of the war, people in Corpus Christi lived on fish and beef, their existence stripped to the bone. Stray cattle were butchered for meat at the Salt Lake one mile west of town. Those with money (and they were few) could buy butter at Nuecestown and they could get a few vegetables at the Priour farm. They ground acorns to make ersatz coffee. White sugar was a rare luxury, but they could sometimes get a few pounds of crude yellow sugar that came from East Texas. Men would travel as far as the Austin area to get flour or corn meal, but making the trip was risky. A man was always in danger of having his team and wagon confiscated by Confederate authorities for use in hauling cotton down the Cotton Road.[72]

In a letter to her parents, Maria von Blucher wrote, "Vegetables I have not tasted for several years. Three years ago in Galveston, Felix (her husband) got me two dozen tin cans of green peas and asparagus, which came from Bremen, and were excellent. These were the last vegetables set before us . . . Butter, milk, vegetables, etc., are luxury articles that we no longer know . . . We have had a hard time here; I can truly say famine . . . Acorn coffee without milk, moldy flour, and bacon are our daily fare."[73]

CHAPTER 6

Union troops capture Fort Semmes - Gen. Bee retreats - The trial and hanging of Chipita Rodriguez - A terrible drought - The killing of Mat Nolan - The bloodiest war in the nation's history comes to a merciful end

I t was a long way from Corpus Christi, but the fall of Vicksburg on July 4, 1863 freed a sizable Union army that could be used elsewhere, like the coast of Texas. It was decided to send an invasion force to South Texas under the command of Gen. Nathaniel P. Banks. Ostensibly, the main purpose of the invasion was to close the back door, to stop Confederate cotton going to Mexico and guns and ammunition coming back. Banks' invasion force left New Orleans on Oct. 23, 1863 and landed at Brazos Santiago Island on Nov. 2.[1]

Gen. Banks, one of Lincoln's political generals, was politically important but militarily incompetent. In Massachusetts, where he was a former governor, he had been a child laborer in a cotton mill and earned the nickname the "Bobbin Boy." He got another nickname after he was thrashed on the battlefield in Virginia by Stonewall Jackson. So much of his supplies were captured by Confederates that they called him "Commissary Banks." After Vicksburg fell, Lincoln became convinced of the necessity of stopping the traffic in cotton going to Mexico. There were also fears that French forces under Maximilian, fighting in Mexico, might make common cause with Confederates. A Union presence in Texas would discourage moves in that direction. It was decided to give the job of invading Texas to the "Bobbin Boy" of Massachusetts.[2]

Banks' first move was a near disaster. Some 20 vessels carrying 5,000 Union troops left New Orleans to invade Texas. Their first objective was Sabine Pass near the Louisiana line. A small fort guarded the pass. When Union gunships approached the fort, the lightly manned Confederate battery opened fire. Two gunboats were forced to surrender and the invasion fleet limped back to New Orleans.[3] To repair this first failure, Banks decided on another tack. He put together a 7,500-man force made up of battle-hardened veterans from the Vicksburg campaign, a force large enough to make a quick conquest of the lightly defended Texas coast. Instead of trying to invade by the Sabine Pass, he would go in through the back door. Banks put this expedition under the command of Gen. Napoleon Jackson Tecumseh Dana, who had served in Zachary Taylor's army when it was encamped at Corpus Christi in late 1845 and early 1846.[4]

The expedition army boarded 13 transports, escorted by three gunboats, on Oct. 23, 1863. Major units were the 13th and 15th Maine, the 94th Illinois, the 20th Wisconsin, and the 19th and 20th Iowa. There was also Battery B of the 1st Missouri Light Artillery. A soldier in the 13th Maine wrote that they marched to the levee in a pouring rain and boarded the steamer *Clinton*. They were packed so tight they couldn't lie down. They spent several days taking on fresh water then, once in the Gulf, a storm scattered the fleet. It was another near disaster. The expedition lost three steamboats, four schooners, all their horses and almost all of the artillery.[5]

They arrived at Brazos Santiago Pass at noon, on Nov. 1, under a sky "of as brilliant a blue as poet or painter ever gave to the sky of Italy. On the right, the low, sandy shore of Padre Island extended further than the eye could reach; on the left, the high, round-topped sand hills of Brazos Island hid the distant mainland from view; and a little farther away, beyond the mouth of the Rio Grande, lay the chaparral-fringed Mexican coast . . . straight ahead, a few miles distant, stood a lofty landmark, the white lighthouse of Point Isabel, while close at hand tossed the fierce breakers of Brazos Santiago bar."[6]

The first units of Banks' forces landed on the north end of Brazos Santiago Island at an abandoned Confederate salt works. Banks sent an exultant message to Lincoln, "The flag of the Union floated over Texas today at meridian precisely."[7] A colonel ordered the soldiers to strip and wade across the Laguna Madre, to keep their pants and shoes dry. They crossed the shallow laguna with bare legs and feet. Sharp oyster shells cut up their feet. When they reached Brownsville, they slept in an empty cotton warehouse and, next day, moved into Fort Brown, the fort built by Zachary Taylor's troops at the beginning of the Mexican War. They met no Confederate opposition.[8]

Gen. Hamilton P. Bee, in charge of Confederate forces in South Texas, almost set Brownsville on fire in his haste to destroy cotton and get out of the city.[9] With Brownsville in Union hands, advance units of Banks' army headed for Mustang Island. The units included the 13th and 15th Maine, and elements of the 20th Iowa, under the command of Gen. T.E.G. Ransom. The invaders planned to go through Corpus Christi Pass and take Fort Semmes, the Confederate earthworks bastion on Mustang Island, from the bay. But the pass was too shallow for their vessels to make it through; they were forced to land on the Gulf side of the island at Corpus Christi Pass.[10*]

During the night of Nov. 16, they marched 18 miles to the head of the

---

* Not far from where Bob Hall Pier is today.

island (where Port Aransas is today). The men were carrying 100 rounds of ammunition, guns, knapsacks, and three days' provisions. Moving up the island, they had to drag two heavy siege guns over the sand dunes.[11] "The marching was very tiresome on account of the men having their feet and clothing wet while landing; but only short halts were made till 4 o'clock the next morning, when the men were allowed to rest till daylight. The distance marched during the night was about 18 miles."[12]

Early next morning, at daybreak, Ransom's Union soldiers approached Fort Semmes (located next to the pass where Port Aransas is today). They shot at Confederate sentries, driving them back, and the Union gunboat *Monongahela* in the Aransas Pass lobbed 11-inch shells at the fort. The Confederates in the earthwork fort raised a white flag. This was nominally the command of Maj. Benjamin F. Neal, who had been the first mayor of Corpus Christi in the early 1850s, but Neal, a district judge, had been called away to preside over the murder trial of Chipita Rodriguez. It fell to Capt. William Maltby, a Corpus Christi newspaperman, brother of the editor of the *Ranchero*, to surrender. In an unfortunate incident, when the white flag was raised, one man in the fort came out and waved at the Union troops, meant to be a friendly gesture, but he was shot and his arm had to be amputated.[13]

Ransom's forces captured three heavy cannon, one schooner, ten boats, 140 horses, nine officers, and 89 men.[14*] The Union soldiers took away a Confederate flag that had been presented to Maltby on the steps of the Nueces County Courthouse at the beginning of the war.[#] While Fort Semmes was under attack, Corpus Christi residents, who could hear the gunfire across the bay, worried about defenders on the island. Semmes was manned by Corpus Christi men and people in the city were concerned about their fate.[15]

Gen. Hamilton P. Bee, the Confederate commander who had a growing reputation for timidity, had left Brownsville to Banks without a fight. On his way north, he stopped at Conrad Meuly's ranch near Banquete. Meuly, a Swiss baker and known Union supporter, evacuated Corpus Christi after the town was bombarded and two New York boys were hanged. His ranch west of Corpus Christi became a sanctuary for Union supporters trying to reach Mexico to evade Confederate conscription laws. When Gen. Bee stopped at the ranch, he called Meuly a traitor and threatened to hang him. Meuly dared him to do his worst. Bee did not carry out his threat and rode on to Corpus Christi.[16]

Gen. Bee sent Lt. Walter Mann under a flag of truce to find out what happened to the men at Fort Semmes, but Mann was held prisoner on a Union ship.[17] Bee reported from Corpus Christi: "About 3,000 (of the

---

[*] Maltby was sent to Vicksburg, where his brother, Union Gen. Jasper Maltby, made sure he was treated with leniency.

[#] The flag taken away by the 15th Maine was returned to Corpus Christi in January, 1928. The Corpus Christi Light Infantry flag is now part of the Texas Confederate Museum Collection of the United Daughters of the Confederacy.

enemy) are now at the Aransas Pass . . . I shall virtually abandon this place tomorrow. There is nothing for the cavalry horses to eat, and, from the latest developments of the enemy, he will either march up Saint Joseph's Island and attack Saluria, or he will land at Lamar, and cross over to Indianola, thus cutting off Fort Esperanza. I need not say that I find my position annoying. There are three points of attack for the enemy—Corpus (Christi), Lamar, and Saluria—the first the least important to us."[18] Gen. Bee, prone to panic and nervously expecting a federal attack on Corpus Christi, withdrew his forces, retreating in unseemly haste across the Nueces River. Not knowing where Banks would strike next, Bee ordered livestock and horses to be driven east of the Nueces, with nothing of value left behind, and the evacuation order said under no circumstances were Negro men to be left behind. As a last resort, Bee ordered, they were to be shot, "for they will become willing or unwilling soldiers against us."[19]*

Before leaving Corpus Christi, the Confederates, fearing Union forces would capture the city, set a charge under the lighthouse on the bluff, which knocked down a corner of the building but failed to destroy the structure.[20] Corpus Christi was furious at Bee. Whatever the strategy might have been, whether it was to run to fight another day, the retreat of the army in the face of the enemy was bitterly resented. The *Ranchero* cast scorn on Bee's strategy, whatever it was. Editor Henry Maltby, the Ohioan turned fierce Confederate, printed a joke aimed at Bee. The joke: a colonel of an Alabama regiment questioned a sentry about his orders; the sentry said he would shoot if unidentified men approached, then he would form a line; the colonel asked what kind of a line one man could form, and the sentry said, "A Bee-line for camp." In case anyone missed the reference to Gen. Bee, the *Ranchero* printed that "A B(ee) line is just 60 miles a day from Brownsville."[21] But jokes aside, the general verdict was that Bee ran away not to fight another day but to run away again.

What Corpus Christi residents may not have appreciated or understood was the fact that Corpus Christi was remote, off the strategic map, and if Bee could give up Brownsville without a fight, at the very vital back door of the Confederacy, well, he would hardly lose any sleep over abandoning Corpus Christi, a shell of a town without strategic importance and one whose prominent citizens had already decamped. Bee made it clear that Corpus Christi was not vital enough for him to risk his troops to defend. The more cynical, and the more honest, might have noticed that Henry Maltby's criticism was leveled from Santa Margarita on the Nueces River where the *Ranchero* had been moved out of harm's way.[22] Nueces County officials had abandoned the courthouse, moving to Santa Margarita. Commissioners' minutes for this time were noted "in vacation."[23] It was symptomatic of the state of things that as the city entered the most desperate time of the war,

---

* It is unknown whether any male slaves were shot as a result of Bee's order.

64

indeed, of its existence, it was without leadership. County officials were at Santa Margarita; there was no city government functioning; other nominal leaders among the wealthy citizens had moved inland or to Mexico for safety.

While Gen. Bee's forces hunkered down north of the Nueces, a Union garrison was established on Mustang Island; Fort Semmes was renamed Post Aransas. The 20th Iowa was chosen for garrison duty, perhaps as punishment detail because Maj. William G. Thompson, commander of the 20th, complained too loudly about having to drag cannon through the sand on the march up the island. Gen. Ransom criticized Thompson for "constantly discouraging his men by complaining in their presence of the hardships of the march."[24] Maj. Thompson, however, put a different spin on it in a letter to his wife, telling her that he and the 20th were given the assignment as a mark of respect for the fine job they had done. It was soft duty for the 20th Iowa, which had fought at Pea Ridge in Arkansas and in the long siege at Vicksburg. Included in the garrison duty with the 20th Iowa were 100 African-American soldiers (two companies of the First Engineers, Corps d'Afrique) who were given the task of rebuilding sand fortifications at Post Aransas.[25]

The 20th Iowa was composed of farm boys from the Marion, Iowa, area. They settled in. Union sympathizers came looking for food. Maj. Thompson said one man, a former slave-owner who had been worth $100,000 before the war, was reduced to begging for bread for his hungry children. In letters to his wife, Thompson said there was plenty of beef on the island, but no trees for firewood. The men were industrious in acquiring wood to build huts. They roamed far down the island, and even tore down the old Singer ranch house for its lumber. Their "wood parties" made frequent raids into Corpus Christi, pulling down abandoned houses for the planks and taking stolen furniture back with them across the bay.[26]

The regimental historian of the 20th wrote that, "Most of the men built comfortable quarters and furnished them with comfort, even luxury. The little frame huts . . . contained mahogany and rosewood furniture of the richest description, procured during scouting expeditions . . . by confiscation from houses abandoned by rebels."[27]

A fierce norther hit on Dec. 3. On Christmas Day, 1863, Maj. Thompson, commander of the 20th Iowa, led a foray into Corpus Christi. He knew from defectors that the town was not defended. It was so cold that Christmas that water froze in buckets inside the homes, where many people were on the verge of starvation. There had been a drought since the previous summer and food was scarce. Thompson wrote his wife in Marion. "I assure you it is a hard sight to see so many starving, absolutely starving, for want of the most common necessaries of life."[28]

Union soldiers on Mustang Island in late 1863 and early 1864 made raiding forays into Corpus Christi in search of lumber and furniture. "Every house abandoned by its owner," wrote Maria von Blucher, "was torn down by the Yankees."[29] In retaliation, Confederate soldiers camping at Banquete came into Corpus Christi and knocked down houses belonging to Union backers. Thomas Noakes, a rancher at Nuecestown, originally an immigrant from England, wrote in his diary, "The Yankees are preying on Confederate property and the Confederates are making a pounce on Yankee property. Furniture can be bought for a song."[30]

Thompson wrote that his men always returned from their raids on Corpus Christi without having encountered any resistance. On one raid, on Feb. 21, 1864, some 200 soldiers under Thompson's command searched the houses of prominent Confederates. From Mat Nolan's house on Mesquite, they took away two U.S. flags that had been captured two months before in the battle of Sabine Pass. They also took copies of the *Ranchero*, which they found amusing because of its "rebel lies."[31]

On one foray, men of the 20th Iowa amused themselves by carting away district court records and mixing up what was left. On the island, Maj. Thompson's men were dealing with large numbers of refugees. Some were Confederate deserters, but most of them were Union supporters. One woman walked into camp after trudging miles through the sand carrying a child on her back. She found her husband at the camp; they hadn't seen each other for a year. Thompson wrote his wife that the refugees "come in fast and I am troubled to find a place for them, but they are not hard to please. The people of Iowa have no idea of the nature of war, but these refugees have seen the elephant."[32]

While the 20th Iowa occupied Mustang Island, the remainder of Gen. Banks' invasion force moved toward its third major objective, the massive Confederate Fort Esperanza, near Saluria on Matagorda Island, guarding the strategic Pass Cavallo.[33]

Another norther hit on Nov. 19, 1863 as troops were ferried across the Aransas Pass that separates Mustang from St. Joseph's Island. They reached Cedar Bayou, separating St. Joseph's from Matagorda, four days later. Confederate Maj. Charles Hill raised a white flag across Cedar Bayou. He wanted to know what happened to the men at Fort Semmes. A sergeant from the 15th Maine, James Saunders, swam across to talk. After angry words, the major shot the sergeant and Union troops fired on and hit the major; his body was found in the dunes.[*] The Union troops crossed Cedar Bayou on flatboats brought up on wagons.[34]

On Nov. 27, 1863 they reached their objective: Fort Esperanza. The massive earthworks on Matagorda near the town of Saluria were built early in the war by some 500 slaves. The walls were 12 feet high and 15 feet thick. The fort was armed with eight 24-pounder cannon and one behemoth, a

---

[*] The Confederate account claimed Maj. Hill was executed without provocation under a flag of truce.

124-pounder "Columbiad" placed to guard Pass Cavallo.[35]

Union troops fired on Confederate pickets, driving them inside the walls. They dug rifle pits and prepared for a siege. Cannon fire was exchanged on Nov. 29. A Union soldier foolishly stuck out his foot to stop a spent cannonball rolling along; his leg snapped like a matchstick and had to be amputated.[36]

Confederates spiked their guns, burned powder magazines, and evacuated before the escape route was closed. It was bitterly cold as Union forces settled into camps. They had little to eat except beef by butchering cattle on the island. They had no tents. They dug holes in the sand and covered them with hides of slaughtered cattle.[37]

In February 1864, they were ordered back to New Orleans. Garrisons were left on Matagorda and Mustang to guard the passes, but they were pulled out two months later. The Confederates moved back into Fort Esperanza.[38] Both sides must have realized that Banks' invasion was a sideshow and the war was reaching a critical stage where victory or defeat would be decided on the battlefields of Virginia. The rest of the war passed in relative peace as the belligerents focused on the great battles in the east.

A few months earlier, Chipita Rodriguez was tried and hanged. She had been convicted on the flimsiest of evidence of murdering a horse trader. She was hanged at San Patricio on Nov. 13, 1863. The judge who ordered her hanged was Benjamin F. Neal, Corpus Christi's first mayor, a man of diverse talents, who had taught school, practiced law, edited newspapers, rode with Texas Rangers, presided as judge, and, when the war started, organized coastal defenses. He came to Texas in 1838, taught school at Live Oak Point, then was elected chief justice of Refugio County. He moved to Corpus Christi in 1844 and became general counsel for Henry Kinney. In 1852, Neal was elected as the city's first mayor.[39]

At the start of the Civil War, Neal feared that the coast was open to invasion. As a private citizen, he wrote President Jefferson Davis, advising him of the need for artillery on the coast.[40] He organized an artillery company to defend Corpus Christi; the company was stationed at Fort Semmes, on Mustang Island.[41] When U.S. forces occupied Brownsville, before they moved up the coast, Neal resigned his command at Fort Semmes, leaving the Confederate battery under the command of Lt. William Maltby, brother of Henry Maltby, editor of the *Ranchero*. Neal had been elected judge of the 14th District and he had a case to hear.[42]

That August, in 1863, a horse trader spent the night at Chipita Rodriguez's cabin, a travelers' way station, on the Aransas River. His body was found next day; his head had been split open with an axe. Chipita and her hired man were charged. The trial was highly irregular. The sheriff who investigated the case sat on the grand jury. There was no jury panel for the trial; people were rounded up. Four of the jury had been indicted for felonies, one for murder. The only evidence was circumstantial, blood spots on the porch, which Chipita claimed was chicken blood, still, the jury found her guilty. Because of her age and the weak evidence, the jury recommended leniency, but Neal ordered her to be hanged, on Nov. 13, 1863, a Saturday.[43]

The *Ranchero* complimented Neal on his handling of the case, saying he presided "in a very satisfactory manner, and by his firmness, impartiality, and mildness gave promise of making an excellent judge."[44]

On the appointed day, at the town of San Patricio, they came for Chipita in a wagon. She was wearing a borrowed dress and her hair had been brushed. She climbed on the wagon and took her seat on a coffin made of cypress planks. The wagon, pulled by oxen, stopped at a mesquite tree by the Nueces River, just below the town. When the rope was fixed and the oxen moved forward, they moved so slowly the fall did not break Chipita's neck; she was slowly strangled to death. One man turned away, muttering, "I've had enough of this." They buried Chipita in the cypress box under the hanging tree. Many in San Patricio believed she was innocent of the crime for which she was hanged.[45]

Thomas J. Noakes, the Englishman who lived with his wife and son at Nuecestown, noted the end of 1863 in his diary. "Dec. 31, the last day of a miserable year. Bitterly cold. I sat by the fire mending Mary's shoes. The company that passed me the other evening went to Corpus where they captured a person named Dix, who had been a traitor and communicating with the Yankees. So ends another year. Jan. 1, 1864: Water froze, milk also. Stayed in and boiled soap, the first I have had to make, and I succeeded very well. I drove the cart to Taylor's and borrowed two bushels of corn. Jan. 2: I am not well. My lungs have bled. Jan. 5, Tuesday: Exceedingly cold, water froze (in buckets) close to the fire. I put my horse in the old house to keep him from perishing. Jan. 7: I helped Mr. Wright pull out a cow of his bogged down in the river. For two or three hundred yards along the river, I counted 42 animals, cows and sheep, bogged down in the river.* Hundreds of thousands of cattle on the other side of the river are starving. Jan. 8, Friday: Ice everywhere. The river froze. Jan. 9: I killed two wethers (sheep) and stretched the hides. Took off as much of the hide as I could get at from the poor dead cows bogged in the river. Jan. 10: There is a lull in the excitement of war. We have had no news of the Yankees. It may be because of the excessive cold. The cattle are dying very fast on the opposite side of the river. Jan. 20, Wednesday: There is no mail now and we get no news of the war. Country is in a deplorable state for want of rain. Cattle and sheep are starving and dying all over the country. The long cold spell has killed great numbers of sheep. Jan. 24, Sunday: No rain worth mentioning for six

---

* "Bogged down" meant they were stuck in the deep mud by the river, too malnourished and weak to pull free. Many were literally dead in their tracks.

months. Dead animals meet your gaze in every direction, look where you will, and the atmosphere is quite oppressive on account of decomposition. War and famine and want is all we see, hear, or talk about."[46]

Because his right lung was useless and he suffered from consumption, he was given a certificate of disability by Confederate military authorities, which allowed him to stay with his family. Noakes, who was skilled with his hands, showed a genius for improvisation. He burned cow dung to get ashes to make lye soap and used cow hides to make what he called "square buckets" and leather sacks. Everything had to be made by hand and it was all but impossible to buy tools. He made saddles for extra income and made his own shot to kill small game by beating lead into thin sheets and cutting it into small squares, which he found "answers very well."[47]

The bad times brought on by war turned even worse by a severe drought. Death and destruction spread across the land like a stain spreads across a map. There had been no rain "worth mentioning" since July of 1863. The land was stripped of grass and hope. Cattle and sheep were dying along the dried-up creeks and rivers. Noakes saw a team of work steers yoked together, one dead and the other standing quietly by its side. "Go which way you will go," he wrote, "you see dead horses, cattle and sheep. All the creeks stink with them." Across the desolate countryside, denuded of grass cover, wind blew dust and sand, filling the sky with a haze that limited visibility. What you could see was parched and brown: "There is not a green thing to be seen."[48]

Noakes had to travel far in an exhausting hunt for corn and flour. Because there was almost no grass, his horses wandered off seeking forage. He would spend days trying to find his cart horses. Then he would travel to the Salt Lagoon (Baffin Bay) 50 miles away to get a load of salt to trade for corn, sweet potatoes and other foodstuffs. In the absence of regular commerce, people fell back on a more primitive barter system. These were hard trips for Noakes, with one lung, who was often spitting up blood and running a fever. In March, 1864, on the way to Goliad, he and a neighbor, Ned Taylor, cut down trees so their horses could eat the moss from out-of-reach limbs. "As soon as we began cutting down the trees, crowds of cattle came running up and only with great difficulty could we get any moss for our horses, as the starved cattle fairly took it by storm. We could not drive them away. Very sad. They ate the moss and leaves and then the branches, eating everything under 1½ inches in diameter."[49]

On his trips, Noakes found houses empty, yards overgrown with weeds, and ranches that were semi-derelict because of a shortage of manpower. On a trip down Banquete Creek, out of 12 or 14 houses, "I only saw one or two that were occupied, the rest having been abandoned; everything has fled east." He found Corpus Christi "in a state of desolation, everything gone to ruin and hardly a living soul to be seen." Noakes thought that Goliad, where he went to trade salt for corn, had "a substantial look about it. Unlike most Texas towns, a good many houses were built of stone and in very good taste."[50]

Beeville was "a poor, deserted-looking place, nearly every house standing on the bare prairie without a fence and having the general appearance of so many wooden boxes standing about at intervals." Helena was also a "tumbled-down-looking affair," with the men gone to war and farms abandoned. He liked Seguin and noted that if it were not for war time, "it would have been a lovely and interesting neighborhood. There are some very nice-looking houses and the fine school house is a tasteful building." He was surprised to find New Braunfels so big with some very fine buildings. The streets were lined with chinaberry trees and the houses were all clean, with nice, shady gardens. Noakes walked all over New Braunfels trying to trade his salt for flour. He found the prices "ridiculously high. We had to pay 15 cents for a small glass of beer and everything else in proportion."[51]

Noakes and two friends went to the Salt Lagoon for a load of salt. Near the Oso they found a place where women were living without their husbands, who had deserted to the Yankees. "One of the women had a child die on the previous evening and there was not a man or boy big enough to make the coffin and dig the grave, so we offered our services. I made the coffin (there being tools and lumber there) while Stevens and Harrison dug the grave. We buried the child and headed home at sundown."[52]

In an entry on Oct. 28, 1864, Noakes showed his keen sense of humor: "I took a ride up the river, giving myself a Texas holiday, which consists in riding a broken-down horse all day, in search of game that you never find, and having nothing to eat." Near the end of his diary for 1864, Noakes wrote, "I was working on my saddle tree and killed two large rattlesnakes, taking their fat, but having nothing to put it in, I had to skin one of the snakes without ripping the skin and of that I made a bag in which I brought home the fat, by tying a knot at each end."[53]

One of the leading Confederate officers in the area was Mat Nolan. He had been a bugle boy in the Mexican War, served as a Texas Ranger under the legendary "Rip" Ford, was elected sheriff of Nueces County in 1858. He hired his younger brother, Tom Nolan, as a deputy; Tom was killed by a drunk in a saloon fracas in 1860. Before the start of the war, in March, 1861, Nolan was authorized by state officials in Austin to raise a cavalry force of 100 volunteers, for frontier defense, which was mustered in at Banquete. Nolan served on the border in the command of "Rip" Ford, his old Ranger captain. In the second year of the war, Mat returned to Corpus Christi to marry Margaret McMahon.[54]

Nolan's company ended the depredations of Cecilio Balerio, a Nueces County rancher who commanded 120 men in an irregular Union cavalry outfit that rustled cattle and attacked wagon trains on the Cotton Road. Was Balerio a bandit raider or a brave Union cavalry leader? It depended on who you asked. Balerio's son Jose was captured in Corpus Christi; he was tried before a military court, and sentenced to be shot. Nolan told Balerio he would let him go if he told him where his father's camp was located; Balerio refused. He broke down, though, when he was taken before a firing squad.[55] He told Nolan that his father's outfit was camped near the present town of Falfurrias. Nolan's forces surrounded the camp late at night, near a place called Los Patricios. At the last minute, Jose yelled a warning to his father, *"Cuidado!"* The ensuing fight was "well-contested" in a dense mesquite grove that lasted about 15 minutes. Two of Nolan's men were killed and two wounded. Five of Balerio's men were killed in the battle, their bodies found in the brush, but father and son escaped and stayed in Mexico for the rest of the war.[56]

Near the end of the war, Nolan was re-elected sheriff of Nueces County. He assumed the office with the approval of his commanding officer, Col. John S. "Rip" Ford. Nolan in a report to Ford wrote that "the enemy returned in their boats, landing with a number of Corpus renegades." Nolan named H.W. Berry, Martin Kelly, Charles Weidenmueller, Joseph Fitzsimmons, William Murdock, and Dennis Kelly. Ford advised Nolan to arrest the "perfidious renegades." On Dec. 22, 1864, Nolan was talking to a horse trader across from Nolan's house on Mesquite Street. Two stepsons of H.W. Berry, Frank and Charles Gravis, shot Nolan and the horse-trader. In his final moments, Nolan named the Gravis boys as the shooters and said he knew why they shot him, but he died before he could explain. A grand jury sitting at Santa Margarita on the Nueces River (where county government was located) returned indictments of treason against the pro-Unionists named by Nolan. Those indicted included Berry, Fitzsimmons, John Dix and eight others. Nothing happened on the indictments as the war was coming to an end.[57]

One day in May, young Eli Merriman was in school at the Hidalgo Seminary on the bluff* when his father, Dr. Merriman, came to get him out of class. A boat had arrived with important news. Gen. Lee had surrendered, the war was over, and Abraham Lincoln had been assassinated. They went to Dr. Merriman's hospital on the bluff in the old Rabb house to relate the news to Confederate soldiers. Some of them were in the outhouses, suffering from dysentery, so sick they could hardly walk. In the hospital, the men were told the war was over, that they were free to go home and attend to their own affairs. One man cried and turned his face to the wall. Then they set out for Banquete where Dr. Merriman had another hospital filled with sick soldiers. They met Col. Lovenskiold with his two sisters-in-law about where Robstown is now; they were coming up from Brownsville. They were surrounded by wild-looking men, Confederate soldiers, ready to kill the colonel. Dr. Merriman pleaded with them to let the Confederate official go. The angry Confederate soldiers, some of whom Dr. Merriman knew, said they had been turned loose without a dollar, hundreds of miles from their

---

* The Hidalgo Seminary, at the northwest corner of Lipan and Tancahua, was started in 1863 by Father John Gonnard and kept going during the war years with the help of Rosalie Priour.

homes and families that they had not heard from in many months. Dr. Merriman told them to take the colonel's money, but let him and his ladies go on to Corpus Christi. They agreed and Lovenskiold escaped with his life.[58]

In Corpus Christi, occupation authorities opened an office in the Russell home* where Confederates were required to take the oath of allegiance.[59] Some took the "Ironclad Oath," but many refused. The oath ended with, "I will faithfully support the Constitution and obey the laws of the United States and will, to the best of my ability, encourage others to do so. So help me God."[60] A number of South Texans sought refuge across the border in Mexico, including the Maltby brothers and Maj. Felix Blucher of Corpus Christi, Gen. Hamilton Bee and his family, Col. P.N. Luckett, J. Williamson Moses, among others.[61] That spring, after one of the worst droughts South Texas had ever seen, the land was green again, and people were again at peace. The bloodiest conflict in the nation's history came to a merciful end.

---

* The home at 802 N. Chaparral was later owned by Royal Givens.

KINNEY

PLATE 1.1 – Henry Lawrence Kinney established Kinney's Rancho in 1839, a trading post on the high bluff overlooking the bay. Kinney's Rancho became the only settlement between the Nueces and Rio Grande in the years before statehood. In 1845, Zachary Taylor brought 3,500 troops of the U.S. Army to the outpost to defend the U.S. claim to the disputed region of the annexed Republic of Texas.

Jim Moloney

TAYLOR

PLATE 1.2 – Gen. Zachary Taylor, nicknamed "Old Rough and Ready" by his soldiers, brought his Army of Observation to Corpus Christi in the summer of 1845.

ARMY ENCAMPMENT

PLATE 1.3 – Drawn by Captain Daniel P. Whiting in late 1845, this is the earliest view of Corpus Christi. The tents of the U.S. Army stretch along the shore from North Beach, across Hall's Bayou, to the south. The army trained at Corpus Christi for the coming war with Mexico.

GRANT

PLATE 1.4 – Ulysses S. Grant was 23 when he arrived in Corpus Christi. Because he was short (5' 5") and "pretty," he was chosen to play the female role of "Desdemona" in a play during the encampment but was replaced by an actress from New Orleans. Grant later grew a beard to hide his almost girlish looks.

Murphy Givens

FAIR PRIZE

PLATE 1.5 – Silver cup is inscribed: H. L. Kinney and the general committee, Lone Star Fair, Corpus Christi May 1852. It was owned by Mifflin Kenedy. Prizes like this were awarded for winning exhibits at the fair. The silver cups were purchased in New Orleans for Kinney by 'Legs' Lewis.

1850 Census -Texas

County	Whites	Free Col	Slaves	Total	County Town	Pop.
Anderson	2,284		600	2,884	Palestine	212
Angelina	945	24	196	1,165	Marion	
Austin	2,286	6	1,549	3,841	San Felipe	
Bastrop	2,180		919	3,099	Bastrop	
Bexar	5,633	30	389	6,052	San Antonio	3,488
Bowie	1,271		1,641	2,912	Boston	
Brazoria	1,329	5	3,507	4,841	Brazoria	
Brazos	466		148	614	Booneville	
Burleson	1,213		500	1,713	Caldwell	
Caldwell	1,054	1	274	1,329	Lockhart	
Calhoun	867	9	234	1,110	Port Lavaca	315
Cameron					Brownsville	
Starr	8,469	19	53	8,541	Rio Grande	
Webb					Webb C. H.	
Cass	3,089		1,902	4,991	Jefferson	
Cherokee	5,389	1	1,283	6,673	Rusk	355
Collin	1,816		134	1,950	McKinney	192
Colorado	1,534		723	2,257	Columbus	
Comal	1,662		61	1,723	New Braunfels	1,298
Cook	219		1	220	Cook C. H.	
Dallas	2,536		207	2,743	Dallas	
Denton	631		10	641	Alton	
De Witt	1,148		568	1,716	Cuero	
Ellis	902	10	77	989	Waxahachie	
Fannin	3,260		528	3,788	Bonham	211
Fayette	2,740		1,016	3,756	La Grange	
Fort Bend	974	5	1,554	2,533	Richmond	323
Galveston	3,785	30	714	4,529	Galveston	4,177
Gillespie	1,235		5	1,240	Fredericksburg	754
Goliad	435		213	648	Goliad	
Gonzales	891		601	1,492	Gonzales	
Grayson	1,822		186	2,008	Sherman	
Grimes	2,326	2	1,680	4,008	Anderson	
Guadalupe	1,171	5	335	1,511	Seguin	
Harris	3,756	7	905	4,668	Houston	
Harrison	5,604	5	6,213	11,822	Marshall	1,189
Hays	259		128	387	San Marcos	
Henderson	1,155	1	81	1,237	Athens	
Hopkins	2,469		154	2,623	Tarrant	
Houston	2,036	12	673	2,721	Crockett	150
Hunt	1,477	2	41	1,520	Greenville	
Jackson	627	30	339	996	Texana	
Jasper	1,226		541	1,767	Jasper	
Jefferson	1,504	63	269	1,836	Beaumont	
Kaufman	982		65	1,047	Kaufman	

78

1850 Census -Texas (continued)

County	Whites	Free Col	Slaves	Total	County Town	Pop.
Lamar	2,893		1,085	3,978	Paris	
Lavaca	1,139		432	1,571	Petersburh	
Leon	1,325		621	1,946	Leona	
Liberty	1,623	7	892	2,522	Liberty	
Limestone	1,990		618	2,608	Springfield	
Matagorda	913	3	1,208	2,124	Matagorda	
Medina	881		28	909	Castroville	366
Milam	2,469	2	436	2,907	Cameron	
Mongomery	1,479		945	2,424	Mongomery	
Nacogdoches	3,758	31	1,404	5,193	Nacogdoches	468
Navarro	1,943	1	246	2,190	Corsicana	
Newton	1,255	8	426	1,689	Burksville	
Nueces	**650**	**1**	**47**	**698**	**Corpus Christi**	**533**
Panola	2,676	2	1,193	3,871	Carthage	
Polk	1,542	1	805	2,348	Livingston	
Red River	2,493	7	1,406	3,906	Clarkesville	
Refugio	269		19	288	Refugio	
Robertson	620		264	884	Franklin	
Rusk	6,012		2,136	8,148	Henderson	
Sabine	1,556		942	2,498	Milam	
San Augustine	2,087		1,561	3,648	San Augustine	
San Patricio	197		3	200	San Patricio	
Shelby	3,278		961	4,239	Shelbyville	
Smith	3,575		717	4,292	Tyler	
Tarrant	599		65	664	Tarrant C. H.	
Titus	3,168	1	467	3,636	Mount Pleasant	
Travis	2,336	11	791	3,138	Austin City	629
Tyler	1,476		418	1,894	Woodville	
Upshur	2,712		682	3,394	Gilmer	
Van Zandt	1,308		40	1,348	Jordan's Saline	
Victoria	1,396	52	571	2,019	Victoria	
Walker	2,663		1,301	3,964	Huntsville	
Washington	3,166		2,817	5,983	Brenham	
Wharton	520		1,242	1,762	Wharton	
Williamson	1,410	3	155	1,568	Georgetown	
Total	**154,034**	**397**	**58,161**	**212,592**		

Jim Moloney

CENSUS

PLATE 1.6 - The 1850 Census was the first taken in the state. More than a third of the people living in Texas were slaves. It was estimated that there were 10,000 "Mexicans" in Texas. They were not counted. Corpus Christi, with 533 residents, was the seventh largest town in Texas.

FLINTOFF PAINTING

PLATE 1.7 – Thomas Flintoff (ca. 1809-1891), an English artist visiting Texas, was at the Lone Star Fair and won a prize for painting. This watercolor of Corpus Christi was probably the painting which won him the prize. After the fair he disappeared, only to resurface in the gold fields of Australia.

KING

PLATE 1.8 – Richard King used his profits from running riverboats on the Rio Grande to purchase the first 15,000 acres of what became the famous King Ranch south of Corpus Christi.

NUECES VALLEY
LAND & EMIGRATION OFFICE,
3, Church Court, Clement's Lane, London.

For Sale:
300,000 ACRES OF LAND IN ONE SQUARE BLOCK.

THE HON. COL. H. L. KINNEY, the proprietor of the above extensive domain, having appointed the undersigned his sole agents for the disposal of the above lands to settlers and capitalists, they are authorized on his behalf to offer to Emigrants the following liberal terms:—

To ANY FAMILY OF GOOD REPUTE FOR HONESTY, industry, and perseverance, he will let them have ten cows on shares; he will sell them one hundred acres of land at six shillings per acre;—also one yoke of oxen, and one horse; two shillings per acre to be paid to the agents in London, on execution of the contract,—and the balance for the land and stock to be paid in ten years, with interest annually; he will also give to each family one building lot in the town of Nueces. A reduced quantity of land may be had subject to arrangement.

IT MAY BE ASKED, WHY THIS LIBERALITY?—The proprietor is the owner of 12,000 head of horned cattle, 2,000 stock horses, mares, and mules, 10,000 sheep; and being resident on the estate, he is thus enabled to offer to emigrants advantages that no other man in the United States can command.

THESE HIGHLY PRODUCTIVE LANDS, being a dark deep loam, well adapted for all agricultural purposes, are beautifully situated on the bay of Corpus Christi, and the Nueces River, Western Texas, from which there is weekly communication by steam with Galveston, New Orleans, and other ports; and there being an extensive demand in the home districts, and for the northern markets, insures a ready cash sale for produce of every description.

CORPUS CHRISTI, situated in the vicinity of this property, is a town of considerable commercial activity, and being the chief mart for merchandize for the western districts of Texas and the Rio Grande country, is fast rising into importance: in fact, the natural position of this locality, having good roads, with extensive water facilities, cannot fail to command a large and extended commerce with the surrounding country in every direction, thus offering to the *agriculturist, the merchant, the trader, the mechanic, and the labourer,* a field of no ordinary character for the successful pursuit of their respective occupations.

THE SOIL AND CLIMATE of this region is unsurpassed,—two full crops of corn and other cereals in perfection, are secured annually. Irish and sweet potatoes, with all other roots and vegetables, make large returns; the peach, the vine, and other fruit trees thrive luxuriantly.

THERE IS AN ABUNDANT and never-failing supply of water; TIMBER of the finest quality for all useful and ornamental purposes; *and three-fourths of the land being gently undulating prairie,* can be made immediately available for the plough, thus effecting a saving of twenty dollars per acre in clearing, an outlay that must be submitted to by settlers in most other parts of the Union.

THIS SECTION OF THE COUNTRY, justly described "the FAIREST REGION OF AMERICA," is singularly free from swamps and stagnant water; there being no fogs or damp air, fever, ague, and other epidemics, are unknown; and no country in the world offers such advantages for the breeding of stock, the range of pasture being almost unlimited. There is perpetual verdure and no provision is necessary for the keep of cattle during the winter; it, therefore, we presume, offers incomparable advantages to all those in search of A HAPPY HOME, with the certainty of speedily acquiring independence for themselves and families.

Cotton of the finest staple, also sugar and tobacco, are cultivated to great perfection without the aid of slaves; the country being so healthy, the unacclimated perform field labour at all seasons without inconvenience. Range of the thermometer, 35 to 85.

IN THE RISING TOWN OF NUECES, situated on the property of Col. Kinney, and on his adjoining lands, there are already located upwards of a thousand individuals; therefore the emigrant will at once enjoy the benefit of association with a thrifty, active, and experienced population.

Murphy Givens

LAND PROMOTION

PLATE 1.9 – Handbills advertising Kinney's land sales were distributed in Great Britain by his land sale agents. Kinney's offer was 100 acres of land at six shillings (about one dollar) an acre. With the purchase of 100 acres, he would provide the buyer with a yoke of oxen, one horse, 10 cows, and a residential lot in Nuecestown.

Ranchero War Extra.

THE RANCHERO.

HENRY A. MALTBY & BRO.
EDITORS AND PUBLISHERS.

CORPUS CHRISTI, TEXAS:

SATURDAY, JULY 20, 1861.

TERMS FOR ANNOUNCEMENTS.—For announcing a candidate for a State or District office, $10; for a county office, $5—each in advance.

ANNOUNCEMENTS.

For Governor.

We are authorized to announce Gen. J. T. Chambers as a candidate for Governor.

For the Confederate States Congress.

We are authorized to announce the name of the Hon. Wm. H. Steward, of Gonzales county, as a candidate for Congress from the first Congressional District.

We are authorized to announce Hon. Edward R. Hord a candidate for Congress, from the first Congressional District.

We are authorized to announce Col. John A. Wilcox, of Bexar, as a candidate for Congress from the 1st Congressional District.

For Representative.

MESSRS. EDITORS:—Please announce G. F. Hanmaker, as a candidate to represent the 76th Representative District in the next Legislature.

We are authorized to announce Wm. J. Davis, as a candidate for Representative from the 76th District, at the ensuing August election.

We are authorized to announce Charles Russell, Esq., as a candidate for Representative from the 76th District, at the ensuing August election.

For State Senator.

I am a candidate for the office of Senator, from Senatorial District No. 29. Election on the first Monday in August next.

HENRY A. MALTBY.

For District Attorney.

We are authorized to announce the name of John S. Givens, Esq., as a candidate for the office of District Attorney, for the Fourteenth Judicial District. Election, first Monday in August.

We are authorized to announce Simon Jones, Esq., as a candidate for the office of District Attorney of the 14th Judicial District at the ensuing August election.

We are authorized to announce J. B. Murphy, Esq., as a candidate for re-election to the office of District Attorney of the 14th Judicial District. Election, first Monday in August next.

District Surveyor.

Felix A. Blucher is a candidate for the office of District Surveyor for Nueces county at the ensuing August election.

Remember that we print no election tickets on a credit.

A wagon-load of corn was sold in Goliad last week at fifty cents per bushel.

The cotton crop on the San Antonio river has been seriously damaged by worms. Hon. H. P. Bee writes us that he will not make half a crop.

Major Felix A. Blucher is announced to-day as a candidate for District Surveyor of Nueces county. He is well known to the voters of the county, and his friends will support him.

We are authorized to announce John Cannon as a candidate for City Marshal; election July 24th. He is eminently qualified to discharge the duties of the office.

MILITARY.—Pursuant to an order of Brig. General Bee, a military company was organized at Casa Blanca on the 15th inst. The following named persons were elected officers: Walter Mann, Captain; James Miller, 1st Lieutenant; C. C. Cox, 2d Lieutenant.

A Word to our Patrons.

Scarcity of paper forces us to issue a war extra this week in lieu of THE RANCHERO. We expect that by next week (unless old Abe's cruisers have seized the vessel) to be in receipt of a large supply of paper, which has been ordered for months, and was to have been brought direct from Berwick's to Corpus by the schooner *Clarinda*. This is the first time we have missed an issue, and we trust it will be the last. Our subscribers may rest assured that no effort will be spared on our part to furnish them with the latest news,—even if we have to come down to wrapping paper. In the meantime, we trust the D—l will lay violent hands on Old Abe and anchor him in the middle of the lake of fire and brimstone; and that a phantom southern navy will maintain a strict blockade of the "impassable gulf" and pour hot shot into him for a thousand years.

It seems that Brother Pierce, of the Goliad Messenger, omitted Karnes county in the circular of Judge Pryor Lea, President of the Pacific R. R. He concludes that there is disaffection in Karnes county toward Judge Lea on that account, and makes a most affecting appeal, in the last Messenger, to the citizens of Karnes in the Judge's behalf. "After all their toil, how uncertain is their treasure," as Brother Cox very aptly observes in his leader entitled, "The folly of laboring to be rich."

Brigadier General H. P. Bee, commanding 29th district Texas Militia, writes us that twelve companies, numbering in the aggregate 720 men, had reported for service up to the 13th inst. Out of that number, 320 were ready for active service. We trust our paper will be on hand next week that we can publish a full list of the company officers.

MORE ESTRAYS.—Mr. Marcus Fusselman has lost the following described animals, viz: a brown, a gray and a bay mare, one yearling horse colt and one sucking horse colt. The gray mare and yearling colt bear his brand as advertised; the other animals Mexican brands. The brown and gray mares were necked together when last seen.

Col. J. A. Wilcox, candidate for Congress, addressed a large assemblage at the Court-House on last Tuesday night. He was repeatedly applauded and we heard many express favorable opinions of him after the meeting.

STRAY HORSE.—Mr. Samuel Cooling has lost a dun horse, bearing his brand on left shoulder, as advertised. Said animal has a glass eye, white face and is about fourteen hands high.

Those who owe us will confer a great favor by paying up. If you cannot pay all, pay a portion.

The mail between here and Laredo has been discontinued.

Mat Nolan's company will be at the Banquete next week, probably.

THE LATEST NEWS.

By Tuesday's Mail.

33,000 Federalists Across the Potomac—More Skirmishing—Bloody Battle Expected—Military Occupation of Baltimore—Indictment of the Crew of the Privateer Savannah—The U. S. Congress—Lincoln's Message—Important from Missouri—Immense Peace Meeting in Delaware—The Galveston Blockade, Etc., Etc.

The New Orleans Delta of Saturday, 6th instant, has a telegraphic synopsis of Mr. Lincoln's message to the Federal Congress, in called session. It opens thus:

At the beginning of the present Administration, the General Government was found suspended in several of the States, except in regard to its postal functions. The national property in those States, except Fort Pickens, Taylor, Jefferson and Sumpter, had been seized and put in an offensive position; other forts had been built, armies organized and being organized, which were avowedly hostile to the Federal Government. The remaining forts in those States were either besieged or menaced. A disproportionate amount of arms and munitions of war had in some manner found their way into the rebellious States; the accumulations of the national revenues within the rebel borders had been seized. The Federal navy was scattered, and the Federal army and navy officers had resigned in great numbers. Ordinances declaring separations had passed.

These States, under the title of Confederates, were applying to foreign powers for recognition and assistance.

The incoming Administration believed it to be its imperative duty to prevent the threatened dismemberment of the Union.

The policy chosen, as indicated in the inaugural address of the Executive, was the exhaustion of all peaceful measures before a resort to coercion—the Government seeking only to hold the public places and property and the unresisted collection of the revenues, relying upon time, discussion, and the ballot box for the rest, and, promising in the meantime, a continuance of the mails. Everything was forborne, compatible with the keeping of the Government on foot.

The first necessity was the relief of Fort Sumpter, Gen. Scott agreeing that it could not be relieved without immediate victualing. The necessity then arose to withdraw the garrisons: which Lincoln considered unallowable, as encouraging the "rebels," and discouraging the "friends of the Union." To reinforce Fort Pickens first, would indicate the Administration's policy and prepare the public mind for the evacuation of Sumpter as a military necessity. Orders to reinforce Pickens were issued and a plan to victual Sumpter put afoot, to be used as contingencies might require, and "Gov. Pickens, of South Carolina, was notified that if the victualing was not resisted, no attempt would be made to throw in men, arms, or ammunition, without previous notice."

The taking of Sumpter, Mr. Lincoln considers as entirely uncalled for and designed purposely to force an immediate dissolution of the Union. No course was left, he says, but to call out the war power of the Federal Government to resist the force employed for its destruction. The question was, he significantly says: "*Must the Government be too strong for the people's liberty, or too weak to maintain its own existence?*"

The response to his call for troops, Mr. Lincoln says, surpassed his most sanguine expectations; but Delaware was the only slave State that responded. The wavering action of the border States is commented on: Virginia's course leaves him no course but that he is pursuing; the "armed neutrality" doctrine of Kentucky and Missouri he considers to be equivalent to "Disunion complete" and as granting all the "rebels" want, without themselves risking anything.

To meet this he called for 75,000 volunteers.

For his successive war measures, his authorizing the suspension of the right of habeas corpus, he pleads the necessity of the case—he says: "*These measures were ventured upon under the popular demand and public necessity, trusting to Congressional ratification.*"

Mr. Lincoln calls for Congressional action, as follows:

"*It is recommended that you adopt measures to make the contest short and decisive; that you place at the disposal of the Government at least four hundred thousand men and four hundred millions of dollars.* That number of men is about one-tenth of the available military force within the willing region—that sum of money the twenty third of the wealth of the men who seem willing to devote the whole six hundred millions less debt per head than the revolutionary proportion. Surely the motive now is as strong as then. The result to the world would be worth ten times the men—ten times the money.

The legislative sanction only is necessary, the material for the work is abundant; the greatest perplexity of the Government is the avoidance of receiving men faster than it is prepared to do. The people will save the Government if the Government on its part will do its duty."

Mr. Lincoln here enters into an elaborate argument against the doctrines of "secession" and "State Rights;" and he questions *whether the people of every State, except South Carolina, are not in favor of the Union.*" The contrary, he says, has not been demonstrated. Here follows a touch of Seward's pen:

"It remains to be demonstrated that those who can fairly carry an election can also repress a rebellion; that ballots are the rightful and peaceful successors of bullets, and that when ballots have fairly and constitutionally decided, there can be no successful appeal back to bullets—no appeal except to ballots themselves, at succeeding elections. Such will be the lesson of peace, teaching men that what they can not take by election, they can not take by war."

Mr. Lincoln kindly promises, in case he whips us, to administer the government "according to the Constitution and the laws." He mainly says that he sees no coercion, subjugation or conquering in the terms." He has employed the war power, he says, with the deepest regret, but he has done it "for the defense of the Government," and further, as an "indispensable means to maintain the guarantees of the Federal Constitution that each State shall enjoy a representative power of Government." He had either to do this or to surrender the government. A Compromise will not answer, for he says:

"No popular Government can long survive the marked precedent, that those who carry an election, can only save the country by giving up the main point upon which the people gained that election. Themselves, not their servants, can reverse their decision."

That is to say, a peaceful settlement of the question would ruin the Black Republican party.

The U. S. Senate organized on the 4th. Powell and Breckinridge, of Ky., Polk, of Mo., Johnson, of Tenn., and Pierce and Kennedy, of Md., present. Lane and Pomeroy, of Kansas, presented their credentials, Pomeroy drawing the long term.

Notice of bills for the employment of volunteers and enforcing laws; to increase the military establishment; for the better organization of the military; to promote the efficiency and organization of the volunteer militia force, to be called the U. S. National Guards, were given.

Senate adjourned.

House.—150 members answered to their name on the roll call.

Murphy Givens

SPECIAL EDITION

PLATE 1.10 - *The Ranchero*, published by Henry A. Maltby, issued an extra edition on July 20, 1861 because the shortage of newsprint forced the publisher to miss a regularly scheduled issue.

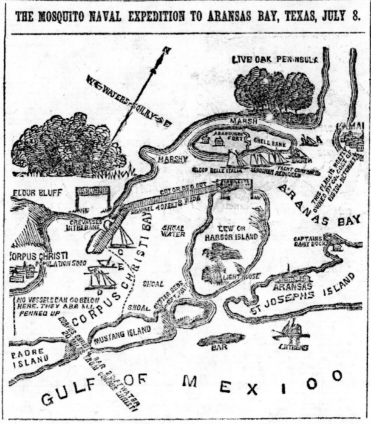

Jim Moloney

UNION EXPLOITS

PLATE 1.11 - *The New York Herald* of August 27, 1862 featured a map of Union naval operations in the vicinity of Corpus Christi. An article detailed Lt. Kittredge's naval accomplishments in capturing nearly 100 bales of cotton and blocking access to Corpus Christi Bay to the rebels.

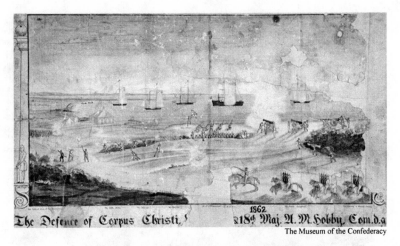

The Defence of Corpus Christi, 1862 ~18th Maj. A. M. Hobby, Com.d.g

ATTACK ON CORPUS CHRISTI

PLATE 1.12 – A watercolor drawing of the Battle of Corpus Christi was "Drawn on the Battle Ground by D. R. Gambel, Ordnance [Sergeant]" showing Confederate forces repelling Union attackers.

NOLAN

PLATE 1.13 – Confederate Maj. Mat Nolan, who was also sheriff of Nueces County, was shot to death in front of his home on Mesquite Street. His younger brother, a deputy sheriff, was killed four years earlier. Both were buried in Old Bayview.

CORPUS CHRISTI MEN ON THE BORDER

PLATE 1.14 – Pat Daugherty, Benjamin F. Neal and William Maltby appear to have imbibed a few before this photo was taken in Brownsville or Matamoras.

87

NOAKES

PLATE 1.15 – Thomas J. Noakes' self portrait. Noakes, from England, kept a detail-filled diary that recorded events around Nuecestown and Corpus Christi. His store was burned by Mexican bandits in the Nuecestown Raid, also known as the Noakes Raid, on Easter weekend, 1875.

CHAPTER 7

County reorganized after the war - Union troops occupy city - Jim Garner hanged – Yellow fever outbreak ravages city - Corpus Christi judge becomes hated governor - Trail drives to Kansas - Market Hall opens

Corpus Christi at the end of the Civil War was ground down by war, hungry and exhausted, utterly devastated. Many of its citizens who could afford to leave evacuated after the town was bombarded by Union warships. Those who stayed behind were destitute, nearly starving; dead animals lay in the streets. Yards were filled with weeds and many houses had been pulled down for their lumber and plundered for their furnishings. Other houses were in varying stages of decrepitude and decay. County officials had moved county government to Santa Margarita on the Nueces, but the minutes for that period are noted "in vacation." There was no functioning city government for the last two years of the war. Even taxes were not collected. In October of 1865, after the end of the war, Nueces County was reorganized. The county seat was moved back from Santa Margarita to Corpus Christi.[1]

Some semblance of order began to be restored. Unionists who had been indicted by a Confederate grand jury, H.W. Berry, Joseph Fitzsimmons and John Dix, among others, were in charge of the situation.[2] Remarkably, considering the bitterness that had existed between both sides during the war, there were no violent reprisals. Both sides began to learn to get along together again. Some in the area were adept at dropping their Confederate sympathies for Union ones—men like Richard King and Mifflin Kenedy. King and Kenedy's riverboats on the Rio Grande were seized by occupation authorities, but quickly returned to their former Confederate owners.[3] King in the fall of 1866 got permission from occupation authorities in Corpus Christi to establish a beef packing house inside the city limits, on the arroyo south of town (near where Cooper's Alley runs today).[4]

John Dix, the chief justice (county judge), was given the oath of office by Charles Lovenskiold, who had been a colonel in the Confederate Army and the city's provost marshal. Commissioners sworn in were James Bryden, John McClane, and Matthew Cody. Henry W. Berry was sheriff. Joseph Fitzsimmons was county clerk. One of the first acts of the reorganized county government was to put the tax collector, Milas Polk, to work. In his first report to the commissioners, Polk said he had to hire armed guards to protect him from attack. Not having paid taxes for two years, and not having had a functioning government at a time when they needed it most, people were reluctant to resume their obligations. But the county began to collect an occupation tax and licenses to do business were issued to John B. Mitchell, commission house; F. Ritter, restaurant and billiards; James Fitzsimmons and company, restaurant; John Riggs, commission house; H.W. Berry, auctioneer; J.R. Barnard, auctioneer.[5] City government was reorganized the following June when a former Union officer, W.N. Staples, was elected mayor.[6]

Corpus Christi was one of the few Texas cities subjected to prolonged occupation. When Gen. Phil Sheridan took possession of Texas for the Union, he ordered the 25th Army Corps to occupy Galveston, Indianola, Brownsville and Corpus Christi. Some 52,000 Union troops were stationed along the coast, out of 70,000 in the state. Small cavalry detachments were sent to San Antonio and Austin. Other units camped at Refugio, Goliad and Victoria. Corpus Christi, with a mere 400 residents at war's end, was occupied by 3,000 Union troops. The sheer numbers were bound to cause trouble.

Texans wondered why such a large force was sent to occupy a defeated and demoralized state, which was as low, one said, as the tail of a whipped cat. But the Union forces were sent to Texas as a show of force, in response to French intervention in Mexico. In June, Gen. Charles S. Russell was ordered to take a regiment to Corpus Christi. By late July, two regiments were in town. Russell occupied the home of Judge R.C. Russell (no kin) at Chaparral and Taylor. Corpus Christi was occupied, off and on, by three Union regiments—the 10th, 28th and 36th—for more than a year. The 122nd may have been here for a short time. The regiments were designated as United States Colored Troops. They were under the command of white officers.

This wasn't the first time that area residents saw African-Americans in the uniform of the Union army. After Banks' invasion in late 1863, when the 20th Iowa was garrisoned on Mustang Island, two companies of black soldiers (the Corps d'Afrique) were stationed on the island. There was a separate cemetery for black soldiers at Mustang Point.[*7]

There was trouble between the town's residents and the soldiers, who had two camps, one on the beach and one on the bluff. Margaret Meuly, a Union supporter during the war, filed a claim against the government because the soldiers gutted her vacant house on the bluff to get firewood.[8] Helen

---

[*] Mustang Point, part of Port Aransas today, later was the site of a quarantine station, before it was moved to the northeast shore of Harbor Island.

90

Chapman, a Union supporter who spent the war in the North, wrote in her diary, "I hear there is a good deal of bitter feeling about the arrival of colored troops."[9]

It was more than bitter feelings, based on J.B. (Red) Dunn's account. The Dunn family returned to Corpus Christi from Gonzales, where they had moved to be near other relatives during the war. They found the town "a desolate looking place. It had suffered bombardment during the war and was badly shattered. There were several companies of Negro soldiers stationed there and the citizens were subject to all kinds of humiliation and insults from them. It was a common occurrence for them to walk into private homes and demand coffee or food."[10]

Dunn said two Negro soldiers broke into his uncle John Dunn's home, four miles west of town, while the family was away at church and stole some clothing and guns. When the family returned, they found the uniforms the soldiers had left behind and their weapons.[11]

"One of the boys, Matt Dunn, went to headquarters and reported the matter to the officer in charge. He was quite insulting and denied flatly that it was any of his men. But next morning, Matt got there before roll call and saw that two names were not answered. He called the officer's attention to the matter, but the officer flew into a tantrum and still tried to deny that any of his men had taken part in the robbery. He told Matt that if he was so sure about the matter to go and get the deserters and not bother him about it. Matt then went in the direction of the [Nueces Bay], thinking the Negroes might have crossed the reef. When he got to the reef he found a fisherman who told him that he had seen the Negroes about two hours before and they had gone out on a peninsula that ran into Nueces Bay . . . Matt found them. When they saw him coming they pulled out their pistols and told him to stay back . . . Matt opened fire on them, and when all his loads were gone but one, he charged them and killed one of them. At that, the other one ran into the bay and got bogged in the mud. Matt roped him and dragged him to shore . . . [Matt] turned him over to the commanding officer."[12]

After several months of fractious relations between the town's residents and occupation troops, the soldiers of the 28th embarked on ships hired from Capt. James "Daddy" Grant, which took them to Brazos Santiago.[13] This brief occupation marked the beginning of the first institutions created solely for African-Americans in the city, the Congregation Church on the bluff and a Freedman's School established to teach the children of former slaves.[14] Rosalie Hart Priour became friends with the wives of Union officers and lamented their leaving, writing in her memoirs that when they departed they gave her a white cat and two white chickens: "They were counted among my greatest possessions."[15]

The departure of the 28th Regiment was not the end of the occupation of the city. Other units were shunted in from Brownsville and Indianola. The conjecture that Union regiments of black soldiers were removed because of friction with local citizens is dubious. It is doubtful that tough Union generals like Phil Sheridan cared much for the sensibilities of defeated Confederates. Sheridan didn't like Texas much anyway. It is more likely that the regiments were transferred because it was time for them to be mustered out. The vast Union army was being disbanded.

On May 15, 1866, a young man named Jim Garner went to Scheur's store on Chaparral Street and tried on a pair of boots. He started to leave wearing the boots, without paying, and the storekeeper followed him out. Garner told him to put them on his bill, but Scheur said he couldn't give him credit. Garner pulled out his pistol and shot Scheur, killing him instantly.[16] Scheur was laid out on his store counter. He had served in a Confederate militia and was well-liked.[*]

As news of the shooting spread, shouts of "Get a rope!" were heard. John Fogg, owner of a nearby livery, went to Felix Noessel's store and grabbed a coil of rope. The killer was found and hustled down Chaparral, an angry mob in escort. They stopped at Conrad Meuly's house, which had an iron railing on the second floor balcony, but Margaret Meuly wouldn't let them use her house for a hanging. They went down Chaparral, looking for a suitable site. Garner, sobering up, was suddenly eager to avoid the experience. "Give me a trial, boys," he pleaded as they pushed him along. They might have listened except that Garner had killed a fisherman in an argument and was considered a worthless loafer, with a reputation for violence, who had killed his first man in a saloon fight when he was 15. They found a mesquite with a limb high enough in the arroyo at the south edge of town. When Garner was hanged, there was no great roaring cheer, just grim silence from those who no doubt felt they had a nasty job to do and did it. Next day, Garner's father reclaimed the body, still dangling from the mesquite limb. It was said the father was more interested in the fact that he had acquired a new rope. W.S. Rankin, a young boy at the time, said the hanging was a terrible thing. "I didn't sleep a wink for a week. I couldn't shut my eyes for seeing that tongue stuck out."[17]

A man named J.S. Snyder, from Washington, D.C., rode in on horseback from Indianola, crossed the reef road, and got a room at Ziegler's Hotel at Chaparral and Lawrence.[18] He died two days later, on July 3, 1867.[19] This man's death was the worst kind of news. He had arrived from a place where yellow fever was in full fury. For a month, beginning in June, Corpus Christi had been hearing about the yellow fever outbreak in the neighboring port city of Indianola,[20] where sick people showed the classic symptoms: raging fever, red eyes, headaches, and the black vomit caused by internal bleeding. In the last stages, faces turned yellow and eyes lost the ability to focus. Corpus Christi was familiar with yellow fever; the town suffered a ferocious outbreak in 1854.[21] Joseph Almond, an immigrant from England who was a

---

[*] Scheur and Garner served together in W.S. Shaw's Confederate militia company. Muster rolls list Scheur as a corporal and Garner as a private.

sheep rancher and carpenter, wrote in his diary on July 24: "On the third of this month, a Mr. Snider [Snyder] died at Ziegler's Hotel [in Corpus Christi] of yellow fever. He came here sick from Indianola at the time the yellow fever was so bad at that place."[22]

They didn't know what caused yellow fever or where it came from. They thought it came from a noxious vapor in the air. They had no idea that the virus was transmitted from one person to another by mosquitoes. Three weeks after the Indianola traveler's death, Corpus Christi was full of sick, helpless people. Those who had the fever and hadn't died expected to. Helen Chapman listed the sick and the dead in her diary entries from July through August. "July 25: Mr. Drinkard died in the night. July 29: Several deaths in town; much distress. July 31: Mr. Eastwood died this morning. Aug. 2: Mr. Mitchell was buried at midnight Thursday. Aug. 4: Mr. Palmer died suddenly this morning, buried this evening. Aug. 5: three deaths today, a young man at Mr. Scott's, Clymer, and a child on the hill." Chapman's diary entries continue in a similar vein for the rest of August and into September.[23]

The streets were deserted like two years before in the final days of the Civil War. In front of homes, smoke rose from tar buckets filled with smoldering charcoal to fumigate the air. Many fled the city to escape the pestilence, some going to the Curry Settlement on Padre Island, where the fever never reached.[24] As the death toll climbed, the supply of polished wood coffins was used up and dressed lumber stacked on the bluff to build a new Presbyterian church was diverted to make plain wooden coffins.[25] "The dressed lumber at the church building site (on the bluff) was hammered into coffins for burial of the dead as the carpenters turned from church-building to this heart-breaking task . . . It was said that the hammering went on all through the day and throughout the night."[26]

A majority of the City Council came down with the fever. The duties of government were taken over by the county commissioners. The town's three doctors worked until they were exhausted.[27] They must have despaired over the lack of their ability to effectively treat the disease. They tried every means. Dr. E. T. Merriman had the victims soak their feet and legs in a tub filled with ashes and hot water, then they were rolled in layers of heavy blankets to sweat out the fever. Dr. Merriman and the town's two other doctors contracted the fever and died.[28] The *Advertiser* noted: "Our local physicians used all their skill and ability to check the disease, laboring day and night, until they fell victims and died—martyrs to the cause of humanity."

Anna Moore Schwien, the daughter of a slave, said Corpus Christi would have been "swept clean as a pin" if it hadn't been for the intervention of Judge E.J. Davis, who later became the reconstruction governor of Texas. Davis, according to Schwien, brought Dr. Kearney to Corpus Christi from Havana at his own expense after Dr. Merriman, Dr. Robertson, and Dr. Johnson died of the fever.[29] "Many mean things have been said about Mr.

Davis, but he deserves credit for what he did for Corpus Christi at that time." Schwien described Dr. Kearney's method of treating the fever consisted of having the patient put his feet in a mustard bath up to the knees and then go to bed, where he was given warm teas or clabber or whey from boiled buttermilk. Dr. Kearney, she said, didn't use as much whisky to treat yellow fever as the other doctors did.[30]

William Maltby, the former Confederate officer and editor of the *Advertiser*, described the calamity. "The cloud burst upon us—a disease of the most virulent and malignant character—and soon death after death occurred among the best and most valuable citizens . . . There is scarcely a house in the city that has escaped either sickness or death of some of its inmates. Our pen is inadequate to the task of describing the distress that now prevails among us." Only the week before, Maltby's 21-year-old wife, Mary Grace (Swift) died, along with Maltby's sister. Maltby listed the names of the victims. His death toll numbered 106, but the spread of the fever was undaunted and the heat of August unabated.[31]

In the town's misery, people worked side by side caring for the sick. Former Confederates and Unionists put aside whatever differences were left from the war. People of all political persuasions and ethnic backgrounds helped care for the sick and bury the dead. When Helen Chapman, an outspoken Unionist, came down with the fever, she was visited by Maltby, a die-hard Confederate.[32] In late August, one of the heroes of the epidemic came down with the fever. Father John Gonnard, a Catholic priest from France, had been tireless in his ministrations to the sick, working day and night with hardly a pause to rest. When he caught the fever, two black men in town, Chandler Johnson and Joe Whitlock, stayed by him and nursed him until he died. He was mourned by the entire city.[33] Rev. Claude Jaillet was summoned from San Diego after the death of Father Gonnard. On his way into town, he saw a long line of wagons carrying the dead in crude coffins.[34]

Corpus Christi in 1867 had a local chapter of an international organization, the Howard Association, a group of volunteers named for British philanthropist John Howard.[35] The local "Howards" built a pest house at the corner of Antelope and Carancahua. It was maintained by a black man named Dan Johnson. Fever victims with no family to care for them were taken to the town's pest house, where they could get well on their own or die on their own.[36]

A man who worked on John Anderson's boat *Flour Bluff* came down with the fever and was taken to the pest house. Andy Anderson, a boy at the time, took some clothes to the sick man. "When I reached him," Anderson said later, "he lay on the floor in the center of the room. He yelled, 'You little fool. What are you doing here? Can't you see all those people died of yellow fever?' He referred to seven or eight corpses in the room. 'Well,' I told him, 'We have it at home, so what difference does it make?' The man later recovered."[37]

J.B. "Red" Dunn sweated out the fever. "When I felt myself coming down with it, I threw myself down between two cousins I was nursing and threw my arms across them to keep the cover on them. I nearly burned up with the fever. My breath burned my face. I went crazy. I crawled across the room, struck my head on a table hard enough to make it bleed. That let the hot blood out, and I think it saved my life." From then on, he said he was impervious to yellow fever.[38]

At the end of August and in the first week of September, cold fronts brought relief for the heat wave and the epidemic abated. No new cases were reported and the death toll began to drop. The fever died out.[39] In the epidemic, parents lost children, children lost parents, and in some cases entire families fell sick and died. Many fever orphans were adopted by families that had lost their own children. Cornelius and Catherine Cahill, who lost two children to the fever, adopted two nieces and a nephew left orphaned; J.B. Murphy and wife adopted two girls, not related to them, who had lost their parents in the outbreak. Martin Kelly and his wife adopted his brother's five children, all under 12, left orphaned by the epidemic.[40]

Many accounts of the 1867 yellow fever epidemic estimated that 300 of the town's 1,000 inhabitants died. This was no doubt an exaggeration. Joseph Almond, a carpenter and cabinet maker originally from Newcastle, England, meticulously recorded each day's deaths during the epidemic. When it was over, by the middle of September, Almond's tally was 135 people who had died.[41] As with the city's epidemic in 1854, deliverance came with the arrival of cold weather. People didn't notice that the departure of yellow fever coincided with the disappearance of the mosquito. It would be another three decades before that connection was made.

Edmund Jackson Davis, a Corpus Christi judge who was a brigadier general in the Civil War on the Union side, became the most despised politician in Texas history. He hated his former enemies the Confederates, and they hated him. They called him "the devil with red whiskers".[42] He was the closest thing to a dictator Texas ever had, though revisionist historians have pointed out some of the good things that he accomplished as governor during Reconstruction, such as safeguarding the newly enfranchised voting rights of black citizens.[43] While historians are divided in their conclusions about the Davis administration, from 1869 to 1873, there is no denying that it was a bleak, divisive, and violent time in Texas history. Davis may get good marks in some revised assessments, but some detractors are not convinced. He sought to divide Texas into two states, north and south of the Brazos. He pushed for the disenfranchisement of ex-rebels, which put him at odds with more moderate Republican leaders. He was not averse to using the power of his office to punish his political opponents, as he did when he jailed state Senators until they passed legislation he favored.

Davis came to Texas from St. Augustine, Fla., with his widowed mother when he was 11 years old. He moved to Corpus Christi when he was 21 to study law. As a lawyer, he practiced in Corpus Christi, Laredo and Brownsville. He became deputy director of customs at Laredo, then federal judge of the Lower Rio Grande Valley. As judge, he rode a judicial circuit stretching from Corpus Christi to Laredo to Brownsville.[44]

Judge Davis married Anne Elizabeth (Lizzie) Britton, the daughter of Sen. Forbes Britton, a veteran of the Mexican War.[45] After the marriage, a house on the Britton Ranch on Oso Creek was moved to the bluff to become the home of the newlyweds.[46] As the Civil War approached, Davis, like his father-in-law, opposed secession. When the issue came up for vote, in February, 1861, Davis spoke at the Nueces County Courthouse against secession.[47] Davis' wife Lizzie's twin brother, Edward W. Britton, enlisted in a Confederate state militia company, W.S. Shaw's Light Infantry of Nueces County, as a surgeon.[48] When the war began, Davis went to Matamoros and organized a unit of irregular cavalry to harass Confederate troops. Davis' 1st Texas Cavalry, U.S.A., was made up of Unionists like himself, whom Confederates called "renegades."

Confederates were so eager to capture Davis that they staged a raid into Mexico. They had learned that Davis and an aide, Capt. W. W. Montgomery, were staying at the Imperial Hotel, in the port city of Bagdad, across the mouth of the Rio Grande on the Mexican side, waiting to board the steamer *Nicaragua*. Davis and Montgomery were captured and taken to Clarksville on the Texas side. The Confederates promptly hanged Montgomery and were putting a rope around the neck of E.J. Davis when Confederate Gen. Hamilton P. Bee intervened and ordered him returned to the Mexican side, with apologies to the Mexican authorities for the incursion into their territory. Some accounts say Davis escaped hanging because he and Bee were members of the Masonic Lodge. It might also have been a gallant gesture on Gen. Bee's part; he had courted Miss Lizzie before she decided to marry Davis.[49]

After the war, Davis returned to Corpus Christi to practice law, with offices in the Hunsaker building on Water Street at the Peoples Street intersection.[50] His clients were Union supporters whose property had been confiscated during the war, such as Helen Chapman.[51] In 1866, Davis represented South Texas in the constitutional convention that drew up a new state constitution.[52] Davis in 1867 formed a company to publish a pro-Republican newspaper called the *Union Record*. It lasted not quite two months before it was destroyed by fire.[53]

This was one of the worst years in Corpus Christi history. After yellow fever struck the town in 1867, Davis sent to Havana for a doctor, according to the account of Anna Moore Schwien (above).[54] Mary Sutherland wrote: "An old friend of mine remembers him (Davis) with gratitude. He came to her assistance and with his own hands helped to lift a dying sister to a cot, and helped carry it three blocks that the sister might spend her last moments with her mother, who was also low with the fever."[55]

In 1869, six years after he had escaped hanging, Davis was elected governor of Texas, beating Andrew Jackson Hamilton by 800 votes out of 78,993 cast. It was considered the most fraudulent election in Texas history. Hamilton always believed he won; the ballots were taken out of the state and later disappeared.[56] Governor-elect Davis and Lizzie left their home on the bluff in a stagecoach for Austin. The story was told that the travelers halted in San Patricio at the home of a Mrs. Sullivan and Davis sent in his respects. Mrs. Sullivan sent a message back, saying, "Mrs. Sullivan is not at home to the traitor."[57]

In his first two years as governor, Davis, said his ex-Confederate enemies, was as busy as the devil in a high wind. He pushed through a State Police bill in the House that gave him extraordinary powers. When the bill failed in the Senate, he had senators jailed until it passed. He had the power to appoint virtually all county officials in Texas. His State Police were used to break up political meetings of his opponents. A corrupt Legislature plundered the state treasury.[58] In 1873, he ran for re-election against Richard Coke, a former Confederate private. Davis lost by more than two to one, but he refused to vacate the governor's office, pleading with President U.S. Grant to send troops to keep him power. Grant sent a terse telegram in response: "Would it not be prudent, as well as right, to yield to the verdict of the people as expressed by their ballots?"[59]

Grant's refusal to intervene to keep Davis in the governor's mansion infuriated Lizzie Davis. She took the president's portrait down from the wall and put her foot through it.[60] Davis, in the night, finally vacated the governor's office; he locked it and left no key behind. The door had to be broken down so the new governor, Richard Coke, could occupy his office.[61] Davis and Lizzie never returned to Corpus Christi to live. They sold their home on the bluff to Norwick Gussett for $4,000.[62] Davis died in Austin in 1883; his monument is the tallest in the State Cemetery. One old Confederate said the size of the monument was entirely appropriate, "since E. J. Davis was the biggest son of a bitch Texas has ever seen."[63]

Confederate veterans came home to find the open ranges teeming with longhorns that had never seen a rope or a hot iron. They were chased out of the brush, branded, and walked to market. It was rounding up money. Driving herds to railhead towns in Kansas began in earnest in the mid-to-late 1860s. South Texas ranchers Richard King, Mifflin Kenedy, Robert and Jeremiah Driscoll, John Rabb, D.C. Rachal, among many others, delivered herds to Kansas.[64]

A Corpus Christi paper reported: "James Bryden starts off with the first drove of cattle for the Kansas market, his herd consisting of 4,120 head from Nueces County."[65] In 1866, some 250,000 longhorns were taken up the trail. In 1869, the number increased to 600,000 cattle going north.[66] The greatest drive in history happened in 1871 when more than 700,000 head of Texas cattle were driven north to market. So many cattle were taken up the trail that they could not be sold; they were wintered in Kansas at a loss.[67] But the following year, herds were gathered again to go up the trail to the railhead towns in Kansas. "Quite a number of our young men are starting for Kansas again with cattle," the *Nueces Valley* reported. "Among the number are Rufus Glover, and John Merriman, from the *Valley* office, also Henry Parker and Frank Gregory, of this city."[68]

This was not the origin of the trail drives. As early as 1779, large herds of longhorns were driven to New Orleans to feed the Spanish army of Bernardo de Galvez.[69] Victoria's Martin De Leon took a herd to New Orleans in the 1820s.[70] After the Texas Revolution, abandoned cattle in the Nueces Strip were driven east for sale. In the 1840s and 1850s, cattle were trailed to New Orleans and Natchez in the east, to Chicago, St. Louis, and other towns in the Midwest. Even longer drives were made to California. During the war, there were trail drives east, taking beef to feed the Confederate Army.[71] But the great cattle-driving era began after the Civil War.

Some ranchers conducted their own drives while others sold their cattle to a drover, who went from ranch to ranch buying cattle. The drovers gathered their herds in the spring, when the grass was coming up. The drive took from three to four months and they wanted to get them to market before rough weather set in. The cattle were fattened on the road, except for those drovers who liked to hurry them along on the trail and then let them fatten up in Kansas. In 1873, a steer worth $8 in Corpus Christi would sell for about $23 in Abilene, a considerable profit.[72]

The mechanics of a drive were similar. For every 1,000 head in a herd, there were usually four to six cowboys on a drive, often called "waddies" or "screws." They were paid $30 to $40 a month, depending on experience. In addition to cowboys, there was a trail boss, a horse wrangler, and a cook, or "biscuit-shooter." Some drives had a scout to choose places to ford rivers, to find a suitable bedding ground each day, to kill wild game to vary the diet. The chuckwagon, often pulled by oxen, carried bedding, rain slickers and provisions—axle grease, beans, flour, sugar, bacon, lard, and burlap bags filled with Arbuckle's coffee beans. The staples would be replenished at Fort Worth or Doan's store on the Red River. The chuckwagon was the social center of a drive. In the early going, the cattle were driven hard, 20 to 30 miles a day, to break them into the routine of the trail and to get them away from their home ranges as fast as possible. Mixed herds were hard to drive. Cows were slower than steers and newborn calves even slower. Some drovers killed calves because they couldn't keep up, but they had to be careful in doing so for the smell of fresh blood would have old bulls pawing the ground and could start a stampede.[73] Sometimes a wagon would be used to haul the calves, but they became a nuisance on the trail. A typical herd after it was trail-broken averaged about 10 miles a day.[74]

The herds were moved up the Texas, Western and Chisholm trails. Many trail drivers were Tejanos and black cowboys, the only jobs they could find. East of the Nueces, Mexican vaqueros gave way to black cowboys.[75] Trail-driving was said to be pleasant when skies were clear and there was plenty of grass and water. With a herd making 10 miles a day, cowboys rode along dozing in the saddle and admiring their shadows. The herd moved in a long line. The two top hands rode point. On either side near the front, a third of the way back, were swing riders, then the flank riders, and at the rear were drag riders chewing dust. Cowboys cut out and ran off ranch cattle that drifted into the herd and watched to keep buffalo from mingling with the herd. They stopped for supplies at Fort Worth and Fort Griffin, depending on which trail they took. In Indian Territory, they kept the peace by paying tribute of a few cattle, "wohaw" the Indians called them.[76]

One of the few women who went up the trail was Mrs. Amanda Burks, of Banquete, west of Corpus Christi. She accompanied her husband when he took a herd to Kansas in 1871. She rode in a buggy pulled by two brown ponies and slept in a tent some distance from the herd. The drive was pleasant until they reached central Texas and she encountered "the worst electrical and hailstorms I ever witnessed . . . The lightning seemed to settle on the ground and creep along like something alive." After the herd was sold in Kansas, the Burks went home by rail to New Orleans and took passage on a ship to Corpus Christi via Galveston and Indianola. "I arrived home in much better health than when I left it nine months before."[77]

Cowboys worked long hours, ate beans, drank Arbuckle's coffee, and liked a trail dessert made of dried fruit in a dough called "son of a bitch in a sack". A rare treat would be something like canned peaches, which the waddies called "air-tights." At night, they played poker by the light of a bull's-eye lantern and slept on a blanket with saddles for pillows, what they called a Tucson bed. It was a dangerous job when there were flooded rivers to cross or when the herd "pulled a big show."[78]

"We took the river route," one old trail hand wrote in disgust, "since we must have crossed every damned river in the country." A trail boss watching his cattle swim the Brazos said it looked as if his herd had disappeared, all he could see were horns in the water. When rivers ran high, a herd would be held back, but they couldn't wait too long; other herds were coming up and mixing herds caused no end of trouble. On one trip, a cowboy counted 15 herds waiting to cross the flooded Trinity River. Further north, the Red River "looked like a young ocean."[79] Worse than taking a herd across a swollen river was a stampede, from the Spanish "estampida." Thomas Welder of Beeville said his herd ran every night for 10 nights in a row, and it was in brush country, which left his cowboys looking as if they had been to an Irish wake.[80]

In one storm, a cowboy from San Antonio wrote that he could see lightning playing on the brim of his hat and the tips of his horse's ears. Riding in the dark, with running cattle, was a dangerous experience. "We had a big stampede and while running in the lead of the steers, I saw by a flash of lightning that I was on the edge of a big bluff of the river. There was nothing left for me to do but jump, so I spurred my horse and landed in the river, which had three or four feet of water in it. Neither my horse nor I was hurt, although some of the steers were killed and others crippled."[81] One cowboy was so sure that he would be killed by lightning during a particularly bad storm that he took a small memorandum book out of his pocket and wrote his own epitaph: "George Knight, struck and killed by lightning, 20 miles south of Ogallala on July 20, 1879."[82] Many cowboys died on the trail, often by lightning or drowning while crossing a flooded river. They were wrapped in their blankets and buried in shallow graves. One man wrote that the saddest sight he'd ever seen was a little mound of fresh earth topped with a pair of boots, the last resting place of some poor cowboy.[83]

On the way home, cowboys would nurse hangovers and memories, sometimes riding over the same trail and telling each other of the experiences on the way up or they would take a roundabout way by train, Mississippi riverboat and coastal steamer from New Orleans, arriving in South Texas in the fall, often broke, having spent their wages on saloon women and fancy clothes and presents for home. Then they would wait for spring and another trip up the trail, repeating the cycle with endless varieties. One cowboy said after a trail drive that he would never forget the comfortable feel of the saddle, the reassuring weight of the six-shooter on his belt, or what a blessing on a rainy night was the yellow slicker called fish.[84] If the cattle barons, the Richard Kings and Mifflin Kenedys and "Shanghai" Pierces, represented one archetypal figure of the last half of the 19th century, the cowboys represented another. We shall not look upon their like again.

In Corpus Christi, on the west side of Mesquite Street, stood a collection of shanties and makeshift sheds occupied by the city's butchers and fruit and vegetable vendors. The small triangular block of land was called Market Square. People complained that the butchers dumped rotting meat in the streets around the square. In 1871, Richard Jordan and William Rogers proposed to the city that they build a structure on the site, with the lower floor leased to the commercial vendors and the upper floor used for city offices. For two decades, the City Council met in various buildings around the city, such as the Hunsaker and Ohler buildings, the Cahill building, Charles Lovenskiold's academy.[85]

In July, 1871, the city agreed to the proposal and Jordan and Rogers hired E.D. Sidbury to construct a two-story building, 80 feet long and 32 feet wide, with a tin roof and a brick floor. The ground floor was divided into open stalls for vegetable and fruit vendors and butchers. The town's butchers kept cattle penned across the bayou on North Beach ready for slaughter to supply the market. The agreement with the city allowed the builders of Market Hall to collect rent for the stalls for 12 years, after which the building would become city property. To make sure that the arrangement would be profitable for the builders, the city made it illegal to sell meat or vegetables anywhere within the city limits except at Market Hall. As the building was going up, a *Nueces Valley* reporter wrote that the nearly finished building would give Corpus Christi "one of the finest meeting halls in Texas. We understand it will be finished next week."[86] When it was finished, the city used the upper floor, where the mayor and aldermen met, and next to their offices was a large hall for dances and public events.[87]

Capt. Andrew Anderson recalled the entertainments. "Upstairs over Market House was a big hall, where the principal entertainments were held. Sometimes we had regular shows. Albert Taylor was one of the shows. Then there was the Stutz Company; Alma Stutz, his daughter, played the part of Mary, the little girl in 'East Lynne.' Fay Templeton was always a favorite. Two of the popular shows then were 'Ten Nights in a Barroom,' and 'The Yankee in Texas.' Another play we liked was 'Rip Van Winkle.' The actors wore high stovepipe hats, beaver hats.[88] And we had medicine shows, too. I remember especially how they would sell Hamlin's Wizard Oil from a wagon. Four fellows would sing beautifully, and the whole street would be full of people listening to the singing. Finally, someone arranged for them to give an entertainment at the Market Hall. You paid 25 cents to hear them sing, and they had a full house every night for a week or more. They sold lots of Wizard Oil."[89]

Market Hall was located on an ideal site for a market, at the very center of the city. A housewife could do all of her marketing within about two blocks. Besides the vegetable and fruit vendors and butcher stalls, on the north side of Market Hall was Heath & Son, advertised as "The Great Emporium," which sold groceries, crockery, and iron stoves. A block south of Market Hall was John Uehlinger's Bakery. Each morning and afternoon, Uehlinger's bread carts made deliveries at the town's homes and restaurants. Across from Market Hall, on both sides of Peoples Street, were two of the city's top grocery stores in the 1880s. W.S. Rankin's store occupied the ground floor of the McCampbell Building. Across Peoples (where Furman Plaza is today) was R.G. Blossman's Grocery, which sold groceries, wine, liquor and fancy delicacies, like pressed pigs feet. An old ledger showed that some of the town's most prominent citizens bought their whisky at Blossman's by the gallon and half-gallon. In 1881, at Blossman's, a housewife could buy sugar for a penny a pound. Bacon cost 11 cents a pound, ham and beef steak 15 cents a pound, coffee 18 to 20 cents a pound, and flour sold for $8.50 a barrel. The best liquor sold for $2 a gallon.[90]

One of the first tenants of the new Market Hall was the Pioneer Fire Company Number One. It was organized after a fire destroyed the home of

101

William Rogers, one of the two builders of Market Hall. The first anniversary of the Pioneer Fire Company was celebrated on June 6, 1872 with a parade, followed by a supper and dance at Market Hall. The *Nueces Valley* reported that "a more brilliant assemblage was never seen in Corpus Christi."[91]

The following year, a new fire company was formed, the Lone Star Hook and Ladder Company. It joined with the Pioneers to become the Corpus Christi Fire Department. This was still a volunteer force.[*] A bell tower housed the fire bell, which was rung to signal the beginning of the work day, lunch hour, quitting time, and when fires erupted. The council in a budget-cutting exercise stopped paying a full-time ringer. The big social event of the year was the firemen's parade and ball. The town's wards competed with each other to show off the most elaborately decorated hose cart for the parade. There was keen competition between firemen over who could pump the most water. The parade and competitive events were followed by a supper and dance at Market Hall.[#92]

---

[*] The city organized a full-time fire department in 1914.
[#] In 1911, in its 40th year, Market Hall was torn down to make way for a new City Hall, built on Market Square at a cost of $55,000.

CHAPTER 8

Birthplace of the cattle industry - Cattle kings and sheepherders of the Nueces Valley - Corpus Christi, a leading wool market - Lawless times follow the Civil War - Dredging of ship channel across the bay

Historian Walter Prescott Webb wrote that the cattle industry began in a diamond-shaped area of South Texas which stretched from San Antonio to Brownsville, Laredo to Corpus Christi. "The Nueces Valley," Webb wrote, "which passes through the region in a southeasterly direction, was the center of the early Spanish [cattle] industry in Texas."[1] The region around Corpus Christi, quite plausibly, was the birthplace of the cattle industry.

This region is where Texas' great cattle barons created the cattle kingdom of Texas, where they learned the requisite skills from the techniques of the Spanish rancheros and vaqueros who came before them.[2] O. Henry called these Texas cattlemen the grandees of grass, the barons of beef and bone.[3] Like the cowboys they hired, they were unique of their kind. One of the first barons in the South Texas region was John Howland Wood, a New York native. He founded the Bonnie View Ranch between Copano Bay and Woodsboro and sold beef to Zachary Taylor's army at Corpus Christi in 1845.[4]

The most famous cattle baron was Richard King, who bought 15,500 acres of the Santa Gertrudis grant for two cents an acre in 1853, the beginning of the world's most famous cattle ranch.[5] Abel Head Pierce (called "Shanghai" because he walked like a Shanghai rooster) was 6-foot-5 with a megaphone voice that carried from one end of the pasture to the other. He came to Texas when he was 20, in 1854, as a stowaway on a schooner from Virginia.* In the 1860s, Pierce established Rancho Grande on Tres Palacios Creek in Wharton County. When "Old Shang" went to buy cattle,

---

* King, Kenedy, and Pierce, among Texas' leading cattlemen, were men of the sea. Perhaps it is not surprising they were attracted to the open expanse of South Texas, often described as being a sea of grass. Pierce's cattle, shipped by sea to the New Orleans, were called "sea lions."

he took a pack horse loaded with gold and silver led by his black cowboy, Neptune Holmes. Pierce would spread a blanket on the ground and count out the gold and silver.[6] Shanghai Pierce was a land-buying cattleman like Richard King, whose ambition was to own whatever land he was standing on.

Another cattle baron was Mifflin Kenedy, a Pennsylvania Quaker who was Richard King's partner in the steamboat business on the Rio Grande.[7] When King bought Santa Gertrudis in 1853, Kenedy chose to stay with the steamboats before he joined King in ranching in 1860.[8]

When the Civil War broke out, King and Kenedy had 20,000 head of cattle and their longhorns were trailed east to help feed the Confederate armies. The two took a close, lucrative interest in the Cotton Road. King used his ranch as supply headquarters for the wagon traffic and Kenedy shipped the cotton on their steamboats on the Rio Grande.[9] The war made them wealthy, providing more money to buy more land and cattle.

John Rabb, a cousin of pistol-packing Sally Skull, began cattle ranching in the western part of Nueces County, in the Banquete area, in 1857 and his operation grew until he became one of the biggest cattlemen in South Texas. He did not buy a lot of land. Rabb ran his cattle under the Bow and Arrow brand on the open range.[10] He bought one small tract of land and built a house on it near Banquete. In 1859, he bought a house on the bluff in Corpus Christi so his children could attend school. During the Civil War, he commanded a company of Confederate cavalry, formed at Banquete, that patrolled the Nueces Strip.[11] Rabb died, at age 46, in 1872, leaving his widow Martha (Regan) a herd of 10,000 cattle running on the open range and 100 acres.[12] Martha Rabb took over her husband's cattle empire at a dangerous time when South Texas was filled with rustlers and outlaws and cross-border raids were frequent. The endemic violence led many cattlemen to sell out. Martha could see the end of the open range coming and knew the land would become more valuable. As others began to sell, she began to buy. She bought one tract of 3,600 acres for 60 cents an acre. Two years later, she added many thousands of acres to her holdings until she had built up one of the largest ranches in this area. She bought the Palo Alto Ranch, in southwestern Nueces County, part of the 1834 grant to Mathias Garcia.

Martha Rabb became known as "The Cattle Queen of Texas." Her pasture was enclosed by 30 miles of fence made of Louisiana pine and cypress posts and it took a fence rider two days to ride it. It was ridden twice a week along an ever-deepening trail.[*] She built a new home on the bluff in Corpus Christi called Magnolia Mansion.[13#] While Martha was the boss, she had help from her three sons, Dock, Frank and Lee, until Lee was killed. Lee

---

[*] Robstown is located in what was a corner of Martha's pasture.

[#] The Magnolia Mansion was bought by Mifflin Kenedy for his son John G. Kenedy. Corpus Christi Cathedral now occupies the site. The Magnolia Mansion building was dismantled and used in the construction of Our Lady of Pilar Church in the Molina subdivision.

Rabb took a girl to a dance in Petronila. While he and his date were sipping coffee, a man slipped up to the window and shot Rabb in the back, killing him instantly. The shooter escaped on Rabb's horse.[14] "Some say that he was caught up with and killed on the banks of the Rio Grande and dumped into the river, but the know-it-alls say he was never caught," John Dunn wrote. "However, he was missing at all the elections since."[15]

Lee's killing led to the fictitious legend that Martha Rabb offered a standing reward of $50 in gold for every pair of "Mexican ears" that were brought to her.[16] Another tall tale connected with Lee Rabb's murder says that Lee's friends in an orgy of revenge by proxy killed some 40 "innocent Mexicans."[17] Not long after Lee Rabb was killed, Martha met and married C.M. Rogers, a Methodist minister, and sold the ranch and moved to Austin, her wealth reportedly dissipated by Rev. Rogers.[18] The Rabb land was sold to D.C. Rachal and was sold again two years later, in the middle of a drought, to the Driscoll brothers.[19]*

Brothers Frank and Edward White, from Liberty, Texas, moved to South Texas and settled across Nueces Bay at Rosita. Their place on the bluff, on the north shore of Nueces Bay, became known as White Point. Some say the name was given because of the white bluffs visible from across the bay, while others say it came from the White family and that in the early years it was known as White's Point, then White Point.[20] In 1857, the Whites hired a young man from their home in East Texas to help drive their stock to their new ranch. He was 18-year-old Darius Cyriaque Rachal, whose family came to Texas from Louisiana. Rachal stayed to work at the ranch. During the Civil War, D.C. Rachal served in Hood's Brigade. He was at the battles of Chickamauga, the Wilderness, and was with Robert E. Lee at Appomattox.[21]

Like other veterans, Rachal came home to begin cattle ranching. Darius (called "Di-reece" by those who knew him) bought a tract of land at White Point. The yellow fever epidemic that decimated Corpus Christi hit White Point, killing Edward and Frank White, along with many in their families. Rachal tore off boards of a new house to make coffins.[22] By the 1870s, Rachal and his brother, E.R. "Nute" Rachal, trailed huge herds to Kansas. The Rachal brothers were famous for moving the cattle up the trail at a furious pace, then fattening them in Kansas for the market. A trail boss trying to hurry his herd along would say, "Rachal 'em, boys, Rachal 'em."[23]

There were other cattlemen of note in that diamond-shaped area where the cattle kingdom was born. After the war, the Driscoll brothers' ranchlands took in parts of three counties; Martin Culver was one of the largest free-range cattlemen in Texas; "Si" Elliff, who ran away from home in Tennessee to become a ranch hand on Martha Rabb's ranch, and ended up owning 50,000 acres; Thomas Coleman helped found one of the great

---

* This land in the 20th Century became the basis for the Robert and Clara Driscoll fortune, after oil was discovered on the property.

ranches of the West, the Coleman-Fulton Pasture Company, which later became the Taft Ranch; George Reynolds, who as a young man hauled fence posts on the King Ranch, bought the Ventana Ranch (sometimes called La Ventana or Palo Ventana). Reynolds became a major sheep rancher in the Nueces Valley.[24]

The age of the cattle kings lasted little more than one generation. The era of the cattle barons and cattle drives represents an epic chapter in the history of South Texas. It is an important part of the history of Corpus Christi and the region around Corpus Christi, which has a much closer connection to the ranching, cattle driving, and cowboy era of the epic and legendary West than Dallas and Fort Worth, two cities that have been adept at marketing their connection to this historic image. Why this is so would make an interesting study, but beginning with the opening of the port in 1926, Corpus Christi turned its back on its Western, cowtown, ranching heritage, and redefined itself as a seaport and nautical town.

L ike the cowboy and vaquero, the shepherd was at home in South Texas. Flocks of sheep grazed the range from Corpus Christi to Laredo, making this one of the top wool-producing areas in the country. Carts (*carretas*) loaded with wool, from as far away as Mexico, rolled into Corpus Christi, one of the world's great wool markets. The sheep era began about 1850 when W. W. Chapman, an Army officer, was transferred to Corpus Christi to head the Army's new 8th Military District depot. Chapman realized that the area's rich grasslands made ideal sheep country. He set up a sheep camp on Santa Gertrudis Creek and brought in purebred Merinos from Pennsylvania. The Merino, unmatched for the quality of its wool, was too delicate for this climate. While Mexican sheep could take the heat, they produced coarse wool. Chapman figured that fine-wooled Merinos bred with tough Mexican sheep would produce a hardy breed with a fine fleece. Merino crossbreeds became the golden fleece of South Texas.[25]

James Bryden, a sheepman from Scotland, was among immigrants attracted here by Henry Kinney's land promotion efforts. Chapman hired Bryden to handle his sheep. In payment for watching the flock, Bryden was given part of the natural increase and a share in the wool profits. Bryden grazed the sheep along Santa Gertrudis Creek.[26] The following year, in 1853, Richard King bought the first acres to begin his ranch near the Chapman sheep camp. King purchased 10 Merino bucks and 42 Mexican ewes.[27] Within a decade, he had some 40,000 sheep. His main sheep camp was called Borregas. Other sheepmen besides Bryden were among immigrants attracted by Kinney's land-selling promotion in the 1850s—Joseph Almond of Newcastle-on-Tyne, the Adams' brothers, George Reynolds, the Wrights, these became sheep ranchers in the Nueces Valley.[28]

Circumstances forced many to turn to sheep. Corpus Christi in 1856 suffered a severe blow when the region's top employer, the army, moved its depot headquarters to San Antonio. Kinney's immigrants who had found employment as teamsters with the army were forced to find new jobs. George Reynolds had worked cutting hay for the army; when the army left, he went to work on King Ranch and then began his own sheep ranch near Orange Grove. Other immigrants turned to raising sheep, something they knew from England and Scotland. "Many were driven to the country; some became farmers, some became stockmen, and not a few turned their attentions to sheep-raising." [29] The decade of the 1850s marked the beginning of the sheep era in the Nueces Valley region of South Texas. The cattle kingdom began about the same time, and in almost the same place, along Santa Gertrudis Creek and in the well-watered Nueces Valley, and for the same reason: necessity. Sheep raisers were encouraged when James Bryden reported wool sales for 1857-1860 totaling $5,567.[30]

In large measure, Corpus Christi's economy depended on Merino crossbreed sheep and longhorn steers.[31] Maria von Blucher wrote in a letter to her parents in Germany on Dec. 26, 1860, "Sheep are the best business here, better than cattle.[32] Mrs. Chapman "has grown rich by keeping sheep, going halves with somebody."[33] (Helen Chapman was the widow of Maj. W.W. Chapman, who died in Fortress Monroe, Va. in 1859.)

By the end of the 1850s, quality wool was shipped from Corpus Christi to world markets; the business grew until, over time, Corpus Christi was shipping out as much as one-third of all the wool exports leaving the United States for the mills of England and Europe.[34] Word spread that South Texas was sheep country; sheepherders came here from all over to make their fortunes by tending sheep on shares. John Buckley, an immigrant from Ireland, came to Duval County from Ontario, Canada, to raise sheep. He became the patriarch of the William F. Buckley family.[35*] John McClane brought 75 bucks from his father's farm in Pennsylvania for Richard King and Mifflin Kenedy. After delivering the sheep, McClane stayed in Texas and went to work helping King build up his flock of sheep.[#36]

A young man named Oscar M. Edgerley came here from New York to tend sheep for William Headen, one of Corpus Christi's wealthy wool merchants. Edgerley kept a diary, recording the daily routines of a sheepherder. He stayed busy moving the sheep and setting up new camps. When the sheep ate all the grass near watering places, they were driven out in search of greener pastures, then brought back for water. Edgerley once moved the flock to San Fernando Creek and Richard King rode up and told

---

* John Buckley's son was William F. Buckley, Sr., father of the later conservative leader William F. Buckley, Jr. William F. Buckley, Sr. moved to Mexico and made a fortune from oil exploration. He then moved his family to Connecticut. John Buckley ran for sheriff of Duval County, as a Democrat, and lost; he claimed voter fraud and the Texas Supreme Court agreed, overturning the election and making Buckley sheriff. He served from 1890 to 1896.
# McClane would be elected sheriff of Nueces County during the violent 1870s.

him to move. Oscar moved up the creek; King told him to move again. "As I thought I was not on his lands, I did not move," Edgerley wrote. "I stayed there until the grass gave out, then took them up on the Aqua Dulce." Edgerley's daily tasks were taking the sheep to water or grass, cooking meals, watching for coyotes and other predators.[37]

Unlike cattle which could be left alone to graze and look after themselves, sheep had to be "lived with." They had to be taken to grass or water and protected from predators. It was a lonely life. Robert Adams went to work when he was 16 in 1863 tending sheep at Belden and Gilpin's Carmel Ranch, near Casa Blanca. Robert and his brother William came to Corpus Christi with their family in 1852, immigrants attracted to South Texas by Henry Kinney's land promotions. In his memoirs, Robert said of his sheep-tending time: "I never saw a house for a year, and was not inside a house for over two years. I did most of my own cooking for four years, and had nothing to eat but meat. I had no bread and didn't know what a vegetable looked like. I didn't see people sometimes for two or three months."[38]

In the years after the Civil War, by 1870, there were 1.2 million sheep in Nueces County.[*] It had more "fleecies" than any other county in the country.[39] In shearing season (April to June and August to September), big two-wheeled ox carts loaded with bags of wool came to Corpus Christi to sell to the wool merchants on Chaparral. Sheepmen came all the way from Mexico to sell their wool. Long trains of oxcarts would arrive by the Laredo Road. The carts with teams of oxen and mules congregated on Chaparral, where the city's wool buyers were headquartered.[40] A Corpus Christi newspaper reported in 1871 that "Mexican carts, loaded with wool, hides and other produce, have been arriving in such numbers that our streets have been crowded with them during the entire week, and our roads are lined with carts bringing produce and carrying back merchandise . . . Every train that comes in is freighted back with either merchandise or lumber."[41]

Mary Sutherland first saw Corpus Christi, in May, 1876. Chaparral was crowded with oxcarts and wagons. "Some of the vehicles had as many as six yokes of oxen, and the patient animals were lying down in a seeming tangle, reaching from curb to curb, chewing the cud and waiting the crack of the whip, the signal to begin the long, hot journey across the prairies to and beyond the Mexican border, carrying in their wake a whiff of civilization: clothes, shoes, hats, cook stoves, sewing machines, oil lamps, clocks, any and everything, bought with the proceeds of sales of hides, tallow, dried meat, wool."[42]

Most Corpus Christi merchants bought wool, but the dealers on a large scale in the 1870s were Ed Buckley, Frank & Weil, William Headen, John Woessner, and Norwick Gussett. One of the largest firms was Doddridge,

---

[*] The county was much larger then, including today's Jim Wells County (created in 1911) and Kleberg County (created in 1913). Both were carved out of Nueces County.

108

Lott & Davis. At the establishments of these merchants, oxcarts would unload wool, hides and other wares and take on a cargo of supplies from their stores.[43] Gussett was probably the city's wealthiest wool merchant. He was called "Col. Gussett" though he had been a sergeant in Zachary Taylor's army. He was shot and wounded in the hip in the battle of Cerro Gordo in the Mexican War. He kept a well-worn piece of his hip bone in his watch pocket, which he would take out and rub with his thumb. To give an idea of the size of his business, in 1873 Gussett purchased three million pounds of wool. He had a fleet of three schooners (named after his daughters Josephine, Leona and Susan) that carried his wool to Boston and New York and brought back merchandise for his store, which was topped with a rooster weathervane and commonly called *Tienda del Gallo*.[44]

Perry Doddridge's place had the symbol of a ram, hence *La Tienda del Borrego*. Uriah Lott (before he became the builder of railroads) was one of the city's early wool tycoons. His office was at the corner of Chaparral and Lawrence. In one year, 1869, he purchased more than one million pounds of wool. Lott later went into business with his brother-in-law, A.M. Davis, and Doddridge (for whom Doddridge Street is named). The wool business was so lucrative that Doddridge, Davis and Lott built their own bank on Chaparral in 1871. Another wool tycoon was David Hirsch, a native of Germany who came to Corpus Christi from New Orleans. Hirsch's store and wool warehouse was on the east side of Chaparral, next to the Crescent Hotel. William Headen was one of the city's oldest wool dealers. His firm, Headen & Son, was located in a frame building at Chaparral and Schatzel.

Sheepmen returning to Mexico after selling their wool in Corpus Christi carried back merchandise to sell. The Corpus Christi wool merchants bought the wool and sold the merchandise for the return trip, making a profit coming and going. The returning sheepmen were often targeted by bandits. One trick of the sheepmen, it was said, was to drill holes in the wooden axles of their oxcarts. The holes were packed with silver dollars, then sealed with wooden pegs. This was the great sheep era of South Texas and Corpus Christi was one of the world's major wool markets.[45]

The sheep ranchers, wool merchants and cattle barons played a major, decisive part in making Corpus Christi a prosperous, thriving city in the 1870s. And it *was* a prosperous time in the 1870s, with huge herds going to Kansas from South Texas and with wool from all over the region and Mexico coming to market in Corpus Christi. But it was also a violent, lawless decade when bandits, many from below the border, robbed, killed, stole cattle, attacked and burned ranches.

After the Texas Revolution, before statehood, in the Mexican War that followed, during the Cortina troubles of the 1850s, in the Civil War, then during the cross-border raids during Reconstruction, the region between the Nueces and the Rio Grande was a zone of conflict. Ethnic hostility that marked the revolutionary period of Texas history and was nurtured along in the Mexican War, was dormant during the Civil War. But the era of bandits, killers and thieves crossing the border brought back the stresses and strains between ethnicities and cultures of the border region. For a decade after the Civil War, South Texas descended into near anarchy. The whole countryside was like an armed camp.

The bandits were a mix of outlaw vaqueros and bad men on the run. They killed indiscriminately, leaving travelers and rural ranchers in fear of their lives, then found refuge across the Rio Grande. The posses and "committees of public safety" took the law into their own hands, dealing out extra-judicial death sentences, and leaving bodies hanging in mesquite thickets all over South Texas. How many? No one will ever know since posses didn't leave written records of their exploits. The volunteer militia companies around Corpus Christi, wrote historian T.R. Fehrenbach, "staged counter-raids not across the border, but against suspected ethnic allies of the bandits. On one of these excursions, 11 men were executed."[46]

Such lynchings began before the violent era of Reconstruction. A Corpus Christi newspaper reported in October, 1860: "A Mexican named Jesus Garcia was hung to a limb of a tree last Monday, at a place near Petronila, on the Agua Dulce. Who done it or what it was done for is a mystery."[47] Casual lynchings, as retaliation by proxy, intensified during the lawless era of Reconstruction. The majority of the victims of extra-judicial hangings were of Mexican descent.[48] The incidents were commonplace. In one, "A Mexican has been found hanging dead to a tree near Nuecestown."[49] In another, "The Mexican who shot Sullivan, the butcher at Culver's Packery, was found hanging in a thicket two miles this side of Nuecestown. The coroner's jury returned a verdict of hanging by unknown parties".[50] In another incident, the *Nueces Valley* reported that, "We have a report that Capt. Wallace caught several Mexicans at Conception and shot some and hanged the others without so much as saying 'by your leave.'"[*51] That was a rare criticism. For if such killings troubled the public conscience, the newspaper usually did not betray it.

"The situation is truly deplorable," said a letter to the editor. "There is no security for person or property between the Nueces and the Rio Grande, and none for residents between the Rio Frio and the Nueces."[52] Stolen cattle were driven across the Rio Grande and hide thieves worked the ranges with impunity. Ranchers hired gunmen to track down rustlers and hide peelers. Hired guns didn't always follow the law. People did not dare to go about without being armed and alert. Conditions were so dangerous that people were afraid to travel; traffic along the roads all but ceased.

The violence in the remote areas was more than a spot on the horizon for Corpus Christi, which was a center of trade and commerce and depended on

---

* Warren W. Wallace was authorized by Gov. Coke to raise a company of 50 men to patrol the Nueces Strip. J.B. (Red) Dunn was in Wallace's company and was involved in the affair at Conception, as he relates in *Perilous Trails of Texas*.

people being able to travel on the roads. John McCampbell, a Corpus Christi lawyer, quit practicing law because it was too risky to attend courts in other towns.[53] Attacks were so frequent and so vicious that travelers dared not ride the roads alone. Rancher Richard King traveled with an armed escort, yet he was attacked by eight men waiting in ambush at San Fernando Creek, six miles from the ranch, on the way to Brownsville on July 31, 1872. A young passenger, Franz Specht, was killed in the ambush. Ironically, King was on his way to testify before a federal grand jury in Brownsville about the violent conditions of the region. King eventually testified on Aug. 26.[54] The commissioners from Washington took thousands of pages of depositions, but it all came to nothing. Grisly attacks on ranch houses, rural stores and unwary travelers told the temper of the times.

On Aug. 19, 1872, William Murdock, who lived on the Santa Gertrudis Road 12 miles west of Corpus Christi, was tied up, a heavy plow placed on top of him, and burned alive.[55] Ingleside's George Hatch, 83, one of the most respected men of South Texas, was robbed and killed in his buggy on the north side of the reef road, at Indian Point, on Sept. 5, 1872. The killers cut out his pockets and robbed him, took his horses and escaped.[56] J.B. (Red) Dunn, a vigilante rider and Texas Ranger, said that outside of five or six persons no one ever knew whether the killers were caught. The names of the killers were discovered, Dunn wrote, "and placed in our plug hats for future reference. But instead of giving them absolution for their sins, we transferred that part of the matter to the Deity and left them to settle it with Him. It is sometimes amusing to hear people say that the murderers of so-and-so were never caught. Well, ignorance is bliss."[57]

The day after Hatch was slain, Corpus Christi citizens held a mass meeting at Market Hall on Sept. 6, "to devise and execute measures for the protection of life and property." The object of the meeting was to form an organization "for the purpose of assisting the officers of the law to maintain order, to bring to justice the perpetrators of the late murders and outrages."[58] Citizens were urged to assume responsibility for maintaining law and order. Maria von Blucher wrote her parents in Germany that, "Murder and bloodshed are now so general here that we do not venture to go out, even for a picnic, not 1½ miles from Corpus Christi. All the scum from Mexico knocks about on this side of the Rio Grande."[59]

One of the worst crimes of a lawless era was committed on May 9, 1874, at Peñascal, a one-store settlement 50 miles south of Corpus Christi on a point of land at Baffin Bay.[*] Store owner John Morton, 24, his brother and two customers were killed in a most brutal fashion. A cook returning from the well with a bucket of water hid and watched 11 bandits ride up and go into the store. It was dusk. He heard shots and saw Herman Tilgner, a

---

[*] The Peñascal settlement, or ranch, was five miles northeast of the La Parra ranch headquarters. Those living at Peñascal were suspected of being linked to cattle rustlers and hide thieves in the area.

customer in the store, running out vomiting blood, then saw the killers finish him off. He watched the bandits shoot Michael Morton, brother of the store owner, four times in the head. The bandits tied up a customer named F.M. Coakley and executed him. They shot the store owner in both arms, then forced him to carry out their plunder. They shot him six more times. His body was found behind the counter, one leg bent under him, and a prayer book by his side. All the merchandise nearby was covered with blood. The killers stayed all night, drinking whisky and trying on store clothes. They packed up their plunder and left at dawn, wearing new store clothes and leaving their own clothes in the blood-splattered store.[60]

The alarm spread. Several posses rode to Peñascal. One struck a trail. In looking at wagon tracks near the store, they found a brownish powder. It was brown sugar that had leaked from one of the bags the bandits had taken. The trail of brown sugar ended a few miles away, but it revealed that the bandits were riding not for the border, as expected, but toward Corpus Christi. The posse following the trail included J.B. (Red) Dunn. They eventually found two suspects hiding with shearers who had come up from Mexico in a sheep pen.[61]

"The hard south wind had blown the big gate open," Dunn wrote, "and we charged right in among them. I happened to dismount beside a blanket where two men were asleep. One of these was Hypolita Tapia and the other Andres Davila. After satisfying ourselves that these were the only men implicated in the murder, we took them back to [Meansville].[*] We placed the prisoners in a room under guard. First we took Hypolita out and told him that we wanted him to tell us all about the murder, but he stated he would confess nothing. Then we took him to a tall mesquite tree and let him kick a few chunks out of the horizon, after which he stated that he was ready to divulge everything." [62]

Tapia said he was a vaquero and sheepherder. He said a Corpus Christi policeman named Tomas Basquez had been in Buckley's wool store in Corpus Christi and overheard there would be a large consignment of goods and money going to Peñascal. Basquez wanted to get 10 men to go down and get it. Tapia said he agreed to do it and got 10 men to go with him, including Davila, an Anglo named Joe, who was the ringleader, and several others. When they arrived at Peñascal, Tapia said, the boat on which the goods had been shipped was away from the shore. They assumed the boat had already landed the money and goods, but it had not. The raiders found only $12 or $13 in the cash drawer. Tapia told how the men at Morton's store were killed. While the posse questioned the suspects, word spread of their capture.[63]

Ranchers showed up with a rope and plans to use it. The Dunn brothers

---

[*] Meansville, a ghost town today, was located three miles southeast of present day Odem. It was named for Col. William Means.

convinced them that if they lynched Tapia and Davila, it would destroy the evidence against the policeman Basquez. Tapia and Davila were tied up and delivered to Nueces County Sheriff John McClane. During the trial, the prosecutor told the jury that Tapia had made a voluntary confession. Tapia jumped up and pointed to the rope marks around his neck and said, "That's the voluntary confession." Tapia and Davila were found guilty and sentenced to be hanged. Their hangings were scheduled for Friday, Aug. 7, 1874. A third suspect identified as the man who shot the storeowner Morton was taken out of the San Diego jail and lynched. The policeman Basquez and the Anglo named Joe were never brought to justice.[64]

Tapia, days before his scheduled hanging, asked to marry his common-law wife. The day before the hanging, on Thursday, the two prisoners were shaved and dressed in white shirts and black pants. Tapia's friends and relatives attended the wedding at the jail. The bride wore a calico dress and black shawl. The ceremony was performed by Father Claude Jaillet. Next day, Father Jaillet returned to escort the two men to the scaffold for the 1:50 p.m. hanging. The scaffold was built out from the balcony of the 1854 courthouse. There was a fence around the courthouse, but the hangings could be seen above the fence. Tapia and Davila were still wearing their fancy clothes. Tapia's last words were: "My friends, I am here today to die by hanging. I have killed no person nor helped kill anyone. The people forced the party that was guilty to swear against me; but it is all right. Goodbye." Davila stood with eyes downcast and said nothing, ready to meet his fate like a stoic.[65]

Not long after the outrage at Peñascal, a sheepman named Thad Swift and his wife were brutally killed at their ranch house in Refugio County. On June 7, 1874, Swift sold his wool clip at St. Mary's for $700 in small leather sacks of silver dollars. On Sunday, Swift, who was deaf, was murdered in his bed, cut to pieces. His wife was stabbed 25 times, her throat cut, and her body left in the yard, where it was mangled by hogs. The Swifts' three small daughters knew nothing of the slayings until they woke the next morning and found the bodies of their parents. The oldest girl, who was eight, took her sisters to an uncle's house three miles away. The news spread and riders came from all over.[*]

Committees of Public Safety, in effect vigilante groups, were already in existence throughout the area. They were called "minutemen" because in an emergency they were supposed to drop whatever they were doing and be in the saddle in a minute. In Refugio County, the minutemen joined the hue and

---

[*] It may seem that this is getting away from Corpus Christi history. But factors that explain an intensified ethnic conflict should be our proper concern. Reconstruction-era violence of the 1870s, marked by the Peñascal and Swift Ranch slayings and the Nuecestown Raid, along with the violent reaction by vigilantes resulted in polarizing effects that lasted well into the 20th century. We can only guess at the pressures, not to mention the prejudices, of the times, which is not to be taken as an excuse for ignorance.

cry after the news spread of the Swift murders. One of Swift's ranch hands, named Juan Flores, was considered a prime suspect. Flores had traveled with Swift to St. Mary's to sell the wool and knew about the sacks of silver dollars. One posse was under the command of Capt. Henry Scott, a rancher known as an old Indian fighter. Scott took his posse toward Laredo, following the trail of Flores. In Refugio County, John Young was with another posse.[#] "What I saw when I arrived at the Swift ranch changed me from a simple-hearted country boy to a hard-nerved man boiling for revenge."[66]

Young steered the posse toward a ranch near Goliad, telling the other minutemen he knew of a "bad Mexican" named Moya who might have been involved in the killings. The posse found the Moyas barricaded inside their ranch house. They refused to come out. One yelled, "What do you want?" A member of the posse yelled, "We want you." One of the Moyas fired and a bullet hit a member of the posse, killing him instantly. The posse laid siege to the ranch house, firing into the chink holes, trying to hit anyone inside. [67]

The sheriff of Goliad County urged the Moyas to come out, telling them they would be under the full protection of the law. They came out. There were two brothers, Antonio and Marcelo, and their aging father. Young described what happened on the way to Goliad: "A lot of us did not propose to put off a punishment that we knew the Mexicans[*] deserved. The prisoners and their guards [the sheriff and his men] rode about three miles when we surrounded them. The guard offered practically no interference . . . In the melee that followed, Marcelo was shot dead, old Moyer [Moya] was wounded and down on the ground. A maddened ranch boy rode his plunging horse over him, at the same time emptying his six-shooter at him. Another man dismounted and cut the Mexican's throat . . ." The Moyas were all killed, their bodies left on the road.[68]

In Refugio, Mexican-Americans suspected of complicity in the Swift murders were chained in the courthouse. One night, a lynch mob took three prisoners and hanged them from a tree at the Swift ranch. On the Rio Grande near Laredo, the posse of Capt. Henry Scott trailed the prime suspect of the Swift murders, Juan Flores, who had crossed into Mexico. Some accounts say Scott paid $500 in gold out of his own pocket to bribe officials to return Flores across the river.[69] Flores was brought back to Refugio, tried, and convicted. Before he was hanged, he admitted his guilt from the scaffold and expressed remorse. No evidence ever surfaced that implicated the Moyas in the Swift murders.

Mexican-Americans began to leave the area. Accounts say the roads west were filled with oxcarts and wagons. When minutemen stopped the wagons, they found only women and children. When they searched, they found men

---

[#] John Young co-authored *A Vaquero of the Brush Country* with J. Frank Dobie.
[*] The word "Mexican" used for Hispanic citizens was clearly pejorative and understood as such.

hiding beneath bedding in the wagons.[70]

This was a terrible time, with conditions near anarchy. Texans, a people prone to fight since the Texas Revolution, often responded in brutal fashion, with posse riders and minutemen cutting a furious swath across South Texas. The pervasive violence in the region primarily centered on nursed animosities between Anglos and Mexican-Americans.[71] T.R. Fehrenbach wrote that the raiding and posse lynchings kept blood feuds and mutual hatred alive, that the racial or ethnic memories of these bloody times would be passed down from generation to generation.[72] The inflamed grievances from those lawless days of the 1870s would last for a long time. Blood memories die hard.

It wasn't all bad news in those lawless times. There was good news for Corpus Christi in 1874 when the Morris & Cummings Cut was completed and the town became a significant port for the first time in its history, marking the beginning of bustling commercial activity on the waterfront.

This climaxed a 30-year effort to make Corpus Christi a port city. Until 1874, shallow water and mudflats between Corpus Christi Bay and both the Gulf and Aransas Bay prevented most sea-going ships from docking at Corpus Christi. The city was at a disadvantage trying to compete with Rockport and Indianola for Gulf commerce.[73] Henry Kinney started the work when he bought a steam dredge to dig out a channel in 1848.[74] The work languished and in 1854 the city issued $50,000 in bonds to dredge a channel. There were setbacks but a channel "of sorts" was scooped out of the bay.[75] In 1858, the city voided the original $50,000 in bonds and issued new bonds to the D.S. Howard Co., of New York, to dredge a channel. These were revenue bonds that were to be paid when the work was finished by collecting a toll on the ships that used the channel. Howard hired Col. John M. Moore to supervise the work.[76]

"I knew of D.S. Howard and Col. Moore, who were interested in a canal down there in what they called the mudflats, where they come out of Aransas Bay to Corpus Christi Bay," said Robert Adams, who came to Corpus Christi from England with his family in 1852. "They had a dredge to dig the canal with. I went through there once with my father; they were mudflats sure enough. Everything behind the boat was just loblolly, thick mud."[77]

The dredging progressed slowly. There was little money. The man in charge of the dredge boat, Capt. J.C. Riddle, complained of "not having a cent," of having to borrow bacon, of being out of wood to fuel the boiler, of not having the funds to pay his workers.[78] The dredging stopped when the Civil War broke out and Capt. Riddle's dredge boat was abandoned on the waterfront. The boiler was visible for years, but the boat gradually disappeared as people dismantled it for firewood.[*79]

---

[*] The dredge boat was beached at the edge of the bay, off Water Street, where the Ritter Pier was later built, from the end of Belden Street.

The dredging resumed in 1872 when the city negotiated a contract with Augustus T. Morris of Bloomfield, N.J., and James Cummings of New York City to gouge out an eight-foot-deep channel through the mudflats in the middle of the bay. The city agreed to pay up to $500,000 for the work, with the contractors authorized to collect a toll on every vessel using the channel, five cents for each cubic foot. When the Morris and Cummings Cut, as it came to be called, was completed in 1874, some of the larger ships did not have to wait outside the bar at the Aransas Pass channel to be "lightered," a lengthy and cumbersome process of shifting cargo from larger to smaller-draft vessels. They could sail or steam directly across the bay and dock at Central Wharf, which reached into the bay from Water Street at William and Laguna (now Sartain).[80]

The *Gussie*, a Morgan Line steamship drawing eight feet of water, arrived on May 31, 1874. This set off a big celebration at Central Wharf.[81] The *Corpus Christi Gazette* in its next edition noted "the triumphant entry of the Morgan ship, *Gussie*, to our bay. For upwards of 20 years we have waited in anxious expectation to chronicle uninterrupted communication with the outside world. Notwithstanding the croaking of numerous people to the contrary, the indomitable working of the present contractors has brought the labor to a successful issue."[82]

Behind this celebration, however, was a furious controversy that split the town into opposing camps. The year before, in anticipation of the completion of the channel, several businessmen bought the Central Wharf. The prime mover was Uriah Lott, of later fame as a railroad builder. Lott was a shipping agent, a wool and hide dealer, and part owner of a bank. Among other partners in the Central Wharf incorporation were rancher Richard King, W.N. Staples, and Doddridge. Lott's business partner, Perry Doddridge, was also the town's mayor, and he was one of the Central Wharf partners.[83] Lott appeared before the City Council and proposed giving the city $1,000 a month, or one-fifth of the gross receipts of the Central Wharf, if the city would give the owners monopoly control for 30 years. The city agreed. The old wharf, built in 1853, was strengthened, a cattle chute added, and a new 20-foot-wide extension added at the end, crossing the T.

One man who didn't like this sweetheart deal was Norwick Gussett, and Gussett had the money and power to challenge it. Gussett came here in 1845 as a sergeant with Zachary Taylor's army. He returned after the war, began several ranches, founded a town called Gussettville, and eventually started a bank, mercantile store, and hide and wool business in Corpus Christi. He owned his own fleet of schooners plying between Corpus Christi and New York. Gussett opposed paying higher wharf fees to the monopoly owners of the Central Wharf. He led a faction called the Anti-monopoly Group. Gussett built his own wharf off North Beach, outside city limits.* His wharf did a big

---

* Near where the Breakers Hotel would be built later.

business, which put an end to the Central Wharf's monopoly and the syndicate quit paying the city $1,000 a month.[84]

This was a time of growth and prosperity for Corpus Christi. The commerce of South Texas flowed past Water Street. The bay was crowded with schooners, side-wheelers, steamships. Morgan Line ships became a common sight docked at the T-Head on the end of the Central Wharf. Exports from Corpus Christi included wool, hides, tallow, and cattle on the hoof. But wool was the major export. Wool shipped out of Corpus Christi in the late 1870s amounted to 12 million pounds a year. On March 28, 1875, shipping tycoon Charles Morgan, owner of 100 vessels in the Morgan Line, arrived on his side-wheeler, *City of Norfolk,* which was described as a floating palace. Mayor Perry Doddridge took Morgan on a tour of the city. Morgan later had a ship built specially for the Corpus Christi trade, named *Aransas*. The Mallory Lines, Morgan's competitor, also built a ship for the Corpus Christi run, named *Western Texas*. It turned out that it was a little too large to make it through the Morris and Cummings Cut.[85] As a result of the deeper channel across the bay, the business of the city increased with shipments of wool, cattle, and hides. This prompted businessmen of the town, led by wool-dealer Uriah Lott, to build a railroad to Laredo.

CHAPTER 9

Skinning War of South Texas leaves a trail of violence - Beef packing houses slaughter cattle for hides and tallow - 1874 hurricane floods downtown - Nuecestown Raid scares Corpus Christi - The Mercer logs

S outh Texas suffered a bad drought in 1871 and 1872. It was followed by a bitterly cold winter. Weak, undernourished longhorns died by the thousands. It was said one could walk for miles on longhorn carcasses.[1] Cowboys called this wholesale death a "die-up." After the die-up in the winter of 1871, the skinning season began the next spring. Cowboys carried skinning knives to strip the hides of dead cattle. John Young recalled that rancher Jim Miller, whose place was along the Nueces River, skinned more than 4,000 head of cattle killed in the die-up of 1872-73.[2] Young said ranchers came to speak of the "skinning season" just as they would the "branding season."[3] Every man with a horse and skinning knife went into the country looking for cattle that, if not dead, soon would be—and often these would be helped to die by unscrupulous skinners. For honest skinners, brands served to identify the owner. The owner was due the value of the skin less the amount owed the skinner for his work.[4]

While cattlemen hired skinners and used ranch hands for the task, many skinners working the ranges were thieves—bandits, freebooters, wanted men on the run. Instead of rounding up herds and driving them across the border for sale, hide thieves killed cattle and skinned them where they fell. It was more convenient to load up a wagon with hides and take it across the border than to take a herd across.[5] Some thieves used a long knife fixed to a pole, called a *"media luna,"* to cut tendons of cattle to hamstring them, then would shoot or stab them to death and skin them. It was horribly cruel.[6] Sometimes the thieves would cut the brand out, leaving a telltale "stove pipe" hole in the hide. The skinning season resulted in a bloody conflict between cattlemen and outlaw skinners called the Skinning War.[7] It was, in cowboy parlance, hell with the hide off.

The range war in South Texas, wrote J. Frank Dobie, was over hides rather than sheep, as it was in many other Western states. In the Skinning

War of the 1870s, "bands of Mexicans rode the country between the Nueces and the Rio Grande, running onto cattle, cutting their hamstrings with machetes, then stabbing them, skinning them, and leaving the carcasses for coyotes and buzzards, the hides being hauled in carts across the Rio Bravo. The waste of longhorns for hides in southern Texas was equaled only by the buffalo slaughter on the Plains."[8]

In March, 1872, the *Nueces Valley* newspaper reported, "We hear many reports of persons who own no stock whatever killing cattle that they may secure their hides. These scoundrels should be looked after and punished to the full extent of the law." The bands of hide thieves, the "scoundrels," worked the ranges, killing cattle, taking hides by the thousands. Judge W. L. Rea said hide thieves drove away herds and shot them on the prairies. They skinned the carcasses and sold the hides. Judge Rea said two of the main hide thieves on the ranchers' black list were Pat Quinn and Alberto "Segundo" Garza.[9] J.B. "Red" Dunn was a member of a company of Texas Rangers that tracked Garza around Lagarto. He was accused of stealing horses and killing cattle for their hides, but they couldn't catch him.[10] The *Nueces Valley* under the heading "Killing and Skinning" reported: "We learn of the wholesale slaughter of cattle by Alberto Garza and his party. At one place there were 275 carcasses, at another 300, and at another 66. These robbers seem to be well-supplied with ammunition, rodeo the cattle, and shoot them down in their tracks, until a sufficient number is killed for the day."

Garza reportedly had 60 men killing and skinning in Nueces and Duval counties. In one account, Garza sent a taunting message from his camp to the town of San Diego, demanding that they bring enough money to buy the hides his men had collected (read: stolen) or to send enough men to fight. Several cattlemen, including Jasper Clark, James F. Scott and nine others, took up Garza's challenge. They attacked his camp and Garza and his bunch of hide thieves escaped in such a hurry they left saddles, bridles and bloody hides behind. Near the camp the posse found the carcasses of 80 cattle that had been killed and skinned.[11]

The winter of 1873 was another die-up. The hide thieves were busy. This was a lawless time, a time of chaos, turmoil and violence, a time when life had little value. Rustlers, hide thieves, and robbers rode in heavily armed gangs of 10 to 100 men. They could take on just about any force they ran up against. If truly threatened, they could find sanctuary on the Rio Grande. The market for the stolen hides was at Brownsville and Matamoros. Dunn wrote that American merchants built stores to deal in stolen goods. Cattlemen who tried to track down their stolen property found a dead end along the border. One hide dealer in Matamoros reportedly told his help: "Shoot the first gringo son of a bitch who comes here and attempts to look at a hide."[12] The Skinning War was a time of murder and mayhem, of general slaughter and gratuitous cruelty.

The activity of outlaw skinners, who found a lucrative market for their stolen hides in Mexico, may have inspired cattlemen and other financiers to build packing houses.[13] The huge numbers of cattle taken up the trail glutted the market. In 1866, the year after the war ended, 260,000 longhorns went up the trail. By 1871, 700,000 went up, 30,000 from Nueces, Live Oak and San Patricio.[14] The numbers declined in 1872 and beef prices plunged the following year in the financial panic of 1873.[15] In a glutted market, the value of the longhorn was reduced to the value of its hide, the tallow that could be rendered for candles, and the horns and bones that could be used to make buttons and knife handles. The combination of range skinning and low beef prices helped introduce the advent of the packing houses. Almost overnight, beef slaughterhouses sprang up on the Texas coast, from Padre Island to the Rockport area, mainly, but as far east as Galveston.[16] E. H. Caldwell wrote in his memoirs: "Often there were occasions when the price of cattle at the end of a long trail drive to Kansas didn't justify the effort. The animals would be worth only what their hides and tallow would have brought back in the Corpus Christi market. To resolve this situation, four steam packeries were established next to the city, within smelling distance."[17]

Slaughterhouses were not unknown in years before. Henry Kinney, the founder of Corpus Christi, opened a slaughterhouse on North Beach in the 1840s where mustangs and longhorns were killed for their hides and in the 1850s, C.R. Hopson, with Kinney as his partner, operated a beef packing house at Peoples and Water, in the very center of town. After the Civil War, in 1866, Richard King built a packing house on the southern edge of town, by the arroyo. Others were built on North Beach and at Flour Bluff. Jim James, who would later build the St. James Hotel, had a packery on Mustang Island. All that was required was to set up packing sheds with great iron tanks, hire cowboys to round up the animals and butchers to slaughter them. Many of the packing houses, also called "factories" and "packeries," were built by cattlemen like Richard King and Mifflin Kenedy to process their own cattle and those of their neighbors. Cattleman Martin Culver operated a packery at Nuecestown. Capt. Andrew Anderson took a boatload of salt up the Nueces River to Culver's packery. Anderson was asked to stay for dinner, but he declined because the place was filthy and full of flies.[18]

In the early to mid-1870s, there were great profits in the hide and tallow factories and huge fortunes were made. The packing houses were fed by a sustained flow of cattle from the ranges of South Texas. The owner of a slaughterhouse at Flour Bluff, James M. Doughty, relocated to a rocky point on Aransas Bay, which became Rockport, a center of the hide and tallow industry. William Hall, a Maine Yankee, built a packing house nearby, which was followed by a dozen others. The Coleman-Mathis-Fulton Company built a large packing house at Fulton, just up the coast. One large slaughterhouse was at what is now the exclusive residential area of Key

Allegro.[19] The Rockport packeries produced a mountain of bones that covered five acres.[20] This was used later to make high-grade fertilizer sold on the East Coast.[21]

A packery employing 40 workers could process up to 250 head of cattle a day. The men were paid very well to work in the muck and blood of slaughter—from $1 to $4 a day, top wages for that time. One Rockport packing house hired 10 cowboys to supply it with 1,000 steers every two weeks; they would pay $4 to $7 a head for any longhorn that would pass the brand inspectors. The cowboys chased half-wild longhorns out of the dense brush all over South Texas. At Rockport's Big Wharf, ocean-going ships loaded salted hides, barrels of tallow, and heaps of horns and bones. The ships brought nail kegs filled with silver dollars for exchange. Stories were told of kegs of silver coins sitting on the pier, unguarded and untended.[22]

J.B. "Red" Dunn worked in a packery owned by Bill Brunwinkel and Henry Ball (known as "Bill and Ball"). Theirs was one of three packing houses on North Beach; the other two were owned by Alonzo A. DeAvalon and John Hall.* [23] Dunn described the process at the packing house. Cattle were driven into a small chute where a man with a spear, called a sticker, stood on a plank walk above the cattle and stabbed them in the neck, severing the spinal column. Before going into boilers, the horns were removed, the skin cut around the neck, feet removed, and the head was hooked to a ring bolt. A mule then pulled on the tail and the skin came off like a shuck, peeled right off, which is why they called it "peeling cattle." The carcasses were hauled on to the main floor by a block and tackle pulled by a mule. There the butchers went to work. The gut man cut the carcass open, the marker cut hams and shoulders, then the ax man broke the bones where they were marked. The meat was pitched onto platforms until there was enough to fill the iron tanks, where it was boiled and the tallow scooped off with huge ladles. As a fireman, Dunn's job was to keep a fire going under the tanks where the meat was boiled.[24] "Sometimes they would run out of cattle and the meat would have to lie on the platform two or three days in the hot weather, and by the time we secured more cattle it would be so rotten and full of maggots that the heat and stench were suffocating."[25] The whole enterprise was called "peeling and tanking." The newspaper reported that DeAvalon** would begin "peeling and tanking at his packery north of town" (on North Beach).[26]

In the early years, the meat was pickled and sold by the barrel, much of it to the army but so many thousands of longhorns were killed that there was

---

* Hall's Bayou, separating North Beach from the city proper, was named for John Hall, whose packing house was next to the slough.
** Alonzo Alphmer DeAvalon, from Tylertown, Miss., had been a collector of customs for the government at New Orleans during the Civil War. When he came to Corpus Christi, he rented a "haunted house" that turned out to be filled with rats. He wrote poetry about Corpus Christi and South Texas.

little to no market for the pickled beef. The meat then was dumped in huge mounds that attracted coyotes, vultures, flies and seagulls and, in the summer, gave off an unbearable stench. At a packing house on the Brazos River, the meat was dumped down chutes into the river and gorged on by catfish, which grew to enormous size. At another plant at the mouth of the Brazos, the dumped meat attracted so many sharks that people were afraid to go swimming along that stretch of the coast.[27]

At the slaughterhouse, or packing house, on Padre Island, the waste meat was dumped in Packery Channel, one of the three channels dividing Padre and Mustang Islands. On North Beach, it was dumped in Hall's Bayou, where the port entrance is today. The packeries on North Beach were easily within smelling distance of Corpus Christi.[28] Even closer to the town was a packing house operated by Richard King and Nelson Plato at the arroyo on the south edge of town. This packery was closed in 1869 after King and Plato were accused of operating a business "injurious to public health."[29]

Capt. John Anderson in his flat-bottomed boat *Flour Bluff* hauled salted and dried hides and barrels filled with tallow from Mifflin Kenedy's packing house at Flour Bluff to Rockport. Andy Anderson, one of John Anderson's sons, said on one of those trips Kenedy said, " 'You can have all the tongues you want, boys, but don't get in the way.' They were big tongues and made good eating."[30]

Within a decade of the beginning of the packing houses, by the late 1870s, summer droughts and winter die-ups greatly depleted the longhorn herds of South Texas. Beef prices began to climb and it was no longer so profitable to slaughter cattle for their hides and tallow and horns.[31] Within a decade, the packing houses closed and the iron boilers were hauled away, some to be used as cisterns or stock tanks, and the grisly peeling and tanking business came to an end.

On Sept. 5, 1874, the sky turned black as ink with gale-force winds and rain coming down like grapeshot. At nine that morning, the wharf of Uriah Lott, a wool dealer, was covered with water. The normally shallow Hall's Bayou between Corpus Christi and North Beach* had 12 feet of water and a strong current. George F. Evans, another wool and hide dealer, had built a new warehouse at Peoples and Water. As the storm threatened, he had barrels filled with sand placed in front of his warehouse. Evans stood in water up to his waist directing his workers. At nine that evening, the building gave way and the storm waters washed away 108 tons of cattle bones. By early Saturday evening, people living on Water and Chaparral were evacuated to the bluff. Livery stable owner John Fogg used his horses and buggies to carry people to safety. On the dark streets, the floodwaters glowed with phosphorescence. A visitor found Henry W. Berry in his house on

---

* North Beach was then known as Brooklyn.

Chaparral, sitting in a rocking chair with water covering the floor.[32]

On Sunday morning, timber from shattered wharves and bathhouses littered the bayfront. Some downtown stores were destroyed and the merchandise ruined. Schooners docked at Central Wharf were wrenched from their moorings and driven inland. Norwick Gussett's lumber yard on Mesquite was a wreck. John Hall's tin shop on Chaparral had a sloop tied to his gallery post. At Mann's red house on lower Water Street, built in 1848, the schooner *St. Joseph* was lodged on the front steps. John Murphy's bathhouse and John Anderson's wharf were both demolished. The *Nueces Valley* reported, "The bay is retiring to its proper limits. Yesterday, it was not easy to tell where the water ended and the land began."[33]

The streets were littered with dead dogs, rats, cats, chickens, and "a disgusting green slime that covered everything." Out of the city, a man drowned in Flour Bluff. Richard Gallagher on the Oso lost 400 sheep. Mifflin Kenedy's new fence on the Laureles Ranch was torn down. Salt deposits on the islands and the shores of Laguna Madre were destroyed. Corpus Christi Pass between Padre and Mustang islands was at an unprecedented depth. The storm washed away the street and six blocks of the bay side of Water Street, north of Taylor Street. The *Nueces Valley* editorialized that, "We need a seawall along the whole front of this city, hemmed in in a pocket as we are, where a storm drives the sea right upon us."[34]

A far deadlier storm hit the following year, destroying Indianola, one of Texas' major port cities. Before the storm, Indianola thrived as a seaport. Gold bullion from Chihuahua was shipped out. Cattle were loaded on Morgan Line ships for eastern markets. The road from Indianola to San Antonio was said to be the busiest freight route in the state.[35] Indianola bustled with commerce until disaster struck on Sept. 16, 1875. The Signal Service (forerunner of the U.S. Weather Bureau) called it one of the most perfect types of tropical storm since the charting and tracking of hurricanes began. The storm claimed 200 to 300 lives.[36] Capt. Andrew Anderson of Corpus Christi took a boatload of supplies for the stricken city — mostly food and clothing. "Everything had been wrecked up there. Back of the town was Green Lake. Its sides were piled high with houses, boats, cattle, everything." After the storm, he said, many people were found clinging to pieces of boats and houses. "One young lady, Susanna Pendleton, was hanging on an old piece of wreck when she drifted right across the bow of a boat which was moving away. She screamed as she brushed against the cable and was rescued. She later became the wife of Mike Brennan, captain of the *Agnes*, one of the mail boats."[37]

The destruction of Indianola was a terrible thing. But as devastating as the storm was, the town was rebuilt. Many of the survivors moved away, but many stayed. While the piers and wharves were gone, Indianola still had its original advantage: access to deepwater. But history repeated itself and the town was leveled by another killer hurricane the following decade.[38]

In the last week of March, 1875, a gang of 150 bandits, followers of Juan Cortina,* gathered at Las Cuevas,* a fortified ranch 12 miles below Rio Grande City, on the Mexican side of the river. The bandits separated into four groups and three of the groups, after some wanton killing on the Texas side of the border, crossed back into Mexico. The fourth group of 33 men rode for Corpus Christi. They arrived about dark on Thursday, March 25, and camped on the Oso, nine miles from town. After sunrise on Good Friday, the bandits hit the ranch of Joseph Campbell, a sheepman who lived near the Juan Saenz community. The raiders went on to the S.H. Page ranch near Tule Lake. They ransacked the Page home and switched their saddles for better ones at Page's. They took the men at the ranch hostage, forcing them to run ahead as they rode up the road to George Frank's store at Juan Saenz. At the store, a bandit yelled *"Viva Cortina! Viva Mexico!"*[39]

The bandits put on store clothes and found $80 in the cash drawer. An elderly Hispanic man named Juan Sena who worked for Frank called one of the bandits by name. The bandit pulled a pistol and shot Sena dead, saying, *"Toma este para que no andas conociendo hente otra cicasion"* (Take this, so you will not know people on another occasion).[40]

Outside the store, traffic was heavy that Good Friday with people on their way to Corpus Christi. The bandits took them hostage. One party captured included sheep rancher George Reynolds, his two teenage daughters, their governess Adele DeBerry, and ranch hand Fred Franks. The bandits told Reynolds to take off his clothes. Reynolds was indignant. "You're not going to make me take off my pants here before my daughters and this young lady?"

The bandits didn't force the issue. But they made Franks, who was courting Miss DeBerry, take off his boots and black broadcloth trousers. The bandits stopped the elderly Henry Gilpin and Miss Laura Allen, heading for Corpus Christi. Another man captured was Sidney Borden, founder of Sharpsburg* and cousin of the inventor of canned milk. They took Mrs. E.D. Sidbury, wife of the Corpus Christi lumber dealer, and her daughter hostage. The two women were on their way to pay ranch hands at Mrs. Sidbury's Rancho Seco.[41]

The bandits took the captives' horses, and made them walk or run as they headed for Nuecestown. One bandit knew Henry Gilpin, the man who unloaded goods for Mexico at the old Indian trading grounds in 1829. The bandit shouted, *"Andale! Don Enriquez! Andale!"*[42] Joe Howell, one of the

---

* One account calls the place Las Quisamas, but U.S. Army officials at Ringgold Barracks identified the Mexican village as Las Cuevas, according to Ruth Dodson, "The Noakes Raid," *Frontier Times*, 1946.
* Sharpsburg was east of San Patricio, northwest of Nuecestown, just above Borden's Ferry on the Nueces River.

original Pioneer firemen, complained about running in his bare feet, so they made him put on Miss Allen's slippers. He ran for a bit, then stretched out on the road, refusing to move. There were shouts and curses in Spanish and English. The bandits jumped their horses over him, then left him behind.[43] They herded the hostages along Up River Road. Since they did not shoot Howell for his defiance, other captives refused to budge. The bandits argued over whether to shoot them, but finally decided to leave them behind. Four men in a posse, led by John Dunn, came across the stragglers. "I shall never forget how miserable Fred Franks looked," Dunn said. "He had been wearing a good suit of clothes and shop-made boots, but the bandits left him with nothing but his underclothes."[44]

News of the bandit raid quickly reached Corpus Christi. Dunn sent a note to Sheriff John McClane: "Sheriff McClane, I just learned from Mrs. Stevens that a party of [bandits] robbed Page's house a few minutes ago. Come with assistance as soon as possible as I am sure no small party robbed this house in daylight." Dunn, then 22, prepared his guns and soon after his cousin "Red" Dunn and his brothers Matt and George showed up. The Dunns went on to the Campbell place, where the women came out crying. The men had been taken prisoner, except for "Old Man" Campbell who hid in the brush behind his house. As the Dunns rode on up Up River Road, they saw that the bandits had Sidney Borden on foot ahead of them, forcing him up the road at a trot. One bandit was riding Borden's prized dapple gray racehorse. Near Frank's store, the Dunns and bandits kept a wary eye on each other. The bandits were too many for the Dunns to attack and the bandits were not disposed to initiate the action.[45]

In Corpus Christi, James M. Hunter, who owned a livery stable, arrived in town after he escaped capture when Sidney Borden was taken by the bandits. Sheriff McClane lathered his horse riding down the streets urging people to stay inside and bar their doors. Guns were loaded; mothers collected their children; schoolgirls on a picnic on North Beach were rushed home. Women and children boarded the Morgan Line steamship *Josephine* and Norwick Gussett's schooner *Leona*. The vessels left the wharves and anchored out in the bay. At a meeting on Mesquite Street, several men agreed to ride with a posse to take on the bandits, but Sheriff McClane tried to stop them, saying he needed every man to protect the town. Jim Dunn, one of the many Dunns in town, had a few words for the sheriff which, John Dunn said, "would not look good in print."[46]

At Nuecestown, Thomas Noakes' store sat on a hill up from the Nueces River. Noakes was waiting for the mail rider to bring the mail. As he waited, a man called Lying John Smith came in to buy flour.* As Noakes was getting it, he saw three bandits ride up. He got his Winchester and, seeing a bandit raise a pistol to shoot Lying John, Noakes fired first, hitting the bandit in the

---

* Smith is variously called "Lying John" or "Windy" Smith.

chest. Noakes' wife ran from the store with their five children. When the mail rider, William Ball, rode up, the bandits took the mail, and the mail rider.[47]

Noakes and Lying John scuttled through a trap door and hid in a trench under the store. The bandits plundered the store, then started a fire. Mrs. Noakes, who had returned to the store after seeing the children were safe, poured water on it. Several times a bandit started a fire, only to have her put it out, before the flames took hold. With the store burning, Lying John tried to run for it and was shot, then shot three more times as he lay wounded on the ground. As the fire spread, Noakes made a run for it. He had his rifle and was ready to shoot it out. Mrs. Noakes yelled that the bandits were gone. As the store burned, Mrs. Noakes ran back inside to save a prized feather bed.[48]

Three miles away, at Juan Saenz, John Dunn and the men from Corpus Christi rode up, their horses winded. Among them were George Swank, a roofer, Pat Whelan, a bricklayer, Pat McManigle, who ran the Gem Saloon, "Wash" Mussett, Clem Vetters, and Jesus Seguira. They could see smoke rising from Nuecestown. As the posse rode up, Swank ordered Noakes to give him his Winchester, saying that all he had was a six-shooter to go up against the bandits. Noakes refused, pointing out that they might come back. Swank pulled his revolver, telling Noakes, "Hand over that rifle or I'll shoot you myself." Noakes gave Swank the Winchester.[49]

John "Red" Dunn and Swank the roofer rode ahead. The bandits had their store plunder and remaining captives and were camped in the brush. As Swank and Dunn rode up, a shot was fired, killing Swank. The rest of the Dunns and the group from Corpus Christi arrived. Shots were fired. "The bullets were singing around us," Dunn said. "We could recognize the sound of Mike Dunn's sharpshooter, which the bandits had stolen from him, for the lead in the end of the cartridges had been split down to the brass shell and their scream was like the wail of a lost soul." As the posse prepared to charge, the bandits took off, leaving their plunder and prisoners behind. Sheriff McClane arrived and took Swank's body. They found a wounded bandit, the man Noakes shot, who was put in a two-wheeled cart to take to Corpus Christi. Lying John, who had been shot four times, was still alive; he later claimed he was shot eight times, living up to his nickname.[50]

On Saturday morning, the day before Easter, Andy Anderson got his sloop *Flour Bluff* unstuck from the mud in a bend of the Nueces River. On the evening before, he was on his way to Sharpsburg and watched as Noakes' store burned. At the landing that morning, he saw the Noakes family cooking breakfast in an iron pot suspended over a fire by three sticks.[51] Sidney Borden, who was captured by the bandits the day before, rode up with a posse raised at Sharpsburg. Someone had asked what kind of men he wanted. Borden said, "I'm looking for men with strong nerves and weak minds." One man who joined him was James Marion Garner (who became Martha Rabb's son-in-law). News of the raid brought minutemen militias riding at a hard gallop from all over. They gathered at Banquete and divided into three groups, each heading in a different direction.[52]

E.H. Caldwell owned a sheep ranch at Borjas. Caldwell and a herder were camped when three riders appeared in the darkness. One man asked to be shown a watering place for their horses. Caldwell refused, figuring they were bandits. Not long before, he spent some time with George Reynolds at Ventana Ranch and he recognized the horse the man was riding belonged to Reynolds. The bandits left to water their horses. When the leader returned, Caldwell kept his rifle aimed at him. The man again demanded water for their horses. Caldwell could hear their horses splashing in the water tank. "I told him they knew very well where the water was. He insisted I show him. I said I wouldn't. He wanted to know why. I replied *'porque'* (because)." Caldwell kept his gun pointed at the man's heart until the three finally departed.[53]

Caldwell learned next day that the three men were members of the bandit gang that had taken prisoners, burned stores, and killed a man in Nuecestown. Next day, Easter Sunday, the posse under the command of Judge Sidney Borden rode up. After they passed Caldwell's Borjas Ranch, they captured two men, one an elderly man with courtly manners and the other apparently his servant. Some of the posse members wanted to hang them. They had a hard glint in their eyes. They were men who were apt to act first and apologize later, if at all. Borden, Marion Garner, and another man argued there was nothing to link the two men to the raiders. Garner said of the pro-hanging faction, "Nothing more was said. But we could see by the frowns on their faces that it didn't set well." Those who wanted to hang the two men took the prisoners and rode off into the brush, and soon rode back without the prisoners. Garner noticed that a long rope was missing. They learned later that the men who were hanged were a merchant and his servant from Laredo. After the hangings, the posse tracked the bandits to the river, then gave up. "Boys, I've brought you on a wild-goose chase," Borden said. "We'd better head for home."[54]

In Corpus Christi, the bandit shot by Noakes was brought to town on a cart. They came down Leopard Street, looking for a place to hang him. They began to fix a rope to the steeple of the Catholic Church, but cattleman Martin Culver stopped them. They went on down Leopard to a gate with a cross pole. William Ball, the mail rider who had been captured at Noakes' store the day before and his mail taken by the bandits, put the noose around the bandit's neck. They drove the cart under the cross pole, a rope was thrown over it, the bandit was lifted into the air, and the cart drove on. The body was left hanging that night. It was taken down on Easter Sunday.[55]

Mrs. E.D. Sidbury and her daughter Mrs. R.R. Savage were found Easter morning. They had escaped from the bandits on Friday and hid in the brush. They were lost for two days and were half-starved. In the aftermath of the raid, George Reynolds, the rancher, spent two years tracking down his team of stolen horses. He found them in Mexican Army stables in Saltillo and got them back.* When Noakes built a new store a mile from the old site, the town moved with him. After the raid, militia companies made retaliatory raids against those suspected of being in league with the bandits. The Nuecestown Raid was one episode in a long-running border conflict that began with the Texas Revolution. But it left a legacy of bitterness that lasted a long time.[56]

One outcome of the Nuecestown Raid was the unleashing of Capt. Leander McNelly's picked company of Texas Rangers on the bandits threatening South Texas. Sheriff John McClane, the sheepman who moved from Pennsylvania to Texas, wired Austin for help: "Is Capt. McNelly coming. We are in trouble. Five ranches burned by disguised men near La Parra last week. Answer."[57] Capt. McNelly and 22 Rangers rode into Corpus Christi, were apprised of the details of the Nuecestown Raid, and headed for the border. South of town, on the Oso, they found two "Mexicans" hanging from a trestle. "Outlaws didn't do that," McNelly told one of his men. "Some posseman worked off an old grudge."[58] McNelly and his men ran into a group of minutemen from the Corpus Christi area. After a tense standoff, McNelly, a man of great courage, had them disarmed. At Palo Alto, near Brownsville, the Rangers caught up with a band of outlaws with a herd of rustled cattle. When the fight was over, one Ranger, Sonny Smith, was dead along with 12 bandits. McNelly ordered the corpses of the bandits brought into town and displayed by a water fountain in the plaza at Brownsville.[59]

McNelly and his Rangers were seen through polarized lens. They were loved or hated, depending mostly on a point of view shaded by ethnicity. They were heroic and fearless men, or they were cruel and vindictive killers. When McNelly was sent to scour the countryside of the Nueces Strip, he did a ruthless job. His Rangers rode down and attacked rustlers and bandits wherever they met them. Because the rustlers relied on a network of spies to keep them informed of the Rangers' whereabouts, it became unhealthy to be captured by McNelly's Rangers and turned over to his guide, Jesus Sandoval, to get information. Sandoval ("Old Casoose") would put a captive on horseback, tie him to a tree by his neck, then whip the horse, pulling the captive loose from his head.[60]

The headless victims were called bandits or spies for bandits, but who decided that? In another incident, McNelly and his Rangers crossed the river to attack a ranch being used as a sanctuary for bandits. They went to the wrong ranch, where they found four men cutting wood, and shot them down. They realized their mistake and went on to the right ranch, Las Cuevas,** a half-mile away.[61] The late Texas historian Walter Prescott Webb observed that "McNelly cannot be condemned too severely if he did permit Jesus

---

* This seemed to confirm suspicions in Corpus Christi that Gen. Juan Cortina and the Mexican government were involved in the Nuecestown Raid.
** The town today is known as Diaz Ordaz.

Sandoval to send the spies to eternity by way of his paint horse gallows" and followed that with, "Affairs on the border cannot be judged by standards that hold elsewhere."[62]

Myths and legends die hard. That helps explain why the Rangers became so feared and hated by Hispanic citizens in the border region of the Nueces Strip. There were hard feelings against McNelly and his men and perhaps it could hardly have been otherwise, given the level of violence and ethnic animosity. The oft-told McNelly story no doubt was responsible for exaggerated praise for the Rangers, which helped establish their reputation in the minds of Anglo Texans, but it can't be denied that whatever means they used, fair or foul, they established undoubted supremacy over bandit raiders and Mexican outlaws in the region between the Rio Grande and Corpus Christi. As to the rights and wrongs of those turbulent times, the list of grievances, by both sides, would be endless.

S andbars off the barrier islands blocked entry to the bays along the coast. This was how the barrier islands formed, starting with sandbars (submerged islands really) building up over eons. The sandbars and twisting passes between the islands made it treacherous for ships trying to reach the inner bays. Shipwrecks were frequent. The danger of crossing the bar blocking the Aransas Pass channel from the Gulf and threading through the pass between Mustang and St. Joseph's meant ships needed expert guidance. This was provided by bar pilots with local knowledge of sandbars, bays and passes. The best-known bar pilots were members of the Mercer clan.

Robert A. Mercer, a lawyer from England with a big family, immigrated to the U.S. and tried farming in Indiana before he moved to Texas. The Mercers lived at the village of Aransas, a settlement of seafaring folks on St. Joseph's Island across the pass from where Port Aransas is today. Aransas was headquarters for bar pilots and lighter operators who unloaded larger vessels that couldn't venture into shallow bay waters. Their livelihood and lives were linked to the sea. The Mercers moved across the pass and built a house on Mustang Island in 1855, which marks the beginning of what would become Port Aransas.* Robert Mercer's ranch was called "El Mar." At one time, Mercer had 2,000 sheep and a similar number of cattle on his ranch.[63] This was when mustangs still ranged over the island. Mercer and his sons were salvage operators, beachcombers and island ranchers. But Mercer's main occupation was bar pilot. He kept a lookout from a widow's walk on the top of the house for ships flying a flag signaling for a bar pilot. He charged a fee based on a ship's draft and the difficulty of guiding it over the bar.[64] His sons Edward and John followed him in the work; the job seemed to be hereditary.

---

* The settlement in the early years took the name of the island. For a time it was called Turtle Cove, Ropesville, Tarpon, and finally Port Aransas in 1911.

In the Civil War, the *USS Afton* landed U.S. Marines and sailors on Mustang Island. They burned the Mercer cabin and slaughtered sheep and cattle on the El Mar ranch, hauling away the beef and mutton. The Mercers evacuated to Indian Point, across the bay from Corpus Christi. Robert Mercer's wife Agnes died in 1863 at Indian Point. After the war, the Mercers returned to Mustang Island and rebuilt the family home. Edward, called "Ned," was the first of two sons to get a pilot's license after the war. In 1873, Ned married Emma Thompson on St. Joseph's. The next year, the oldest son, John, married Emma Scott. Robert Mercer, the father, died in 1876 and was buried in the sands of the island. The Mercer diary notes: *"Father departed this life at three and one-quarter o'clock a.m. He had been confined to his bed for about four months and has been gradually sinking . . . Steamer Mary left for Brashear. Captain Clubb came to sit up with father. Day ends. Wind N.N.W. Strong."* [65] Robert Mercer was later reburied in Holy Cross Cemetery in Corpus Christi. [66]

It was Robert Mercer who started keeping a diary written like a ship's log. After his death, sons John and Ned kept up the daily entries. The early history of Port Aransas was recorded on these logs. The diaries go from 1866 to the 1880s in five books covering two decades. At least two other volumes were lost, one covering the earlier years. The logs were written in the third person. There is little difference in style, no matter which Mercer was making the entries. They reveal a sense of style and wry, understated humor. The Mercer diaries, or logs, convey the rhythm of the lives of the bar pilots and give a rare glimpse of life at the Mercer settlement, a community as tight and snug as a ship's company. The Mercer settlement later became Port Aransas. [67]

Each day's entry begins with weather conditions and ends with the depth of water on the bar. One tells of a lunar eclipse: *"The moon went blind tonight . . . It is an awful sight . . . but at daylight she was right side up. The world is all right yet."* [68] Another tells of Corpus Christi's ongoing struggle to gain access to deepwater: *"The citizens of Corpus Christi held a meeting. The object was to have a canal from Aransas Bay to Corpus Christi Bay cleaned out and widened. All humbug. No dinero."* [69] On an August night, the log says, *"Mosquitoes are powerful bad; had to build fires to make smoke and keep the mosquitoes off."* [70] When Robert ran out of chewing tobacco, he wrote, *"I'd fight any man in the U.S. for a good hard chew."* . . . *"Hot weather. There's no use talking about it. A fellow would not be worth a damn for the next two weeks if he was to work all day in such weather as we have today."* [71]

"The day begins with the wind N.N.E. Very cold weather with rain and fog. Ned and Tom killed a beef and salted part of it. Cooked part of it for mincemeat. Had a time cutting meat, suet, oranges, raisins, currants and ingredients to make mince pie.". . . "Clubb [another bar pilot] spent the evening with us. Played scrimmage. Made a huge whiskey stew and drank it

without a struggle."[72] Beginning on the day after Christmas, 1872, Clubb celebrated his 55th birthday with a party that lasted three days. It was so cold, the log noted, guests had to dance to keep from freezing. Another entry: *"Clubb and the Dutchman had a row. Did not amount to much."[73]* ... *"Ned went to St. Joseph's to see his Dulchina [sweetheart].[74]* ... *"A schooner off the bar. Put up the flags."* On the day Indianola was nearly destroyed by a hurricane, Sept. 16, 1875, the log notes that on Mustang Island the *"chickens had the life blown out of them"* and water was waist-deep at El Mar. The entry ends with, *"All's well; nobody here hurt, thank God."* [75] *"This day begins with the wind N.E. Foggy as mush. Harry Reynolds took a small hunt but got no game. The girls scrubbed their houses and manufactured some cakes. So ends the day.''* [76]

The logs tell of arriving or departing ships that hove to and hoisted a flag signaling they wanted a bar pilot to thread the channel. The Mercers kept watch from a pilot's lookout on top of the house. The pilots charged $3 per draft foot (later $4) to guide ships through the pass.[77] Low water on the bar often kept ships waiting for days, even weeks. The logs tell of deaths, weddings, hunting trips, and lively parties attended by families on the islands. They tell of the weather conditions on the coast, of the depth of water on the bar, of events in people's lives in the 1870s and 1880s on Mustang Island. The Mercer logs represent an amazing record of an almost lost period of history.

The Mercer diaries are filled with activities of the pilots and the arrival and departure of ships: *"Schooner Clements came for Corpus. Got aground on the flats. The Arthur anchored with a flag up for a pilot."* ... *"John and Frank started to put stakes in the dugout (the channel between Mustang and St. Joseph's) but the wind died and they got only as far as Heath's wharf. Steamer Clinton got aground in the channel last night and is there yet."[78]* *"Steamer Aransas came from Brazos and hove to off the bar. John and Ned went out to her. The captain was anxious to come in and go to Corpus Christi to get a load of wool, but there was only five feet on the bar. He anchored and layed [sic] until 2 p.m. when he struck for Galveston."[79]*

The logs describe the loss of the *Reindeer* in 1870, the *Fountainebleau* in 1873[80] and the side-wheel steamship *Mary,* bound for Rockport from Galveston, which wrecked on the Aransas bar on Nov. 30, 1876. The log noted: *"Steamer Mary while trying to cross the bar at dead low water failed. She pounded her bottom out. Set the colors of distress. John, Ned, Tom Brundrette, Tom Lacey, Parry Humphrey started for her in the Doaga [a pilot's boat]. The sea was very heavy. Made several trips to get alongside her. The cargo between decks was leaving in big piles. The Mary struck at 7 a.m. and her fires were put out in 30 minutes. She settled very fast. No lives were lost."[81]*

The *Mary* had arrived off the Aransas bar the night before, just as a fierce norther hit. A passenger said the ship plunged and dipped from side to side.

It was impossible to anchor in the crashing seas, when the captain decided to take her in over the bar and through the pass himself, as he had done before, rather than waiting for a bar pilot. Then came disaster. In making the attempt, the ship struck a buoy, opening a hole in her side, and then struck the bar, pounding her bottom out as high waves foamed and lashed the stricken ship. Mrs. S. G. Miller, whose husband, a rancher, owned a ferry on the Nueces River, was on board. She had been visiting relatives in Louisiana. After the ship struck the buoy and scraped its bottom on the bar, water rose in her cabin and the bulkheads began to pull apart.[82]

"I heard terrific noises all over the boat. The chambermaid came running and cried: 'Get up! The boat is sinking!' Dr. East [a brother] ran in and told me to run for my life to the pilothouse. He caught my hand and we waded through water pouring through the ship like a mighty river. When we reached the pilothouse, we found everybody huddled there awaiting his doom. As a last resort, we were to try the lifeboats, a dangerous undertaking in such a sea. Crested with great banks of foam, the waves dashed over the sides of the ship as though they were great monsters."[83]

The *Mary* was flying distress flags when pilot John Mercer, his brother Ned, and two others (Tom Brundrette and Tom Lacey) reached the ship with the *Doaga*, but they couldn't get close enough to make the rescue. "Trial after trial was made to get to us," Mrs. Miller wrote, "but each time the great waves carried our rescuers beyond our reach. At last, after three or four hours of hard work, the rope was caught by one of our men, and the small boat was lashed to the *Mary* by her gangplank. In order to reach this gangplank, we waded through water waist-deep on deck. As I started across the gangplank, the *Mary* broke away from the pilot boat and down I went into the sea. As I fell, the heel of my shoe caught on one of the slats. This broke my fall and enabled me to catch hold of the two sides of the plank with my hands. Scrambling to a sitting position on the gangplank, I bobbed up and down as each big wave struck. It seemed an eternity before the sailors caught hold of it again and I was helped into the rescue boat.[84]

"The rescued party filled the boat to capacity, and the outgoing tide and the terrific gale made sailing very difficult. We managed to get across the bar at last while waves that seemed mountain high were rolling and lashing the unfortunate *Mary*. Before we could reach the pilot's house, we had to walk the length of a 300-foot wharf made of two 12-inch planks. We suffered an agony of cold as the blizzard whipped about us in our wet clothing. Upon our arrival (at the pilot's house), we found a roaring fire in the fireplace, and there we sat and dried our clothes. Our hostess served us a hot meal, and after this we went out on the beach to watch for a ship."[85]

At the scene of the wreck, barrels of flour, bolts of calico, wagon wheels, a dentist's chair, washed ashore. The *Corpus Christi Gazette* warned people not to sample the contents of unlabeled bottles because the cargo included 500 bottles of strychnine.[86] In the wreckmaster's sale, the Mercer family bought most of the soaked cargo for $1,245.[87] They managed to retrieve from the wreckage several wheels, the size used for Mexican two-wheel carts, by using grappling hooks.[88] The submerged *Mary* could be seen for years on the south side of the bar.[89]

The lucky passengers of the *Mary* were not the first or last shipwreck survivors to meet the Mercers, who had been rescuing shipwreck survivors and guiding ships over the bar for two decades, and would do so for two decades more. The first lifesaving station was built at Port Aransas in January, 1880. Capt. John G. Mercer was in charge of a crew that included William Grant, Henry Nolls, Frank Smith, V.A. Scott, Dan McCarty, and Bert Ayers.[90] (A representative entry of the Mercer logs reads: *"This day begins with the wind N. moderate. Cool weather. Got Clubb's and our oxcart and moved the pilothouse. It was too close to the pass to be comfortable. Moved it nearer Turtle Cove. Schooner George Peabody came from Corpus and anchored near the dugout. So ends this day. Wind N.N. W."[91]*)

Ice was a real luxury in Corpus Christi in the years after the Civil War. Schooners with cargoes of lake ice from Maine or upstate New York arrived each spring. The ice was cut in four-foot blocks and packed in straw and sawdust. In the early 1870s, ice sold for 15 cents a pound, a hefty price then. In 1875, the newspaper reported that "on account of the non-arrival of the steamship on time, causing the supply of ice in the city to give out, the imbibers of mint juleps and soda water have been wondering 'why the deuce can't Morgan put an additional steamer on the line.' "[92] The ship finally arrived and its appearance "was hailed with joy, cooling drinks may be anticipated the coming summer."[93] It was reported soon afterwards that "Weber with his ice loaded cart makes his daily rounds supplying those who wish it with this wholesome luxury."[94] In 1878, rancher Richard King bought a new ice-maker for Corpus Christi. It was a two-and-half-ton Boyle machine which could turn out 500 to 600 pounds of ice each day. The operator of the plant was John Greer; George Blucher delivered the ice by mule-drawn wagon. After King's death, the ice plant passed into the Blucher family.[95]

CHAPTER 10

Schools and education - Train to Laredo - Wool trade ends - Richard King dies - Shooting clouds - Fire burns a block of Chaparral - The Ropes boom - Fitzsimmons on North Beach - The boys of '98 - Blizzard of '99

An act of the Texas Legislature in 1876 permitted parents to make application to the county judge to create an independent school district. It was said that in 1876 there were not more than a dozen public schools between the Rio Grande and the Nueces River.[1]

In Corpus Christi, elementary schooling, what there was of it, started three decades before, in 1846. It was a private enterprise, with a teacher giving lessons paid for by parents. The town's first teacher, Amanda Katherine Brooks, taught classes in a corner of John Peter Kelsey's store on Chaparral. Forty students were enrolled; each paid tuition of $2 a month.[2] The teacher and storekeeper married and moved to Rio Grande City. Madame de Meza, a doctor's wife, took over the school in October 1848, but it didn't last long.[3] The newspaper bemoaned the fact that Corpus Christi "has no church nor school."[4] The following year, C.C. Farley and W.W. Whitley opened an academy, which was short-lived.[5]

The first real school was the Corpus Christi Academy opened in 1853 by Charles Lovenskiold, who came to Corpus Christi from Denmark. At his school, students quickly learned order and cleanliness, if they learned nothing else. Lovenskiold insisted they come to class clean; they lined up military fashion for inspection before class; those with improper clothes or dirty fingernails were sent home to clean up before coming back to school.[6] Unruly students were made to wear a dunce cap. This was a private school, as we understand the term, but it had some public support. Students who could afford to pay tuition were required to pay; those who could not had their tuition paid by the county from its public free school fund.[7]

A story is told about an incident in Lovenskiold's school: "One cold morning two brothers, men in size, came to school armed with pistols, looking for trouble with the teacher for some fancied insult of the day previous. The colonel came in, and seeing the situation at a glance, told the boys to put down their arms, which, after a moment's hesitation, they did. He ordered them to sit down. He addressed them as if pleading a case before a jury. The girls wept, then the small boys, and lastly the would-be desperadoes broke down and sobbed their promises to lead better school lives."[8] Another story was told of Lovenskiold. Willie Hoffman, the son of Prokop Hoffman, who had a grocery store on Chaparral, was too young to go to school, but he showed up at Lovenskiold's academy early one morning with his older brother Alex. Lovenskiold said, "Well, little boy, have you come to school too?" Seeing the book Willie was carrying, he said, "And you've brought a book with you," then he took the book, which opened to the page that carried his past-due account at Hoffman's Grocery.[9] Lovenskiold's academy was closed at the beginning of the Civil War.[10]

During the war, starting in 1863, the Catholic Church operated the Hidalgo Seminary, on the bluff at the northwest corner of Lipan and Tancahua, on a site given to the church by Henry Kinney. [#] The Hidalgo Seminary was under the leadership of Father John Gonnard, who founded the school.[11] The newspaper at one point called it the Catholic college on the hill. At the Hidalgo Seminary students were taught moral and spiritual lessons alongside academic subjects. The students came from all over South Texas to attend the school; they would find homes to board in in the town. Rosalie Bridget Hart Priour taught in the school during the last two years of the war.[12] Eli Merriman said it was the first school he attended. ". . . The Hidalgo Seminary was one of the biggest schools in this part of the state. It was for boys only, and pupils came from Laredo, Victoria, Goliad and many other towns in South Texas. It was managed by the Catholic Church, with Father Gonnard at the head, and was located in a concrete building at the edge of an arroyo long since filled up, where N. Tancahua and Lipan streets meet. Father Gonnard didn't teach himself, but he would come to the schoolroom and give talks to the pupils."[13]

While boys could go to the Hidalgo Seminary on the bluff, a school for girls was operated at the John J. Dix home on Water Street.[*^] Mary Eliza Hayes Dix, described as looking like the very image of Queen Victoria, taught black girls in the morning and white girls in the afternoon. Black girls were taught sewing, while white girls were taught reading, writing, and arithmetic. Mrs. Dix was one of the first teachers here to teach phonetic reading. "She did not believe in making the child learn the alphabet as was the custom in those days."[14]

After Mrs. Dix became ill, teaching duties were taken over by Jane Marsh, who believed in the twin tools of education, the Blue-back speller and the dogwood switch, except in her case she used a cowhide whip. Marsh,

[#] The Hidalgo Seminary was located on the site later occupied by the Incarnate Word Convent, 701-715 N. Carancahua.
[*^] The Dix home was later remodeled to become the Seaside Hotel.

who was later the city's postmistress, was strict with the girls, as shown in the story of a student named Annie. Little Annie was deathly afraid of the cowhide whip, which was used very freely when the girls talked in class or did not learn their lessons. One day during a spelling exercise, Annie was given the word 'scissors.' She spelled 'scisors.' The teacher gave her 15 minutes to learn to spell the word correctly. She knew what punishment she would receive if she again misspelled the word; the cowhide whip was hanging from a nail, ready for use. The room in which Miss Marsh was teaching was on the second floor . . . Little Annie did not wait the allotted time, but took her leave by jumping from the second floor window. The cook picked her up and took her home. Fortunately, no bones were broken, but that ended Annie's schooling with Miss Marsh.[15]

After Father Gonnard's death in the yellow fever epidemic of 1867, the Hidalgo Seminary was operated for a short time by Robert Dougherty, from San Patricio, then Professor W.S. Campion.[16] Dougherty went on to build his own school at Round Lake, St. Paul's Academy, near San Patricio.[17] The Hidalgo Seminary closed with the establishment of a public school system.[18]

Secondary education was taken over from the private sector in 1871 when Corpus Christi got its first public school. It was organized by Stanley Welch. Teachers were Rosa Beynon and Rhoda Burke, each paid $50 a month.[19] Classes for white students were conducted upstairs in the Methodist Church at Mann and Chaparral.[20] Classes for black students were held in the old Mann house on Water Street. The newspaper reported there were 200 students attending the white school and 75 at the school for colored children. In August 1872, a request for bids was advertised to build two public schoolhouses.[21] They were to be built on Carancahua on land donated by Richard King of the King Ranch.[*] Two frame buildings were constructed, one for white students and one for blacks. A fence separated the two.[22] When school was over for the day, P.G. Lovenskiold once remembered, boys played baseball or caught crabs off the wharves on the bayfront or watched for small boats to arrive at the Central Wharf.[23]

The board of directors of the public free schools of Nueces County met on June 14, 1873. Members included Perry Doddridge, president; Horace Taylor, treasurer; William Headen, secretary; and John J. Dix. They agreed that public schools be operated in each school district in Nueces County, at Corpus Christi, Nuecestown, San Diego, and Santa Gertrudis. Professor William N. Hanna was the school principal at Corpus Christi. His teachers were Mrs. Hannah M. Conklin, and Ellen C. Clark. W.B. Lacy was the teacher in the colored school.[24] The board of directors also agreed that the county superintendent would hold a session at the Corpus Christi schoolhouse on the fourth Saturday of every month for the examination for

---

[*] The site was at 525 N. Carancahua.

competence of the school teachers.*[25]

The new school system soon ran out of money. The state paid for only four months of operations. The teachers often had to wait for their salaries; they were sometimes forced to sell their vouchers, or warrants, on the street for half their value.[26] With no money to pay teachers and principals, the schools were closed in October, 1873. In desperation, trustees asked parents to come up with "subscription" money. With this infusion of funds, the schools reopened in November. It was essentially a private school operating in a public school building.[27]

The following year, the city took over the schools inside the city limits under a new law passed by the Legislature.[28] Council members voted that "all religious exercises must cease from this time in the public schools." The council quickly backed down after a public uproar and nullified the action.[29]

Solomon Coles, a black Congregational minister from Petersburg, Va., near Richmond, was named principal for the black school. Coles, an ex-slave, was illiterate until he was 14. As a slave, he was trained to be a coachman for the wife of his owner. When emancipation came, he went to Pennsylvania where he attended Lincoln University, a new college founded for blacks and freed slaves. After he graduated, he went to Yale Divinity School and was later ordained as a minister in the Congregational Church. Coles was brought to Corpus Christi by the new Congregational Church on the bluff. When he arrived, the children of former slaves were being taught in the old Mann house.*[30]

When Coles was named the principal of the black public school on the bluff, he was paid a salary of $42.88 a month. The school year lasted from mid-October until the end of May. Coles was known as a fine teacher and a strict disciplinarian. One of his reports to the school board said, "None of the school property has been the least bit damaged by the pupils. Not a pane of glass, a window blind, or desk has been broken, and if there has been a pencil or chalk mark on our school building, I am not aware of it."[31] Hattie Littles, one of Coles' pupils, said they feared him, "but they learned some sense and fundamentals of the three R's. Nobody was tardy. You were in your seat by 9 a.m. or you got a whaling."[32]

One of the early schools out in the country was the Oso school, which began in 1884 in a sheepherder's jacal, or shack, on the Henry Davis Allen Ranch west of town.[33] The first teacher, Bridget McCabe, was paid $35 a month. She married the rancher's son, Henry Davis Allen, Jr. Roy Terrell

---

* W.G. Sutherland noted that teacher certificates were usually awarded based on politics. Teachers who contributed part of their salary to politicians in power, or teachers with political influence, were more likely to pass, whatever their qualifications: "Century of Education in South Texas Reviewed by the Sage of Bluntzer," *Corpus Christi Caller*, date unknown, clipping in author's possession.
* It was also known as the Virginia House, as the hotel operated in the building was named. It was located o the water side of Water Street, at the intersection with Cooper's Alley.

recalled attending the Oso school. He said boys rode their horses to the school in the mornings and would stake them out so they could graze while the boys learned their lessons. They soon learned that coyotes would chew the ropes in two. At the end of the school day, the boys would have to find where their horses had wandered.[34]

A crusade to improve public schools began in 1889 when Professor C.W. Crossley was named principal of the schools. He instituted a high school program with academic and commercial tracks. Academic courses included algebra, history, philosophy, civil government, English and German literature. Commercial courses included bookkeeping, business arithmetic, commercial law, civics and political economy.

The city's first high school was constructed in 1892 at a cost of $1,563. It was built next to the two elementary schools on the tract of land given the schools in 1872 by Richard King. Professor Moses Menger was lured from Austin to become the principal of the new high school. It was said he had no superior as a teacher.[35] Under Menger's guidance, the school soon established a reputation for excellence. Corpus Christi High School under Professor Menger was one of the few schools in the state whose graduates were accepted without an entrance examination by the University of Texas. The required course completion for graduation was stiff: four years of Latin, six years of Spanish, three years of English, two years of algebra, courses in geometry and trigonometry, one year of ancient, modern, and English history, and one year of chemistry and physics.[36]

Graduation ceremonies for the first graduates were held at Market Hall in June, 1893. Four graduates sang a chorus of "Upidee," a Civil War era song, followed by a piano recital of "The Waves of Corpus Christi," then Irving Westervelt delivered the valedictory address.[37]

Uriah Lott, a native New Yorker, was a prosperous wool merchant in Corpus Christi in the 1870s, but his abiding ambition was to build railroads. In the 1870s, Lott scrounged for money to build a railroad from Corpus Christi to Laredo. He got the financial backing of the area's big ranchers, Richard King and Mifflin Kenedy, and he sold bonds and got land grants from the Legislature. Surveying, brush-clearing and grading for the Corpus Christi, San Diego and Rio Grande railroad began in March, 1875. A new locomotive arrived on Thanksgiving Day, 1876, and the first spike was driven at the arroyo on south edge of town.[38]

Lott printed his first schedule in the *Corpus Christi Weekly Gazette*. Excursion tickets to the end of the track cost 50 cents. Passengers sat on homemade wooden benches as they rode 18 miles to Martha Rabb's pasture, where Robstown is today.[39]

Despite the excitement of something new, there were those who grumbled that Lott's railroad would hurt the oxcart trade. The city was known for its opponents to progress of any kind. Who needed trains? Freight came in by oxcarts and one could catch the stage to Brownsville or San Antonio. Bales of wool packed in 500-pound bags came into Corpus Christi on huge Chihuahua carts with big round wooden wheels that squealed in protest, pulled by teams of oxen, horses or mules. The city's economy depended on the wool trade.[40*]

When the tracks of Lott's railroad reached Banquete, a pipeline was laid to Agua Dulce Creek for water. Mesquite logs were burned to heat water to make steam. Indians attacked the work crew, killing all but two, and soon after that Lott and a man from Pennsylvania, who made the iron rails, were robbed by bandits and stripped of their clothes; they had to walk into San Diego in their underwear.[41] Construction was stopped in 1879 in San Diego when Lott ran out of money. He sold the line to a syndicate, which later became the Mexican National Railway. The line was completed in 1881. The new owners of the line allowed the former owners to celebrate the inaugural run, from Corpus Christi to Laredo. Ranchers Richard King and Mifflin Kenedy, big investors in Lott's little railroad, invited friends to ride to Laredo in a private car. On the way they drank lemonade secretly spiked with Richard King's brand of whisky, Old Rose Bud. They rolled into Laredo full of good food and high spirits.[42]

The railroad, known as the Tex-Mex, spurred the growth of Corpus Christi and Laredo, though it did spell the end of the oxcarts. The first trains going to Laredo and back must have passed the old lumbering oxcarts loaded with wool and hides on their way to Corpus Christi, the last witnesses to a vanishing way of life.[**] The Tex-Mex was a most unusual railroad. If an engineer spotted a buck grazing near the tracks, he would stop the train and let the passengers take a few shots. He would stop the train in the middle of nowhere for a cowboy who needed a lift. Ranch wives along the route would give conductors shopping lists to be filled in Corpus Christi or Laredo and brought back on the return trip. In the early years, passengers would help out by tossing mesquite wood to the tender to speed things along. The little railroad started by Uriah Lott was known as the one of the friendliest and most unusual railroads in the world.[43] The schedule was something aimed at, rather than achieved, which earned it the nickname of "Till-Mañana" train.[44]

Boxcars and gondola cars for the new railroad were constructed in a factory on Railroad Ave. (later renamed Kinney Ave.) The shop turned out a boxcar or gondola car a day. The wheels came in by ship. Some 2,000 freight cars were built in the shop for the Texas-Mexican Railway.[45]

---

[*] One pundit said Corpus Christi "has some men who take a sincere pleasure in sitting on the coat tail of progress and crying halt, whenever any move is made by which the public are to be benefited or the city improved."

[**] The huge oxcarts hauled more than hides and wool. They brought in loads of copper, lead and silver from Chihuahua, Mexico, via Laredo to Corpus Christi. From there, the cargoes went to ore smelters in, mainly, Hamburg, Germany.

In late 1882, the old Noessel building on Chaparral (originally the Kinney House hotel built in 1845) was rented for $300 a year and remodeled at a cost of $84.35 to become the first home of the *Corpus Christi Caller*. The newspaper was born on a night so cold that a kerosene fire was needed to thaw out the ink, and so cold that a bucket of oyster stew, brought in to feed the pressmen, was frozen solid. That first night, on Jan. 21, 1883, the new Cottrell press was stopped for breaking news. Mrs. Mark Downey had given birth to triplets.[46]

Those who worried that Lott's railroad would damage the wool trade found other reasons to worry. In 1884, Grover Cleveland, a free-trader, a Democrat, vowed to lower or end the wool tariff, which protected American wool from the cheaper Australian imports. He kept his campaign promise when he was elected president and the wool trade declined, suddenly and rapidly, from that point on. It was a devastating blow to the sheep and wool industry of South Texas, an important part of the economy.[47] In 1880, some 12 million pounds of wool were shipped out of Corpus Christi. Much of the city's wealth depended on the wool trade.[48]

Several things happened at the time of Cleveland's election, a "perfect storm" for sheep ranchers and wool merchants. A severe drought reduced available grazing lands, followed by a parasite that decimated the flocks, along with the closing of the open range; sheepmen depended on free grass; when ranchers began to fence their pastures, the days of the sheepmen were numbered. Mifflin Kenedy fenced his Laureles Ranch in 1868 and other ranchers soon followed. By the 1880's the days of the open range were numbered.

Still, sheepmen might have survived for a bit longer except for Cleveland's election. The day before the election, wool in Corpus Christi was selling for 26 cents a pound, considered a good price. The day after the election, with the prospect of cheap Australian wool flooding the American market, the price dropped to seven cents a pound.[49] The bottom fell out of the wool market, and the effects were devastating to South Texas, including Corpus Christi, San Diego and Laredo. Almost overnight, many of the wealthiest men in South Texas went bankrupt and sheepmen became cattlemen. The wool trade never recovered. The *Caller* still followed the wool market, with declining interest, reporting from time to time, "Wool lower; no demand."*[50]

Richard King, one of the great cattle barons who did as much as any individual to found the cattle empire of South Texas, died on April 14, 1885, at the Menger House in San Antonio. He was 61. At his death, he

---

* In an ironic twist, during World War II, the Port of Corpus Christi received millions of pounds of Australian and New Zealand wool for storage during the duration of the war.

owned 614,000 acres, which he willed to his widow "Etta," along with a debt of $500,000. His fortune in gold, gained during the war by hauling cotton on his riverboats, had been spent on fencing, land and more land. He never forgot his friend Robert E. Lee's advice to buy land and never sell. In his lifetime, this Irish orphan from New York became the most famous rancher and greatest cattleman in the West. King was buried in San Antonio, but in 1925, 40 years after his death, his body was disinterred and reburied in Chamberlain Burial Park in Kingsville. He was buried in a family plot near that of a daughter, Mrs. L.M. Welton, and his youngest son, Robert E. Lee King.[51]

Uriah Lott, after he went broke and was forced to sell his railroad from Corpus Christi to Laredo, the Tex-Mex, didn't give up on building railroads. He helped build the San Antonio and Aransas Pass Railroad, the SAAP, which reached Corpus Christi in 1886 after a trestle bridge was built across Nueces Bay, giving the town its second railroad link, and he was the driving force behind another railroad, the "Brownie" line to Brownsville.[*52]

There is a bird's-eye view of Corpus Christi (assuming a high-flying bird could sketch the scene) as it looked in 1887. Augustus Koch, a German-born artist, sketched the city as if looking from a high perch. The map shows a busy harbor, with the steamship *Aransas* docked at the Central Wharf. It shows another ocean-going ship docked at the Sidbury wharf, used mostly for lumber shipments. It shows the Tex-Mex depot and the San Antonio & Aransas Pass depot. Streets, houses and stores are shown with meticulous detail.

The arrival of the SAAP, which was largely paid for by Mifflin Kenedy, led to unintended consequences. The Morgan shipping line had been serving Corpus Christi with ocean-going freighters since the Morris & Cummings Cut was dredged across the bay in 1874. But the coming of the SAAP ended the Morgan line's monopoly on the carrying trade. The line stopped its ships from going to Corpus Christi, which the city interpreted as retaliation. They were well aware of the fact that the Morgan line owned the Southern Pacific, a competitor of the SAAP. To make up for the loss of the Morgan Line ships, Corpus Christi merchants raised money to buy a small steamer to carry cotton bales to the Galveston port. The vessel was sunk in the great storm of 1900.[53]

A drought in 1891 led to an unusual experiment. A book titled *War and the Weather* held that heavy artillery fire during the Civil War often brought heavy rainfall afterwards, leading to the theory that clouds could be bombarded into dropping moisture. A cloud-bombarding experiment was conducted in Corpus Christi in 1891, paid for by area ranchers and

---

[*] In the age of railroads, there were several ephemeral lines with strange nicknames: the San Antonio, Uvalde and Gulf Railroad, the SAU&G, was known as the Sausage line. Count Giuseppe Telfener's projected line from New York to Mexico was known as the Macaroni Line. It was acquired by Southern Pacific in 1885.

undertaken by the U.S. Department of Agriculture. In September 1891, a crew came to Corpus Christi to bombard the clouds. For the first few days after they arrived, no test was possible because of stormy weather. On Sept. 26, experimenters took a dozen shells and two howitzers west of town. They fired the shells timed to explode at 500 feet. After the thump! thump! of the guns, raindrops began to fall. By the time the last shot was fired, people watching the experiment were soaking wet. Skeptics pointed out that on the day of the exercise, thunderclouds were over the city and it had rained the day before.[54]

The experimenters went to San Diego. This time, besides an artillery battery consisting of mortars and cannons, they used 10-foot balloons filled with gas and carrying explosive charges. The plan called for synchronized explosions with the artillery fired to coincide with balloon explosions. Judge James O. Luby, one of the onlookers, carried an umbrella just in case. The mortars and cannons thumped and the balloons exploded at one-minute intervals from 9 p.m. until midnight. After local observers went home, at about 4 a.m. the last balloon went up and exploded, followed by a few more artillery shots. A heavy rain began to fall. San Diego was ecstatic. Another cloud-bombarding experiment was conducted in San Antonio. The first shot took off the top of a mesquite tree and concussions from the cannon shots shattered hotel windows. While there was no rainfall in San Antonio, there was a violent downpour in Laredo. A telegram sent from Laredo to the man in charge thanked him for the rain.[55]

At the beginning of the 1890s, Corpus Christi had no municipal water supply. Residents in town had cisterns to catch rainwater from the roof. Roy Terrell remembered that in a long dry spell, the cistern would get nearly empty. "We had to put potash in this water to kill the wiggletails so we could use it."[56] When the cisterns ran dry, Terrell said, they would buy water from a barrilero who came by in a two-wheeled cart with his barrel of water.[57] The water vendors, the barrileros, traveled down the streets selling water at 25 cents a barrel. This was hauled from the Nueces River, in a severe drought, or from a spring in the arroyo in Blucher Park.[58]

On July 14, 1892, near midnight, fire broke out in the Lay home at 215 N. Chaparral. The fire spread from the Lay home to the J.B. Mitchell Warehouse. Volunteer firemen rushed to fill their water wagons from the box wells at the end of stubby little wooden piers on the bayfront. They were soon directing a stream of water on the fire, but it burned out of control, spreading from the Mitchell Warehouse to the William Biggio residence, then the Molander and Daimwood places. The flames jumped from the Daimwood home to the Royal Givens' wholesale grocery store. The Givens' building was shellcrete with a tin roof, giving the firefighters a good chance to bring the conflagration under control. But while they were fighting the fire in the front of the store, a wooden annex at the rear caught fire, then quickly spread to Louis de Planque's photo studio next door on William. The firemen were able to gain the upper hand and bring the fire under control.

The scene in town on the morning of July 15 showed many homes and buildings in the 200 block of North Chaparral destroyed, leaving the remains of charred timbers and ruined furnishings. Stocks of tin goods from Givens' grocery were stacked in the street, with armed guards standing by. Furniture and possessions rescued from burned buildings lined the street. The *Caller* said it was the most destructive fire in the city's history. [59]

After the fire, the city got serious about establishing a municipal water system. The city had wells dug west of town, but the water was salty and brackish. Then, less than a year after the fire, on May 26, 1893, the city celebrated the city's new waterworks, with 200,000 gallons a day of untreated water piped in from the Nueces River. The steam-powered pumping plant at Calallen was fired by wood then lignite coal shipped from Laredo. When it was finished, city officials traveled by hacks past cotton fields to see the new plant. The *Caller* reported that, "Hydrants are opened and water rushes out with tremendous force. The city is safe against fire."[60] The new waterworks didn't put the water vendors, the barrileros, out of business, since the piped-in water didn't reach most homes. People still relied on cisterns and when they ran low in a drought they turned to the barrileros. One difference was that the barrileros didn't have to travel to the Nueces River for their water; they could fill their barrels at standpipes in the town.

Elihu Harrison Ropes, a New Jersey man recovering from diphtheria, visited Corpus Christi, a village of 4,500 people, in 1888. He and his wife and two children stayed at Mrs. Merriman's boarding house on Chaparral. Ropes was a Civil War veteran, publisher and business developer. He soon developed big ideas for Corpus Christi. One was that Corpus Christi was the ideal place for a deepwater port, which the town had long pushed for, and he saw the bluff shoreline south of town as perfect for development. He bought 1,280 acres from Prokop Hoffman (where the Naval Air Station is now) for $12,800. His ideas and plans created the boom times of the early 1890s.

Ropes hiked over Mustang Island and found where a natural pass existed. The *Caller* said he was "fluent of tongue and his credentials impressive—the town becomes enamored of his ideas. His enthusiasm is contagious." A New York reporter wrote: "The life and enterprise of Corpus Christi dates from the coming of one man—Col. E. H. Ropes." Ropes set to work. He hired a crew to begin dredging a pass across Mustang Island; he called it Ropes Pass. (The pass was cut all across the island, said E.H. Caldwell, but there was no current running through it and the dredge was kept busy trying to prevent it from silting in.) A Corpus Christi tobacconist began selling a popular five-cent cigar called "Ropes Pass." Ropes' plans called for a port to be built on both sides of the pass. He planned to build a railroad from Corpus

144

Christi to Brownsville, then on to South America. At the railhead south of town, he envisioned a new city to be called Anthony.[61]

Ropes bought 20 blocks of land in the old W.S. Harney tract, where he planned a development along the south shoreline called "The Cliffs." He laid out streets for the development and built a three-story resort hotel, "the finest in the Southwest," called the Alta Vista (high view) patterned after a luxury hotel in Santa Monica, Calif.[*62]

Ropes had a streetcar line run out to the hotel. The rail coaches were pulled by a steam locomotive which had a streetcar built over it. Because the engine was hidden underneath the passenger compartment, it was called a "steam dummy railway." It made a trial run in June. The *Caller* said no horses were frightened and no eyes filled with cinders. The tracks began north of the Courthouse on Tiger Street, ran along Chaparral, then along the Alta Vista Road, now called Santa Fe. The tracks reached the Alta Vista in October. The hotel had a grand opening on Aug. 14, 1891, even though it was unfinished. The guests dined and danced on the hotel's third floor with its view of the bay. Ropes planned a parkway that would extend five miles along the bayfront called Ocean Park. The street alongside this park would be called Ocean Drive. Ropes also bought tracts of land on the Oso and at Flour Bluff, which he tried to rename Flower Bluff.[63]

Ropes' activity spurred an economic boom. It was as if the entire city had suddenly mastered the art of getting on in the world. The new Miramar Hotel on North Beach was filled with workers hired to attend to Ropes' projects. Big deals were cut in hotel lobbies. Land values soared. In one incident, two elderly men got in a fight, hitting each other with canes over who would get to buy a lot near the Alta Vista selling for $900. Land in "Flower Bluff" that sold for $8 an acre before Ropes, sold for up to $1,000 an acre at the height of the boom. The city's population doubled. During the boom, the city got its first national bank, the Corpus Christi National Bank, with David Hirsch, a former wool merchant, as president.[64]

Joseph W. Page came to Corpus Christi during the height of the boom, in 1890, and noted in his diary on Feb. 15: "Went to town in the afternoon. A street railway is all the talk there now. Notice they are putting up electric light poles. Corpus Christi will be a city yet." A few months later, in May, he wrote, "The town is booming. Land is selling like hot cakes at $20 and $30 an acre. The town is full of prospectors. Lawrence sold his 22 acres for $100 an acre, and I understand Mr. Storm was offered $10,000 for his place."[65]

The crash came in 1893 with a "money panic" (we would call it a depression today). Overnight, Ropes' sources of capital dried up. A Boston newspaper questioned Ropes' character and he sued for libel. Ropes left Corpus Christi one day in 1893, leaving a nearly bankrupt town behind him.

---

[*] It was located at Three-Mile Point, three miles from town where S-curve begins on today's Ocean Drive, a spot that was reputed to have been a lookout place for Jean Lafitte's pirates.

With Ropes gone, the boom quickly went bust. The dredge *Josephine* was trapped in sand halfway across the island. Ropes Pass silted in. Lots in "The Cliffs" were put up for sale by the sheriff for delinquent taxes. The abandoned streetcar line to Alta Vista was sold at auction to merchant Norwick Gussett, who replaced the steam-dummy locomotive with cheaper-to-operate mules. The vacant Alta Vista stood surrounded by weeds. Ropes' abandoned assets were sold for debt. The city underwent a flood of bankruptcies. People who had paid stupendous prices for real estate saw the value crash to nearly nothing. The speculators packed up and left and Corpus Christi's population dwindled to what it had been before Ropes came. E. H. Ropes died in New York in 1898, at age 53, a shattered man. Corpus Christi, which lost a lot of money betting on his visionary schemes, hardly noted his passing.[66]

"Blacksmith Bob" Fitzsimmons rented a house on North Beach in 1895 to begin training for a heavyweight fight with "Gentleman Jim" Corbett, a match the world was waiting for. Fitzsimmons ran wind sprints on the beach with his pet lion loping beside him. When the alarm spread that the lion had escaped, mothers kept their kids inside and a posse of "lion-hunters" was formed. After four days, the lion crawled out from under a porch where he had been hiding. In September 1895, Fitzsimmons invited any citizen to spar with him at his training camp. He promised that no one would be hurt. Walter Timon, who later became Nueces County judge, was the only man to take up the challenge.[67]

The fight with Corbett was set for Dallas, but the Legislature passed a bill making prize-fighting illegal. The match was called off. The following year, Judge Roy Bean, known as "the law west of the Pecos," staged a fight between Fitzsimmons and Peter Maher on a sandbar in the Rio Grande, outside Texas jurisdiction. But it wasn't much of a fight; Maher went down in two minutes. Corpus Christi got the news that Fitzsimmons' pet lion was killed when he got entangled in some electrical wires. In 1897, the long-anticipated fight between Fitzsimmons and Corbett was held in Carson City, Nev. People in Corpus Christi gathered outside the office of the *Caller* as the results, at the end of each round, came in by telegraph. A cheer went up when it was announced that "Blacksmith Bob" knocked out "Gentleman Jim" Corbett to become the heavyweight champion of the world.[68]

In 1898, the Kenedy Rifles of Nueces County marched through Corpus Christi on their way to "a splendid little war." The *Caller* had been filled with war news since the battleship *Maine* exploded in Havana Harbor on Feb. 16. The *Caller* had been pushing for war, editorializing that there had been "too many bluffs and grandstand plays, but perhaps we will get down to business in a few days." When war against Spain was declared on April 22, volunteer units were formed all over Texas. There were the San Antonio

Zouaves, the Belknap Rifles, the O'Connor Guards of Victoria, the Sealy Rifles. The "Rough Riders" were training in San Antonio. The papers were full of patriotic rhetoric. The *Caller* reprinted Kipling's racist ode, "The White Man's Burden" and the *Houston Post* noted that Spain once ruled half the world, "but fooled it away, too many bullfights." A battery was moved to Galveston and the *San Antonio Express* whooped, "Now the enemy will never get into Texas by way of Galveston."[69]

The Corpus Christi volunteers, the Kenedy Rifles, had to borrow money to take the train to Austin. As the train left the San Antonio & Aransas Pass depot, someone yelled, "Remember the *Maine!*" They arrived at Camp Mabry in Austin with 84 men and were formed into Company E of the First Texas Volunteer Infantry. Another volunteer unit, the Longview Rifles, which became Company A of the Third Regiment of Volunteer Infantry, was moved to Corpus Christi for coastal defense. Some of the men camped on North Beach while others were quartered in the Constantine Hotel, which was leased by the army.[70]

The Kenedy Rifles, the men of Company E, were in training when the battle of El Caney was fought, when the Rough Riders stormed up San Juan Hill, when the U.S. Navy defeated the Spanish fleet at Santiago harbor. The fighting in the Spanish-American War lasted four months, from April to August, but a peace treaty was not signed until December. The Kenedy Rifles, or Company E of the First Texas Volunteer Infantry, were shunted from Mobile to Jacksonville to Savannah. At "Camp Onward," a tent encampment in a cotton field outside Savannah, they received gift boxes from home filled with "cakes and hams and all kinds of dainties." From Uncle Sam they received the new smokeless powder Krag-Jorgensen rifles in preparation for duty in Cuba.

They boarded the transport *Michigan* on Christmas Day, 1898, and arrived in Havana Harbor five days later, where they sighted Morro Castle, the wreck of the *Maine*, and "crossed the bar with the band playing the Star-Spangled Banner." Departing Spanish soldiers waved in a friendly fashion, glad to be going home. The arriving Americans waved back. "We were expecting trouble," Lt. Tobe Fitzsimmons wrote home, "but there was nothing but cheers from the natives for 'los Americanos.' "[71] Fitzsimmons described Cuba as being like Mexico, with stone buildings, cobbled streets, and no sidewalks. "We are not allowed to visit Havana unless we are on special business," he wrote. Those few who were allowed to visit Havana found it swarming with Americans looking for jobs.[72] When they marched through Havana on the way to their camp, Pvt. Robert "Robby" Hall from Corpus Christi wrote that the Cuban people were very friendly; "they waved, threw us cigars in the parade and gave us stuff to drink."[73]

Their camp was on a mountainside three miles from the Atlantic. They discovered rum and Cuban girls. Sgt. Sam Tinney wrote home, "There is some kind of drink here that will set a person wild. Some of the boys got

147

hold of some and nearly went crazy."[74] Another reported that, "the girls here are the prettiest I ever saw." Tinney wrote that the Corpus Christi soldiers had an advantage over other American soldiers on the island because most of them could speak Spanish and could talk to the Cuban girls.[75]

They were not impressed with the defeated Spanish. "They look little," one wrote; "one American could whip four of them."[76] They did garrison duty during the occupation and were called on to break up a near-riot of soldiers from Indiana and Missouri who were angry at not being allowed to attend a circus. Almost a year after they had marched out of Corpus Christi, they were ready to be demobilized. They turned in their guns, belts, bayonets, scabbards and boarded a transport for Galveston. [77]

They arrived at the San Antonio & Aransas Pass Depot in Corpus Christi on Sunday night, April 16, 1899. They were greeted by a cheering crowd and the strains of Jose Crixell's brass band, the same band that played when they left the year before. The *Caller* reported that, "it was impossible to form them into procession, as parents would not give them up." Three days later, on Wednesday evening, Market Hall was draped in bunting and decorated with a portrait of Mifflin Kenedy, namesake of the Kenedy Rifles. The returning heroes from the Spanish-American War were showered with laurel leaves and given the freedom of the city. After dancing, a banquet was served at midnight.[78]

The worst-recorded cold front in the state's history occurred in 1899. No blizzard or "norther" since has paralyzed Texas like the one that struck in the middle of a Saturday night on Feb. 13, 1899. Temperatures plunged to Siberian levels. On the cold high plains of the Panhandle, the temperature fell to 31 degrees below, *below!*, zero. That was at Tulia. At Abilene, they fell to 23 degrees below. It was frigid across the northern part of Texas, with 16 degrees below at Denison, 11 below at Dallas. It was very cold in the southern part of the state, with temperatures reaching four below zero at San Antonio. Corpus Christi was the hot spot of the state, with temperatures 11 degrees *above* zero.[79]

It was stone cold all over the country. Trains were stalled, with passengers marooned inside their cars. A shortage of coal in the larger cities caused real hardship. "There is great suffering," the *Caller* reported, "especially among the poor of New York, and other large cities, where the cold is the worst known in decades." Many were frozen to death while others were burned to death. Pot-bellied stoves, loaded up with coal, became glowing, red-hot. It could be frigid a few feet away from the stoves, so people crowded in too close to the warmth. This led to tragic accidents. In Alice, a woman burned to death when her dress brushed against a stove. There were similar accidents all over the state. The *Laredo Times* reported that many thousands of lambs, goats and cattle were frozen to death. The weather, the *Times* said, was "the coldest in the memory of man." The *San*

Antonio Express reported that "for the first time in human memory, the San Antonio River was turned into a cake of ice of sufficient thickness to hold human weight."[80]

Capt. Andrew Anderson, who came to Corpus Christi with his parents in 1852, got caught in that terrible blizzard. "We were 50 miles down Laguna Madre [when the storm hit]. We were iced in. The Laguna had frozen over. It was snug and warm in the cabin [of the boat] all night, but in the morning we couldn't get the cabin door open. By chopping with a hatchet we were able to open it, and what a sight we beheld. There was snow and ice over the sails and rigging. It was impossible to move them. After much beating and shaking of the canvas, however, we were able to hoist the sails. Then we went to work on the anchor, and finally got that loose. It was so intensely cold we had to stop every little while and get a drink of hot coffee. Finally we started out with a head wind. We got up 25 or 30 miles, as the wind was rather favorable, and anchored at sundown. We had to climb the hoops around the masts to get the sails down that night . . . It was about noon when we reached the [bay] and the wind died down. We had to pole in from the beacon to the wharf.

"During this same terrible cold spell, a fellow in an open boat with vegetables from Ingleside landed in front of my house [on Water Street]. There was so much steam from the water he couldn't see anything, and so he anchored. He was so cold he didn't see how he could live if he remained on the boat. So he jumped overboard, thinking he would just as soon freeze to death in the water as in the boat. After swimming a ways he was able to walk. Reaching shore, he asked me to go out to the boat and get another fellow off, who had remained behind. The bay was frozen out 30 or 40 feet from shore; my skiff was on top of the ice, and the oars were about six inches thick with the ice. . . . We found the man on the boat nearly gone, just sitting huddled up, covered with canvas; he didn't respond when we called to him. We pulled him off the boat and tumbled him into the skiff and made for the shore in a hurry. He just lay there in the skiff, appearing to be dead. But on shore they put some whiskey in him first, and then some coffee, and brought him to."[81]

The *Caller* correspondent at Alice reported that the temperature fell to five degrees above zero. Across South Texas, in the extreme cold, cattle froze to death by the thousands. For those still alive on the range, their breath condensed and hung in clouds over their heads. Frozen prickly pear pads fell to the ground and shattered like glass. At Port Aransas, named Tarpon then, the boat harbor froze solid. People walked on the harbor between boats encased in ice.[82]

Corpus Christi ran out of coal. People burned dry and green mesquite in their stoves.[83] The winter storm of 1899 killed all the cabbage crops around the city. It killed the city's oleanders and orange trees. It froze meat at the meat stalls at Market Hall; saws were used to cut it. It froze the river solid at

Nuecestown; people could walk from bank to bank. It froze Nueces Bay between Corpus Christi and Portland, with the ice extending from North Beach to Indian Point; the mailman rode his horse on the ice across Nueces Bay.[84] It killed "tons and tons of fish" and froze seagulls, which fell like stones. It froze the saltwater in Corpus Christi Bay out past the piers. Fishing boats were locked tight in ice and boys walked out on the ice past the bathhouse on Central Wharf.[85] The *Caller* editor wryly noted that, "Northern ice ought to be cheap this year." The four-day bay-freezing blizzard of 1899 was undoubtedly the coldest weather Corpus Christi ever shivered through.

CHAPTER 11

Anderson windmill torn down - City lands Epworth revival - Former McNelly Ranger goes on trial - Ranch lands turned into farms - City copes with first automobiles - President Taft comes to visit - Streets paved and bluff balustrade built - 1916 hurricane - Soldiers trained at Camp Scurry - City stricken in Spanish flu epidemic

When Capt. John Anderson died in 1898, his grist mill on Water Street was torn down by the family. The old windmill was a waterfront institution recognizable to all. Anderson first came to Corpus Christi in 1845, captain of a ship carrying supplies for Zachary Taylor's army. He came back after the war with Mexico and became a pilot for ships sailing across Corpus Christi Bay. He ran his own schooners, used to haul freight. Anderson built his shellcrete home on Water Street and in 1874 built the windmill. His sons also entered the shipping business.[1]

Anderson's grist mill was used to grind salt and corn and cut timber into stove-length firewood. If a good wind was blowing, the mill could saw up to 10 cords of wood in a day, cut in lengths for iron cook stoves.[2] The mill was also used, in a small way, to gin cotton. The wood was hauled in from the Nueces River bottoms and the salt from the shores of the salt-making Laguna Madre. At the mill, the salt was ground fine for home use and coarse for curing hides at the packing houses. It sold for 20 cents to 25 cents a bushel.[3]

Anderson used half a dozen or more cannonballs that were among some 500 fired at Corpus Christi during the bombardment of the city by Union warships in 1862. Residents called these cannonballs "Kittredges," after the Yankee commander of the blockading fleet. Anderson used his cannonballs as ball bearings at the windmill. They were used to turn the mill into the prevailing wind.[*4]

As the start of the 20th century, Corpus Christi was waking up from a long slumber. When the Ropes' boom went bust in a national financial panic

---

[*] Not long after the grist mill was torn down, the Anderson home was razed, in 1913, to make way for the Nueces Hotel.

in 1893, the city underwent its own depression and the town's ambition seemed to shrink. This lassitude lasted a decade, but in the early years of the new century there was a renewed energy and optimism. The Woman's Monday Club sold shares of stock to raise funds to build a facility called the Ladies Pavilion.[5] It was intended to become the social center of the community, to replace Market Hall, built in 1871. The Ladies Pavilion was built in 1902 off Water Street, between Schatzel and Peoples. And, as intended, it quickly supplanted Market Hall as the venue for plays, dances, and skating parties. It was also where conventions were held. The Texas Bankers, the Texas Medical Association, and the Texas Press Association held conventions at the Ladies Pavilion.[6]

More important, though, was a reception given at the Ladies Pavilion in 1905 for members of the Methodists' Epworth League. Corpus Christi was competing with Rockport to obtain the Epworth League convention. This Methodist revival would bring thousands of visitors each summer. The city that gained this convention would gain a real prize. The San Antonio & Aransas Pass Railroad (SAAP) brought the Epworth committee to Corpus Christi on Jan. 20, 1905.[7] The members stayed at the New Constantine Hotel on Mesquite Street and were entertained that first night at the Ladies Pavilion. Next day, they were shown an 18-acre site marked off with flags on North Beach. They left afterwards to visit Rockport. A month later, Corpus Christi learned it had won the prize.[8] The first Epworth League revival opened on Aug. 8. Hundreds of tents went up on North Beach, which probably had not had so many tents since Zachary Taylor's army camped there in 1845.[9] Roy Terrell, a Corpus Christi resident, remembered the encampment. "A frame building, called Epworth Inn, was constructed and contained both lodging places and a large auditorium. Smaller buildings went up and the overflow lived in tents stretched along the sand. Preaching took place night and day, but there was time for games and bathing. There was a big tent where they served meals. The first time I ever tasted ice tea was at one of these Epworth meetings."[10]

The city was in the midst of its own revival. When the Methodists arrived in the summer of 1905, there were many signs of progress. Corpus Christi had a population of 6,000, three railroads, an ice-making factory, three brass bands, six automobiles, 10 churches, a steam laundry, five dentists, one cannery, one cistern factory, three lumberyards, a fire department, and a three-man police force.[11] The newspaper listed the town's improvements made in the past two years: the Epworth League encampment; the inauguration of the railroad to Brownsville; a large new hospital built on North Beach; a new SAAP railroad depot built; Central Wharf rebuilt; the Ladies Pavilion completed.[12]

The restored Alta Vista Hotel built by Ropes was being prepared for reopening. In March 1905, a telephone line was extended to the hotel.[13] In early May, wagons loaded with fancy furniture passed through the town, on their way to the Alta Vista, which opened the following month with a grand ball and supper. Couples danced all night in a ballroom decorated in lavender, pink and green. It was the year's big social event.[14] As part of the Alta Vista project, the city, county and developer J.J. Copley paid one-third each of the cost of building a new shell-topped road to the hotel. The road was called Ocean Drive.[*][15]

The Board of Trade traveled to Brownsville on the new St. Louis, Brownsville & Mexico Railroad, the "Brownie" line, Uriah Lott's third and last railroad. The train stopped for lunch at Katherine (later called the Armstrong stop).[16] The Magnolia Mansion on the bluff built by Martha Rabb was being renovated by John G. Kenedy.[17] The city contracted to have part of Chaparral and Mesquite graded; the dirt streets turned into quagmires after a rain. A fancy yacht, the *Lone Star Margaret,* built by Capt. Andrew Anderson, was launched near the Seaside Hotel.[**] The snow-white yacht with black and gold trim was said to be the finest vessel ever built in Corpus Christi.[18] High school commencement was held at the Ladies Pavilion; Marie von Blucher was the valedictorian.[19] The annual Columbus Landing was enacted on the Fourth of July. Spohn Sanitarium was built on the grounds of the Miramar Hotel, a fancy hotel built during the Ropes boom that burned shortly after it opened. James F. Scott donated lumber for the east gallery of the hospital and Joseph Hirsch paid the labor costs to build it.[20] Spohn was opened and turned over to the Sisters of the Incarnate Word to manage; the $15,000 hospital was built with contributions from the people of Corpus Christi.[21] In October, the Seaside Hotel changed hands. The new owners were J.J. Copley and W.A. Fitch; Fitch also managed the New Constantine Hotel and the Alta Vista.[22]

A trial began in December of George Talley, a former Ranger charged with the murder at a Ranger camp at Banquete 26 years before. The shooting was a tragic outcome of an idle, drunken prank. Talley tied a tin can to the tail of a colt belonging to Josh Peters, the son of a nearby rancher. After the horse almost ran himself to death, an argument between Talley and Peters led to a shootout, with Peters being shot to death. After the killing, Talley left for New Mexico, where he lived under an assumed name.[23]

In 1905, Talley returned to the Corpus Christi area and went to work building the St. Louis, Brownsville and Mexico Railroad. After he was tipped off, Nueces County Sheriff Mike Wright approached Talley in the street. Talley said his name was Smith. Sheriff Wright took him into an alley and told him to lift his pants leg to show a scar on his leg that identified him.

---

[*] It would be another two decades before the first palatial residence that started Ocean Drive as a place of consequence was built, V. M. (Manasel) Donigan's white-stucco mansion at Three-Mile Point. It was built in 1930 on the site of the Alta Vista Hotel after it burned.

[**] The *Margaret* was built for L.E. Campbell of Denver, Colo., and named for his wife, Margaret Dent, a sister of Julia Dent Grant, who married U.S. Grant. Anderson was paid $9,000 to build the yacht.

Talley asked Wright, "Who gave me away?" Talley told Wright that he came back to Texas because he was tired of living on the dodge and he wanted to clear the charge against him. Talley was re-indicted.[24]

The trial in Corpus Christi offered an opportunity for a reunion of Texas Rangers who had served with Capt. Leander McNelly in the Nueces Strip in the 1870s. The courtroom filled with old McNelly Rangers, including Lee Hall of San Antonio, W. L. Rudd of Yorktown, Harry Wright of Palestine, E.R. Jenson of Starr County, Sgt. O.S. Watson and W.H. Griffin of Corpus Christi, and George Durham of Raymondville.[25] It ended with a mistrial. In the second trial, Brownsville lawyer and political boss Jim Wells was appointed special judge. On Dec. 11, 1905, a jury found Talley guilty of murder in the second degree. He was given seven years. Defense attorneys objected. A man had been dismissed from the jury pool because he said he was in favor of hanging Talley. Later, he was heard to say that his dismissal was all right because his son and two friends were on the jury who felt the same way he did. Talley was granted a new trial, which began a year later in December 1906. The jury returned a verdict of not guilty. After 28 years, the old case was closed. Talley lived out the rest of his days working on a ranch near Falfurrias.[26]

The early years of the 20th century were a time of great change across the landscape of South Texas. The half century before had seen the coming of sheep flocks, when Corpus Christi was one of the world's great wool markets. It had seen the era of beef packing houses and trail drives to Kansas. Many of the old cattle barons were gone and thousands of acres of their ranches were being converted into plowed fields. This great change started with the railroads, which needed people to settle along their lines. An alliance was formed between ranches, railroads, and land promoters. This was the homeseeker era, with farmers from the Midwest buying farm plots and moving to South Texas.[27]

Uriah Lott's railroads were a major factor in bringing about the homeseeker era, in addition to a few other factors. The Texas-Mexican Railroad, the Tex-Mex, Lott's first railroad, was completed between Corpus Christi and Laredo in 1881. Five years later, his second railroad, the San Antonio and Aransas Pass Railroad, the SAAP, reached Corpus Christi. Lott's last railroad, the St. Louis, Brownsville & Mexico Railroad, the Brownie, made its inaugural run on July 4th, 1904. With this network of railroads, ranchers could get their beef to market. But the railroads couldn't survive by hauling cattle. They needed people, cities and towns with a greater population. In sparsely settled South Texas, where most of the land was ranchland, no people meant no passengers and, except for cattle, no freight and no profits.[28] When ranchers lost money in the drought that began in 1886 and continued into the 1890s, they began to sell some of their vast acreage for farm plots. Fencing, stock breeding, and ranch improvements meant they didn't need as much land, and they decided it was not profitable to run cattle on land that could sell for $10 or more an acre. They could recover some of their drought losses by selling excess land. The railroads helped the ranchers and land promoters by offering below-cost passenger rates to homeseekers. With this combination of factors behind it, the South Texas land boom was on.[29] Land promoters saw possibilities in buying large tracts of virgin ranchland and subdividing them into small, farm-sized plots, then bringing in land-hungry farmers from the Midwest to make the sale.[30] One writer noted that all of Texas is connected in some fashion to the land rush.[31]

In San Patricio County, the Coleman-Fulton Pasture Company, later known as the Taft Ranch, sold 2,000 acres to three firms to bring Midwestern farmers to Texas. The 300,000-acre ranch was the first to turn to tenant farming.[32] Just before the turn of the century, the Texas Land & Cattle Co., a Scottish syndicate, began to sell farm acres in the Encinal and Garden tracts (today's Four Bluff area).[33] On the outskirts of Corpus Christi in 1904, more than 7,000 acres of the Grim Ranch were sold to Stanley Kostoryz, a Czech newspaper publisher, for $52,000. Kostoryz named this tract the Bohemian Colony lands and sold 80 and 160-acre plots to Czech farmers from the Midwest.[34] He later cut them into even smaller tracts. A newspaper article reported that, "Mr. S.L. Kostoryz has 35 men employed on his property a short distance from the city grubbing a clearing and preparing quite a large acreage for cultivation. This land will be cut into small five and ten acre farms prepared ready for cultivation of actual settlers. The 35 men are Bulgarians who recently landed . . . On all sides lands are being cleared and placed in cultivation, and there is a general awakening all down the line."[35]

F. Z. Bishop, for whom Bishop was named, bought land from the Driscoll Ranch for farms.[36] The Elliff ranch near Banquete and the old Rabb pastures were subdivided for farming. The Benton pasture lands near Alice, part of the old Galveston Ranch near Falfurrias, the N.G. Collins properties around San Diego, and chunks of the Welder Ranch in San Patricio County were sold by land promoters for farming. [37]

Land promoters brought homeseekers by the thousands. The greatest of these promoters was a young man named George H. Paul, who grew up on a farm near Washington, Iowa. He was a hired hand, making $18 a month until 1904 when he went to work selling land. He was selling land in Canada when he heard about the vast tracts of ranchland for sale in Texas, so he came to Corpus Christi to see for himself.[38] He stayed at the Seaside Hotel. Paul made a deal with rancher Robert Driscoll to sell Driscoll ranchlands north of Robstown, founded at the junction of the Tex-Mex and Brownie railroad lines.[39] The George H. Paul company soon had prospective land buyers arriving by the trainload. The railroads offered cheap excursion rates to homeseekers, at $15 round-trip from Kansas City to Corpus Christi, and Paul bought his own private Pullman cars.[40]

Paul developed a system. The homeseekers (some called them "homesuckers") would stay in Corpus Christi hotels until they boarded the Tex-Mex to ride to Robstown. They would arrive in Robstown on a Friday morning to be met at the depot by Paul's salesmen with rented gigs and spring wagons to take them to look at the land. The salesmen carried maps showing tracts for sale. They would spend Friday and Saturday looking at land and return to Corpus Christi for a Sunday excursion on the bay aboard the *Pilot Boy*. Paul in one year sold 56,000 acres of Driscoll land, at an average of $35 an acre, and within two years, he sold 200,000 acres in Nueces and San Patricio counties. Before the rush was over, Paul sold half a million acres of South Texas ranchland. On the land that was sold, homes were built, fields were cleared and put into cultivation, and new towns with Midwestern names sprang up.[41]

What brought homeseekers to Texas to begin a new life was the attraction of cheap land, and it was land billed as the richest soil in the world. In the Midwest, land prices were so high they were out of reach for many would-be farmers who wanted their own place, but in Texas, subdivided ranchland was cheap, on average from $15 to $35 an acre, and it was rich soil. Between 1900 and 1910, homeseekers came to the Corpus Christi area by the thousands. After buying their plots, the homeseekers brought families, farm equipment, even livestock. Railroads provided boxcars that were separated for household goods on one end and livestock on the other. The *Caller* reported on Jan. 6, 1904 that, "Two immigrant cars rolled into Corpus Christi this week. One was D.A. Stone's, from McGregor. Mr. Stone recently bought 120 acres from O.S. Watson in the Encinal, below Aberdeen.[*] The other immigrant car belongs to Mr. Osburn, but where he is going to locate, we cannot say." In the first eight months of 1905, ending on Aug. 31, Uriah Lott's new railroad to Brownsville, "the Brownie," handled 251 immigrant cars for homeseekers. For 1906, the railroad spent $25,000 in advertising the advantages of the country and it transported 11,700 homeseekers for that year.[42]

Some homeseekers no doubt thought the land would be ready to plow like in the Midwest; hitch up a team and break up the sod and plant a crop. But the ranchland of South Texas had to be cleared of scrub brush and running mesquite before crops could be planted, and it was difficult work to grub out extensive networks of roots below the surface. In earlier days, prairie fires were set to burn off brush invaders. This had the beneficial effect of helping bring in new grass in the spring. Fencing ended this practice since ranchers didn't want to burn down their fences.[43] From the time that fencing began in the 1870s, brush spread over what had been a coastal savannah of lush grass. The savannah quickly became brush country.[44]

---

[*] The community of Aberdeen was located south of Corpus Christi where Seaside Cemetery is today.

Huge steam tractors pulling fuel and water wagons behind them (like a sow with piglets) were put to work clearing the brush. The steam age came late to rural South Texas, about the time the motor age was beginning. Despite their great size, the steam tractors ran quietly, making a soft putt-putt noise.[45] In some places, the dense spreading roots of the running mesquite had to be dug out by hand, root by tenacious root, with grubbing hoes, mattocks and long-handled axes. It was hard work.[46] Thousands of laborers came to South Texas from Mexico to clear the land. Many brought their families and entire family units became grubbing crews. They were paid by the acre; the going rate was $12.50 an acre, in 1910. They lived on the land until it was cleared, then moved on to the next tract. At night, the campfires of the land-grubbers were more numerous than the stars.[47]

Acre by acre, pastureland was turned into farmland. Amused ranch hands, the last of the independent-minded cowboys, watched men on tractors and laborers with grubbing hoes work the land. They called it, with wry contempt, "turning grass upside-down."[48] It also turned their way of life upside-down. Crops were soon growing on land where cattle had grazed for a half century or more. One major crop was cabbage. Truck farmers were convinced that cabbage grown along the coast was better than cabbage grown anywhere else.[49] It was said that more cabbage was shipped from Corpus Christi than any other city in the world. The San Antonio and Aransas Pass Railroad, the SAAP, ran special cabbage trains from Corpus Christi. There were also extensive shipments from the area of beans and cucumbers, "long greens," amounting, in one year, to more than 200 carloads.[50] A succession of frigid winters that began in 1899 and continued until 1906 helped to end the cabbage and truck-farming era.

With the coming of farmers, new towns and communities began to spring up: towns such as Sodville, St. Paul, West Sinton, Violet, Orange Grove, Edroy, Riviera, Bishop, Robstown, Driscoll. Premont, north of Falfurrias, was a land-rush town founded in 1909 on what had been the Galveston Ranch. Theodore Koch bought 18,000 acres of ranchland to found the town of Riviera and, nine miles east, Riviera Beach on Baffin Bay. Towns like Aransas Pass and Portland began before the homeseeker era, but they didn't flourish until the big ranch holdings began to be converted into farmland during the land boom times, which served to bring in more people and businesses prospered.

The new century brought the first automobiles to Corpus Christi, the beginning of the time when a world powered by animals was converted to machines. In 1901, George Blucher took his family to the Pan-American Exposition in Buffalo, N.Y. (where President McKinley was shot). At the Exposition, Blucher met Ransom Olds, who sold him one of his cars. It was shipped in crates and arrived in Corpus Christi in October, 1901. It had a tiller instead of a steering wheel, and the motor was under the back seat.

Jasper Blucher later remembered that the car was used to take his three sisters to school while he and his brother had to walk.[51] Dr. A.G. Heaney bought a one-cylinder Cadillac in 1902 and Dr. Arthur Spohn and John G. Kenedy bought new automobiles. On Sept. 12, 1902, Sam Anderson, a foreman of the Coleman-Fulton Pasture Co., was knocked unconscious when his horse fell on him. Dr. Heaney was called. He drove his new automobile to the reef road at North Beach, then rode a special bicycle across the railroad trestle, then a horse and buggy carried him on to the Anderson place. Anderson had suffered a concussion.[52]

Peter McBride, a dairyman, on his way to Corpus Christi in a mule cart encountered his first automobile, driven by Dr. Spohn. "I kept holding the mules back, but they were scared and there was no stopping them. Dr. Spohn stopped his automobile so we could get by."[53] Corpus Christi got its first taxicab in 1906, operated by Pitts Livery Stable and Funeral Home. A man named Dan Darby was the driver. Roy Terrell got his first automobile ride in the Pitts taxi. "My father sent the taxi to our house to pick us up and take us to the railroad station, a distance of four blocks, but what an experience!"[54]

A *Caller* reporter took a spin around town on Dec. 21, 1906, in E.R. Oliver's new car. "Of all easy riding and noiseless autos, we believe it takes the lead, at least it is ahead of anything this rider ever rode in. Very little machinery. The mechanism is compact and enclosed, which is a great advantage. The auto is a rapid mover, yet it can be stopped in a few seconds, even in going up or down the bluff."[55] One of the first auto ads in the *Caller* ran in 1906 for Noakes Brothers. They were selling Cadillacs and Noakes promised to keep the machine in repair for six months, barring accidents or punctured tires. The ad said Cadillacs were so popular there were already four in town. "The Cadillac Motor Car," said the ad, "needs no recommendation. The merit of the four cars used in this city is good enough. The Cadillac is past the experimental part, and is sold in Corpus Christi by Noakes Bros. "[56]

In March, 1908, the *Caller* reported that John D. Barnard and Dr. W. E. Carruth were on Broadway at night when an automobile collided with their buggy, throwing both men out, and knocking the horse down. After the accident, the *Caller* started an editorial campaign pushing for a vehicle ordinance to deal with "reckless auto-ing." An ordinance was passed requiring motorists to sound a horn, bell, gong or trumpet as the driver approached intersections. After it went into effect, the *Caller* editor complained that drivers were "blowing their horns louder and longer than ever; if they can't be a nuisance one way, they will another."[57]

One man noted that people in town knew everyone who had a car. "If we saw a Hudson coming down Chaparral, we knew it was Mrs. Maude Miller. If we saw an open Benz with the brass shining, we knew it was Mr. Driscoll. If you were near Artesian Park and heard a Cadillac moving slowly, you would know it was Judge McDonald."[58] Before highways sliced across the land, traveling by car was tough going. The automobiles were underpowered and the streets were shell or dirt; country roads were even worse. After a heavy rain, the gumbo-like heavy clay became all but impassable. Mrs. A.R. Yeargen, who ran a grocery store on King Street, said the streets, except for two blocks of Chaparral, were mud. "From our store, I could see horses bogging down in the mud when it rained."[59]

South of town, farmer Herman Poenisch bought his first automobile, a Ford sedan, equipped with carbide lights. A tube ran from the carbide system to the lights. One night, coming back from town, they hit a bump, which knocked the tube loose, and Poenisch hit a cow; the family helped to pull the scared but unhurt cow from under the car. Their next car had magneto lights; the faster the car went, the brighter the lights.[60] Besides automobiles, there were other signs of progress and change. For housewives, the coming of screen doors and windows to keep out black clouds of mosquitoes was a great improvement. For men, life was improved with factory-rolled cigarettes that replaced the drawstring tobacco sacks and the practice of having to roll their own.

President William Howard Taft stopped by to visit Corpus Christi on Oct. 22, 1909; he was in the neighborhood. He came to South Texas to visit the ranch of his half-brother, Charles Taft, on the north side of Corpus Christi Bay. The president was a guest at the Taft ranch house, La Quinta. When the president arrived at La Quinta, he turned to his half-brother and said, "Charley, old boy, you said 'Let's go to Texas and rough it.' I don't call this roughing it."[61]

Corpus Christi planned for the president's visit for some time. City officials wired Rep. John Nance Garner in Washington, who arranged to have a Coast Guard cutter, the *Windom,* brought over from Galveston to ferry the president across the bay. City officials also ordered matching outfits for the welcoming committee to wear: Prince Albert coats, formal stovepipe hats, kid gloves and shoes of the same color. On Oct. 22, the *Windom* picked up Taft and brought him to Corpus Christi's Central Wharf, where the members of the welcoming committee, dressed in the Prince Albert coats, were standing by cotton bales on one of the hottest days anyone could remember for October.[62]

The portly president made his way down the gangway, presenting quite a contrast with the spruced-up welcoming committee. He was wearing a battered Panama hat, well-worn alpaca coat and wrinkled gray trousers that looked as if they had never met an iron. The welcoming committee in their swallow-tailed matching outfits looked as trim and nifty as bridegrooms. An observer said the president was amused at the discomfiture of the welcoming committee.[63]

The president and entourage rode in a parade down Chaparral. Roy Terrell, who grew up on the Terrell Ranch on the Oso, said his father, Stewart Blackburn Terrell, a city policeman, rode his horse "Old Gray" escorting

Taft's car.[64] The presidential parade ended at a stage with a roof (called a pergola) on the side of the bluff.* [65] Thousands gathered to hear the president. Schools and businesses closed for the occasion. Taft noticed men in the crowd in Civil War uniforms; he asked them to join him on the stage, in the shade, which displaced the welcoming committee, forcing them to stand under the hot sun. It was sweltering and several people fainted. The president spoke of the city's need for harbor improvements and a deepwater port, an opinion and topic that certainly appealed to Corpus Christi.[66]

Next on the president's agenda was a trip to North Beach in a seven-passenger Rambler. The president struck the first ball at the Country Club's new golf course. As Taft bent over to strike the golf ball, someone snapped a picture of the president's rear end, and for years the Country Club displayed the golf club, ball, and photo in a glass case. Next came a reception and lunch at Henrietta King's house on the bluff, where, according to Tom Lea's *King Ranch*, Taft was given an extra large saddle with a "Running W" brand.

Taft returned to La Quinta, where he stayed for four days. He saw one of the first gasoline-powered tractors in South Texas, a Hart-Parr, and ranch hands held a roping, branding and riding exhibition and dipped cattle to kill ticks. That 22-inch saddle came in handy when Taft was taken for a ride around the ranch. They drafted a large horse, Old Sam, as a mount for the 320-pound president. The horse, according to *Taft Ranch*, groaned when the president settled into the saddle. It was said that as a reward for carrying Mr. Taft that Old Sam was put out to pasture and never saddled again. The welcoming committee probably never wore those Prince Albert coats again.[67] A day or so after Taft's departure, Eli Merriman, editor of the *Caller*, ran into Mrs. Dugan, who lived across Mesquite Street from Spohn Park where the president spoke. She said, "Mr. Merriman, why didn't you put in the *Caller* that the President of the United States made a speech in front of my gate? I would have liked to have sent a copy to Ireland."[68]

Drilling for oil resumed at White Point across Nueces Bay in 1913. Oil exploration began here in 1902 when Randolph Robinson drilled a test well at White Point the year after the Spindletop gusher at Beaumont ushered in the oil boom in Texas. Robinson abandoned his well after hitting a gas show; at the time, there was no market for gas. On Sept. 6 1913, a test well blew out and drill pipe was blasted up like a missile from the great gas pressure below. In 1914, the White Point Oil and Gas Co. was purchased by the James M. Guffey Petroleum Co. Guffey's company became Gulf Oil. The Guffey No. 1 well at White Point blew out in January, 1916. The *San Antonio Light* called it the biggest strike of gas in the world. "The well is beyond control at present . . . The roar of escaping gas can be heard for seven

---

* It was located where Spohn Park is today.

160

miles . . . pure gas is rushing from the well in a column about 300 feet high."
This monster well ignited. People traveled from all over to see the great gas
fire at White Point. There was an ad in the Corpus Christi paper by one
enterprising fellow: "See the big gas well. Take a trip over the causeway.
Phone 348. Paul Cabe Auto Service."[69] When it burned itself out, it left a
crater 200 feet wide and 100 feet deep.[70]

In Corpus Christi, the city's major streets were known mostly by their
nicknames: Front Street (Chaparral), Back Street (Mesquite), then Water
Street and the streets uptown were generally lumped together as "The Bluff."
From the earliest times, the streets were a cause of complaints and concern.
Sheep, hogs, goats, dogs and cattle roamed the streets. Citizens complained
that animals died or were killed and left to rot in the streets.[71] At the end of
the Civil War, the town's main streets, Chaparral and Mesquite, were
obstructed by mud, water and littered with dead animals.[72] To correct the
situation, Chief Justice John Dix and the Commissioners Court ordered the
town divided into five road precincts, with an overseer appointed in each
precinct; men living in the precinct were designated as "road hands," willing
or not, and could be conscripted to work on the streets without pay.[73]

After a heavy rain, the clay streets became almost impassable with
glutinous mud. In the wet season, it was said, Corpus Christi streets were the
wettest on earth. Wagon wheels on the big delivery wagons caked up and
had to be scraped off. Gullies washed out on the bluff and the runoff carried
mud and soil onto the streets and sidewalks below. During the rainy season,
half of Chaparral would be under water and the sidewalks were passable
only when planks were laid across them.[74] Doddridge, Lott and Co., on
Chaparral, filled the mud holes in the street in front of their store with oyster
shell at their own expense. "Our streets need more attention from the city
fathers. Corpus Christi should not lie in a lake at every good rain," the
newspaper complained.[75] Mayor John B. Murphy put city prisoners to work
digging drainage ditches to the bay. To insure they "volunteered," those who
refused to dig were fed bread and water only. In his regime, those in jail
were not going to be allowed to loll about doing nothing.*[76] In 1894, the city
treasurer paid the Fishermen's Union for 24 loads of oyster shell for the
streets. C.R. Simpson, who moved to Corpus Christi in 1909, said the streets
were in a deplorable condition before they were paved. "The mayor spread
clay all over the town streets and when it rained the streets were almost
impassable. I saw a four-horse team, pulling an express wagon, bog down so
they couldn't move right by the side of the Nueces Hotel."[77] Mrs. A.R.
Yeargen, who ran a grocery store on King Street, said when she arrived in
1911 Corpus Christi had two blocks of paved streets on Chaparral. "The
other streets were mud. From our store, I could see horses bogging down in

---

* Mayor Murphy ordered city policemen to arrest any grown man walking around without shoes.
"A man who would go barefoot in public must be a vagrant," he said. "Either wear shoes, or leave
town."

161

mud when it rained."[78]

The first assessments for paving city streets were made in 1913, with the city paying one-fourth the cost of paving and adjacent property-owners assessed three-fourths of the cost. Plans were made and assessments levied to pave Belden, Twigg, Taylor, Mann, Lawrence, Schatzell, Peoples, William, Aubrey, Laguna (now Sartain), Last (N. Alameda), Upper Broadway, and to finish the paving that had already begun on Chaparral, Mesquite and Water streets. In all, the plan called for paving 150 blocks of city streets, a project that took years to complete. By 1930, the city had 35 miles of paved streets.[79] Some of the money for street improvements was set aside to build a concrete balustrade on the side of the bluff that separates "downtown" from "uptown." The bluff was ugly and untidy and muddy when it rained. In places, there were makeshift steps to assist pedestrians going up or down the often slippery slope. It was steep in places. Mrs. Angie Westbrook once recalled when they first came to Corpus Christi in 1900, they were riding in a wagon down the side of the bluff at the end of Leopard Street. "We had to lock all four wheels of the wagon, and then we could hardly hold the horses, the bluff was so steep."[80]

Alexander Potter, a New York engineer hired to design a water supply system for the city, was put to work on developing a plan to convert the bluff from an eyesore into an attractive feature. Mayor Roy Miller said, "It would be highly desirable to give the people a concrete idea of the great possibilities of bluff beautification." Concrete walls reinforced with base anchors were built and the bluff itself was terraced to prevent erosion. Potter included plans for a pedestrian tunnel between downtown and uptown. It was built after the original bluff improvement project and opened in 1929. While the bluff balustrade was being built, the Daughters of the Confederacy contributed the gift of a fountain at the bottom of the slope and the top of Schatzell and Peoples Street. They hired Italian sculptor Pompeo Coppini, who had moved to San Antonio, to design the fountain. His Confederate memorial fountain depicts Corpus Christi as a beautiful young woman, flanked by Father Neptune and Mother Earth. It was finished in 1915 and became the crown jewel of the bluff improvement project.[81]

The wet-dry election of 1916 was one of the most potent issues in the history of Corpus Christi. This was two years before Prohibition was ratified by the states. In Corpus Christi, there were fierce arguments over Demon Rum. The Nueces County Prohibition Club formed in December 1915 and began a petition drive for a wet-dry election. They wanted to close 43 saloons, 37 in Corpus Christi, three outside the city limits, and three in Port Aransas; the rest of the county was dry. Bee and San Patricio counties had recently voted dry. The drys (or "pros") gathered 1,089 names on the petition and an election was set for March 10, 1916.[82] The dry forces, dominated by women, got a boost from Rev. Mordecai Ham and Benjamin Ramsay, who set up a tent tabernacle for a six-week revival. The pulpit exhortations were aimed at card-playing, dancing, going to the movies on Sunday and drinking Demon Rum.[83]

Rev. Ham thundered from his pulpit that, "When it comes to rotten conditions, Pompeii has nothing on Corpus Christi. I have traveled over Europe, North Africa, much of Asia, and many states in the Union, but I have never before heard of a man and four women sitting half a day at a beer table together perfectly nude" except in Corpus Christi. Ham charged that there were 300 gambling halls and 40 houses of prostitution operating brazenly in the city and local officials were too blind or too corrupt to stop it. Ham's partner Ramsay said their sermons would make Corpus Christi so hot that "if one spits on the street it will sizzle."[84]

The town did sizzle. Passions were at fever pitch. Children wore ribbons showing which side they supported, white for dry and red for wet. Families that had been friends for generations quit speaking. Men fought on the streets. Merchants who tried to stay out of it were threatened with boycotts if they refused to close for the revival. Parades were conducted by the "drys" that culminated at the Nueces Hotel, where the marchers would sing "Goodbye Booze" and "Nueces County Going Dry."

Town leaders led by Mayor Roy Miller and Nueces County Judge Walter Timon tried to calm things down.[85] The *Caller* warned that the business climate was being hurt. The paper said the city of Temple went dry the year before "and now there are 400 vacant buildings in Temple." The name-calling escalated. *Caller* editorials were critical of Ham's revival from the start, but the barbs became sharper. One editorial said, "Just because a muck-rake is full of holes, is no sign it is holy." The *Caller* called Ham a "hired foreigner" and noted that the first collection plate for Ham-Ramsay contained more than $3,000. Ramsay retorted that the editor of the *Caller* was "too rotten to go to hell." The editor said that was fine with him, then he wouldn't have to rub elbows with Ham and Ramsay.[86]

The drys were on the offensive. The wets were overconfident; they couldn't see how they could lose. Most of those attending Ham's revival and marching in the dry parades were women and children, and they couldn't vote. The *Caller* predicted the anti-Prohibitionists would win by a 580-vote majority. Tempers were high by election day, Friday, March 10. Ham and Ramsay didn't stick around to see the outcome of their campaign; they left town before the voting started. Large crowds of women gathered around every polling place to harangue the male voters. Some women threatened to divorce their husbands if Prohibition failed. A total of 3,377 men voted, 92 percent of those registered, and the drys won by 218 votes. Women who had led the campaign celebrated their victory with a march, which ended with singing "Nueces County Going Dry."[87]

It would be a long time before half the town would speak to the other half. The saloons on Mesquite and Chaparral were closed at 9:30 p.m. on

April 21, a Saturday night.[*88] Nationally, the 18th amendment banned the manufacture, sale and transportation of liquor, but the country was never dry. It simply changed legal liquor to illegal liquor and introduced the era of bootleggers, homemade gin, smuggled hooch, and shameless hypocrisy. Saloons were closed, but a man could always find a drink. In Corpus Christi, people drank Jamaica Beer made from vanilla extract, bay rum, and bitters. While these products were prohibited, druggists sold them anyway. Welding shops manufactured copper cylinders that could be used as portable stills, small enough to be loaded on pickups. People set up moonshine stills in backyards, using mesquite wood fuel for copper pots that held corn or grain mash. A problem for backyard bootleggers was disposing of the mash, which authorities could sniff from a mile away. Bootleggers would caramelize sugar to add to the liquor to give it an amber color to look like bourbon or scotch. They stored moonshine in oak barrels with charcoal to simulate the taste of aging. Bathtub gin was made of grain alcohol mixed with distilled water.[89] One of the best-known bootleggers in town was a bellhop at the Nueces Hotel, Lincoln Daniels, known as "Old Dan." It was said he could supply just about any brand, from white corn made in backyard stills to choice imported liquors.[90]

Pack mule trains brought tequila, mescal, and whisky with unfamiliar names from Mexico. Distilleries there produced an ersatz bourbon, "Waterfill," and an ersatz Scotch, "Frazier." Trying to stop the smuggling was a never-ending battle between smugglers, *los tequileros*, and Rangers, *los rinches*. Ships lying off the barrier islands brought in Canadian whisky sealed in cans labeled "Insect Spray." Cases of smuggled "Old Hospitality" that had been thrown overboard washed up on Padre and Mustang islands.[91]

It was back in 1908 when the Commercial Club (forerunner of the Chamber of Commerce) asked Congressman John Nance Garner of Uvalde to obtain an appropriation to build a new federal building in Corpus Christi (Garner represented the district in Congress; he was later vice president in the Franklin D. Roosevelt administration). Garner succeeded in getting an act passed by Congress. The construction of a new federal building at Corpus Christi was authorized by Congress. Eli Merriman, editor of the *Caller,* wrote that Garner asked the people of Corpus Christi what was wanted and was told a federal building. "He got it for us. 'What else now?' he asked. A federal court, people said. And he got that for Corpus Christi, which was in competition with Brownsville for the designation."[*] The money to buy a site and construct the building was limited to $70,000. Preliminary steps were taken in 1908 to

---

[*] Bars would not reopen until Prohibition was repealed on Dec. 5, 1933 when Utah became the last of 36 states to ratify the 21st amendment, repealing the 18th amendment.

[*] For his work in getting a port and a new federal building for the city, Eli Merriman wrote, Garner was presented with a gold watch inscribed from the people of Corpus Christi. He carried that watch for the rest of his life.

choose a site, but the under-funded project was delayed for years and not completed until 1918, three years after construction began in September 1915. The post office, customs office, and federal court offices were moved into the new federal building, a structure of tan brick, white stucco with a red tile roof. The building was finished just after downtown streets were paved and the bluff improvement project was completed, all part of the city's dynamic growth surge.[92]

On Aug. 17, 1916, the U.S. Weather Bureau in Corpus Christi warned that a hurricane was 150 miles out in the Gulf and would likely make landfall somewhere between Corpus Christi and Brownsville.[93] Corpus Christi Mayor Roy Miller ordered the evacuation of frame buildings along the shore. Police, firemen and volunteers went door to door warning residents to move to higher ground.[94] Refugees took shelter in the new Nueces Hotel at Peoples and Water, at City Hall on Mesquite Street, at the Nueces County Courthouse and other strong buildings away from the waterfront.[95]

The center of the storm moved inland just south of Riviera Beach on Baffin Bay at 1 a.m. on Aug. 18, a Friday.[96] The storm destroyed a new pavilion and pleasure pier and damaged the new Buena Vista hotel at Riviera Beach.[97] Bay View College at Portland, a home-boarding school, was badly damaged by the storm and forced to close.[98] A bathhouse and wharf at La Quinta on the Taft Ranch were destroyed and the La Quinta mansion, where President Taft had stayed in 1909, was damaged.[99] A new wharf at Portland built in 1913 to handle cotton shipments from the Taft Ranch was badly damaged. It was repaired, then destroyed in the hurricane of 1919.[100] Cotton compresses at Port Aransas were destroyed.[101] The *Aransas Pass Progress* reported, "Hurricane and tidal wave sweep coast. One dead here, hit at 1 a.m. on August 18."[102] Three miles out, the *Pilot Boy* broke up and six crew members drowned.[103]

In Corpus Christi, there was considerable damage along the waterfront. The Ladies Pavilion was destroyed. Loyd's Pavilion and Pleasure Pier, which opened two years before, was badly damaged and all but destroyed. The Natatorium was wrecked and the Seaside Pavilion Hotel lost its pier. The Central Wharf was badly damaged along with the railroad trestle of the San Antonio and Aransas Pass across Nueces Bay. The new Nueces Bay Causeway, which had been open little more than a year, was wrecked.[104] On North Beach, the nine-foot storm surge reached the SAAP railroad tracks. The 1916 storm was a dress rehearsal for a far deadlier storm. Three years later, when a more dangerous hurricane threatened, residents of North Beach were lulled into a false sense of security by recalling that the 1916 storm surge never got above the railroad tracks, which offered an escape route from low-lying North Beach to higher and safer ground in Corpus Christi.

Nueces County voters in 1913 approved a $250,000 bond issue to build a new courthouse. County officials traveled the state looking at courthouses before they settled on a design. The resulting building on Mesquite Street was the county's third courthouse. The first was built in 1853, when the county was six years old. Commissioners had been meeting in each other's houses. The job of designing a building was given to Felix von Blucher, a surveyor. The courthouse was built of shellcrete on three lots on Mesquite Street bought from H. L. Kinney.[105] The county's first courthouse took three years to build. It cost $4,000. But the plans that called for a jail were left out. The sheriff, with no jail for prisoners, put them up in a boarding house, at his own expense, or let them go. Meetings on whether Nueces should vote to secede were held in the courthouse. At the onset of war, a ceremony was held on the steps of the courthouse. A Confederate flag, made of silk and sewn by young ladies in town, was presented to the Corpus Christi Light Infantry. When Union gunboats shelled the city, the courthouse sat deserted. County officials had evacuated to Santa Margarita, a ferry crossing on the Nueces River.[106]

After the war, when a yellow fever epidemic hit in 1867, the courthouse became the only center of local government for the county and the city. A majority of City Council members died of the fever, which led county commissioners to assume control of city affairs. The county in the 1870s outgrew its first courthouse. A new courthouse was built of concrete blocks, with a wooden front, next to the old 1853 structure. It was called the "Hollub Courthouse," nicknamed for the engineer who designed it. The Hollub Courthouse, finished in 1875, cost $15,000. The old and new courthouses stood side by side on the north end of courthouse block, facing east on Mesquite, with Belden Street to the north. The old courthouse was used as a jury room and offices for county officials.[107]

After more than three decades, the Hollub Courthouse was too small for the growing county. Voters approved a bond issue to pay for a new building, The county's third courthouse was built south of the three older structures, which were then torn down. The 1914 courthouse, six stories high and built of brick and stone, was meant to create a sense of awe. It became a showpiece of South Texas. Two cells with gallows and a trap door for hangings were built in the 1914 courthouse, but they were never used; the state took over the duty of carrying out executions. Five years after it was built, the most dramatic event in the history of the building occurred when the courthouse became a refuge in the 1919 storm.[108]

When war broke out in Europe in August, 1914, Corpus Christi and South Texas were focused more on events in Mexico, where U.S. troops stationed along the border were kept busy chasing Pancho Villa. But Corpus Christi soon became a training ground for soldiers who would fight in France. Corpus Christi, from its early years, was an army town. It was hardly a settlement or village at all until Zachary Taylor's army pitched their tents along the shore in 1845. In 1916, it once again became a soldiers' city with the establishment of Camp Scurry not far from where Taylor's soldiers camped. Camp Scurry was laid out in a cow pasture near the bay, south of town. The camp covered an area of the city behind Ocean Drive (across from Holiday Inn-Emerald Beach) beyond where Spohn Hospital is today. The camp had shell-topped roads, screened and floored tents, and wooden mess halls. It was built for Texas units called into federal service during the disturbances on the border, the Second and Third Texas Infantry National Guard units. Some 3,500 soldiers were moved here from Harlingen after the 1916 hurricane flooded the soldiers' camps in the Valley. They were welcomed in Corpus Christi with an ice cream and cake party, which ended in a near brawl between competing bands of the Second and Third Infantry.[109] Gen. Frederick Funston, in charge of all the units on the border, visited Corpus Christi for a review of the troops. He and his staff had lunch at Mayor Roy Miller's home and were taken for a swim at North Beach. The outing was marred by a swarm of jellyfish which attacked the officers and drove them out of the water.[110]

Trenches were dug in the area and soldiers held bayonet drills. At the request of Mayor Miller, some troops were diverted from training to lay shell on Up River Road; it was called Shell Road for a long time. In one incident, the army bought mules from King Ranch to use as pack animals to carry heavy machine guns, but the mules bolted, wrecking tents in the melee, and escaped into the heavy brush around the camp. For days, soldiers could be heard cursing as they tramped through the thick brush chasing the wild mules and collecting scattered machine guns.[111]

When the United States entered the war on April 6, 1917, Camp Scurry became a training post for the Fifth Engineers and the Fourth Field Artillery. One New Yorker stationed here with the Fourth Field Artillery, Dermot M. Meehan, once reminisced about life in the camp: "I remember a bunch of us bought a boat and rented a net and we'd drag it around the bay and catch shrimp; then we'd have a shrimp feast. Everybody would donate a nickel for catsup and we'd eat shrimp until we were sick of them . . . There were lots of pretty girls and there was always a dance somewhere. Whenever you wanted one, there would be one." [112]

When the Second Texas Infantry was stationed at Camp Scurry, the outfit fielded a football team made up mostly of former college players from the University of Texas. They built a practice field at Santa Fe and Booty. The Second Texas team played the best military teams in the nation and trounced them, one and all. They beat teams by scores of 53-0, 68-0, 102-0. They went undefeated in their one eight-game season, which is not that unusual, but what was unusual was that in these eight games the Second Texas team scored 432 points while allowing their opponents only 6. Camp Scurry's football team defeated Wisconsin Infantry, 60-0. It defeated

167

Virginia Military, 53-0, Nebraska Infantry, 68-0, and New York Infantry, 102-0. Based on its record, the Second Texas team was considered to be one of the best football teams ever.[113]

Soldiers trained at Camp Scurry fought in many of the major battles in the last year of the war. Besides those killed in action in World War I, many died in the Spanish flu outbreak in 1918 that was especially deadly in cramped army barracks. Some said the flu started in Spain, which gave it the name, and spread to the battlefields in France. Some accused the Germans of spreading the germs while others thought it was brought to France by Chinese workers imported to perform war work. Another theory, which has gained wide acceptance (John M. Barry, *The Great Influenza*) is that the flu outbreak actually began early in 1918 at Camp Funston (now part of Fort Riley) in Haskell County, Kansas. The outbreak spread rapidly. The death rate in Philadelphia jumped 700 percent. In Baltimore, bodies went unburied. Historical accounts said the flu claimed more victims than German guns, ending the lives of an estimated 20 million to 40 million people around the world. At the height of the pandemic in this country, in the last two weeks of October, 1918, 40,000 deaths were recorded. It was made worse in army camps and on transport ships where men were packed in close quarters.[114]

Roy Terrell of Corpus Christi was on board an army transport ship steaming for Brest, France. He said the ship was so crowded bunks were three deep. "It was during the flu epidemic and soldiers were dying like flies; coffins were piled everywhere. When we got to France, the epidemic was there also, and you could see burial details everywhere burying the dead."[115] Here at home, the *Caller* printed rules of hygiene. People were advised to avoid crowds, to refrain from spitting in public places, to practice "uncompromising cleanliness," to avoid using the common towel. Obituary notices mounted and Mayor Miller issued an appeal to the people to take precautions. Many of the city's normal activities were suspended. Businesses closed. On Oct. 18, the mayor and City Council—calling the flu a "crowd disease"—closed movie theaters and public dances. Schools were closed. Poolrooms, domino parlors, and soda fountains were closed; restaurants could stay open only if they moved the tables at least five feet apart. People were urged to walk to work and avoid crowded streetcars. Some wore gauze masks.[116]

On Oct. 26, 475 people were stricken with the flu in Corpus Christi; 21 deaths had been recorded in two weeks. The *Caller* warned that it might have to suspend publication because so many of the linotype operators were sick. Army Hospital No. 15 on North Beach, where convalescent soldiers were being treated, and Camp Scurry were placed under strict quarantine: soldiers could not leave and civilians could not enter.[117]

Anita Lovenskiold, a 16-year-old who lived on Carrizo Street, a daughter of Dr. Perry G. Lovenskiold, kept a diary in 1918 when the Spanish influenza was raging. She wrote: "My, how dead things are. The boys at the

168

camp are quarantined, and nothing seems to be lively." A childhood friend, Charles Wheeler, died of the flu. Anita went to visit his mother. "I had to cry, as Mrs. Wheeler was crying, and reminding me of the good times Charles, Ella, Katherine and I used to have." Two others claimed by the flu were mourned by the entire city, Father Paulinus Doran and his assistant, Father John Scheid.[118] They died within hours of each other.

On Sunday, Nov. 10, the *Caller* advised readers, "When peace comes, and peace is just around the corner, avoid crowds, but yell a little and insist that the bells ring and the whistles blow. It would be entirely too cow-like to chew a cud in silence when the world receives official notice." The next day, Monday, Nov. 11, the world did receive official notice. It was the end of the war to end war. On Nov. 11, Armistice Day, Anita wrote: "Oh, what a grand and glorious day is today! The war has ended. This morning the whistles blew, bells rang, and music began to play. We heard a lot of yelling. It was a parade and we sure did some running [to catch up]. I lost my money and goodness knows how many hairpins."[119] A few days later, the flu epidemic came to an end and the ban on public gatherings was lifted. Schools, theaters, soda fountains, domino parlors, shoe-shine stands were re-opened. On Nov. 16, a dance was held at the Soldiers Seashore Club to celebrate the end of the war and the end of the quarantine.[120]

Jim Moloney

MERRIMAN GRAVE

PLATE 2.1 – Dr. E. T. Merriman tended the sick and dying during the yellow fever epidemic in 1867 until he was stricken and died on August 12. He is buried in an overgrown grave in Old Bayview Cemetery.

170

Texas State Capitol

GOVERNOR DAVIS

PLATE 2.2 – Edmund J. Davis, a Union general in command of irregular cavalry units on the border during the Civil War, was elected governor after the war and led the "Radical Republicans" during Reconstruction in Texas.

OXCART

PLATE 2.3 – Two-wheeled oxcarts were standard vehicles for transporting goods in northern Mexico and South Texas in the 19th Century. They were used to carry hides and wool to the market in Corpus Christi.

MARKET HALL

PLATE 2.4 – A public-private building on Mesquite, between Schatzell and Peoples, served as City Hall, provided a public meeting space, housed the fire department and the city's meat and produce vendors. After 40 years, Market Hall was replaced by a three-story brick City Hall in 1911.

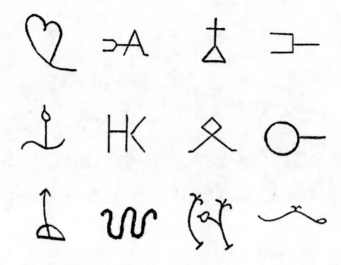

Jim Moloney

STOCK BRANDS

PLATE 2.5 – Ranchers marked their stock with unique brands to identify their property. Brands were registered with the county in brand books. These belonged to area ranchers (from top left) Juan Aguilar, William P. Aubrey and Henry L. Kinney (1848), Frederick Belden and H. A. Gilpin (1848), Robert Driscoll, Mifflin Kenedy (1868), Henrietta King, Henry L. Kinney (1848), Thomas Henry Mathis, John and Martha Rabb, Santa Gertrudis (King) Ranch; Andreas Villarreal, and Refugio Villarreal.

KENEDY

PLATE 2.6 – Mifflin Kenedy came to Texas soon after the start of the Mexican War as a steamboat captain on the Rio Grande carrying army supplies. He and his friend and eventual business partner, Richard King, grew rich on the profits of carrying cotton during the Civil War and invested in ranchland. Kenedy, the wealthy rancher, helped finance Uriah Lott's railroads.

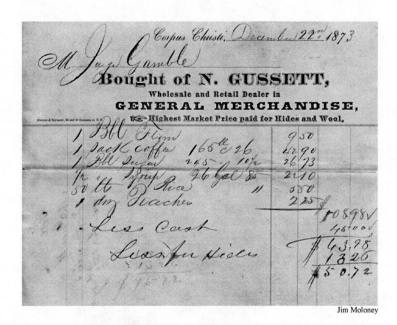

Jim Moloney

GROCERY RECEIPT

PLATE 2.7 – Receipt from Norwick Gussett's store to John Gamble is dated December 22, 1873. Gamble bought coffee, sugar, syrup, rice and canned peaches for $108.73 and paid $45.00 cash, $13.25 in hides and left a bill owed of $50.72.

ARANSAS

PLATE 2.8 – In 1875, the steamer *Aransas*, built to navigate the shallow Morris & Cummings Cut across Corpus Christi Bay, arrived in Corpus Christi and docked at the T-head portion of the Central Wharf.

BIRD'S EYE VIEW

PLATE 2.9 – Augustus Koch's bird's eye view of Corpus Christi was drawn in 1887. Koch, a German immigrant, learned his skill by drawing battlefield scenes from balloons during the Civil War. After the war, he traveled around the country producing bird's eye images on a subscription basis. His work was remarkably accurate, considering it was drawn from ground level. Larger reproductions than the one here show the buildings are accurate in scale and design.

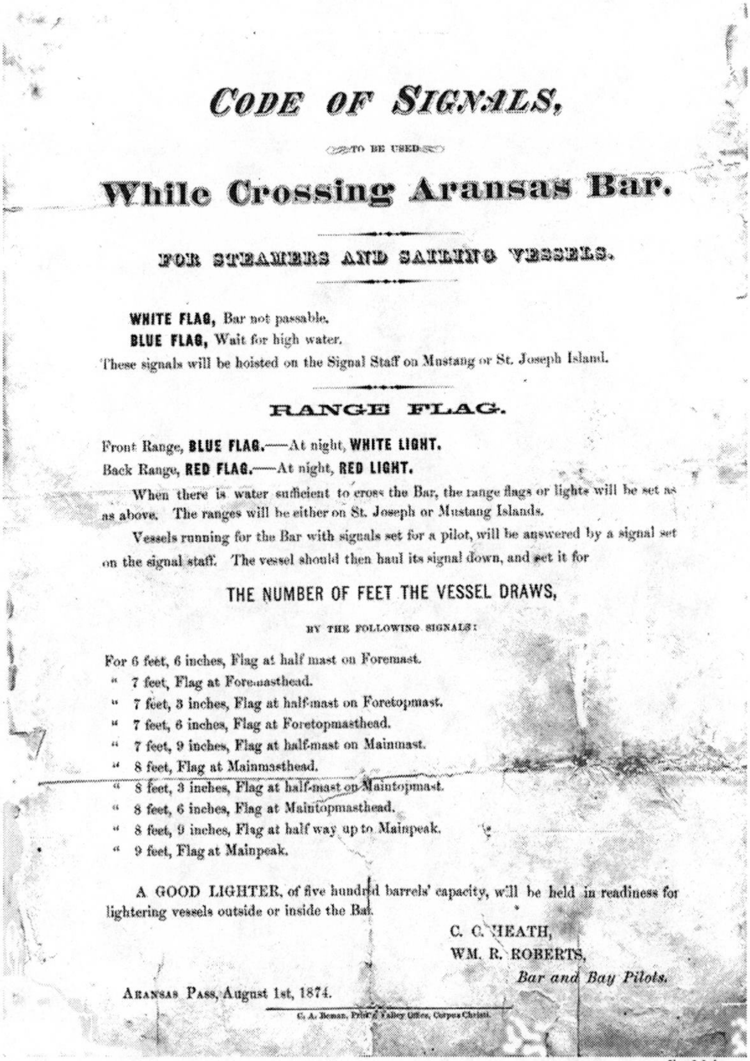

CODE OF SIGNALS,

TO BE USED

While Crossing Aransas Bar.

FOR STEAMERS AND SAILING VESSELS.

WHITE FLAG, Bar not passable.
BLUE FLAG, Wait for high water.

These signals will be hoisted on the Signal Staff on Mustang or St. Joseph Island.

RANGE FLAG.

Front Range, **BLUE FLAG.**——At night, **WHITE LIGHT.**
Back Range, **RED FLAG.**——At night, **RED LIGHT.**

When there is water sufficient to cross the Bar, the range flags or lights will be set as as above. The ranges will be either on St. Joseph or Mustang Islands.

Vessels running for the Bar with signals set for a pilot, will be answered by a signal set on the signal staff. The vessel should then haul its signal down, and set it for

THE NUMBER OF FEET THE VESSEL DRAWS,

BY THE FOLLOWING SIGNALS:

For 6 feet, 6 inches, Flag at half mast on Foremast.
" 7 feet, Flag at Foremasthead.
" 7 feet, 3 inches, Flag at half-mast on Foretopmast.
" 7 feet, 6 inches, Flag at Foretopmasthead.
" 7 feet, 9 inches, Flag at half-mast on Mainmast.
" 8 feet, Flag at Mainmasthead.
" 8 feet, 3 inches, Flag at half-mast on Maintopmast.
" 8 feet, 6 inches, Flag at Maintopmasthead.
" 8 feet, 9 inches, Flag at half way up to Mainpeak.
" 9 feet, Flag at Mainpeak.

A GOOD LIGHTER, of five hundred barrels' capacity, will be held in readiness for lightering vessels outside or inside the Bar.

C. C. HEATH,
WM. R. ROBERTS,
Bar and Bay Pilots.

ARANSAS PASS, August 1st, 1874.

C. A. Beman, Print & Valley Office, Corpus Christi.

Jim Moloney

BAR SIGNALS

PLATE 2.10 – When a ship arrived at the bar off the mouth of the Aransas Pass channel, flags or lights could be seen hanging on the signal staff on Mustang or St. Joseph's Island. Services of a bar pilot could be requested by flag signals hoisted on the vessel.

179

Jim Moloney

MERCER HOUSE

PLATE 2.11 – The Mercer cabin featured a bar pilot's lookout perch on the roof.

URIAH LOTT

PLATE 2.12 – After a successful career as a hide and wool dealer, Uriah Lott was involved in building all three railroads, connecting Corpus to the west, north and south.

181

OCEAN PARK

PLATE 2.13 – Elihu Harrison Ropes planned a six-mile residential development along the 30-foot high cliffs along the present Ocean Drive area.

ALTA VISTA

PLATE 2.14 – Ropes' 125-room Alta Vista Hotel, built in 1890 at Three Mile Point, was patterned after a resort hotel in Santa Monica, Calif. It burned in 1927.

ANDERSON WINDMILL

PLATE 2.15 – Captain John Anderson's windmill on Water Street was built in 1874. It was used to cut firewood and grind salt. The windmill was demolished in 1898.

EPWORTH-BY-THE SEA

PLATE 2.16 – Bathers at the Epworth encampment, with the bathhouse and tents on North Beach. Hundreds of Methodist families arrived each summer to attend Epworth by the Sea, a vacation mixed with Bible studies, religious activities and fun in the sun.

183

Jim Moloney

GEORGE H. PAUL CO.

PLATE 2.17 – Iowa land promoter George H. Paul sold hundreds of thousands of acres of South Texas ranchland to Midwestern farmers during the "homeseeker" era.

Murphy Givens

LAND EXCURSION

PLATE 2.18 – George H. Paul stands in a buggy carrying prospective land buyers in Robstown. His office building stands behind him.

184

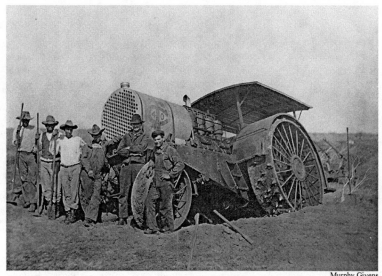

LAND CLEARING

PLATE 2.19 – A grubbing crew and tractor crew stand next to a kerosene-fueled tractor at Banquete. Mesquite roots were plowed up or dug out by grubbing crews.

ROAD BUILDING IN ST. PAUL

PLATE 2.20 – Mechanical road-graders replaced graders drawn by mules. The town of St. Paul, platted in 1910 on Welder Ranch land, was named for George H. Paul.

COUNTRY ROAD

PLATE 2.21 – An automobile navigates a muddy road between Alice and Kingsville in 1911. After a rain, dirt roads became almost impassable.

TAFT'S VISIT

PLATE 2.22 – President William Howard Taft is driven down Mesquite Street in a car provided by John G. Kenedy. Constable Ed Brennan, on a white horse, and Stewart Blackburn Terrell escorted Taft by horseback. The president visited Corpus Christi during his stay with his brother Charles on the Taft Ranch across the bay.

WELCOMING OUTFIT

PLATE 2.23 – Thomas Hickey wears the official outfit purchased for members of the reception committee chosen to welcome President Taft. The outfit included stovepipe hats, Prince Albert coats, and kid gloves.

1916 HURRICANE

PLATE 2.24 – Storm wreckage covers the shore in front of the Seaside Pavilion.

Jim Moloney

CAMP SCURRY

PLATE 2.25 – Soldiers line up for mess at Camp Scurry. Eight men lived in each of the 16' X 16' tents. After the U.S. entered World War I on April 6, 1917, thousands of soldiers trained at Camp Scurry for trench warfare on the Western Front.

CHAPTER 12

1919 storm - "Temporary" causeway to Portland - Streetcars reach the end of the line - Electric light plant burns - Sheriff tried for murder - Four men killed in brothel shootout - Pleasure Pier lives up to its name - City celebrates port opening - "Skyscrapers" built on the bluff

On the last day of August 1919, a tropical storm formed east of the Windward Islands and moved across the Atlantic into the Caribbean. It hit the Florida Keys on Sept. 10. The storm churned across the Gulf, pushing a storm surge one-foot high and 50 miles wide. The sea in front of the storm rose as much as 15 feet.

Saturday, Sept. 13, was a beautiful day in Corpus Christi, but people saw strange things. Schools of fish swam close to shore. It was said that people were gigging flounders with a cooking fork. Kids diving off the old Loyd's pier found the water filled with crabs. "We were not scared," one girl said, "but it was strange not to be able to take a stroke without touching a crab." Otherwise, it was a routine Saturday. A barnstormer offered airplane rides on North Beach. It being cotton-ginning time, bales of cotton crowded the cotton yard at Cooper's Alley and Chaparral. On the Central Wharf, at the cotton compress, some 14,000 bales were waiting to be shipped to cotton markets around the world.[1]

Lucy Caldwell, a teacher from Terrell, Texas, vacationing in Corpus Christi, decided not to go bathing in the bay that day. "The waves were not high, and the wind was not strong, but the water gave one the impression of a child denied something, and chafing in a suppressed manner."[2] That Saturday night, a dance was held on a waterfront pier. Couples walking home afterwards found the sidewalks black with crickets. You could hardly take a step without crunching crickets.[3] There were other unusual signs. Dogs and horses were unsettled, and tense. A hurricane (before they were named) with a 10-and-half-foot tide was heading for the islands. A drought had weakened the grass cover on the barrier islands, nature's protective seawall for the coast. The storm leveled dunes on the southern end of St. Joseph's and northern end of Mustang, opening a funnel on either side of the pass that aimed the storm tide straight at Corpus Christi.[4]

Mrs. Pauline Emmert was at Port Aransas visiting her parents, Captain and Mrs. Max Luther. Her father was the inspector of customs. When the water began to rise, her parents refused to evacuate the customs house, so Mrs. Emmert took her two-year-old daughter Maxine to find safety on higher ground. "The wind was so strong I could scarcely hold my baby. Water was everywhere. We waded knee-deep to one house, then another. About daylight Sunday morning, we reached the last house, Capt. Ned Mercer's. This building left its blocks and whirled out upon the waves just as lifeguards lifted Maxine and me into a boat to leave it." Capt. Luther and his wife were rescued from the customs house and joined their daughter in the sand hills, at a mott of salt cedars. They scooped out holes in the dunes to crouch in while the wind whipped them with wet sand. They were cold, frightened, and could hear shouting above the roar of the storm.[5]

On St. Joseph's, the ranch of Richard Wood was evacuated, with ranch hands and their families taken to the mainland on cattle barges.[6] Hands at Pat Dunn's ranch on Padre Island rode out the storm on Green Hill, the island's highest point. "We laid there flat and watched all that water, and prayed. It was like the whole ocean crashing in." As the storm swept across Harbor Island, it ruptured huge oil tanks and storage facilities. Massive timbers from the port facility were turned into battering rams when the storm surge hit Corpus Christi.

A generation of Corpus Christi citizens would remember Sunday, Sept. 14, as the day of the storm. There were other storms, over the years, but this was "The Storm." Late Saturday, it began to rain. Percy Reid and his family on North Beach were awakened by rain and high winds.[7] Lucy Caldwell, the vacationing teacher, slept soundly in her room at the Nueces Hotel until about two a.m., when she was awakened by wind and rain with a loud crashing noise as windows shattered on the hotel's fourth floor. There was no sleeping after that. On Sunday morning, as hotel guests went to breakfast, the bay was gray, with gray clouds crouching on the horizon. The rain was falling so thick you could hardly see across Water Street. "When I say the water was hurled," Lucy Caldwell observed, "I mean it literally. The wind threw the water of the bay exactly as you would dash a bucket of water on a fire."[8]

Mrs. W.A. Kieberger, her husband, and three-month old baby went down for breakfast in the hotel dining room. "As we sat down, Bill said, 'Now, let's eat a good breakfast; we don't know when we'll get another one.' I hadn't guessed what was happening, but my husband seemed to know what was ahead of us." As they finished eating, water was spreading across the dining room floor.[9]

On North Beach, Percy Reid called the weather bureau, but the report was that there would be a 40-miles-per-hour gale, with no immediate danger. That was abruptly changed after a drop in the barometric pressure. At 9:45 a.m., the first warning to evacuate low-lying areas was issued. North Beach, only five feet above sea level, was certainly low-lying. The water rose, the wind gathered force, and by noon a foot of water covered Chaparral.[10] Mrs. Marion Clemmer and husband Almyr were at the home of her parents, Mr. and Mrs. Eli Merriman, on Water Street. The house was leaking from the heavy rain, so Mrs. Clemmer took down the imported drapes and spread sheets over the piano. Her husband went out to feed the chickens, and came back yelling, "The bay is coming in!"

They ran out into chest-high water and made it to the State National Bank on Mesquite, where they joined other wet and scared refugees.[11]

Matt Pelegrino, who lived on Mesquite, took his mother and four sisters to the Maxwell Dunne funeral home on Mesquite. Deciding that wasn't going to be a safe place, they went to the high school on the bluff. People came into the school throughout the night. A baby boy, covered with oil, was brought in. They found him floating in a tub. Pellegrino said they put grease on the baby to get the oil off. "Later that night, a woman came in, covered with oil, her hair all greasy. All she would say was, 'Where's my baby?' And sure enough, it was her baby."[12] At the Nueces Hotel, lobby furniture floated in water filled with storm debris. Lucy Caldwell reported that someone said a dead horse floated in, but she didn't see it. The hotel staff, wearing bathing suits, would dive under the water, checking to see if bodies of storm victims washed in.[13] Miss Caldwell and other hotel guests spent that night huddled in the halls on the upper floors. There was no light except for the brief flare of struck matches. They listened to the howling wind and the sounds of the storm; children cried, and mothers shushed them. There was no food or drinking water.[14] At the courthouse, people slept on floors, desks, benches. Two women gave birth on the third floor during the night. About midnight, several men went to the roof; all they could see was an expanse of water, with the line between the sea and shore obliterated by the storm.[15]

Past noon on North Beach, 10-year-old Ted Fuller's family left their house in rising waters. His father told Ted to go to higher ground, to a house west of the railroad. His father and 14-year-old brother and mother went looking for a safer place. Ted, his aunt, sister, and a soldier took refuge in an empty house. "The rain and spray were coming down in sheets," Ted said. "We realized the house to the east of us was being pushed toward us. It was the Lerick home. As it came alongside, the Lerick family came out and waded to our porch. We had chairs on top of the chests and tables to stay above the water."[16]

The former Beach Hotel (later named the Breakers) was leased by the government to use as U.S. General Hospital No. 15, a rehabilitation facility for soldiers wounded in World War I. The roof was swept away, the basement flooded, windows blown out, but the building was standing. More than 100 refugees were taken in during the storm. One of those was five-year-old Lemmawayne Burnett. Her father took her, her sister and mother to the hospital, where they rode out the storm. "I'm sure my parents were terrified, but we sat on the beds, and the soldiers told us stories. You could hear the storm and ever so often, a big wave would smash into the windows."[17]

Soldiers of I Company, 37th Infantry, occupied tents on North Beach.[18] The soldiers sought refuge in homes and other buildings. The commanding officer, Capt. B. M. Egeland, and his wife climbed on a makeshift raft. They were swept into the bay, holding on to each other.[19] At the Spohn hospital on North Beach, operated by Sisters of the Incarnate Word, an editor from McAllen said it was the most horrible night that could be imagined. "Wing after wing of the hospital was swept away. Once we were all huddled in the rear portion of the building and the Sisters were saying their prayers in concert. I did not know how to say them their way, and I was sorry, for it was a time for prayer."[20] As the storm began to tear away one wing, Sister M. Thais went back to check on a paralyzed patient. Her body was later found washed ashore at Portland.[21]

The home of Bob Hall was being pulled apart. Hall, his wife, and his parents escaped through a second-floor window into water 15 to 20 feet deep. They clung for dear life to storm wreckage. "My husband's parents, being feeble, were the first to drown," Mrs. Hall said. "They were swept off a piece of a house and drowned, with us helpless to aid them." She watched others swallowed by the storm. Mrs. Terrell Brooks, wife of a railroad conductor, tied one of her babies to her with a rope. She was on a piece of wreckage. The baby was swept overboard and the rope pulled Mrs. Brooks under behind it. "Mr. Brooks, exhausted from the struggle and disheartened at losing his wife and baby, was swept off. He drowned before my eyes."[22]

With the storm raging, Percy Reid, his wife, and five-year-old son jumped from the second story of their home on North Beach into 10 feet of violently swirling water. Mrs. Reid grabbed a piece of driftwood for a raft. She saw the family collie, Scotch, on another raft. She whistled to him and he left his raft and swam to hers. Mrs. Reid and her dog were swept into Nueces Bay by the force of the storm. Her clothes became a sail in the wind; she found she could hold on better after she tore her clothes off. Fighting against the wind and the waves, at one point she lost her grip on the raft and slipped into the water. The dog got a grip on her hair with his teeth, and pulled her back to safety. Time and again, in the fury of the storm, she slipped from the raft, and each time the dog saved her. Finally, the dog was knocked off the raft by passing timber. Soon afterwards, the raft struck land and Mrs. Reid crawled ashore and covered herself with the warm sand of mother earth.[23]

Mr. and Mrs. W.P. Helscher and their daughter Fern were in a house west of the Government Hospital when the storm struck. When the building disintegrated, the Helschers clung to a piece of rooftop. They were separated in the water and, as the storm moved them apart, Helscher yelled to his wife and daughter: "Goodbye, I'll see you in the morning."[24]

Ted Fuller, 10, his 18-year-old sister Esther, and his aunt found refuge in a house west of the embankment. The walls began to move apart. His aunt "Doshie" got her hand caught in the parting wall and it was crushed when the walls closed together; three fingers were severed. The storm abated as the eye passed. They were standing on pieces of furniture stacked on top of each other, their heads near the ceiling in a thin layer of space. Suddenly, after the lull, the wind, water and waves began to rise again. Aware that the house was on the verge of collapse, they escaped through a hole in the ceiling. The people in the house struggled against each other to get out first. Ted's sister Esther yelled at one of the men, "Let Ted out! He's just a little boy!"[25]

The building was falling apart as Ted finally made it out. People held on to the roofs of three houses. They fought during the fury of the storm to stay afloat. At one point, Ted saw his aunt Doshie drown. She threw her arms up and screamed. "Her voice was piercing, even above the sound of the storm." As Ted and his sister were forced to abandon the roof, a large floor of a house came into view. Fuller thought it might have been the floor from their own house. "We swam to this new raft and scrambled toward the center of it. By now we were seeing nothing but flashes of lightning. It was terrifying to see in a flash of lightning an enormous wave poised above us. It was equally terrifying to feel our raft heave and know we were going to be submerged for as long as our breath would last."[26]

Wave after wave crashed over their raft, as if determined to devour them. Storm-tossed timbers, lumber, telephone poles, all crashed into those fighting to stay afloat on makeshift rafts. The debris knocked some people into the water, while it provided others with a means of survival. During that long night, Ted was partly unconscious. His sister Esther would hold his head out of the water. At one point, he watched his schoolmate Billy Lerick drown. Ted awoke from a deep sleep. It was Monday morning. His sister Esther was sitting beside him on the remains of their raft. They were floating among the tops of mesquite trees on the back end of Nueces Bay.[27]

Those who survived the enormous force of the storm in the bay were usually found naked; they tore off their clothes to reduce wind resistance. The storm subsided near dawn early Monday morning. The fine mansions on North Beach were destroyed; only three structures, from hundreds, were left standing. Many of the stores between the bluff and the bay were destroyed, along with 900 homes. Many thousands of bales of cotton were scattered on the streets. Mud and muck from the bay bottom and huge mounds of storm debris, sheared-off lumber and incongruous bathtubs and fine furnishings from hotels and homes littered the downtown area. That Monday morning, after the storm, dazed people wandered about in mismatched clothes looking like refugees. Guests at the Nueces Hotel found two feet of water in the lobby. The scene outside was a mass of wreckage. Jumbled together were houses, cars, boats, bales of cotton, and bodies of horses, cows, seagulls, people, all covered with oil. Lucy Caldwell described it as a sickening sight. Men at the hotel waded through the water to the bluff and returned with buckets of water and some bread and cheese. All day, people showed up looking for lost relatives. A man came to the hotel who had floated with his wife and baby for hours, and finally lost them. A boy came in who had seen his mother, father and sisters drown.[28]

At the U.S. Government Hospital on North Beach, rescuers arrived in rowboats. Lemmawayne Burnett, five years old, and her mother were taken to the courthouse, where they looked at rows of bodies in the basement. Many of those who drowned, as well as many survivors, washed up in the back area of Nueces Bay.[29] The rescuers at the Rachal ranch at White Point found one woman's body hanging by her hair in a mesquite tree, a mesquite thorn piercing her neck. They found one woman dead on a roof, her hair tangled in nails. They found a dead cow with a rope on it floating in the bay; as they pulled it in, they found a woman's body at the other end of the rope. Bodies were stacked up 50 at a time for burial. Gasoline was used to clean the bodies. Ranch workers were kept busy digging mass graves. In Rockport, people found snakes everywhere; they were raked into piles and burned.[30]

A relief train from Brownsville brought food and emergency supplies. Relief kitchens were set up by the Red Cross at three locations to feed the homeless, at the Courthouse, the high school, and the First Presbyterian Church. A relief boat with 100 tons of food arrived from Galveston. Every able-bodied man in town was required to clean up storm debris. Buried among the storm rubble were bodies covered with oil. It would take a week before the burying would be completed. There was no drinking water, no electricity, no trolleys. The city was placed under martial law. Every citizen in town was required to register and no one was allowed into the storm area without a military pass. There was no *Caller* on Monday; the big press on the first floor was damaged by the tidal wave. But, when printing resumed in Kingsville, the *Caller* told the stories of those who survived and those who died. Some of the bodies could not be identified. The papers were filled with descriptions, such as: "Unidentified white girl, 14 or 15, wearing a Wall of Troy ring on the fourth finger of the left hand."[31]

Theodore ("Ted") Fuller and his sister Esther washed up on the northeast side of the Nueces River, at the back of Nueces Bay, 18 miles from North Beach. They were taken to Sinton. "On Friday morning, we were put into a car and taken to the station," Ted wrote. "A train had just pulled in and there stood Papa. It was a total surprise to us for communication with Corpus Christi had been completely out . . . His way of telling us about our family was to say, 'Brother is waiting for us in Corpus Christi. He will be eager to see you two.' 'And Mama? Is she there too?' He looked over me with his eyes on the horizon as he answered. Papa had a clear, deep, voice which was soothing. 'No, son, she is with Aunt Doshie and we won't see them for a long, long time. They are in heaven.' "[32]

Casualties for the area, including Rockport, Port Aransas, Aransas Pass, totaled 357. The official death toll in Corpus Christi was 284, but many believed the actual toll was somewhere between 500 and 600 because many bodies were buried in mass graves and the city may have encouraged a deliberate undercount; only identified bodies were counted. Many people simply disappeared, never to be heard from again. Those were not counted. The 1919 hurricane was the greatest disaster in Corpus Christi's history, but the widespread destruction galvanized the city, pushing it to greater exertion to gain a deepwater port and protective seawall. The 1920s found Corpus Christi trying to recover. The downtown, the old "beach section," was hardly recognizable, but it was not a city broken in spirit. A civic fundraising campaign increased its goal from $10,000 to $15,000 after $9,000 was pledged the first three hours. This determination would lead to building the breakwater, the port, and the seawall. In the wake of tragedy came dynamic change.[33]

When the fancy new concrete causeway across Nueces Bay first opened to traffic in 1915, it was the pride of the city. It was damaged in the 1916 hurricane, after which it was repaired, and then destroyed in the 1919 storm. For two years after the hurricane, people of Portland, Gregory and Taft had to travel about 40 miles around Nueces Bay to reach Corpus Christi. There was opposition to the plan to replace the causeway, with some Corpus Christi merchants arguing that rather than bringing in new customers and commerce, the causeway would make it easier for Corpus Christi people to spend their money elsewhere.[*][34] But in 1921, a temporary wooden causeway was built, for the modest amount of $400,000, and opened to traffic on Oct. 8, 1921. It was a few feet above water level and at times the splashing of waves impeded traffic. It was a low, narrow, shaky wooden causeway that few thought would survive the next storm, but it lasted almost three decades.[35]

The storm also destroyed Corpus Christi's streetcar line, though not immediately, and there were other factors to blame, especially the increased sale of automobiles.[36] The city had a variety of makeshift, short-lived transit lines, dating back to the 1880s when mule-powered "herdies," a name taken from inventor Peter Herdic, ran from the Tex-Mex railroad depot to the St. James Hotel on Chaparral. The city briefly had a steam-powered railway during the Ropes boom in the 1890s; the line ran from the downtown to the Alta Vista Hotel. When the Ropes boom collapsed in 1893, the railway was sold at a sheriff's sale to Norwick Gussett. He replaced the dummy-steam engine with mule teams. Gussett sold the line in 1898 to P. A. Graham, who cut the system back to one mule car. The new owner operated the line to suit his fancy. On days he felt like it, he would run the mule car up and down

---

[*] A reminder that there were still those in the city would sit on the coat tails of progress.

195

Chaparral. On days when his energy flagged or he was nursing a hangover, he was hard to find. After several days absence, he would return and hitch up his mules to the one open-sided car. He would transport women on shopping trips down Chaparral, then vanish until the mood struck him again. The line was shut down for good in 1900.[37]

The city's first real electric trolley line was started in 1910 by Daniel Hewett, who came from Tyler. The line was called the Corpus Christi and Interurban Railway. Hewett laid tracks on wooden blocks on unpaved streets and copper wires were strung overhead. He had four railway cars and bought electric power from the Peoples Light Co. for three cents a kilowatt hour. The first run was made on March 28, 1910.

Within a year, Hewett sold the line to the Heinly brothers of Denver. V.S. (Vinton Sweet) Heinly ran the operation; his brother Earl would visit to check on his investment. The Heinlys built a power plant that ran on Mexican oil.[38] Like Hewett, the Heinlys became discouraged and sold out in 1914 to a Philadelphia syndicate. The new owners added eight new cars and extended the lines. They changed the name to the Corpus Christi Railway and Light Co. The fare was a nickel. The line was a losing venture until Camp Scurry opened in 1916. With thousands of soldiers at the camp, the trolley business took off. Between the summer of 1916 and March of 1917, the number of riders exceeded one million. The trolley system had two more profitable years before the 1919 storm struck. The railway cars and rail lines were badly damaged and the power plant knocked out.[39]

The system was put back in operation on Nov. 19, 1919, but the flush times were gone, killed by the storm and the beginning love affair with the automobile. An article in a 1917 issue of the *Electric Railway Journal* was headlined, "Meeting the Menace of the Private Automobile in Corpus Christi." The writer said more people were buying cars, now that the city had paved streets. The writer also bemoaned the fact that "neighborly feeling in Corpus Christi is so developed that even the stranger who is observed waiting for a streetcar is invited to step in and ride in a private automobile." After the storm, the streetcar line went into receivership and was purchased by new owners. Sporadic attempts to revive it in the 1920s failed.[40]

A fire in the early morning hours on Nov. 20, 1921 during a thunderstorm and fierce norther destroyed the downtown power generating plant, leaving the city without electricity, in complete darkness, and with no power to operate the streetcar system. After the fire, the *Caller* hooked up a Fordson tractor with a belt drive to the press and with careful "driving" got the presses operating.[41] This trick was learned after the 1919 storm. A line of automobiles operating a "jitney" service replaced the streetcars.[42]

At the time of the fire, Corpus Christi's electric power service was 30 years old, dating back to 1890 when the Corpus Christi Electric Company was organized by Dr. Alfred Heaney, J.W. Stayton and T. P. Rivera. The power plant was located in a corrugated iron building on Water Street. The company was sold and reorganized in 1907 as the Corpus Christi Electric and Ice Company. Electric service was then provided only at night, and only for a few customers.

A competing firm, the Peoples Light Company, was formed by Clark Pease, John G. Kenedy, and George Blucher. Each company had about 300 customers. A third power generating plant was built by the Heinly brothers after they purchased the streetcar system. In 1914, all three plants and the streetcar system were purchased by a Philadelphia consortium. The system became the Corpus Christi Railway and Light System. New diesel engines were installed in the oldest of the three plants, the Corpus Christi Electric and Ice Company plant, and the other two were dismantled. In the 1919 storm, the plant was wrecked and service disrupted for a week. A temporary shed was built over the Ball engine and power was restored on a limited basis.[43]

After the fire, temporary electric service was resumed quickly and a new building was started. The electric plant could not provide enough power for the heavy evening load, so a different section of the town was left without power each night. The system was sold four years later to the Central Power and Light Company.[44]

The nation went dry on Jan. 16, 1920. The 18th amendment banned the manufacture, sale and transportation of liquor, but the country was never dry. Prohibition ushered in the era of bootleggers, homemade gin, and smuggled hooch. It prohibited those who were already inclined that way and may have actually encouraged those less inclined to abstinence. It was a national joke.

Nueces County was ahead of its time. It went dry four years earlier when the county voted in Prohibition in 1916. Remote Padre Island was a favorite landing place for rum-runners and bootleggers bringing in illegal cargo from Mexico. Louis Rawalt, who lived in a wooden shack on Padre Island, spotted gunnysacks partly covered with sand. It was not uncommon for some captain to dump his cargo when the Coast Guard approached. Rawalt investigated and discovered that the burlap sacks contained tin cans and inside each can was a bottle of "Old Hospitality" bourbon. Rawalt salvaged 110 sacks and hid them behind sand dunes. He filled a duffle bag with 72 bottles and headed to Port Isabel, at the southern tip of the island. The ferry captain was suspicious, so Rawalt told him what he had found and gave him a few bottles. Rawalt took the rest to sell in Port Isabel. On his way back, his pocket full of money, he saw the ferry captain returning in what appeared to be a loaded-down pickup. He had followed Rawalt's tracks into the dunes and recovered the hidden stash. There wasn't a bottle left.[45]

In Corpus Christi, one bootlegger on the Hill kept track of the money owed him by making a mark on the wall by the buyer's name. The bootlegger showed up one evening to find the owner of the shack had it painted and the bootlegger's list of debts owed him were all wiped clean.[46]

A sensational murder case dominated the news in October, 1922. Fred Roberts, a prominent real estate dealer who was believed to be a Klan leader, was shot to death in his car in front of a store on Railroad Avenue (later renamed Kinney) at Staples Street. The store was owned by Mr. and Mrs. G. E. Warren. The chain of events began when Sheriff Frank G. Robinson arrived, he asked Warren how business was going. Warren said it was slow. "That's how it is with you Ku Kluxers," said the sheriff. Deputy Sheriff Joe Acebo, with the sheriff, piped in, "Warren is a Ku Kluxer. Everybody says he is." The sheriff said, "You are a Ku Kluxer, aren't you, Warren? By God, you know you are." The sheriff slapped the storekeeper, who grabbed two bottles, as if to defend himself. The sheriff and deputy left the store and went across the street, leisurely watching the Warren store, loitering with intent.

Mrs. Warren called the police. Police Chief Monroe Fox showed up and found Sheriff Robinson and Deputy Acebo calmly talking across the street. He told the Warrens the sheriff was minding his own business and he could do nothing unless the Warrens were willing to sign a complaint. Warren then called Fred Roberts, who came to the store, talked to the Warrens, then went back to his car. He started the engine and Sheriff Robinson walked over, reached in, and turned off the ignition. Then, witnesses said later, he stepped back and fired three shots at Roberts from his .45 caliber Colt revolver. From the passenger side of the car, Acebo fired one shot.[47]

The slaying of Fred Roberts caused an uproar. The *Caller* printed a page one editorial urging people to stay calm. County Judge Hugh Sutherland and Mayor P.G. Lovenskiold asked the governor to send Texas Rangers. Ranger Capt. Frank Hamer arrived with a five-man force. There is some dispute about whether "the murderers" and some 30 or 40 armed henchmen barricaded themselves in the courtroom and whether Hamer actually kicked in the double doors of the courthouse when he arrived, supposedly declaring, "I'm Frank Hamer, Texas Ranger. I have warrants for the arrest of those involved in the murder of Fred Roberts. The rest of you put up those guns and get the hell out of here." That account is told in the Hamer biography, *I'm Frank Hamer,* but is not supported by contemporary newspaper accounts. Sheriff Robinson, Acebo and two others were indicted for murder. The trial was moved to Laredo on a change of venue. The jury brought back its verdict on Jan. 13, 1923. All four defendants were found not guilty. Frank Robinson's daughter, Marion Uehlinger, said the former sheriff so feared Klan retaliation that he fled to Mexico and remained there for a decade.[48]

Three years later, a shootout in front of a house of sporting girls also involved law enforcement officers instigating the violence. It was Sunday at sundown, July 5, 1925 when three men left Bessie Miller's, a house of prostitution on Sam Rankin Street. One was Paul McAllister, a game warden, another was George Ryder of San Diego, a third was Rufus

McMurray of Three Rivers. As McAllister and Ryder were getting into their car, Constable C.M. Bisbee and Deputy Constable R.R. Bledsoe drove up and angry words were passed. Constable Bisbee looked at Ryder and asked, "Where you going?"

"San Diego," Ryder replied.

"No, you're not," said Bisbee. "You're under arrest."

"What for?"

"It don't make no difference 'what for'," said Bisbee. "I can lock you up for any reason I want to." Bisbee said he was tired of seeing Ryder drunk, making a nuisance of himself.

"You can't be," said Ryder. "I don't get drunk."

"You're a liar," said Bisbee.

Shots were fired and the shooting continued until five men were down on the ground. The sporting girls in Bessie Miller's watched from the windows. The shootout left four men dead: officers C.M. Bisbee and R.R. Bledsoe, game warden Paul McAllister, and George Ryder of San Diego. The fifth man, Rufus McMurray of Three Rivers, was seriously wounded but survived.

Detectives learned that Deputy Constable Bledsoe started the affray when he shot Ryder in the leg, then shot the game warden McAllister, who fell to the ground in getting out of the car. Then it became a general shootout. For weeks, people would drive down Sam Rankin Street and point out Bessie Miller's yard, the site of the bloody shootout.[49]

In 1922, the city built the Pleasure Pier at the foot of Peoples Street, at the modest cost of $8,200. It became a favorite place for Sunday strolling and fishing. The newspaper reported that the pier was one of the first places visited by tourists "who want to get out over the water and watch the activities of boats and boatmen." From 1922 until it was dismantled for the seawall, the Pleasure Pier lived up to its name. Like the old Central Wharf in its time, the Pleasure Pier was ideal for an evening stroll, for air and exercise, with the stars reflected in the waters of the bay.[50]

A train called the Blackland Special pulled out of Corpus Christi on Nov. 9, 1924. On board were 105 farmers and businessmen from the Corpus Christi area, many from Robstown, all wearing pearl-gray Stetsons. The group toured north and central Texas, promoting blackland farming of South Texas. They would parade through a town and rent a movie house to show a film called "Land of Plenty." The film touted carrots "that make your hair curl" and "beets that put roses in your cheeks." The Blackland Special included three special rail cars carrying exhibits of cotton, grain and other crops grown in the "black soil" of Nueces, San Patricio, Jim Wells and Kleberg counties. It was the idea of a young Robstown cotton-grower, Maston Nixon, who would later build Corpus Christi's first towering office building on the bluff. The Blackland Special was called the greatest promotion ever launched for any one section of the state. An estimated 55,000 Texans saw the movie, "Land of Plenty," 65,000 viewed the agricultural exhibits, and within five years 100,000 new acres were brought into production, in large part as a direct result of the Blackland Special.[51]

From Henry Kinney's founding of Kinney's Rancho in 1839 into the 1920s, much of the town's creative energy and civic drive focused on gaining a deepwater port.[52] That effort intensified after the 1919 storm devastated the city.[53] The big event of the century, for Corpus Christi, came seven years to the day that the city was hit by the 1919 storm. On Sept. 14, 1926, the Port of Corpus Christi was opened and the city became a gateway to international trade and commerce.[54] The modern city Corpus Christi became and the economy it depends upon show how important that fight was. It was the climax of a long struggle.

Corpus Christi's problem from the beginning was that it was 20 miles from deep water, separated by a shallow, tricky, if not treacherous, bay. The city's efforts to overcome that obstacle to become a major seaport began after the city's founding, from the time supplies for Zachary Taylor's army in 1845 had to be lightered over mudflats and clogged oyster beds in Corpus Christi Bay.[55] U.S. Grant wrote that the lighter transporting troops from Shellbank Island to Corpus Christi "had to be dragged over the bottom when loaded."[56]

In 1848, the *New York Sun* scolded the army for not dredging a channel.[57] But the army decided it would be easier to move army supplies for Texas forts through the growing port of Indianola on Matagorda Bay.[58] The city in 1854 issued $50,000 in bonds to dredge a five-foot channel; the effort proceeded in fits and starts and was abandoned with the Civil War.[59] After the war, Corpus Christi watched as Indianola became the port city it sought to be. Wharves, stretching a quarter mile into Matagorda Bay, were piled high with cotton, hides, tallow, pecans, and wheat. It was a great seaport that could compete with Galveston. Two new arrivals in Texas in 1868 found Indianola booming, with freight wagons leaving daily for San Antonio, with stores selling anything a frontiersman could want.[60] Corpus Christi tried to compete, but ships bringing in goods had to anchor at the bar outside the Aransas Pass where cargo was transferred, lightered, to shallow-draft boats. The Morris and Cummings Cut, completed in 1874, brought the first ocean-going vessels to the city's waterfront, but ships were getting bigger and the Morris and Cummings Cut was not deep enough, and the zig-zag route added 10 miles to the 22 mile trip from the Aransas Pass channel to the Corpus Christi bayfront. In the narrow channel, ships collided with the sides of the banks, losing cargo in accidents.[61]

In 1875, Indianola was hit by a killer storm and the city and the port were all but destroyed. Indianola was rebuilt, but it was hit by another hurricane 11 years later and it never recovered. The trade of Matagorda Bay shifted to Corpus Christi Bay.[62] Corpus Christi's struggle to replace Indianola as the

200

major port in the western Gulf got a boost with the election of John Nance Garner of Uvalde to Congress. In the Democratic primary race in 1902, Jim Wells, the Brownsville political boss, sent a telegram to Corpus Christi saying, "Garner's our man." Garner won the primary race and faced a Corpus Christi Republican in the general election. Garner won again.[63] On Jan. 26, 1903, Garner arrived in Corpus Christi for a victory celebration at the St. James Hotel. A meeting was held in the Doddridge Building. Garner promised he would do his best to get whatever Corpus Christi wanted because it supported him in the election over one of its own. "What is the one thing dearest to your heart?" he asked the crowd. H. R. Sutherland Sr. said, "We want a straight channel dredged through Turtle Cove* in the bay to give Corpus Christi a deepwater connection to the Gulf."[64]

Garner went to work on the one thing dearest to Corpus Christi's heart of hearts. It was a tall order. Washington policy dictated that Texas needed only one major port, and that was at Galveston. Garner learned to play the game. (He was an excellent poker player; in one special session of Congress he won $15,000 from his fellow members.) Garner was able to overcome entrenched opposition; he got an appropriation for a survey of Turtle Cove and convinced the number two man in the Corps of Engineers to break with government policy and support Corpus Christi's effort. Garner got funds appropriated in a 1907 bill to dredge a channel from the Aransas Pass between Port Aransas and St. Joseph's through Turtle Cove, but it was a shallow channel.[65] Then, in 1909, a special board of engineers surveyed possible port sites and found that the Turtle Cove mud bank made dredging a deep channel across the bay too expensive, and Corpus Christi, 22 miles from the Aransas Pass channel, was about as far from the sea as a seaport could be. The engineers concluded that Harbor Island off Port Aransas, which was 20 miles closer to the Gulf, was the best location. That's where the port would be built.[66]

Corpus Christi's backers, said Roy Miller, took this setback in stride; they did not "sulk in their tents." They were convinced the time would come when nature would demonstrate the unfitness of the Harbor Island location.[67] Fate did take a hand with the storm of 1919. It wiped out the dock and warehouse facilities on Harbor Island.[68] Even though much of Corpus Christi's downtown was also destroyed, city boosters were able to argue that Harbor Island was in a more exposed position and that Corpus Christi, with a breakwater, would be a safer location for a port.[69]

A new Corps of Engineers' study focused on four sites for a deepwater port, a port that would be financed in large part by the federal government: Port Aransas, Rockport, Aransas Pass, and Corpus Christi. Corpus Christi's main argument was that it was the largest city, with a population of 10,522 to

---

* Turtle Cove was the name for the extensive mudflats that effectively blocked navigation between the Aransas Pass channel and Corpus Christi Bay.

Rockport's 1,545 and Aransas Pass's 1,569. Corpus Christi had four railroads, three banks, and natural gas had been discovered nearby. Corpus Christi had several things in its favor. The hurricanes of 1916 and 1919 demonstrated that low-lying Port Aransas, Aransas Pass and Rockport were more vulnerable than Corpus Christi, where much of the city was built on the bluff, the highest elevation on the Gulf Coast. Corpus Christi's biggest disadvantage was that it would cost $5 million to dredge a 25-foot channel across the bay; by comparison, it would only cost $1.6 million to dredge to Aransas Pass and $2 million to Rockport.[70] The recommendation of which city should get a port and deepwater connection to the Gulf would be made by the district engineer of the Corps of Engineers, located at Galveston.

Corpus Christi had articulate and persuasive promoters. It sent its former mayor, Roy Miller, to lobby in Washington. It already had a strong ally in Congress with Garner. Robert J. Kleberg of King Ranch organized a committee to raise $1 million in navigation district bonds to build port facilities.[71] It was never a sure thing for Corpus Christi. Because of the cheaper costs and the closer location to the Gulf, many thought Aransas Pass had it in the bag until a bond issue to finance a deepwater port was rejected by Aransas Pass voters. That rejection opened the way for Corpus Christi.[72]

Perhaps something else made the port possible. Maybe it wasn't exactly a fair fight; perhaps the city violated the Queensberry rules. M. Harvey Weil, who served for years as the port's attorney, once explained how Corpus Christi was able to beat out the competing cities for the port designation by gaining the support of the district engineer of the Corps, Major L.M. Adams of the Galveston headquarters. One December day in 1920, Weil wrote, Roy Miller took Adams on a hunting trip on King Ranch. It was a hot day for December and they drove around all day before Adams shot a nice buck. That night at the "big house" Miller took a bottle of bourbon to Adams' room. After a few drinks, Miller came out and whispered to banker Richard King, "We've got it." Adams returned to Galveston and recommended that the best place for a new port was Corpus Christi.[*][73] Perhaps a deal was made. But after the devastation of the 1919 storm, after Corpus Christi's valiant effort to rebuild, no one with a generous heart could deny that the city deserved its long-sought reward, some mitigation for nature's havoc.

On May 22, 1922, President Warren G. Harding signed a bill that included an appropriation to begin dredging a channel to Corpus Christi. A telegram from Roy Miller to Corpus Christi officials said, "We win!"[74] Construction began in the summer of 1924 with $1.8 million in federal funds; $2 million in state aid; and $1 million raised locally by the new Nueces County Navigation District.[75]

The breakwater was the first step. In constructing the breakwater, a

---

[*] Was a deal made? The answer will probably never be known, but when Adams retired from the Corps of Engineers in 1930, he was named director of the port of Corpus Christi. If there was a deal, it worked, with lasting and satisfactory results.

railroad trestle was built into the bay in the curved shape the breakwater would become. Granite rocks quarried near San Antonio were hauled to the end of the line, where a barge-mounted crane dropped the boulders to the bay floor. As the breakwater took shape, the rail lines were pulled up and the work backed its way toward town.[76] Work began on the turning basin (1,000 feet wide by 2,500 feet long) north of the city in Nueces Bay, followed by building the wharf and transfer sheds on the south side of the basin. Hall's Bayou was dredged to become the entrance to the port. A bascule lift bridge was built across the entrance channel to the turning basin, a place where boys in rolled-up pants liked to go crabbing.[77]

Port opening day on Sept. 14, 1926 was the biggest celebration in Corpus Christi since the Lone Star Fair 74 years before. Special trains brought guests from Houston and San Antonio and excursion boats arrived from Galveston and Beaumont. A parade whipped up enthusiasm in the downtown and ended up at Cargo Dock 1. Sirens blew, flags waved, people cheered. Gov. Pat Neff, John Nance Garner and Roy Miller spoke. Miller called the new port a thing of destiny and then, perhaps recalling the hurricanes that destroyed Indianola, said it was not "a child spawned by disaster." Miller said, "While it cannot and ought not to be said that the Port of Corpus Christi is a creature of circumstance or the child of disaster, it is undeniably true that the realization of a dream of more than half a century was hastened by the disastrous storm of Sept. 14, 1919."[78] The sleepy languor, as the cliché goes, of a fishing village would be gone forever and in its place would be the beginning of the growing, modern city. They were thrilled with the new port, the new industries moving in, the city's new sense of vitality. There was no sense of impending loss, no time for nostalgia; the town was ready for the future. It is another cliché, but it did mark the beginning of a new age.

Eli Merriman, the former longtime editor of the *Caller,* and a longtime advocate for deepwater, wrote, "It has been a long and hard fight, but we have seen our dreams come true."[79] The new port quickly began to change the city. Before the port opened, Merriman wrote, you could shoot a cannon down Chaparral and not worry about hitting anyone. The year after the port opened, Corpus Christi was filled with cotton producers, cotton buyers, cotton brokers, cotton exporters. One result of this boom was the need for office space. With the building of the port, Maston Nixon could see the need for new office space. Nixon, a go-getter, had pulled himself up by the bootstraps. His first job was to harness mules to ice wagons. He saved his money and invested in a cotton farm near Robstown. It was his idea in 1924 to promote "blackland farming" in the Coastal Bend, which opened up vast tracts of ranchland to agriculture because of the Blacklanders' odyssey. The year after the Blacklanders, Nixon began looking at the bluff as a site for an office building.[80]

Maston Nixon focused on property at Upper Broadway and Leopard. He got options on the site and brought in a partner from San Antonio, H. L.

Kokernut. Nixon and Kokernut ran ads announcing the construction of a new office building, the largest in the city. The ads said that when the concrete frame reached the 8th floor, if seven floors were rented, they would build to 10, and when it reached the 10th floor, if nine were rented, they would build to 12. The 12-story Nixon Building* opened on April 2, 1927. It was filled with cotton brokers and shipping firms.[81] From the towering Nixon Building on the city's highest ground, they could look down, in supervision as it were, over the downtown below.

After the Kokernut-Nixon venture, there was a rush to build new commercial structures on the bluff, where the stately mansions of the cattle barons and the city's wealthy citizens stood. Corpus Christi Bank & Trust built at Leopard and Tancahua. Perkins Brothers built a department store on the old Savage homestead on Leopard. Up and down Broadway, old homes were torn down to be replaced by modern buildings. Nixon looked across Leopard Street at the old Redmond house, built in the 1860s, and thought it would be a good spot for a hotel. He helped organize two companies, one in Corpus Christi to finance building the hotel, and one in San Antonio to run it. The result was the Plaza Hotel, which opened in May, 1929, giving the city two "skyscrapers" on the bluff.[82]

A major investor in the Plaza was Robert Driscoll, rancher and banker. After Robert's death, the Driscoll family interests were managed by his sister Clara Driscoll. There was a falling out between Clara and hotel chain owner Jack White, who had taken over the operation of the hotel and changed its name to the White Plaza. In time, the feud between Clara Driscoll and Jack White led to building another hotel on the bluff, but that was some years away.[83] Maston Nixon was responsible for, or a key figure in, constructing four major buildings on the bluff: the Nixon building, the White Plaza Hotel, the Robert Driscoll Hotel, and the Southern Minerals Corp. building, known as Somico, which much later became headquarters for H-E-B before the grocery chain moved its main office to San Antonio.[84] The old cattle baron mansions of Martha Rabb and Mifflin Kenedy and Henrietta King, with their pronounced sense of style, were the victims of this new development on the bluff. There would be no nostalgia, not for a long time, for this vanished world.

---

* It was renamed the Wilson Building after oilman Sam Wilson bought it in 1947. Wilson built the 21-story Wilson Tower five years later.

CHAPTER 13

Causeway opens Pat Dunn's island - Ben Garza heads LULAC - Wall Street crash ushers in Great Depression - Dance marathon on North Beach - Oil found in Saxet Field - La Fruta Dam collapses - "Old Ironsides" visits port - City gains its first chemical plant - President Roosevelt lands a tarpon - Seawall gives city a new look

The wooden Don Patricio Causeway opened to traffic on July 4, 1927, giving Corpus Christi easy access to Padre Island. The first car was driven across by Col. Sam Robertson, builder of the causeway, and riding with him was Lorine Jones Spoonts, president of the Corpus Christi Chamber of Commerce.[1] This first causeway took Corpus Christians across the Laguna Madre to enjoy the surf and sand of Padre Island, which had long been the cattle ranch of Patrick F. Dunn. The island was a remote place. Fishermen and hunters who wanted access had to get permission from one of Dunn's agents at Port Isabel or Corpus Christi.[2]

Visitors to the island could ford the shallow reefs of the Laguna Madre in wagons, buggies and by horseback. Padre Island had long been used as a route south. In the winter of 1845, Zachary Taylor's reconnaissance officers explored the island, looking for a route the army could take from Corpus Christi to the Rio Grande. Texas Rangers would travel down the island to get to Brownsville. One Ranger wrote that his company rode across the Laguna Madre. At the place where they crossed, it was about five miles across and "it looked as if they were going to sea on horseback." He wrote that the waves beat up against the horses' sides and it was all they could do to keep their six-shooters out of the saltwater.[3] Ernest Poenisch, a prominent farmer, told of driving a mule team across the laguna near Pita Island at Flour Bluff. Poenisch said they were late in the day coming back from the island and the sun reflected on the water in their eyes. They couldn't see enough to follow the reef across the laguna. They took a slanting course that took them into deeper water and they almost drowned. They were so exhausted when they finally reached shore they camped for the night rather than travel on home.[4] Trail boss Hub Polley was hired to drive a herd of cattle from Padre Island to Kansas. He and his trail hands crossed the Laguna Madre on horseback and rounded up 2,300 longhorns, which were forced to wade across the lagoon before starting on the trail.[5]

Dunn, called the Duke of Padre Island, owned an empire of sand, cattle and 112 miles of Gulf beaches. Over a 50-year span, from 1879 until 1929, he developed the island into a unique ranch, with cattle wading in the surf, with corrals made of driftwood. Dunn gave himself the title of duke. He received a letter from someone in England, with fancy titles after his name, so Dunn attached his own string of letters, D.P.I., which he told his lawyer stood for "Duke of Padre Island."[6] Dunn, when he was 21, moved his family's cattle to the island in 1879, a drought year. He bought out his brother and mother and called his ranch "El Rancho de Don Patricio."[7]

Dunn wasn't the first to use the island as a ranch; cattle had been on the island from the earliest times. Padre Nicolas Balli, for whom the island was named, began a cattle ranch on the island's southern end from 1806 until he died in 1829. His nephew took over after that and the Balli ranch continued to flourish until 1844. Then came John Singer, whose brother Merritt invented the sewing machine. The Singer family shipwrecked on the island in 1847. The Singers began running cattle in the same area of Padre Balli's Santa Cruz ranch, 20 miles up from the island's southern tip. They moved out at the beginning of the Civil War.[8] In 1874, John King and W. N. Staples established a beef packing house next to a deep channel at Corpus Christi Pass. This part of the pass became known as Packery Channel. The packery was gone when Dunn began grazing cattle on the island in 1879.[9]

Richard King and Mifflin Kenedy (and before them a man named Healey) ran cattle on the island.[10] Pat Dunn, however, turned it into a special kind of ranch, unique to Texas and no doubt unique to the world, with cow pens made of mahogany driftwood and longhorn cattle grazing among the dunes and wading in the surf. The year after Dunn moved to the island, he bought 400 cows from D.C. Rachal at White Point, across Nueces Bay. Dunn and his hands herded the cattle from White Point to Flour Bluff, where they forded the Laguna Madre near Pita Island. In the next few years, Dunn established four cattle stations, with corrals and holding pens, a day's journey apart, including Owl's Mott, Novillo, Black Hill, and Green Hill. Between these four stations were camping places, such as Campo Bueno and Campo Borrego.[11] At roundup time in April and October, Dunn's ranch hands moved the cattle up from the southern tip at Brazos Santiago. Dunn built traps and cutting chutes to eliminate the need for roping, which he thought cruel.[12] The island cattle grew fat from beach or sedge grass, supplemented by sand crabs, dead fish and whatever edibles came in on the tide. The hides of the island cattle often showed spots of tar from lying on the beaches.[*][13] Dunn had water tanks dug in the sand, long trenches shored up with ship

---

[*] Blobs of tar on the beach, natural seepage from the floor of the Gulf, were collected on the island to use in patching leaky roofs in Corpus Christi. It was also used to make a chewing gum called "chicardy."

hatch covers to keep out the sand. The cattle would kneel to drink.[14]

Five years after he moved to the island, in 1884, Dunn married a widow, Mrs. Clara Jones, and adopted her daughter Lalla. The Dunns moved to the old Curry Settlement, 17 miles down the island.[15] He later built a home in Corpus Christi on the bluff and another one on the island, facing east on Packery Channel. After the 1916 hurricane destroyed the two-story house on Packery Channel, Dunn built a one-story house a mile away.[16] On the south porch by the kitchen was a long table made of driftwood, unpainted and weathered gray like the house. Ranch hands were served their meals there, prepared by Dunn's cook Aurelio. They would sit on the porch, in the long purple evenings, and wait for night to close in.[17] Pat Dunn spent most of his time on the island, except during the time when he served in the Texas Legislature and lived in Austin during legislative sessions.[18]

In 1926, Pat Dunn sold his title to El Rancho de Don Patricio to Col. Sam Robertson, who planned to develop the island into a tourist resort. Robertson built the Don Patricio Causeway in 1927, which opened up the island to visitors from the mainland. Crossing the causeway, open troughs built on wood pilings, cost motorists $3 for a round trip. Dunn retained grazing rights for his cattle and mineral rights.[19] He moved into town and stayed at the Nueces Hotel. Dunn later regretted selling out and said, "I want to find another island, one that no one can reach. If the Lord would give me back the island, wash out a channel in Corpus Christi Pass 30 feet deep, and put devilfish and other monsters in it to keep out the tourists, I'd be satisfied."[20] He died on March 25, 1937, in his room at the Nueces Hotel, at age 79, of a heart attack.[21]

On Feb. 17, 1929, Ben Garza, owner of the Metropolitan Café in Corpus Christi, forged a compromise among separate Hispanic civil rights organizations to form the League of United Latin American Citizens (LULAC). The organizations were the Order of the Sons of America, Council No. 4; Knights of America, San Antonio; the League of Latin American Citizens, formed in Harlingen in 1927. The meeting was at Obreros Hall at Lipan and Carrizo. At the first convention in May, at Allende Hall, Garza was elected the organization's first president and Luis Wilmot, also from Corpus Christi, was elected treasurer; M.C. Gonzalez was elected vice president and A. de Luna secretary. Delegates to the first convention gathered for a group photo at the bluff balustrade.[22] From its inception, the organization espoused many causes, but the predominant cause was the belief that Mexican-Americans were entitled to share in the full benefits of citizenship. LULAC was not the first such organization in Corpus Christi committed to the goal of equality. The growing political awareness of Latin-Americans can be traced back, at least, to the 1870s with the founding of what were called mutual benefit clubs. The *Club Reciproco* was founded in Corpus Christi in 1873 committed to "the protection of the poor and mutual benefit of its members, calculated to assist society and elevate all who may wish to associate with the members of the club."[23] Others that followed were the *Sociedad Beneficencia*, founded in 1890 by Hispanic women in Corpus Christi, and, after the turn of the century, the *Sociedad Ignacio Allende* and *Sociedad Ignacio Zaragoza*.[24]

Ben Garza, LULAC's founder and first president, was a self-made man, an inspiring success story. He grew up in Rockport. His father died when he was 15; he quit school to go to work to help his mother support the family. He moved to Corpus Christi, took a job as a waiter, worked at a shipyard during World War I, and began to save his money and buy property. He and three business partners bought the Metropolitan Café on Chaparral in 1919. He became the leader of an Hispanic civil rights organization, Council No. 4 of the Order of Sons of America. Garza began to work toward melding the other Hispanic organizations in South Texas to increase power, reach and influence. In 1929, Garza called to order an historic meeting of the three organizations that resulted in forming the new League of United Latin American Citizens.[25] It took time, but through the efforts of LULAC, primary schools in Corpus Christi were open to children of Latin descent, Hispanics were accorded the right to serve on juries, and other gains were made.[26]

As the new president of LULAC, Garza went to Washington to testify against legislation that was aimed specifically to restrict immigration of Latin-Americans as "undesirables."[27] Garza closed the Metropolitan Café in 1931 and entered a sanitarium for the treatment of tuberculosis. He died at the age of 44 in 1937. Flags at the City Hall and Courthouse were lowered to half-mast and the governor and the White House sent representatives to his funeral. Ben Garza's widow, Adelaida Garza, later said that her husband's original intent in founding LULAC was not only to fight segregation and discrimination, but also to improve the educational opportunity for all Hispanics. "He wanted to better the Mexican-American in all aspects of life, and the way to do this was through education."[28]

On Oct. 29, 1929, the stock market crashed. Shares lost half their value, then dropped to pennies on the dollar. Within days, $30 billion in paper value was lost. Banks closed, jobs vanished, families lost homes and were put on the road, farms were repossessed. The hard times became known as the Great Depression.[29] In Corpus Christi, Sunday, Monday and Tuesday were designated as "Prosperity Days" to encourage positive thinking. The newspaper said the difference between hard times and good times was 90 percent psychological: "If we can just actually feel that we are on the way back to prosperity, by golly, we are."[30] The "Crow's Nest" columnist (unsigned in the early years) urged readers to quit talking about poor economic conditions: "If we can't find anything else, let's talk about this beautiful weather we're having."[31]

The news wasn't all about bad economic times. In January of 1930, a new bakery opened at Leopard and Palm. Fehr Baking Co. made Fair-Made Bread.[32] That summer of 1930, a dance marathon was held at the Crystal Beach Park Ballroom on North Beach. It lasted 31 days, from July 24 until Aug. 25. One couple got married while they danced. The winning (and exhausted) couple received $675. That was a lot of money when you could have your shoes half-soled for 10 cents.[33] (It may be hard to understand today, just how it was supposed to boost morale by watching exhausted couples trying to keep their feet moving beyond the limits of human endurance, but then, it would be hard to understand the appeal of bear-baiting and other forms of cruelty aimed at crowd amusement.) Farm laborers lucky enough to get work made about 40 cents a day. Bank tellers made $17.50 a week. A fireman in Corpus Christi made $2 a day, and he was on call 24 hours a day. But steak was 15 cents a pound, pork chops 10 cents a pound; you could get a room at the Riggan Hotel for $3 a week. You could buy a new Erskine automobile at Winerich Motors for $895.[34] At Roy Murray Ford, for $44.50 you could get a radio attached to the dashboard of your car so you could listen to the city's new radio station, KGFI, which some wag said stood for Kome Get Fish Immediately.[35]

In 1930, a fire at Vaky's Café on Chaparral threatened to get out of hand. "Water was freezing as it came out of the hoses," a man who was there recalled. "Firemen kept slipping on the frozen pavement. It took all night and all day before they put the fire out."[36]

The big news that year was the discovery of oil in the Saxet Field on John Dunn's property on Calallen Road. On Aug. 16, 1930, the *Caller* reported the discovery as a 500-barrel-a-day gusher. Thousands of people drove out to see the producing well. Saxet Field was already well known to the city; gas was discovered there eight years before. The first well soon ran dry, but it was the first of many producing oil wells in the area. Most importantly, the discovery of oil provided jobs and hope during the dark days of the Depression.[37]

James H. Doolittle touched down at Corpus Christi in his biplane, the Skyways Buzzard, on Oct. 19, 1931, on a 2,500-mile flight from Ottawa to Mexico City, seeking to be the first man to visit the capitals of Canada, the U.S. and Mexico in a single day. He arrived at Corpus Christi at 2:10 p.m. and left 16 minutes later, after refueling.[38] Another famous visitor, cowboy humorist Will Rogers, spent time on King Ranch in 1931. He would die four years later in an airplane crash.[39]

The 1930s brought back an age-old problem for Corpus Christi. From the earliest times, water was an ongoing concern for the town. An arroyo was dammed up to form a small reservoir. It was called Chatham's ravine* (later this was along Chatham Street, then Blucher Street).[40] There were persistent complaints of hogs wallowing in the town's water supply.[41] When Zachary

---

* It was located at today's Blucher Park, behind the Corpus Christi Central Library.

Taylor's army arrived, soldiers dug a 380-foot well (where Artesian Park is today), but the highly mineralized sulfur water was unfit to drink. The army was forced to haul casks of water from the Nueces River.[42] After Corpus Christi was incorporated in 1852, the town suffered a severe drought. Water hauled from the Nueces River sold for $1.50 a barrel, a very steep price for the time.[43]

In 1854, Henry Kinney tried to drill a well on the site of the old Zachary Taylor well, but he gave up when it was half-completed and gave the well to the city to finish the job. A few months later, the city learned that it had gotten a dud.[#] In 1867, the *Corpus Christi Advertiser* advocated a land reclamation plan that would make the Nueces Bay a freshwater lake.[44] Residents and businessmen in town relied on cisterns designed to hold runoff from the roofs. A good heavy rain was called a "cistern-filler." Andrew Anderson said many people purified their cistern water by keeping a bag of charcoal under the spout leading to the cistern. "The old cistern at the Anderson home was square in outline, instead of the round shape usually used; it was finally made useless by the penetration of roots from nearly trees, causing it to leak."[45] When the cisterns ran dry, people would buy water from street water sellers called barrileros, who filled their 55-gallon barrels from the arroyo or a water well north of Kinney Ave., when available, or the Nueces River in times of drought.[46] In 1891, the city tried drilling wells on the bluff, but the water was no good and the system was rejected.[47] Bay water was used for fire-fighting, with wharves built into the bay so the fire wagons could run out onto a wharf and drop a suction hose into the bay.[48]

After a disastrous fire on North Chaparral in 1892, the city established a municipal water system with 200,000 gallons a day of untreated water piped in from the Nueces River. The new water system did not pump water directly from the river, but from a well 50 feet from the bank and sunk below the bottom of the bed of the stream. The idea was that the water at this point had been filtered through natural sand and gravel, purifying it. A plank dam was built across the river to keep saltwater from backing up into the water supply. The city's first waterworks system in 1893 cost $143,000. To pay for it, the city had to double the local ad valorem taxes. The waterworks brought water from the Nueces River to the downtown, but it didn't bring water to residents' houses; people still relied on cisterns and in a pinch barrileros.[49] In 1910, citizens were urged to install their own cypress cisterns to hold rainwater for household consumption. But the city began to buy pipe for the city's first water mains and a purification plant was built a few years later. Alexander Potter, a New York engineer who helped design the bluff balustrade and was doing consulting work for the city, suggested in 1913 using desalinized water from Corpus Christi Bay. He wrote Mayor Roy Miller

---

[#] The water, which smelled like the back room of a drug store, was later prized for its supposed medicinal qualities.

that "a chemically pure water, a soft water, and from a supply wholly inexhaustible are arguments so convincing that they must at once appeal to all." But the cost of installing distilling plants scuttled the project in early 1914.[50]

By 1926, the need for a reservoir to store the river water became apparent. The city had grown and in times of drought the river flow dwindled so low it threatened to leave the city without water. Experts recommended a dam be built on the Nueces.[51] The city built the La Fruta dam to impound water in a reservoir, 14 miles long and three miles wide, named Lake Lovenskiold, in honor of Mayor P.G. Lovenskiold. The project cost $2.7 million.[52] A portion of the dam washed out on Nov. 23, 1930, at noon on Sunday. A fisherman, Jessie Oliphant, noticed a small boil at the concrete apron of the dam. Then he saw another boil and the apron began to vibrate from the pressure. He scrambled up an embankment to get out of the river channel and saw the concrete apron disappear beneath the rush of water. He ran to the caretaker's house to report that the dam had collapsed. The end of the spillway quickly disappeared in the turbulent water. The reservoir, which had been full, was nearly empty by the next morning.[53] The dam caretaker, Frank Eddie Wright, called his supervisor, H.V. Harvey, chief of the water plant, and reported that water was coming through the north end of the dam. "Harvey said, 'I can send you 500 men'. I told him I didn't need 500 men," Wright replied. "It was too late."[54]

Faulty engineering was blamed.[55] Experts found that water seeped under the steel piling, which was 30 feet in length and, they said, should have been 40 feet to reach the clay bed. There was a 10-feet gap between the bottom of sheet piling and the clay; the water seeped into and under this gap, undermining the dam.[56] The engineering post mortem pointed out that out of false economy the city used 30 feet sheet piling instead of 40 feet to achieve a savings of $60,000, which, in hindsight, cost it a $2 million structure.[57] The collapse of the dam not only deprived the city of a dependable source of water, it also set the stage for one of the blackest chapters in the city's financial history. The city defaulted on payments of the bonds that were issued to build the dam.* The city was again without a dependable water supply. For the next five years, the city kept its fingers crossed and relied on the daily flow of the Nueces, praying there would be no severe drought to reduce that flow. The Mathis Dam was built in 1935 and the reservoir behind it renamed Lake Corpus Christi.[58]

With the country deep in the Depression in 1932, it was said that men and women one passed in the streets looked as if they had just received bad news. This mood of despondency was lifted for a time in Corpus Christi with the arrival on Feb. 14 of the historic three-masted *U.S. Frigate Constitution,*

---

* The default on the bond payments was contested in court for 18 years. Finally, in 1948, $2.1 million in bonds were issued to pay off a judgment against the city.

which had earned the nickname "Old Ironsides" in the war of 1812. The visit of the historic old frigate created intense excitement throughout South Texas. On its arrival, a day ahead of schedule, on a Sunday afternoon, the ship was towed by a minesweeper, the *USS Greebe*, through the narrow "eye of the needle" opening of the bascule bridge.[59] The old ship struck the side of the opening, slicing off a chunk of its wooden prow. Mayor Edwin Flato and other city officials greeted the officers of the ship. During its visit, long lines of people waited for their chance to board the ship. During the busiest day of its visit, Sunday before its departure, the lines waiting to board the ship stretched from the port's Cargo Dock No. 1 to the bascule bridge, the equivalent of several blocks.[60] Women of the Church of the Good Shepherd had charge of concessions at the docks: Hamburgers, soft drinks and souvenirs of the *Constitution*.[61] There were parades, ceremonies and a balloon race. Hundreds of couples attended a dance on Cargo Dock No. 1. The Corpus Christi Yacht Club featured a boat parade. Perkins Brothers department store offered new spring frocks to visit "Old Ironsides" for $9.85. Two special trains ran from San Antonio to bring visitors to see the old frigate and Corpus Christi schools closed to allow the students to visit the ship.[62]

Juliet Knight (Wenger) and friend Margaret McGloin were two of the thousands of students who toured the *Constitution*, but they came back with a unique story, which was told in the Centennial Journey in 1983. "Outside the quarters of Capt. Louis J. Gulliver we stood for a time. There was a reception area, roped off, with sideboys standing at parade rest, for honored, invited guests. These guests, on arrival, were escorted across the thick carpeting into an intriguing room. As we watched and listened, we heard the visitors identify themselves. Their appointments were confirmed. They were taken in for tea. Being presented to royalty could not compare to the thought of being received by Capt. Gulliver. We conferred and a plan took form.[63]

"We began looking at our watches regularly, making comments about the fact we had arrived early. At an agreed moment, we walked over and introduced ourselves, stating the time of our appointment, as we had heard invited guests do. There was a conference on the other side of the important door. The decision may have been that the appointment was overlooked or that the captain would like to be kind to two eager girls. Whatever, we were escorted in. We were served tea, and drank it with stiff-backed pomp. We had been discussing Texas wildflowers. When we got ready to leave, the captain asked, 'Would you come back and have tea with me tomorrow afternoon and bring me some wildflowers? Otherwise, I won't get a chance to see them.' We nodded in stunned delight. We could come back and our names would be in the impressive books with a real appointment. We hunted out every variety of flowers and returned next day with arms full."[64]

Despite a week of foggy, rainy weather, the *U.S. Frigate Constitution* attracted 93,362 visitors during its visit. Considering the city's population of

27,000, more than three people for every person in Corpus Christi went aboard. The ship departed on Tuesday, Feb. 23, 1932 for its next port of call, Houston.[65]

During this time, the Intracoastal Canal was being dredged,[66] the "Hug the Coast Highway" to Houston was under construction, the ship channel was being dredged to 30 feet and port tonnage was up.[67] The port's major export was cotton, which increased from 45,000 bales shipped in 1926 to 600,000 bales four years later. Nueces County was the top cotton-producing county in the nation. Corpus Christi was the headquarters of cotton country.[68] In cotton-picking time, fields of white stretched to the horizon and on a Saturday, Leopard Street would be packed with cars of cotton-pickers and families who came to town to shop. Then, cotton prices fell from 18 cents to five cents a pound. Farm workers on Chapman Ranch west of Corpus Christi were let go. The first farmer in the country to get paid for plowing under his cotton crop was a Nueces County farmer, W.E. Morris, who went to Washington and was presented the "plow-up" check by President Roosevelt.[69]

Mrs. Rose Shaw, principal at Cheston Heath School, was among the first to provide a "bean line" for her students during the Depression. Merchants in town donated bread, milk and beans. The beans were cooked in the room with the school heating plant.[70]

Ranchers were hit hard when calf prices dropped from 9.3 cents a pound in 1929 to 3.6 cents a pound in 1933.[71] On Armstrong Ranch, Charlie Armstrong cut his salary almost in half and laid off most of the hands.[72] At King Ranch, Robert J. Kleberg, Jr. ordered 250 head of cattle rounded up to furnish meat for hungry families. The meat was distributed from the King Ranch warehouse in Kingsville.[73]

Area banks were caught in the panic. The Odem State Bank and the Sinton State Bank closed in October 1931. A letter from Jim Goodwin at George West was sent with a returned check issued by the White Point Oil & Gas Company for $10. The check had been stamped by a San Antonio bank — "Returned: Drawee bank reported closed." The letter said, "Friend Roy: It seems as though you are giving hot checks now, and I am returning this one to swap for another one. Did you get hurt in the closing of the Sinton State bank? It is dry as Hell up here and not a dollar in the county. If I had a dollar in my pocket I would expect someone to hijack me. Well, old stud, when you locate about one-half dozen bottles of tequila, send me a wire and I will come in a jiffy."[74] The City National Bank in Corpus Christi went under in 1933.[75] During the "bank holiday" in March 1933, the Chamber of Commerce issued trade certificates for $1 each that would be accepted by the town's merchants. Many were never redeemed; they were saved as souvenirs.[76]

Although Corpus Christi missed a direct hit, the hurricanes of 1933 gave this area a pounding. Seven hurricanes made landfall along the coast between Corpus Christi, and Tampico, with three of the seven making their presence felt.[77] The city experienced hurricane weather on July 6, Aug. 5 and Sept. 5, 1933. The July storm, which made landfall below Brownsville, stripped the grass from Padre Island. The August storm also made landfall near Brownsville, with little effects locally except to assist work in dredging a fish pass across Padre Island. The worst of the three was the September storm. Corpus Christi was well-prepared, having been warned that it would receive the brunt of the storm. Downtown businesses boarded up and moved their goods to higher ground. The lobbies of the Nueces and Plaza hotels were opened as a refuge. The storm again made landfall near Brownsville, but Corpus Christi experienced strong winds and torrential rains. The storm tide resulted in floodwaters of five feet on North Beach and three feet downtown. The storm destroyed the Don Patricio Causeway to Padre Island, built in 1927. The Nueces Bay Causeway was heavily damaged and beach cabins on North Beach were swept away. Curiously, the city ran out of yeast because of the storm; a plane was sent from Dallas with yeast supplies for Corpus Christi bakers. In the storm three years later, 600 refugees spent the night in the Wynn Seale auditorium singing, "Don't Fence Me In."[78]

A few popular business establishments in Corpus Christi in 1934 included George Plomarity's Manhattan Café on Peoples, the Wonder Bar on Peoples, The Texas Café and Grigg's Pig Stand, on Leopard, the Heap O' Cream on North Beach.[79] The South Texas Exposition was first held in 1934. It was held again in 1935 and '36. Some 40,000 people visited that first fair at the Gulf Compress warehouse by the port. A big hit was radio entertainer W. Lee O'Daniel (later governor and senator) and his Hillbilly Band. O'Daniel would be back four years later, campaigning for governor. Another popular attraction was the Kibbe Wild West Show.[80]

In 1934, the city gained its first big industry, Southern Alkali.[*] Three years earlier, a delegation of businessmen led by Maston Nixon convinced the company of the advantages of Corpus Christi.[81] Those advantages included the new port, cheap natural gas,[#] a supply of alkali and brine, oyster shell lime, and an adequate water supply, the last of which presented a problem because of the failure of the La Fruta Dam. Maston Nixon said the Flato administration that took office in 1931 "put [its] shoulder to the wheel to refinance and make possible the reconstruction of the dam, so we were over the hurdle."[82] Another hurdle was the company's requirement of a 30-foot deep inner harbor channel to Avery Point. Richard King III, banker and port commission chairman, agreed with a handshake to make the improvement. "We don't know how we're going to do it," he said, "but we will."[83]

When the deal was finalized on April 28, 1931, the Green Flag that was a symbol of civic success was flown over Leopard Street between the Nixon

---

[*] In 1951, the name was changed to Columbia Southern, a subsidiary of Pittsburgh Plate Glass.
[#] A report presented to Southern Alkali showed gas reserves of 75 billion cubic feet at White Point and 100 billion cubic feet at Saxet Field.

214

Building and the Plaza Hotel.[84] When the flag went up, the *Corpus Christi Times* reported, "business practically stopped everywhere except at the telephone switchboards while citizens congratulated each other," knowing that the Green Flag meant they had landed Southern Alkali and what that would mean for a job-hungry city in the middle of an economic depression.[85] An employment office was opened in the Aztec Building on Leopard Street. Ben Garza, who helped to found the League of United Latin American Citizens (LULAC) four years before, sat at a card table on a folding chair and helped select workers to construct the plant.[86] The company hired 250 workers, in the beginning, in a city desperate for jobs.[87] The $7 million plant opened on Sept. 1, 1934.[88] It produced soda ash and caustic soda from oyster shell and brine piped from a salt dome near Benavides 60 miles away. It was the first major industrial plant in Corpus Christi and the first of many large chemical plants that would be built along the coast.[89]

The New Deal began to take hold. The Works Progress Administration (WPA) opened a sewing room at 613 Waco where women were paid up to $43 a month to make overalls, underwear, shirts and dresses for the needy. At Christmas, they made "cuddle toys" for kids from scraps of cloth, which were delivered to local charitable organizations. Mrs. Gladys Bonham was the director of the sewing room.[90] Another WPA project was to terrace the slope and build a concrete base to keep Cole Park from sloughing off into the bay. Some 70 men worked in the park for six months in 1935.[91]

Corpus Christi in 1935 was a city of 30,000. The city annexed North Beach that year with its migrant camp. Homeless camps around the country were called "Hoovervilles," but in Corpus Christi it was simply the "migrant camp on North Beach". The camp consisted of tents and shacks that looked as if they were constructed of tin cans and cardboard boxes. At this time, the city extended to the south to Louisiana Parkway. Arcadia Village was a subdivision between Staples and Ayers. South Padre Island Drive was Lexington Boulevard.[92] Del Mar College, first called the Corpus Christi Junior College, began night classes in 1935 at Corpus Christi High School. The enrollment for that first year for the junior college was 154. The college was moved in 1937 to a garage room at the First Methodist Church at Mesquite and Mann next to Doc McGregor's studio. Two years later, in 1938, it moved again, this time to a stucco frame building constructed on South Staples. The college moved to its present site at Baldwin and Ayers in 1942.[*93]

Pat Limerick, who had been a sales manager for Shell Oil Co. in Moline, Ill., built a grocery store at what is now called Six Points, outside the city. People thought he was crazy. "It's so far out in the country," they said. "Why put a grocery store way out there?" people asked him. It *was* out in the country; the Staples Street pavement ended there. On early mornings,

---

[*] The name was changed to Del Mar on June 6, 1948. A board of regents was appointed Oct. 8, 1951.

Limerick could hear coyotes howl in the brush to the south and west of his new store. He once recalled that there was only brush and chaparral going west. His back door opened on what was then called Dump Road (Staples). "We chose 1211 Ayers as the front door address because that was inside the city and we could get city mail service. There was only RFD service on Dump Road." Limerick soon had company with the Tower Theatre and Parr Drug Store built soon afterwards. As the surrounding area grew, so did the store."[94]

One of Corpus Christi's first major hotels, the St. James, was demolished in 1937. It dated back to 1869 when it was built by J. T. James, a stockman on Mustang Island. Before construction was finished, James sold it to William Long "Billy" Rogers. Rogers survived a supply-train massacre on the Arroyo Colorado in 1846, at the beginning of the Mexican War. In that massacre, members of his family were killed, including his father and a brother, and many others in the attack. Billy Rogers had his throat cut and he was thrown in the river from a high cliff. But he survived, and was nursed back to health. The story told was that Rogers prowled the border, searching for the killers and took his revenge, one by one. A slit throat on the Rio Grande was called "Billy's mark." Rogers became a rancher, businessman and sheriff of Nueces County. His St. James Hotel opened on Sunday, July 27, 1873. The hotel became one of the city's most famous landmarks. When Rogers died in 1877, William Biggio became the manager of the St. James.[95]

Under Biggio, the St. James Hotel became known throughout Texas. It was the headquarters of ranchers, politicians, gamblers and gunmen. John Nance Garner, who would become vice president in Franklin D. Roosevelt's administration, stayed at the St. James. Gov. Jim Hogg was a frequent guest. John Wesley Hardin, who backed down Wild Bill Hickok in Abilene, stayed there. So did Ben Thompson. An article in the *Caller* said, "While governors and congressmen banqueted in the dining rooms of the St. James, gamblers and happy-go-lucky cowboys faced each other across tables in backrooms, with poker chips drawn up in neat stacks before them and loaded revolvers beside them." The old hotel was said to be a wreck and a firetrap when it was demolished in 1937. Three years after it was torn down, a new Lichtenstein's department store was built on the site. Like the St. James, it became a center of activity of the downtown.[96]

In early May, 1937, President Roosevelt's yacht *Potomac,* escorted by the destroyer *Moffett* and the light cruiser *Decatur,* anchored off Harbor Island so the president could go tarpon fishing. Roosevelt was accompanied by his son Elliott and the usual entourage of aides and Secret Service detail. The president was officially greeted at Port Aransas by Gov. James A. Allred.[*97]

Nine tarpon were caught by the presidential party the first day of fishing close to the jetties. None were caught by the president, though he said he felt "four good tugs." Next day, May 3, the president landed a four-foot,

---

[*] President Roosevelt would later appoint Allred to a federal district court in Corpus Christi.

eight-inch tarpon. Minutes after the catch, Corpus Christi photographer "Doc" McGregor snapped a shot of fishing guide Barney Farley shaking the president's hand. Roosevelt caught another five-foot, two-inch, 77-pound tarpon a few days later. He also caught four kingfish. The tarpon were mounted for the president by Port Aransas taxidermists Ancel Brundrett and Alfred Roberts. On one day, when guide Teddy Mathews took Roosevelt out, the president got a soaking. "We were fishing off the south jetty," Mathews said. "I pulled in the open and a northeast wind sent a spray up and it hit in the boat. It soaked him. The president said, 'Don't worry, I've been wet before.' "[98]

Just as the 1920s witnessed some sensational crimes, the murder of Fred Roberts and the shootout at the Bessie Miller brothel, the 1930s had its own unusual murder cases.

On a hot sluggish day, Sept. 1, 1931, Matt Dunn and a vaquero on his ranch south of Corpus Christi on the Oso walked into the sheriff's office to report that the vaquero had discovered a human skeleton. Deputies found the skeleton had a hole in the back of the skull. Near the body they found an empty envelope addressed to Fred Sinclair of Sinclair Metal Works in Corpus Christi. The investigation revealed that the dead man was Alfred Steinbach, who shared a rented room with V. Don Carlis, a mechanic at Binz Service Station on Water Street. After questioning, the evidence began to point to Carlis. One of his tools, a ball-peen hammer, fit into the hole in the skull; there were bloodstains and a strand of hair on the hammer.[99]

Carlis was charged and indicted for murder. When the trial came up, the courtroom was packed. Halfway through the trial, there was a scream when the undertaker, Maxwell P. Dunne, wheeled the skeleton into the courtroom. District Attorney D.S. Purl said young Steinbach had returned from the dead to tell of his fate. "Look at my teeth. Look at my left arm. Now, look at these pictures. You see, I'm Alfred Steinbach," the bones of the dead man seemed to be saying. "Now look at these nicks in my ribs. That's where I was shot. Here, see this round hole in my skull, that's where the murderer hit me with a ball-peen hammer." The jury found Carlis guilty. He was sentenced to 99 years in prison. The case was overturned on appeal, with appellate judges deciding that bringing the skeleton into the courtroom prejudiced and inflamed the jury. In the second trial, there was no skeleton and Carlis, though found guilty, was sentenced to eight years in prison.[100]

Another case in the 1930s involved a body found on a remote ranch outside Corpus Christi. The body of a young red-haired woman, about 20, was found in the brush, wrapped in an Indian blanket, five miles south of Sandia. She was wearing a silk dress, expensive slip and stockings, but there was no identification, no jewelry. Her skull had been crushed by a blunt instrument. She was found on the Gallagher ranch by cowhands working for Richard Miller of Orange Grove.[101]

217

Since the body was found just inside the Nueces County line, Nueces Sheriff William Shely investigated. The body was taken to Maxwell Dunne's funeral home. The sheriff checked on transient laborers, but there were no missing persons. A number of Corpus Christi citizens went to the funeral home to view the body. No identification was made. Finally, a woman who ran a tourist camp on North Beach identified the body as that of Annabelle Evans, who had lived at her camp. As the sheriff unraveled the story, he learned she was from Kansas, had been married with two children, but, in the hard times of the Depression was divorced and ended up in Corpus Christi looking for work. She turned to prostitution, visiting oil-field workers on payday. She was killed by a blow to the head with a flat iron, hence the case became known as the "Flat Iron Murder." The man eventually arrested, tried and convicted of the crime, H.T. Whitaker, was given a 25-year sentence. Sheriff Shely wrote, "While I bear Whitaker no grudge, I feel that 25 years is scarcely enough time in which to atone for the life of a woman whom fate had treated so shabbily as it had Annabelle Evans."[102]

In 1938, Joe Ball, a beer joint owner in Elmendorf near San Antonio, killed a waitress and buried her body in the sand near Ingleside. He killed another waitress with an ax, dismembered the corpse and stuffed it in a barrel in the back room of his beer joint, Joe's Place. After customers complained about the odor, he took the body parts and buried them on the banks of the Salado River. When these were found, police showed up to question Ball. He pulled out a pistol and shot himself in the heart. During the investigation, officers learned that Ball had killed another waitress and fed her to alligators. A school teacher who was infatuated with Ball disappeared. A number of women customers and waitresses at Joe's Place all disappeared, but how many were killed by Joe Ball was never confirmed. Only one of Ball's victims was buried in a sand dune near Ingleside. That was Minnie Gerhardt, shot in the head.[103]

It was also during the 1930s when Ben Lee, sheriff of Nueces County, discovered an easy way to get confessions from suspects. He would force them to stand on their bare feet on blocks of ice until they became more amenable to questioning. When a reporter asked him about the practice, Lee bristled. "I didn't spend one penny of county money for that ice. I paid for it out of my own pocket."[104]

North Beach honky-tonks were a source of trouble for law enforcement officers in the 1930s. One troublesome place was called the Kat's Meow. There were frequent brawls and complaints of gambling and loud music. Mayor Giles in 1936 said he would push to close the worst honky-tonks, but not all. "We don't want an air-tight city," Giles said. "There are certain pleasures the citizens and visitors demand."[105]

One of Corpus Christi's more shocking crimes of the decade occurred in 1939 in the federal courthouse. Gilbert McGloin, widely known and popular with "a ready sense of humor," was appointed acting postmaster by President

Coolidge on Dec. 1, 1927. He was re-appointed in April, 1933. On May 19, 1939, Postmaster McGloin and Assistant Postmaster Albert E. Dittmer were shot to death in McGloin's office on the second floor of the federal building on Starr Street. Their bodies, in a tableau of carnage, were discovered by V. William Prewett, an attorney from Tyler. Both McGloin and Dittmer were shot in the head. A .45 caliber handgun was found under Dittmer's body. Two bullets had been fired from the gun. Investigators said McGloin was sitting behind his desk (he had taken off his glasses) when he was shot. Dittmer was shot in the back of the head just behind the ear. No official explanation was given, but it was considered an open-and-shut case: one murder, one suicide, one gun, two bullets fired. Investigators believed there was an argument between Dittmer and McGloin leading Dittmer to shoot McGloin, sitting behind his desk, and then put the barrel of the .45 behind his right ear. It was a case of "going postal" before the term was invented. But even this basic conjecture was hush-hush and no motive beyond a generic "argument" was ever advanced.[106]

Mrs. Gilbert (Ameta) McGloin was appointed postmaster to succeed her late husband at the urging of Congressman Richard M. Kleberg, a successor to John Nance Garner. Mrs. McGloin was the fourth woman to serve the city as postmaster. Before her were Georgia Welch (1915), Hannah Taylor (1867) and Jane Marsh (1865).[107]

There was a hard-fought city election campaign in 1937 between Mayor H. R. Giles and A.C. McCaughan with two slates of council candidates lining up behind Giles and McCaughan. It was widely expected that Dr. Giles would win; the newspaper predicted it a week before the election. The McCaughan slate won.[108] Before he moved to Corpus Christi, McCaughan was the U.S. vice consul at Durango, Mexico. He moved to Corpus Christi in 1914, entered the real estate business, and developed Hillcrest and Oak Park. He was elected to the City Council in 1933 and ran for mayor in 1935, losing to Giles.[109]

One thing McCaughan did after his election was to crack down on brothels on Sam Rankin Street, forcing them to move west of town to "the flats." Police Commissioner C.O. Watson said the move was necessary for public decency. "We can't exterminate them entirely," he said, "but we can move them to a location that is the least objectionable in the public eye."[110] McCaughan and Giles faced off again in 1939 and again McCaughan won. His tenure marked great progress for the city. Work began in 1939 on a project that would change the city's appearance, adding the seawall, two T-heads and an L-head. But it was a mess at the time, with dredges pumping mud from the bay bottom.[111] The idea for a seawall goes way back, at least to 1874, after a hurricane flooded the downtown, and again in 1890 when the *Caller* ran an article on how the city might look at the beginning of the 20th century and the article forecast building a seawall "500 feet from the shoreline, filling up back of this wall and utilizing the ground." It didn't happen then but the idea stayed around. In 1909, County Judge Walter Timon tried to convince Corpus Christi Mayor Dan Reid of the need for a seawall. The idea went no further, but after two severe storms in 1916 and 1919, people remembered Timon's proposal. He was asked to look at seawalls along the Atlantic coast and make some recommendations. On his return he drafted what was called the Timon Plan to build a seawall and a breakwater.[112] The federal government required the breakwater to be in place before it provided funding for building the port. The breakwater was started in 1924, two years before the port opened for business, but there was no money for a seawall.[113]

Still, the idea wouldn't die. In 1928, the city hired sculptor Gutzon Borglum to design a seawall. The man who would eventually sculpt Mount Rushmore had family ties here. The plan Borglum drafted called for a grand boulevard behind the seawall, with parks along the bayfront and an imposing—not to say monstrous-size—32-foot statue of Jesus standing inside rock jetties in the bay with his arms uplifted as if to calm the raging waters. Borglum's seawall design did not include steps; it was a smooth wall with a castle-like parapet at the top. Borglum described the seawall as serving as a sort of amphitheater facing the bay. Another part of Borglum's bayfront improvement plan urged the city to locate the municipal airport in the bay. Borglum's plan called for building a bulkhead around an area just beyond the breakwater, adjacent to the ship channel, and filling it with dredged material from the bay bottom. Of course, there was a fierce fight over the statue of Christ and the city was unable to get state or federal help to pay for the seawall. Borglum's plan was shelved and he departed for South Dakota's Black Hills.[114]

In 1938, voters approved the first of two bond issues to finance the seawall. The first, for $650,000, passed 1,431 to 108 and the following year voters easily approved another $1.1 million bond issue, 1,078 to 83.[115] One of Timon's ideas was revived. It called for the state to give Corpus Christi the state's share of ad valorem taxes from seven South Texas counties—Nueces, Jim Wells, Jim Hogg, Brooks, Kleberg, Willacy and Duval—to help pay for the seawall. That was done with little opposition in the Legislature. The main purpose of the seawall was to protect the downtown so there would be no replay of the 1919 devastation.[116]

Work began on the north end near the ship channel. Creosoted pilings were driven to provide a footing for the embankment, which was built of dredge spoil from the bay bottom. Contractor J. DePuy designed a 40-foot metal shed on railroad wheels under which 40-foot lengths of the stepped seawall were poured of reinforced concrete. The L-head and two T-heads were part of the plan. The plan called for a fourth L-head off the end of Twigg, but the money ran out. The plan also called for a tube tunnel under the ship channel, to be paid for by federal dollars and a toll, but that part of

220

the plan was dropped.[117]

Part of the project in 1939 was to build a levee that reached from the west side of the bluff to the high ground on the east side of the port's main turning basin. The levee was intended to keep storm waters from flooding through the city's back door after stacking up in Nueces Bay, as it happened in the 1919 storm. Like the seawall, the levee was built slightly more than 14 feet above sea level. In the middle of the levee was an opening for a railroad spur to the port. When a storm threatened, city workers could plug the gap in the levee with sand bags.[118]

When work on the seawall was completed in March 1941, the city had been extended two blocks into the bay and the shoreline behind and above the stepped seawall, in effect a levee, had been elevated to 14 feet above sea level, 3.7 feet above the high-water mark of the 1919 storm. The seawall's clean lines along two miles of the bayfront, facing the rising sun, dramatically improved the city's appearance, providing the classic amphitheater Borglum once described, though the final product was not based on his original design. The seawall was designed by Edward Noyes of Myers & Noyes, the project engineers.[119] When it was finished, the seawall gave Corpus Christi a bayfront "second to none in point of beauty."[120]

CHAPTER 14

War in Europe affects port business - Flour Bluff chosen for Navy base - City experiences growing pains - Driscoll Hotel built on the bluff - Pearl Harbor attack stuns city - U-boat threat leads to blackouts - People learn to cope with war rationing - President Roosevelt visits NAS - Escaped POWs caught on North Beach - Roosevelt dies - War ends

The year 1939 was a busy time for the Port of Corpus Christi.[*] Ships painted with a Nazi swastika docked to load cargo, such as lead ingots from Mexico, and Japanese ships loaded scrap iron by the thousands of tons. Little did they know that in not too many months that scrap iron would be returned in the form of weapons aimed at U.S. forces in the Pacific.[1] It was easy to believe in 1939 that the war in Europe was very far away, in fact half a world away, but the country was beginning to prepare for the possibility of involvement in that far-off war. When Hitler's Nazi Germany invaded Poland setting off what would become World War II, President Roosevelt invoked the Neutrality Act in September, 1939. At the port, several ships scheduled to arrive cancelled and customs officials were trying to determine what materials would be banned for shipment to belligerent nations. French and British ships leaving the port were bound for a rendezvous at Norfolk, Va., to join a convoy for protection against German U-boats in crossing the Atlantic.[2]

There were other signs of a country gearing up for war. A big bin was moved to the bayfront for the collection of aluminum scrap for defense. An airplane dropped 10,000 leaflets urging housewives to contribute pots and pans to the national aluminum drive. Small hills of scrap aluminum rose near the port as aluminum from other counties was transported to Corpus Christi to join the growing piles awaiting shipment to smelters.[3] The most popular song on the radio in the summer of 1940 was "A Nightingale Sang in Berkeley Square." The song was a reminder that Britain was battling for its

---

[*] The Port handled 13.3 million tons of cargo in 1939, a record that stood until 1946, after the war ended.

life; the Germans were in Paris and had similar plans for London. Veterans in Corpus Christi collected old license plates for shipment to Britain for use as war materiel. A "Bundles for Britain" drive was conducted to collect articles for the besieged British.[4] Corpus Christi that summer became a reserve center for Australian wool. More than 200,000 bales of wool were stored in Aransas Compress warehouses at the port as a strategic reserve for the British government.[5] Roosevelt signed the draft bill in September, 1940, which specified that all men 21 to 35 had to register for military service. The first draft lottery number was 158; five men in Corpus Christi held that number.[6]

Corpus Christi had already won a more highly prized lottery when it entered competition for a proposed naval air station in 1939. Clara Driscoll, of the wealthy Driscoll ranching family, was in California when she heard that $50,000 had been put up by the Corpus Christi Chamber of Commerce to buy a site for the proposed naval base. Driscoll, known as the "savior" of the Alamo, sent a telegram to Maston Nixon of the Chamber offering to match any contribution two to one.[7] She had more than money to offer. She was a friend, contributor and confidante of former Vice President John Nance Garner and of President Roosevelt. She had political clout on her own as a national committeewoman from Texas in the Democratic Party. She used that influence to help see that Corpus Christi won the competition for the new navy base.[8] The city had considerable clout in Washington with the support of Sen. Tom Connally, Congressman Richard M. Kleberg and Lyndon Johnson.[9]

Rep. Kleberg announced that the base would be located somewhere on Corpus Christi Bay and members of the Naval Affairs Committee visited the city. The exact site had not yet been determined.[10] The Corpus Christi Chamber of Commerce voted to underwrite expenses incurred in buying land for the base, up to the aforementioned $50,000.[11] The Nueces County Waterways Committee offered to extend water mains from the city lines to the base.[12] The committee offered to convey to the government, free of charge, 640 acres of vacant land on the Encinal Peninsula at Flour Bluff for the base site.[*13] The total package of incentives from the chamber and the Nueces County Waterways Committee amounted to $1.7 million. The package included the value of the lands, and road, water, and housing improvements.[14] In May, 1939, a board of Navy officers recommended the Flour Bluff site. The selection, other than the political weight brought to bear, was based on several factors, including prevailing wind direction, the sheltered bay, and the open air space.[15]

Congress allocated money in 1940 to begin construction.[16] Sand dunes and fishing shacks on the site at Flour Bluff were leveled by June, 1940.[17]

---

[*] Additional land was purchased to increase the size of the base to 2,050 acres. Other tracts were bought or leased to give the base a reserve area of 11,200 acres.

224

Some 9,000 construction workers arrived to build the base, among many thousands who were just hopeful of getting a job.[18] The city was buzzing with activity. Hotels were packed. Extra beds were put in lounges. The Nueces Hotel even put beds in its famous Sun Room. Lobbies were filled with luggage of those who were out looking for rooms in private homes. People rented out extra rooms and garages to the influx of workers. What had been a migrant camp on North Beach filled with workers and families who arrived from all over the country hoping to get work building the base.[19]

The city was in a state of flux, like one gigantic construction site. New sewer lines were being extended, pipes laid, ditches dug, streets were being paved or repaved or dug for water or sewer lines. Five trenching machines were kept busy gouging out deep trenches in various parts of the city to prepare for 39 miles of new sewer mains. The south end of the Water Street area, the old "Beach Section" of the city, was blocked off as work began to spread fill dirt. Small mountains of dredge material from the marina and the seawall project were piled high along the bayfront, reserved for use in raising the grade on the south end of the city, the area between Water Street and South Bluff around Zackies Drive In. The entire south end was raised several feet to conform to the grade of the seawall project.[20] Not long afterwards, a reporter with a talent for pulling pranks, Bill Barnard, wrote an April Fool's Day story that the seawall improvement project, with the T-heads and yacht basin, was a cover-up, that it was really a Maginot Line like that in France. He wrote that bayfront construction was meant to hide an underground fortress from which troops could emerge to fight off an enemy approaching by sea. In the furor that erupted, with the newspaper besieged by callers, Barnard was fired for his ability to make up a good story.[21]

The greatest activity was in Flour Bluff where the Naval Air Station was being built at a frenzied pace. The base was substantially built in seven months, a project that in normal times would have taken three or four years to complete.[22] Corpus Christi NAS, soon to become the largest naval flight training center in the world, was patterned after the Navy base at Pensacola. [23] It represented an investment of $100 million by the government. The naval air station was 70 percent completed when it was dedicated on March 12, 1941 by Frank Knox, the Chicago publishing tycoon, a Republican who was Roosevelt's Secretary of the Navy.[24] In his dedication speech, Knox said, "This station has not been built in the spirit of aggression. I want to dedicate this station not to war, but to peace, the peace of justice and righteousness."[25] The first commanding officer of the naval air station was Capt. Alva D. Barnhard.[26] Three auxiliary fields around the city were quickly built and commissioned: Rodd Field in June, Cabaniss in July, and Cuddihy in September. Kingsville NAS was commissioned in 1942, Waldron in 1943, and Chase Field in Beeville the same year.[27] Despite Secretary Knox's speech aimed at the prevailing anti-war mood of the country, the new bases were built not with an eye on peace but on the very likely prospect of war.

The government's great investment in building the base would pay off. Naval aviators trained at Naval Air Station Corpus Christi and its outlying and supporting fields would play a major role in the coming war in the Pacific. The first group of 52 cadets began flight training with a fleet of N3N Yellow Peril biplane trainers on April 7, 1941. On Nov. 1, the first class of aviation cadets, 45 of the original 52, received their wings.[28]

As the naval base was being built, Corpus Christi was shifting into high gear and growing at a fast pace. The population more than doubled from 27,789 in 1930 to 57,301 in 1940.[*] Within another year, it had gained an estimated 30 percent, to 75,000, giving the city boasting rights as "the fastest growing city in Texas." In 1940, the 14-year-old port was handling 14 times more tonnage than it did in 1930, from 490,000 tons to 6.7 million tons. The city's largest building, the 20-story Robert Driscoll Hotel, was beginning to rise on the bluff. The Plaza Hotel next door, preparing for its competition, installed an air conditioning unit to cool the public areas of the hotel and 130 of the guest rooms. Air conditioning was added to the first four floors of Lichtenstein's new department store.[29] Buccaneer Stadium was being built. Flour Bluff High School opened. City limits were pushed out to consume cotton fields west and south of Six Points. Everywhere people drove that summer they bounced over torn-up streets and some had all the boom they could stand.[30] Mayor A.C. McCaughan answered the chorus of complaints by pointing out that the city was going through intense growing pains, that the difficulties and inconveniences were unavoidable as a small city was trying to serve the needs of a suddenly much larger population.[31] To meet the demands of housing alone, the city was adding an average of eight living units every day.[32] New subdivisions were sprouting up every week. In 1941, a new five-room house on Clodah Drive cost $35 a month for interest, principal, taxes and insurance. For cash, it would sell for $4,575.[33]

This was a time of great bustle and energy in Corpus Christi. Slums were cleared to make way for new subdivisions. Streets were paved. New churches opened. The seawall, yacht basin and Shoreline Boulevard were dedicated, along with the recently completed Intracoastal Waterway, giving Corpus Christi a direct waterway connection to other Texas coastal cities.[34]

Besides complaining about torn-up streets, people were grumbling about other things, such as the increase in prices. Barbers collectively agreed to raise the price of a standard haircut from 50 cents to 65 cents and a shave from 25 cents to 30 cents. Men could remember that in the "good old days" before the Depression, a haircut cost a quarter.[35] At one of the town's more popular restaurants, "Papa" Shoop's Grill on Water Street, roast Long Island duckling with wild rice cost 80 cents and roast prime rib was even higher at

---

[*] By the end of the war, the city's population would be doubled again. In 25 years, the city's population increased tenfold from 1920, when it was 10,522, to 1945's estimated 104,559.

95 cents. Hamburgers were 20 cents and open face steak sandwiches were 35 cents.[36] At Lichtensteins' new million-dollar store on Chaparral, on the site of the old St. James Hotel, silk hose were selling for $1.35 a pair while the new nylons were selling for $1.95 a pair for the two-thread type or $2.95 for the 1-1/2 thread type.[37] Prices were up because of the boom connected to building the naval air station.[38] Much of the commercial activity was downtown, where the parking on the streets was free; the city had no parking meters. The corner of Mesquite and Peoples, where the buses stopped, was one of the most crowded places downtown. Olympia Confectionary in the Nueces Hotel was normally full of sailors.[39]

At the request of Navy officials and a recommendation from a Nueces County grand jury, Chief of Police George Lowman ordered houses of prostitution in the vicinity of Josephine Street and Sam Rankin Street closed. The city tried to crack down three years earlier, in 1938, forcing some brothels to move to an area known as "the flats."[40] The brothels had long operated under the watchful eye of the city police and the sheriff's department. The women in the houses were fingerprinted and photographed and their records kept on file. The rest of the town put on blinders to the existence of a thriving red-light district. After the crackdown, at least two of the houses moved their operations to just outside the city limits. Many of the houses shut down, with moving vans carting away their furniture. After Chief Lowman's order, by Aug. 1, 1941, at least 39 houses in the red-light district became vacant.[41]

On Saturdays, the amusement park on North Beach would be crowded. At night spots Palmero, El Rancho and Swingland, young couples danced to tunes such as Glenn Miller's "Chattanooga Choo Choo" and "Moonlight Serenade," the Andrew Sisters' "Boogie Woogie Bugle Boy" and "Rancho Pillow," and the Ink Spots' "I Don't Want to Set the World On Fire." In the first week of December, 1941, Christmas lights were turned on downtown. On Friday, Dec. 5, Santa Claus landed in a Navy seaplane on Corpus Christi Bay and toured the city by car. (The Lookout columnist complained about modern-day Christmas; it featured too many Santas who moved too fast in planes and cars). Mayor McCaughan decided that the city would leave the running of the recreation center for servicemen on Shoreline to the USO, ending a dispute between the city and the USO. Mrs. Edith Phillips, a teacher at Wynn Seale, was called for jury duty, but sent home; women were not seated on juries.[42]

As Americans were humming the catchy little tune of "I Don't Want to Set the World On Fire," a man in Germany with a silly little mustache was doing all he could to set the world on fire. As Adolf Hitler's German army pushed deeper into Russia, Americans that December were divided between isolationists, who opposed any U.S. involvement in the war, and internationalists who felt the U.S. must help Britain and Russia defeat Nazi Germany before the U.S. was truly isolated and it became too late. The tide of opinion favored the isolationists and then came the fateful stroke that ended all debate. Sunday, Dec. 7, 1941, began in Corpus Christi as a cool, clear, placid day. Scheduled events that day included the opening of two new subdivisions, Hilltop Terrace near the new Robert Driscoll Junior High and Dahlia Terrace near the Del Mar addition; and the Corpus Christi Sailing Club was holding its mid-winter regatta. It was a lovely December afternoon when, just after midday, people heard on their radios that Japanese planes had attacked the U.S. Navy base at Pearl Harbor.[43]

At the new Naval Air Station, all leaves were cancelled and extra guards posted at the gates. At the *Caller-Times*, printers and reporters showed up in Sunday clothes to prepare a special edition on the attack. Mrs. Guy T. Coffee, who lived on Santa Fe, told a reporter later, "We had just come home from church when we heard it on the radio. We were stunned. We couldn't imagine anything that terrible happening."[44] Telephone operator Virginia Adams said when the news was announced on radio, the switchboard lit up. "The lights were all over the board. You couldn't take care of them, there were so many."[45]

Edith Parker, who would later head the History department at Del Mar College, was a secretary for Texas Sen. Tom Connally, chairman of the Senate Foreign Relations Committee. "I was planning to go to the office to type some letters when the news of the attack on Pearl Harbor came over the radio. I knew the senator would call. At the office the telephone began to ring. The White House, the State Department, the Labor Department, everyone was looking for Sen. Connally. I called everywhere. I couldn't find him . . . An Associated Press man called and asked, 'How do you declare war, anyway?' We didn't know, but we found out. It is handled just like any other bill and then presented to the Senate for a vote." She found a book on World War I which had the declaration of war in it. She copied that and made it conform to the current situation. It was a page long. "I put my copy on the senator's desk with a note that the president wanted him at the White House at 8 a.m. The senator came in at 7 p.m. and picked up my copy. I didn't realize it at the time that I was making history, for it was my copy that was voted on in the Senate."[46]

That Monday, Dec. 8, at the cavernous Assembly & Repairs hangar at the Naval Air Station, hundreds of sailors and civilian workers gathered to hear President Roosevelt deliver his address to the nation, his war message, every word delivered with unusual formality, with deliberate spacing around each word, which served to give it extra emphasis and weight, the tone matching the gravity of the situation. "Yesterday, December the seventh, nineteen forty-one, a date which will live in infamy, the United States of America was suddenly and deliberately attacked by naval and air forces of the Empire of Japan." Like a prosecutor reading an indictment, Roosevelt summarized Japan's acts of war.[47] After the president finished, it was said, there was a moment of stunned silence in which people looked at each other, every face reflecting unasked questions, each one knowing that nothing would ever be the same, that the status quo was gone forever, blasted to smithereens like the U.S. base at Pearl Harbor, that all their lives would be changed from that moment on. Whether they understood it at that moment, the long war to come would take possession of them and everything would yield to that priority.

After the attack on Pearl Harbor, men in Corpus Christi were angry, raring to fight back. On Monday morning, Dec. 8, more than 300 men crowded the Army and Navy recruiting offices at the federal courthouse on Starr Street. Most of them were turned down because of age, physical condition, or marital status. One man was turned down by the Army because he had a trick knee, even though he had played football in college with that knee for two years. He next tried to enlist in the Navy, which also turned him down. "If you sat here in my chair as I have these last few hours and interviewed men like that," said a Navy recruiter, "you would never wonder again how our country became the great nation it is."[48] The city learned about its first casualties of the war. "Billy Jack" Brownlee, a Corpus Christi High School graduate, was killed in the Japanese bombing of Hickam Field at Honolulu. Warren Joseph Sherrill, who also attended Corpus Christi High School, was killed on board the USS Arizona.[49]

Six giant air-raid sirens were installed at sites capable of sounding the alarm to every part of the city. They were at City Hall (Mesquite and Schatzell), a site at Port and Morgan, and at Menger, Wynn-Seale, Crossley and North Beach schools.[50] The paper carried instructions for the first blackout drill. It was held on Jan. 19, 1942, between 9 p.m. and 9:30 p.m. The paper warned that it was not an occasion for parties, but a serious event that required wholehearted cooperation. The sirens were used to signal the beginning of the blackout drill.

Navy planes flew over the city, looking for points of light.[51] Photographer "Doc" McGregor positioned himself on the roof of the Plaza Hotel, where he shot time-exposure photos of streams of light from traffic and buildings just before the test began, and another showing almost total blackness, except for two tiny pinpricks of light where two places on North Beach didn't follow the drill.[52] For most people, it was absolute blackness. "That night, it was terrific," Louis Anderson,* a *Caller-Times* reporter, wrote. "The atmosphere was tense and the darkness so thick that you were a little leery about going outside."[53]

Ten days later, on Jan. 29, the blackout was not a drill. It was the real thing, prompted by a U-boat sighting in the Gulf near Port Aransas. The city's two radio stations, KEYS and KRIS, were ordered off the air. The Naval Air Station was blacked out, cafes and nightclubs were shut down, and

---

* Anderson was later sports editor of the *Caller-Times,* a position he held from 1948 until he retired in 1977.

lights were ordered turned off at Port Aransas, Aransas Pass, Ingleside, Portland and Corpus Christi.[54] It was reported that this was the first dusk-to-dawn blackout ever called or ordered in the continental United States in history.[55]

During 1942 and 1943, U-boats roamed the Gulf at will, sinking some 33 American and Allied ships, mostly tankers carrying oil and gasoline. In the last few days of January, 1942, a U-boat was sighted near the Aransas Pass ship channel. A smoke bomb, used as a danger signal from one U-boat to another, was seen four miles away, suggesting that another U-boat was in the vicinity. Merchant ships in the Port of Corpus Christi were ordered to remain in port. Navigation lights were doused. Airplanes were grounded. Trains were allowed to run, but coach lights could not be turned on. To prevent approaching ships from being silhouetted against the background of city lights, a dusk-to-dawn blackout was ordered by military authorities for Corpus Christi and coastal towns. Air-raid wardens wearing white armbands and carrying billy clubs patrolled the towns, banging on doors and warning the people inside if they saw a speck of light.[56] Anderson wrote that people in Corpus Christi could tell about those two blackout nights "to our children, when they get old enough to know not to question a few more details we can work up by then."[57] During a later blackout after a German U-boat had been sighted, the police were warned that code signals were being flashed from a window at the Driscoll Hotel. When policemen, FBI and Navy officials converged on the hotel, they discovered a torn blackout curtain flapping in the wind near a fluorescent light.[58]

Beginning in 1942, the Navy operated a radar training school on Ward Island. A security fence guarded by Marines surrounded the facility, and people in town had no idea what the big secret about Ward Island was until after the war.[59] Tight security measures were imposed around Corpus Christi, beginning just after the attack on Pearl Harbor. There were military guards posted at the port and at the Coast Guard station at Port Aransas. Extra guards were on duty at the big Humble Oil Refinery at Ingleside. Cars were stopped and searched for cameras before they could leave the mainland for the islands. Fishing boats were stopped by patrol boats and searched for cameras. Navy regulations prohibited taking photos of shipping facilities, ships, wharves, docks, storage tanks, or at any point on the barrier islands along the coast.[60] People were not permitted to take a boat out in the bay or the Gulf without having a photo ID.[61] Much of Padre Island and the Laguna Madre were off limits. The Naval Air Training Center posted four restricted areas on Padre Island that were used for aerial bombing and gunnery practice.[62] It was said that Pat Dunn's cattle, which were still grazing on the island, grew so accustomed to bombing sorties that they would run in the opposite direction when they heard planes overhead.

The war brought new rules from new government agencies created to control prices and ration supplies of critical material. Sugar registration was held in the schools. Each person was authorized one pound of sugar every two weeks.[63] Rents were frozen, beginning in August 1942. Unless one were a doctor or had a defense-related job, there would be a large white "A" stamp against a black background on the car windshield that entitled one to four gallons of gasoline each week (later reduced to three).[64] Gasoline rationing forced teachers to join kids in riding bikes to school.[65] A whisky drought lasted from 1942 to 1944. A popular song went (You get no bread with) "One Meatball." People talked of red tokens, airplane stamps, shoe stamps, sugar stamps. Civilians were allowed only two pairs of shoes a year. Men wore pants without cuffs, coats without lapels while women dressed in clothes that were somber if not drab; they were nervous about wearing too-colorful clothes or of being too ostentatious while servicemen were dying overseas. There was little butter and no bacon.[66] About half the restaurants in town observed a voluntary effort to reduce meat consumption by observing a "Meatless Tuesday." One hotel manager complained that his place observed the meatless days while his competitor continued to serve choice steaks.[67] Housewives saved cooking fat to increase the national supply of grease. Butcher shops were grease collection points. One shop in Corpus Christi posted a sign that read, "Ladies, Put Your Fat Cans Down Here."[68]

On Monday, May 25, 1942, the new 20-story Robert Driscoll Hotel was opened. It was built by Clara Driscoll and named for her late brother. The hotel featured huge murals depicting scenes of Corpus Christi. The cafe on the first floor had paneled walls and white-leather booths.[69]

President Roosevelt and Mexico's President Avila Camacho arrived on April 21, 1943 to inspect the Naval Air Station and discuss the war. It was FDR's second trip to the area; he went tarpon fishing off Port Aransas six years earlier. When the president's special train left, a large crowd gathered at Port and Agnes, where the rail spur from NAS joined the main line of Missouri-Pacific, and waited for hours to see the president. The crowd was pushed back by soldiers carrying rifles with fixed bayonets and submachine guns. When the train stopped, Secret Service men jumped off to join the soldiers on the tracks and the president's little dog Fala was led off on a leash. Roosevelt didn't wave to the crowd and people saw him only briefly behind half-closed curtains. Some said he looked very tired. Mrs. Roosevelt was seen sipping a soda but not looking at the large crowd outside the train windows. As the train pulled out, one man was heard to mutter, "Well, I've seen the president, even if he didn't see me."[70]

At the time of President Roosevelt's visit to the base, some 20,000 civilians were employed at the Naval Air Station, many of them young women who came from all over the country. They enlisted in the National Youth Administration for civil defense jobs and, in Corpus Christi, they worked in the Assembly & Repairs Department at the base learning to service and repair Navy planes. A billboard outside the north gate read:

NYA / War Work Shops / Federal Security Agency / National Youth Administration for Texas. Throughout the war, young women wearing coveralls, the regulation work clothes, with photo IDs were a common sight in Corpus Christi.[71]

Aviators trained at the Naval Air Station at Corpus Christi and its outlying fields played a major role in winning the war in the Pacific. A month before the attack on Pearl Harbor, the first class of aviation cadets received their wings. In that group was Gerald F. Child. Less than a year later, on June 7, at the Battle of Midway, Child and his PBY crew were the first to locate the Japanese fleet. Before his plane was shot down by Japanese fighters, Child kept visual contact of the Japanese carriers for three hours, which helped give American forces a great victory that turned the tide of war in the Pacific. More than 35,000 aviators were trained for combat and received their wings at the Naval Air Station and auxiliary fields, Rodd, Cabaniss, Cuddihy, Waldron, Beeville, and Kingsville.[72]

In early February, 1944, two German POWs escaped from a POW camp at Mexia, 360 miles to the north. They fled to Corpus Christi, hoping to find a boat to take them to Mexico. They were captured without mishap at a tourist court on North Beach, posing as "Free French" soldiers. They were identified as Lt. Eugene Kurz, 26, and Lt. Heinz Joachim Grimm, 21. Before they were caught, the police switchboard was flooded with tips. A student called to say he had spotted the escaped POWs near his school; officers found men in a crap game behind some bushes. Someone reported a merchant seaman with an accent; he was arrested and held briefly. One man called and said he knew a dive where the Germans hung out; it was a local bar. Two Russians in Corpus Christi studying refinery operations were arrested after they were heard "talking foreign" in a restaurant.[73]

After they were arrested, the German pilots refused to answer questions and demanded that their interrogators call them "sir."[74] *Caller-Times* columnist Bob McCracken, who wrote "The Crow's Nest," was introduced to Lt. Grimm. McCracken found it a depressing experience. "Here was a young man of fine appearance and background, cultured, polished, intelligent. Change his heavy-ribbed German sweater for a lightweight pullover model, his ersatz trousers for a pair of slacks, his cumbersome army shoes for white bucks, and he could have passed in anybody's gaze for an American college student, such as the campus knew before it went military. But when he spoke, the illusion faded. Then his professional arrogance, his ingrained contempt for everyone not of his race or class, his sarcastic politeness, stamped him for exactly what he was, a misguided zealot and an utter fool." McCracken reported what the two POWs were carrying in their pockets when they were captured. They had ID cards, dog tags, ration books, combs, mirrors, French invasion currency, cheap good luck charms, and one of them had an Iron Cross made of cheap metal.[75]

Near the end of the war, German prisoners of war were housed at the

Naval Air Station. The POWs were kept in a 10-acre garrison enclosed by six-foot-tall barbed wire near the South Gate, behind the station commissary. The POW camp was in operation from Aug. 2, 1945, when the first contingent of 100 POWs arrived, until March 16, 1946. The POWs worked 48 hours a week at various manual labor jobs, for which they were paid 80 cents a day. In one chore, they dug up hackberry trees from the banks of the Nueces River and transplanted them around the Naval Air Station. People in Corpus Christi found the POWs to be cheerful, good workers.[76]

On April 12, 1945, on the eve of victory in Europe, an Associated Press flash bulletin, accompanied by four bell rings, sounded in the *Caller* newsroom. The bulletin at 5:49 p.m. read: "President Roosevelt died suddenly this afternoon at Warm Springs, Ga." The president's death was the biggest news since the bombing of Pearl Harbor. People passed others in the street who seemed to have been crying. Business houses in Corpus Christi were closed and schoolchildren gathered around campus flagpoles to sing the national anthem. At George Evans Elementary, fifth-grade students sang two of the president's favorite songs, "Home on the Range" and "Abide With Me."[77]

On Monday, Aug. 6, an atomic bomb was dropped on Hiroshima by a B-29 named the Enola Gay. Three days later, a second bomb was dropped on Nagasaki. People learned later that a native of the city, James Burney, a geophysicist, brother of assistant district attorney Cecil Burney, was among the scientists who unlocked the secrets of atomic fission.[*78]

The long-awaited victory over Japan came on Aug. 15, 1945. Minutes after President Truman's announcement that the most terrible war in history was over, a spontaneous celebration erupted in the downtown, centered on Chaparral. A steady stream of cars and trucks filled with shouting, singing, kissing, drinking passengers drove up and down the streets, moving among thousands of jubilant pedestrians milling the streets. Police said they were reasonably well-behaved.[79] Irma Kathryn Biel (later Morley) and her friends got in her brother's old Model T and headed for Chaparral. "It was solid cars, bumper to bumper," she once told a reporter. "People were honking horns, screaming and yelling, running up and down the streets. You would drive down Chaparral to Artesian Park, make a U-turn, and drive back down Chaparral. You did that for hours, just made a circle." The *Caller* reported that the stream of cars ranged from ancient Fords to the latest models, from Jeeps driven by sailors to trucks crammed full of whooping girls, with bicycles and motorcycles "all racing madly through the streets, hooting and honking, as policemen attempted vainly to control the crowds."[80]

Juliet Knight (later Wenger), a reporter for the *Caller-Times,* was at City Hall when it was announced that the war was over. "The building emptied

---

[*] The first atomic bomb, in a test, was exploded south of Los Alamos, New Mexico, on July 16, 1945. Corpus Christi learned later that one of the other possible sites considered for that test was Padre Island.

into the streets, as did others around us. Everyone was shouting and singing, hugging each other. Tommy Matthews, a police detective, came down from the police station on City Hall's top floor. He was carrying a high-powered rifle, which he began shooting into the air. Bullets were whizzing by in all directions. No one objected. The joy of long-awaited peace exploded. For a moment in time, everybody in the city, regardless of class or race, loved one another."[81]

Returning veterans would come home to find a much-changed city, with the Dragon Grill on North Beach burned, with El Rancho turned into an apartment house, with the new Driscoll Hotel towering over the bluff, with one-way traffic instituted downtown. "Saddest of all the changes will be those missing faces among the old corner gangs, the boys who used to gather at the drug stores and never took life seriously until their country was in danger. Many are gone, and many who return will never be the same."[82]

Just about everybody had been part of the great machine of war. Now they faced the uncertainty of peace. The floodgates of eloquence were opened with a bit of graffiti, asking a universal question: "What the hell now?"[83]

CHAPTER 15

Postwar Corpus Christi - Causeway to Padre Island opens - Marine reservists leave for Korea - Refineries, chemical plants build on salt flats around the port - The great legacies of Clara Driscoll and Ada Wilson - Schools and education - Harbor Bridge replaces the bascule bridge over Hall's Bayou - North Beach falls on hard times

In December of 1945, there was a definite reminder that war was over. For the first time since 1941, streets were decorated with Christmas lights. Only a few stores, however, had strings or bulbs of Christmas lights for sale; only those who kept their pre-war strings could decorate their trees.[1] Nationally, the Office of Price Administration, the huge bureaucracy that controlled wartime rationing, was still operating. In Corpus Christi, food shortages seemed to get worse with peace. The meat panic of 1945 became a bread panic in 1946. In the summer of 1945, butchers, grocers and restaurant owners appealed to the Office of Price Administration at Dallas for relief from the "meat famine." With the city out of fresh meat, some restaurants and butcher shops closed.[2] There were bread lines in April, 1946. Stores received only a fraction of their usual supply and that sold out quickly. "Career-wives" who shopped for groceries on their way home from work found empty shelves.[3]

A special election was called for March 2, 1946 to fill the vacancies in city government after the resignation of Mayor Roy Self, a building contractor, and four members of the City Council. The year before, city voters approved the switch to a city manager form of government. Self and the City Council hired an unknown, George Hight, the first applicant for the job of city manager, after a short 40-minute interview. A movement was launched by a group of 50 Corpus Christi businessmen, which called itself the Better Government League, to recall Mayor Self and City Council members Raymond Rambo, Neal Marriott, Nels Beck and B.G. Moffett for their failure to hire an experienced city manager. Rather than face a recall election, Self and the four council members resigned. The Better Government League nominated a slate, which won the election, headed by oilman Robert T. Wilson.[4]

Six boats that served the Coast Guard were "honorably discharged" and returned to their Corpus Christi owners. The private yachts had been used to patrol the Gulf Coast from New Orleans to Point Isabel.[5] The POW camp for German prisoners at the Naval Air Station was closed on March 16, 1946. Much of the town turned out on June 18 for a parade honoring Fleet Admiral Chester W. Nimitz. A crowd estimated at 10,000 lined Chaparral for the Nimitz Day parade. Afterwards, the five-star chief of naval operations promised that "Corpus Christi will always be an important byword in naval aviation."[6] Despite the admiral's assurances, the Naval Air Station in the postwar years became a ghost of its former self. Cabaniss, the last of the auxiliary fields, closed in 1947. There was some consolation in 1949 when the Navy's precision flying team, the Blue Angels, moved their headquarters to Corpus Christi. The Naval Air Station would grow again with the Korean War buildup.[7]

In the years after the war, as building supplies became abundant and government permits were no longer needed, builders and developers got busy on the Southside. In 1949, building permits totaled $16 million, then jumped to $29 million in 1950.[8] The city's population, based on the 1950 census, was 108,053.[9*]

The Padre Island Causeway opened in 1950, giving the city a new playground. The island that had been the haunt of Karankawas, Spanish explorers, pirates and cattlemen would never be the same. Padre Island had always been a remote place. The Singer family lived there before the Civil War. There was the Curry settlement and a meat-packing plant on Packery Channel. Richard King and Mifflin Kenedy ran cattle on the island before Pat Dunn began ranching there. Dunn dug trench wells in the sand and his cattle waded in the surf to feed on delicacies brought in by the tide. Dunn sold the island in the 1920s to Col. Sam Robertson, who planned to develop the island into a resort. He built the wooden Don Patricio Causeway from Flour Bluff to the island, built the Twenty-Five-Mile Hotel up from the southern end, and planned to build a toll road from North to South Padre. The Great Depression ended Robertson's plans to develop the island and the Don Patricio Causeway was destroyed by a storm in 1933. Former Sen. John Hastings of New York and his associates bought the island in 1938, planning to build a fashionable resort, but they ran into title difficulties and scuttled the project. Another development plan in 1940 that called for building a new causeway from Flour Bluff to Mustang Island fell apart when the proposed site of the mainland terminal was needed for the construction of the Naval Air Station.[10]

It was a brilliant summer day, the sky blue as cornflowers and the sun

---

* For the long view, the population was 550 in 1850, after the town's first census, and 4,703 in 1900.

shining like a new gold piece, when the causeway opened on June 17, 1950. People were waiting in line at five that morning for the opening at noon. Among the first in line at the toll gate were Frank Morris, a cotton farmer from Portland, Mrs. D.O. Knox, a shell collector from Fort Worth, Newton Lee from Lacoste, a town east of San Antonio, A.B. Curtis and family from Corpus Christi. After the opening dedication, cars streamed across to this newfound playground and almost immediately plans for development came back to the forefront. Padre Island, it was said, would be the next Miami Beach. The new $1.2 million causeway was built by Nueces County, the cost to be repaid through a vehicle toll.[11] In the first 36 hours, the drivers of 4,800 cars paid their toll and passed by the Flour Bluff toll gate.[12] The charge was $1 for a car (regardless of how many passengers), $2 for a car with trailer, $1.25 to $3 per truck, depending on size, and 10 cents for a bicycle. The Padre Island Causeway (later renamed the JFK Causeway) opened the lonely and mysterious island to thousands of visitors. There were predictions that summer that access to Padre Island would mean trouble for the amusement park business on North Beach, but any harmful effects were not immediately apparent.

In the last weekend of June, Corpus Christi was enjoying its new playground on Padre Island when a crisis erupted half a world away. At 4 a.m. on Saturday, June 24, North Korea, as Gen. MacArthur put it, "struck like a cobra" across the 38th Parallel that divided North and South Korea.[13] During a week of crisis, Seoul fell on Wednesday, President Truman convened the "war cabinet," and the question *du jour* was, "Are we at war?" On Thursday, during a rare press conference, a newsman asked President Truman a spoon-fed question. "Would it be correct to call it a police action under the United Nations?" he asked. Truman was ready for it. "Yes. That is exactly what it amounts to." On Friday, June 30, the seventh day of the crisis, Truman made the fateful decision to send American troops into Korea to stem the tide of the North Korean aggression.[14] The *Corpus Christi Caller* editorialized: "The question of whether this country is at war is now more or less academic. Technically and legally, it isn't; actually and as a matter of cold fact, it is. American flesh and blood and American implements of war are locked in deadly combat with the Red forces of aggression. It's war, all right, the continuation of a war that has been going on for a long, long time. There can be no backing down, no retreat."[15]

On Aug. 6, the reserve Company B of the 15th Marine Infantry, composed of 80 young men from Corpus Christi and area, departed from the Missouri Pacific Depot on Aug. 6 for training in California for the Korean War. Hundreds of relatives and friends gathered to see the train off. A reporter observed that many of the Marines at the railroad station "wore a look of incredulity as though they were asking themselves: 'Can this really be me, going off to war?' A few short days ago these same boys were engrossed primarily in dating their girlfriends, making plans for college, and indulging in other sweet delights . . . The older men had been immersed in the raising of their families, the business of earning a living, and the carving of a niche for themselves in the life of their community. Their only contact with military life had been the one night a week they got together for drill as members of the Marine Reserve Corps."[16]

One mother of a departing young Marine had to be carried sobbing from the platform. An older man embraced his uniformed son for uncounted minutes, neither of them speaking. Tears did not dry, even in the hot sun. As the train departed, faces were pressed against the windows, "eyes searching out loved ones gathered on the platform. Then, as the train picked up speed, the faces became a blur that soon faded from sight."[17] Some of the men in Company B ended up with the 7th Marines in the desperate fighting around the Chosin Reservoir.[18] During the buildup of forces in Korea, soldiers arrived here to board troopships, which departed from the Port of Corpus Christi and traveled through the Panama Canal to Japan and Korea. The Corpus Christi Naval Hospital at the Naval Air Station received hundreds of wounded from the "police action" in Korea.[19]

If it was bitterly cold in Korea that winter, it was also cold at home with the arrival of a cold front—in Texas parlance, a norther. At the end of January, 1951, the worst ice storm in many years crippled and isolated the city. Buses and taxis were parked, there were no flights in or out, and telephone circuits across the state were knocked out. The frozen rain and low temperatures caused traffic accidents, closed the schools, ruptured water pipes all over the city, but it didn't break the records. The city's all-time low was a frigid 11 degrees on Feb. 12, 1899. The second all-time low was recorded on Jan. 18, 1930 when the temperature plunged to 14 degrees. The longest spell of bitterly cold weather was in 1940 when it stayed below freezing for 10 straight days. In late January, 1951, the slippery streets and sidewalks kept most people home. Those who ventured out, the newspaper reported, often lost control of themselves and their cars and wound up "where the law of gravity demanded."[20]

Industrialization came late to Corpus Christi, but it took off after World War II. In the 19th century, the city was the supply headquarters of cattle ranches in the Nueces Valley. It was a market town for wool and hides, often hauled from the interior of Mexico by oxcart. In the first three decades of the 20th Century, it was an agricultural town, its economy dependent on cabbages and cotton and other products of blackland farming. Several things happened in the 1930s to change the port's activity and the agricultural-based economy of Corpus Christi. The coming of major industries and refineries would alter the city forever. When the Port of Corpus Christi opened in 1926, it was a cotton port. The year it opened, the port handled 44,000 bales of cotton but within five years, by 1931, it handled 598,000 bales in one season alone.[21]

In the 1930s, oil came into its own in South Texas. A port official said the port would have grown steadily without oil, based on cotton and other agricultural products, but oil accelerated that growth and helped make it one of the leading ports in the country.[22] Then came the location of the Southern Alkali plant in 1934, the first major industrial plant in Corpus Christi. Part of the deal that brought Southern Alkali* to Corpus Christi was that the port would dredge a channel to serve its needs. The industrial canal leading to the new turning basin at Avery Point was completed in 1934. Modern industrial development began when the Southern Alkali plant was completed. The plant produced chlorine and soda ash, using salt brine and oyster shells as the raw ingredients.[23]

Southern Alkali wasn't the first in the Coastal Bend. One of the earliest plants in the area was the Humble Refinery at Ingleside, built in 1928. The refinery struggled with persistent labor problems throughout the 1930s and 1940s. During the war, in 1944, with the refinery workers threatening to strike, the National Labor Relations Board held a referendum at the plant. Workers were asked to answer this question: "Do you wish to permit an interruption of production in wartime as a result of this dispute?" By a vote of 187 to 119, the answer was yes. A strike followed and Humble closed the refinery and put it up for salvage sale.[24]

During World War II, in 1942, the government built and operated a plant on Up River Road, adjacent to Nueces Bay, to produce zinc and cadmium for defense. It was one of only five plants in the U.S. that produced zinc and cadmium. After the war, the plant was sold to private interests to become the American Smelting and Refining Company. ASARCO almost tripled the size of its operation by the early 1950s.[25] Work on the Bluebonnet plant of Corn Products Refining Company began in February 1947. The plant on UpRiver Road, four miles west of town then, produced starches and dextrose sugar from grain sorghum. Before Celanese opened its huge Bishop plant, it operated a research center on Clarkwood Road beginning in 1946.[26] In 1950, Halliburton Portland Cement plant, built on the north side of the industrial canal of the port, produced a million barrels of cement in its first 10 months of operation. It used oyster shell, dredged from the reefs of Nueces Bay, in great quantity.[27] On the north shore of the bay, on the old Taft Ranch, the largest industrial operation in the area, Reynolds Metals, opened its huge complex, the La Quinta** alumina plant and the San Patricio reduction plant nearby.[28] The $80 million aluminum reduction plant was built in 1951 and before it was completed work began on the $42 million alumina plant.[29] The Suntide refinery opened in September 1953 and Central Power & Light built the Nueces Bay power plant, on the north side of the port, in 1950.[30] Beginning in World War II, pipelines began sending natural gas from South Texas to the northern and eastern United States.

---

* The name was changed to Columbia Southern in 1951.
** The name was later changed to the Sherwin plant in honor of R.S. Sherwin, Jr., one of the world's leading authorities on the production of alumina.

During the war, when government officials realized the deadly threat posed to oil tankers by German U-boats in the Gulf, work began on building two pipelines from Texas to the East Coast. The 24-inch "Big Inch" pipeline, to transport crude oil, was completed in 1943 and the 20-inch "Little Big Inch," designed to carry refined products, was completed in 1944. Building the two lines was said to be the largest single government project in history.[31] Not only did these two pipelines help to win the war, by transporting 350 million barrels of crude oil and refined products, but they helped the South Texas petroleum industry to grow after the war.[32]

The refineries and chemical plants built on the salt flats around the port and across the bay on the north shore helped create modern Corpus Christi, or at least the economy on which the city thrived. Maston Nixon and Richard King III (the banker and grandson of the famous rancher) didn't know it, but they were arranging the transformation of Corpus Christi when they landed Southern Alkali in 1933. A short drive on I-37 north of the city, or on Navigation Boulevard, with that industrial backdrop, serves to emphasize the point. The time when the Corpus Christi economy depended on cabbage crops and blackland farming was a distant memory in the petrochemical age.

Along with industrial growth, civic improvements in the postwar years were keeping pace. A new red-brick City Hall opened on Shoreline in 1952.* Exposition Hall held its first show in 1952 and the Memorial Coliseum, called the world's largest Quonsetorium, opened in 1954. La Retama Library moved from the W.W. Jones mansion on Upper Broadway, where it had been since 1939, into the newly vacated City Hall on Mesquite between Schatzell and Peoples. The year the new City Hall was occupied on Shoreline was also a year of scandal for the city administration. Mayor Leslie Wasserman was indicted on charges that he accepted bribes in return for giving oil and gas leases on city-owned land. Others were indicted with him. The cases never reached court and a recall movement failed. The following year, the group behind the recall movement succeeded in helping Albert Lichtenstein win the mayor's contest.[33]

In May, 1952, an 80,000 barrel storage tank holding 47,000 barrels of kerosene went up in flames on North Port Avenue. Some 700 firemen struggled for 16 hours as they fought to bring the blaze under control.[34]

South Texas suffered a severe drought in 1953. Crops burned up. The city's reservoir near Mathis ran low and water rationing was instituted. The reservoir, built in 1936 after the La Fruta Dam collapse in 1930, was small, about one tenth the size of the reservoir after the Wesley Seal dam was built in 1956.[35]

Driscoll Children's Hospital opened in 1953, founded as a legacy of Clara Driscoll, the heiress of the Driscoll ranching dynasty. Clara Driscoll's

---

* The 1952 building on Shoreline, designed by Richard S. Colley, was demolished in 1988 despite efforts of local preservationists to save the structure, described as an "architectural legacy."

story is worth some attention. Her father, Robert Driscoll, and his brother Jeremiah acquired huge land holdings. Robert bought the Palo Alto ranch in Nueces County, 22 miles from Corpus Christi near today's Driscoll, the 53,000 acre Sweeden ranch, the La Gloria ranch in Duval County, the Los Machos ranch near Alice, and a ranch in Bee County he named the Clara Ranch after his daughter. Clara grew up on the Palo Alto Ranch, where one of the family's favorite activities was a South Texas version of fox-hunting. They kept a pack of greyhounds for chasing coyotes. In the early 1890s, Clara went away to school at Peebles and Thompson's in New York, then to study at a French convent near Paris. Her mother, Julia Fox Driscoll, took Clara and Robert Jr. on a round-the-world trip. Clara sent travel dispatches to the San Antonio and Corpus Christi papers under the *nom de plume* "A Texas Girl." Julia died in London on May 23, 1899.[36]

Not long after her mother's death, Clara led the fight to rescue the Alamo. She joined the Daughters of the Republic of Texas in a campaign to arouse public opinion to save the convent portion of the Alamo. The convent, where much of the Alamo fighting took place, was in danger of falling to a syndicate which planned to demolish it to build a hotel. The campaign by Clara Driscoll and the DRT received much attention, but little in the way of donations. Clara put up $18,000 of her own money with $7,000 raised by the Daughters of the Republic of Texas. With this $25,000, they made a down payment on the convent property, but they needed $75,000 to buy the site. They didn't have the remaining $50,000 by the deadline so Clara signed five personal notes for $10,000 each. The state was shamed into refunding her money and taking the property off her hands. Clara Driscoll became known as "the woman who saved the Alamo." Some years later, the state proposed buying land around the Alamo for a park, but the appropriation was not enough; Clara Driscoll came to the rescue again, writing a check for $65,000, an outright gift.[37]

Clara's brother, Robert Jr., a bachelor, became president of the Corpus Christi National Bank and a leader of the community in building the Port of Corpus Christi. He died in 1929 after a leg infection required two amputations. Some years after his death, Clara built the Robert Driscoll Hotel on the bluff named in his memory. As the last surviving member of her family, she became immensely wealthy from oil deposits on the family's ranch holdings. In the last years of her life, she occupied a penthouse in the Robert Driscoll Hotel.[38]

Clara Driscoll died, at age 64, on July 17, 1945. They put her body in the chapel of the Alamo where thousands of Texans paid last respects. Her portrait adorns the wall of the Texas Senate Chamber, along with Sam Houston, Davy Crockett, and Stephen F. Austin. The portrait is inscribed "Savior of the Alamo." Her bequest was to use the Driscoll wealth to create the Driscoll Foundation to operate a children's hospital "for crippled, maimed and diseased children." She set up the foundation to honor her father, mother and brother, so it is officially the Robert Driscoll and Julia Driscoll and Robert Driscoll, Jr. Foundation.[39] The Driscoll Foundation Children's Hospital, at 3533 Alameda, opened in February 1953 to provide free medical and surgical care for the children of those who could not afford that care through conventional means. It operated as a purely charitable institution until 1970.

Another perspective of the Clara Driscoll story introduces a larger-than-life character: Ada Wilson. The question is whether there was a spirit of competition between two wealthy dowager queens—Clara Driscoll and Ada Wilson, the wife of oilman Sam Wilson who had a talent for finding oil, including one well in his own backyard.[40] Mrs. Wilson founded the Ada Wilson Hospital of Physical Medicine and Rehabilitation in 1938. After Clara Driscoll built the 20-story Robert Driscoll Hotel in 1942, Ada and her husband bought the Nixon building down the street and renamed it the Wilson Building, with a big revolving "W" on the top. The Wilson Tower was built in 1952 and both the Wilson and Driscoll buildings dominated the skyline. Clara Driscoll wrote two books and an operetta. Ada Wilson wrote a short story and a number of musical compositions.[*] In an interview in the 1970s, Ada was asked if she and Clara were rivals. "Oh no, honey, not at all. That's a mistake. Let me tell you about poor Clara. I felt sorry for her. She'd go on and on about my brilliance and what I had done . . . She was a brilliant woman, a very forceful woman, and marvelous to me. She had a lovely disposition for those she liked, but if she had it in for people, oh, boy."[41]

It was a town joke that Ada Wilson was much impressed with herself. Her conversation would include statements such as "I was great" or "I was beautiful" or that she kept the Naval Air Station open "with my prestige." She had the world's largest ruby, which weighed 10 pounds, carved with her own likeness. Now, none of that should detract from her real accomplishments, including the founding of the Ada Wilson Hospital and her two-year fight to get the state to buy what became Mustang Island State Park. She and her husband purchased Mustang Island, except for the area around Port Aransas, in the 1940s for $31 an acre.[42] After Sam Wilson's death, she planned to sell the island to private developers, but decided the state should buy it as a park, but the state didn't want it. It took a court suit that went to the Supreme Court before the state finally agreed to purchase the land for Mustang Island State Park. Former *Caller-Times* Publisher Edward H. Harte wrote that Ada Wilson could have made a lot more money by selling the island to private interests, but she was persuaded that the highest and best use for her part of Mustang Island would be a state park.[43] Ada Wilson was a flamboyant original, but she was a benefactor of the city and a humanitarian who wanted everyone to like her as much as she liked herself, an ambition shared by most people.

---

[*] One of Ada's compositions, "Come to Corpus Christi," was named the city's official song in 1952.

The early years of education in Corpus Christi, private and public, were outlined in Chapter 11, summarizing events from 1846 to 1893, when the first high school graduates received their diplomas in a ceremony at Market Hall in June of 1893. It is time to tell the rest of that story.

In 1896, a room was rented on Leopard Street from Francisco Grande for use as a classroom to teach first, second and third-grade Mexican-American pupils. Rose Dunne (later Rose Shaw) was hired to teach at what was called the "Fourth Ward School." The main purpose of the school was to teach children enough English so they could attend the Central school, where they would go after they completed the course study at the Fourth Ward School.[44] There were 36 students in the school in 1901.[45] As a student progressed from one grade to the next, he or she would move from one side of the room to the other. At this time, water coolers were placed in all the classrooms in all the schools to reduce the "trips to the water jars in the yard."[46]

Rose Shaw said her first rule was order. "I would tap a bell for just about everything. One tap meant one thing and two taps meant something else and three taps meant to march outside because it was time for recess."[47] During those early years at the Fourth Ward School, she would turn to Cheston L. Heath for help. Heath and his father, Capt. Cheston C. Heath, owned a hardware and grocery store on Market Square, north of Market Hall. The younger Heath became president of the school board. He would buy books for those students who couldn't afford them.[48] Rose Shaw quit teaching for a spell, but she went to the 1908 graduation ceremony to see Julia Pena become one of the first, if not the first, Mexican-American student in Corpus Christi to graduate from high school.[49]

A new high school was built in 1911 in the 500 block of North Carancahua. People called it the New Brick Palace, a criticism of the building's cost. The original high school on the site still stood. It was a two-story building painted yellow.[50] One of the wood frame buildings was moved to the Salt Lake, one mile west of town, to become the Salt Lake School, or the Fifth Ward Mexican School.* In October 1913, the school had 78 pupils and one teacher, Rose Shaw's sister, Geraldine Dunne, who rode a horse to school from her home on Chaparral. After one year, the building was moved to North Carrizo to become the Mexican Central School with Rose Shaw back teaching.[51] After the death in 1918 of Cheston L. Heath, the school benefactor, Rose Shaw convinced the school board to name the school after him.[52]

Not long after Rose Shaw started teaching at "the Mexican school," Mary Carroll, who was brought up in Mexico, was hired to teach Spanish, even though she was just 18 and did not have a formal education. She taught at the main campus, which included the elementary school, built in the

---

* It's not clear which of the older school buildings on the site was moved to the Salt Lake.

1870s, and the high school, which had three rooms. She taught at both schools, from the sixth grade through the 11th grade, for $50 a month.[53] Spanish was a compulsory subject then, from the 8th grade up.[54] Mary Carroll was later appointed principal of the high school, in 1921, and then superintendent of the school system the following year.[55]

When the New Brick Palace was finished, school board members began planning three new schools, which were built in 1913: David Hirsch, Edward Furman, and George Evans.[56] When high school classes began in the New Brick Palace, Ella B. Wheeler Carter (class of 1912) said, "We thought we were grown, to be permitted to move from room to room for our classes, and to meet for assembly for the first time in history."[57] They would gather every morning to recite the Lord's Prayer. One hangout for high-school students of that era was the Alcove, a chili parlor on Mesquite Street. The senior class of 1919 took the day off on April 1 and went riding around the town, then to Loyd's Pier where they danced until noon, then to the Amusu for a box lunch, then back to Loyd's for more dancing.[58]

A class in domestic science (cooking) was conducted in the basement of the Brick Palace. On Monday after the 1919 storm struck on Sept. 14, the domestic science lab was turned into a soup kitchen for storm survivors. Janet Boerum (Mrs. Edward Ettel) said, "We got plenty of experience cooking, and cleaning up." The class of 1924 took a bayfront boat ride on the *Japonica* and picnicked at Calallen. Letha Agnew recalled that she had a new pink dress for the occasion. When fire escapes were added to the upper floors, school officials conducted sliding drills, with the older boys stationed to help girls onto the slides. After a week of ruining shoes and snagging clothes, the thrill of the exercise wore off.[59]

In 1929, with the city growing after the opening of the Port of Corpus Christi, the district built a new high school "out in the country." School officials expected the city to grow to the west. The school district opened its new three-story high school on Fisher Street, near the end of Leopard Street. Corpus Christi High School[*] had 26 larger-than-normal classrooms and a huge auditorium that would seat 1,600.[60] A brick structure was built for the Cheston L. Heath School and the Brick Palace became the junior high school. When Wynn Seale was completed in 1936, a Public Works Administration project, the Brick Palace was renamed the Northside Junior High School.[61]

Despite building the new high school and Wynn Seale, the lack of classroom space became a serious problem with the city's growth in the 1930s. Schools were overflowing. In 1929, when the new high school opened, the district had some 5,000 students. Ten years later, enrollment was at 9,113.[62] At Cheston Heath, there were 16 rooms with 782 students (all Mexican-Americans until 1940). The school district had four first grades in

---

[*] It was renamed Roy Miller, after the late mayor and civic leader, in 1950.

portable buildings.[63] Before wartime shortages stopped construction, the district built the Beach School on North Beach in 1939, the Robert Driscoll Junior High, and three new elementary schools.[64]

As the city grew to take in suburban villages, the Corpus Christi school district absorbed outlying schools. The Fairview school on UpRiver Road became part of the Corpus Christi district in 1932; the school was renamed for Alice Borden Savage, the first and only woman to serve on the Fairview school board. The Kostoryz school district, founded in 1907, became part of the Corpus Christi district, as did the Sunshine and Aberdeen districts, which had been combined into the Sundeen district.[65]

If the schools were overcrowded in the 1930s, they became even more crowded in the 1940s. The Naval Air Station brought in thousands of workers and their families and then base military families. Many incoming students went to the Flour Bluff district, but thousands attended Corpus Christi schools. To add to the problems, the state switched from a 11-grade to a 12-grade system, which kept students around for another year.[66] After efforts to raise taxes to build new school buildings failed and after an appeal to get the government to finance new construction failed, the school district resorted to half-day sessions. School board president W.B. Ray told the community, "There is no alternative to half-day school. One group of children will come for four hours in the morning and another for four hours in the evening."*

The federal government did help. The Federal Works Agency provided $3 million that helped to fund building Travis, Austin, Fisher, Oak Park and Lamar schools, a gym at Coles, a wing at Driscoll, and rooms under Buc Stadium.[67] After the war, wooden barracks that once housed aviation cadets at the auxiliary air fields were turned over to the district to convert to classrooms.[#68]

Bond issues were passed in four consecutive years and the school district built new schools at a fast pace. The new $3.5 million W.B. Ray High School, at Minnesota and South Staples, opened in September 1950. Only one part of the new state-of-the-art school had air conditioning, the library.[69] Besides Ray, the school system built another new high school, Mary Carroll, seven junior highs, 17 new elementary schools, plus additions to existing schools. Mary Carroll, the city's third high school, was named for the school system's only woman superintendent.[70] Richard King High School was completed in 1965 and Foy Moody opened in the fall of 1967.[71]

Television came to Corpus Christi in June 1954 when KVDO began broadcasting on ultra high frequency (UHF) channel 22. Most sets were made for very high frequency (VHF) and needed a converter before they

---

* The last half-day sessions finally ended in 1959.
# The last World War II barrack classrooms at Crockett Elementary were removed in 1970.

245

could pick up KVDO. Earl and Billy Aldridge ran a radio store on N. Carrizo. They had TV sets for sale before there were any local TV broadcast stations. The Aldridges recalled how people would park and stare at their sets in the window, even when there was nothing but a test pattern on the screen. In 1948, a seven-inch black and white set cost about $300. To get a signal required a 40-foot-high antenna to pick up Houston or San Antonio stations. Needless to say, reception was gray and fuzzy, with much of the picture left to the imagination.

It was a big event in town when KVDO—nicknamed "K-Video"—began broadcasting on June 20, 1954. The first full day of KVDO's operation a man climbed the broadcasting tower and threatened to jump. He changed his mind. The station had no coaxial cable link to any of the three national networks. All of the KVDO programming either originated in its own studios on Staples Street or were canned programs shipped in on film and aired weeks late.[72]

One of KVDO's programs was "Video Kitchen" with Pat Kline, shown each afternoon from 3:00 to 3:30. One afternoon, she came in to begin preparing for her cooking show and discovered that over the weekend they had switched her gas range to an electric range, due to a change in sponsors from Houston Natural Gas to CPL. As the show began, she put a Pyrex pan of water on to boil. No one had removed the paper packing from the burners and they caught fire. The show host grabbed the pan of water and poured it onto the cooking element. The electric circuits throughout the building shorted out and KVDO was off the air until the next day.[73] Other programs aired during KVDO's early days was "Roving Reporter" with Jeanne Ramsay and NOW (Nonsense or Worse) with Charlie St. John, who was also featured on the station's news, weather, commercials, and special programs.[74] A local talent show "Sneak Preview" was aired in the evenings.

KVDO had the market to itself and tried to keep its monopoly by filing suit to keep competing VHF stations from getting FCC approval, but the lawsuits were unsuccessful and KRIS (Channel 6, VHF) and KSIX-TV[*] (Channel 10, VHF) went on the air two years later.[75] KSIX-TV began broadcasting from a studio between Corpus Christi and Robstown called "the farm." The only thing in the room was an orange crate and a microphone when the engineer flipped a switch and, with Vann Kennedy, the owner standing nearby, Gene Looper began to read: "This is KSIX-TV signing on the air on Channel 10, September 30, 1956, and operating in the public interest."[76] KVDO soon folded and was sold in 1957. KVDO returned as a VHF station briefly (KVDO Channel 3) in 1964 with a new office and studio at Lexington and Everhart.[77#]

C.G. "Gus" Glasscock—a pioneer Corpus Christi oilman who built one

---

[*] It was later changed to KZTV.
[#] It was later changed to KIII.

of the first offshore oil platforms, in 1949—filled in 22 acres of the bay in 1954 and announced plans for a resort hotel and office complex. The plans fell through and the vacant Glasscock fill land was put up for sale.[78]

Just before Christmas, 1958, the Navy announced it would close the Overhaul & Repair Department at the Naval Air Station, which had been in operation since World War II. The Navy employed some 3,000 civilian workers to overhaul and repair Navy aircraft and aircraft engines. The closure was a severe blow to the Corpus Christi economy. The Navy's O&R was the largest employer in the area. There were protests from business, civic and religious leaders. The governor, congressmen and senators all remonstrated with the Secretary of the Navy, but the decision stood.[79] In 1959, the O&R facility was shut down. Employees were offered jobs at other Navy repair facilities elsewhere. Two years later, the city cheered when the new Army Maintenance Center (now the Army Depot) moved into the old O&R facility.[80]

Corpus Christi's resident federal judge, James V. Allred, died of a heart attack in Laredo on Sept. 24, 1959, where he was conducting court. Allred, a former governor of Texas, had been appointed to the federal bench by President Franklin D. Roosevelt, who stepped to the rear platform of a special train, when it was stopped at Wichita Falls, to announce the appointment. Allred moved from Houston to Corpus Christi in 1949. Judge Allred once described his political philosophy. "I thought I was a moderate, but the history books have made me a liberal. That's all right." Just before he died, the judge recessed court, explaining that he was feeling "a little under the weather." He died in his hotel room a few hours later.[81]

Two years after Allred's death, Brownsville attorney Reynaldo Garza was appointed to fill the vacancy. "If I am confirmed," Garza said, "I will be succeeding one of the finest judges who ever served on the bench."[82]

Corpus Christi's big quarrel in the early 1950s was over what would replace the long inadequate bascule bridge. It was built in 1925-1926 over what had been a muddy inlet called Hall's Bayou, a place where boys in rolled-up britches once went crabbing. While the bridge was being built, huge dredges worked behind it, scooping out a turning basin for the new port in the marshy salt flats. When the new port was opened to ships, on Sept. 14, 1926, the major attraction was the bascule bridge. It didn't have a formal name. "Bascule" is the French word for see-saw, which described the counter-balanced bridge built by the Wisconsin Bridge & Iron Co. The bascule bridge was built across the port entrance. The bridge was 121 feet long, 52 feet wide, weighed 1,500 tons, and cost $403,000. It was painted black and coated with grease to protect it from salt air.[83]

The Corps of Engineers opposed plans for this type of lift bridge, arguing that a 97-foot-wide channel opening would not be wide enough to accommodate the ever-larger ships that would enter the port. But the city, which was paying for the bridge, wanted the cheapest bridge possible. This false economy would be costly. The city's reluctance to spend enough money to build the kind of bridge and port entrance the Corps of Engineers recommended created a problem that bedeviled the city for three decades. At first, the city was enamored of the bridge. In the *Caller's* special port-opening edition, it was said that the bascule "is so designed and constructed that within one minute's time this massive structure, weighing hundreds of tons, may be hoisted 141 feet in the air, allowing incoming and outgoing ships to enter and leave the turning basin. Then, with only a slight interruption of traffic, it is dropped back into position and the vehicles of commerce and pleasure again take motion." But the "slight interruption in traffic" turned out to be wishful thinking as the bascule bridge increasingly became an impediment to traffic, both cars and ships.[84]

The 97-foot opening under the bridge, as the Corps had warned, was a very tight fit for cargo ships, which often scraped the sides of the bridge, sometimes putting it out of commission. It was closed for 10 days in 1931 after a major mishap involving the *SS Youngstown*. Part of the hull of "Old Ironsides" was scraped off when the wooden ship smashed into the bascule when it visited Corpus Christi in 1932. Tankers and freighters often brushed against the bridge's fenders. It was such a dicey maneuver for larger ships that some shipping companies refused to come to Corpus Christi for cargo when they could go to other ports. After 1942, the Navigation District issued a regulation requiring larger vessels to use tugs when passing through the bascule channel. The master of a Dutch cargo ship said that the tight squeeze under the bascule bridge "scared the hell out of me." Sailors called it "threading the needle".[85]

The bridge was also a nuisance for motorists. When the siren sounded that a ship was approaching, the bridge was raised, stopping traffic. Drivers fumed because the ships were usually far out in the bay. But ships were required to signal the bridge when they were a mile away and the bridge tender was required to raise the bridge. The bridge stayed up about 20 minutes (or less for a barge or smaller vessel) but the wait seemed endless to motorists roasting in their un-air-conditioned cars on a hot day while watching a tanker or a barge approach the bridge. Bascule became an adjective for "bottleneck". While children loved waiting at the bascule bridge, they could play outside the cars and watch for the ship, eventually, to pass by, but adults with appointments to keep and things to do hated it. Traffic would back up, sometimes as many as 30 times a day. One bascule bridge tender said the bridge became an alibi for wayward husbands who would say, "Honey, the bridge held me up." The tender said anytime a woman asked him if the bridge had been raised at a particular time, he always said yes, and figured that he kept not a few husbands out of trouble.[86]

The bascule bridge became increasingly inadequate as the volume of traffic grew and as the frequency of it being raised increased, and as the size of the ships visiting the port became larger. But how to replace it? Beginning in the 1930s, the city argued about how to solve the bascule bottleneck. In 1941, the idea of digging a toll tunnel under the port entrance was considered, but World War II intervened. In the early 1950s, the town debated whether to dig a tunnel under the port entrance or build a new bridge over it. Those who favored the tunnel argued that a high bridge would tower over the city like a big ugly birdcage, depicting it as a larger version of the squat black bascule bridge. They argued that the network of bridge approaches would destroy homes in an historic part of town. The issue was settled when the state highway department said it would put up $9 million to finance construction of a high bridge, but not a dime for a tunnel. That was the deciding factor. On March 24, 1954, the City Council voted to build a high bridge. A disappointed Mayor Albert Lichtenstein, a leader of the tunnel faction, resigned in protest. He walked down and sat in the audience, his arms crossed in resignation and indignation.[87]

Construction of the high bridge began in June, 1956 when the first load of shell was hauled to the bridge site. It took three years and four months to build; four workers were killed falling from the structure. A 16-year-old painter from Dallas, working beside his father, lost his footing. His father watched helplessly as his son fell to his death. The sides of the cantilever truss bridge were joined on March 13, 1959. When the two met in the middle, the spans were off a few inches, but that had been expected. One side was jacked up until the two fell perfectly into line. The finished structure included 21.5 million pounds of steel and 134.4 million pounds of concrete, for a total weight of about 155 million pounds.[88]

The new Harbor Bridge opened to traffic on Oct. 23, 1959. It was a big day for the city, like the port opening celebration 33 years before. The first car across was driven by Eleanor Tarrant, a 46-year-old housewife whose name was pulled in a drawing. The cars in the official motorcade, led by Mrs. Tarrant, crossed over the old bascule bridge to North Beach so they could make the return trip, heading into the city, over the new Harbor Bridge. The old bascule bridge was sold for scrap. A few hated to see it go. In its early days, it was a symbol of the city's growth and prosperity, before it became a bottleneck. In a way, it straddled not only the port entrance, but old and new Corpus Christi.[89]

The Harbor Bridge loomed over North Beach. Two major events —bookends around the decade of the 1950s—had profound consequences for North Beach, known as the "Playground of the South." The first event was the construction of the new causeway to Padre Island. When it opened in 1950, it gave Corpus Christi a new playground of surf and sun to compete with North Beach's carnival attractions and the eroding bayside beach. The second event at the end of the decade was the construction of the Harbor Bridge.

Even before the bridge was built, North Beach was in decline. The amusement park that once made it a center of fun closed in 1957, two years before Harbor Bridge opened. The often long waits to cross the bascule bridge hurt, but traffic was funneled through North Beach. The lanes of the new Harbor Bridge rushed traffic away. You didn't go to North Beach except on purpose. North Beach was bypassed and isolated. The merchants on North Beach could look at the traffic exiting Harbor Bridge, whizzing by thick and fast, and remember how nice it used to be when all the cars streamed past their front doors.

The strip of land that juts between Corpus Christi and Nueces Bays, a peninsula of 310 acres, was once called Rincon. Later in the 19th Century it was known as Brooklyn. By the 1890s, it was called North Beach. The official name now is Corpus Christi Beach, although many call it North Beach and it is North Beach in the institutional and collective memory of the city.[90]

The history of North Beach is the city's history. Henry Kinney had a mustang pen on the Rincon where his workers slaughtered mustang horses for their hides. Once in the 1840s Kinney's wranglers hid in a mesquite thicket and watched Comanche warriors, on a horse-stealing raid, throw buffalo robes into the shallow end of the mud slough so their horses wouldn't bog down in the mud. This was the area where Zachary Taylor's troops landed in the summer of 1845 and beat off the buzzing rattlesnakes as they set up their tent encampment that stretched from North Beach to the area around today's Artesian Square.[91]

Twenty years later, a large beef packing house was located on the salt flats of the Rincon. Hall's Packery was built by John Hall, a former Union soldier and immigrant from England. Hall's Bayou,* was the mud slough, or tidal inlet, leading to the packery.

Between the north end at Rincon Point and Indian Point across the bay, was the reef road, a raised oyster bed that divided Nueces Bay from Corpus Christi Bay. The reef provided an underwater bridge, which the Indians had long used to cross the bay. Nueces County for decades maintained signposts in the water showing its location, which zig-zagged across the bay. If a rider or wagon driver tried to take a short cut, he ran the risk of drowning his horses. The *Caller* reported in March, 1896: "R.K. Reed of Portland visits Corpus Christi and reports that a wagon belonging to D.C. Rachal is stuck in the reef, the driver taking the wrong side of the stakes in crossing Nueces Bay. . ."[92]

During the Ropes' boom in the 1890s, local people put up money to build a resort hotel on North Beach. The Miramar Hotel opened in May, 1891. Three months later it burned to the ground. In 1895, heavyweight champion "Blacksmith" Bob Fitzsimmons opened a camp on North Beach to

---

* Hall's Bayou would be under Harbor Bridge, the entrance to the Port of Corpus Christi.

250

train for his fight with "Gentleman" Jim Corbett. A man who came with the Fitzsimmons entourage, F.E. Ring, built a group of tourist cottages to capitalize on the popularity of the heavyweight boxer's presence. The Ring Villa tourist courts were the first in Corpus Christi.[93] Beginning in 1905, and lasting for a decade, North Beach was the scene each August of a summer Methodist encampment and revival called Epworth-By-The-Sea (see Chapter 11).[94]

Spohn Sanitarium was built in 1905 on the site of the old Miramar Hotel. Before the hospital was built, the town's doctors operated on their patients in the homes of the patients, with bad lighting, untreated water from a cistern, and the kitchen or dining room table used for the operation. Dr. Arthur Spohn led efforts to raise money to build a hospital. A tract of land was bought on North Beach, fronting the bay, and a two-story building erected. Dr. Alfred Heaney admitted the first patient to Spohn Sanitarium. In March 1905, the hospital was turned over to the Sisters of Charity of the Incarnate Word to operate.[95]

President William Howard Taft delivered the dedication speech at the opening of Corpus Christi's first country club. The date was Oct. 22, 1909. The clubhouse, painted dark green with white trim, was a wooden building with a veranda on four sides. A 9-hole golf course was laid out across Timon Boulevard from the clubhouse.[96] The clubhouse was sold in 1914 to local businessmen who turned it into a bathhouse. In 1912, John Dickenson built the Beach Hotel. The hotel was converted into an army convalescent hospital for soldiers recovering from wounds in the fighting in France in World War I. The top floor of the hospital became a refuge during the 1919 storm.[97]

The most momentous event happened on Sept. 14, 1919 when a fierce storm surge swept across and inundated North Beach. Like the city proper, the history of North Beach is clearly divided between before and after the great storm. On the Monday morning after the storm, only three of hundreds of structures remained: the McDonald home, the Spohn Sanitarium, and the Army convalescent hospital. Before the storm, North Beach was one of the city's finest residential areas. After the storm, all but one of the great mansions were destroyed and what had been a growing development was leveled.[98]

The North Beach Bath House (the former Country Club clubhouse) was rebuilt the year after the storm by Bruce Collins, whose family owned theaters in town. Collins and his cousin, John Mosser, spearheaded the revival of North Beach. They built the North Beach Pleasure Park, the Saltwater Pool, and in 1927 Collins purchased an old wooden sailing ship abandoned in the port turning basin, moved it to North Beach and sank it in the sand to keep it stable. The side of the ship was painted in large letters, "Dance On The Ship." Dancing on the deck under the stars, with an evening breeze blowing off the bay, was made the ship a popular venue for a Saturday night. When the *USS Constitution*, "Old Ironsides", came to visit

Corpus Christi in 1932, its escort of destroyers created a wake that lifted the dance ship from its sand base and it broke free of its moorings. The vessel was finally returned to its berth at the pier. It was destroyed the following year by a hurricane in 1933.[99]

The old Beach Hotel, turned army convalescent hospital, was rebuilt and renamed The Breakers. Its Spanish village ballroom, designed to resemble a rose garden in moonlight, was famous. North Beach was the place to be, a place of perpetual summer, with a carnival every day, the smell of salt air, the lapping waves and feel of warm sand. Tourists crowded the waterfront, which stretched from the port entrance, the old Hall's Bayou, to the Nueces Bay Causeway, about a mile in length. The Crystal Beach Park Ballroom and pier were built south of the bathhouse in 1929. The following year, a dance marathon contest was staged by Harold J. Ross in the Crystal Beach Pavilion. The marathon, which attracted large crowds, lasted for 31 days.[100] In 1931, the Crystal Beach Park Ballroom and pier were sold, remodeled and renamed the Bayside Park and Ballroom.

A top attraction in the Bayside Park in the early 1930s was the Roll-A-Coaster, built south of the Breakers Hotel and near the pier for the Dance Ship. In 1931, a 13-year-old girl was killed; she stood up on a turn and was thrown out. In another fatal accident, a woman was killed when one of the cars jumped the track. The Roll-A-Coaster was closed and removed.[101]

A September storm in 1933 damaged the Nueces Bay Causeway; it was out of commission for several months. The storm tide resulted in floodwaters of five feet on North Beach. Tourist cabins were swept away, the pier and the Dance Ship were destroyed. The recently remodeled Bayside Park and Ballroom were destroyed, the timbers scattered for blocks along the beach.[102] The damaged structures of the North Beach attractions were rebuilt and North Beach remained the city's playground. On an average weekend, the North Beach Amusement Park, the carnival midway, the Ferris wheel, merry-go-round and other rides would attract as many as 4,000 visitors. On a holiday weekend, the number could climb to 20,000 or more.[103] The city's boom years in the 1940s, when thousands of Navy cadets were in training at the Naval Air Station, were busy, crowded, prosperous days for North Beach.

The numbers of visitors began to drop, gradually, after the Padre Island Causeway opened Padre Island in 1950. The Saltwater Pool was closed and removed and, in 1957, the amusement park and boardwalk were closed and torn down. Bruce Collins blamed the bascule bridge for the declining number of visitors coming to North Beach.[104] In 1959, Collins and other beach property owners convinced the City Council to change the name from North Beach to Corpus Christi Beach, to emphasize that it was a part of the city.[105]

Maybe they were grasping at straws, but how the name change would have helped to revive North Beach's flagging fortunes is beyond this writer

252

to fathom. From the perspective of hindsight, it no doubt made a bad situation worse by severing North Beach from its historical associations. But changing the name would not change the reality. Whatever it was called, the little strip of land between Corpus Christi and Nueces Bays would never be what it once was in its glory days, "The Playground of the South."[106]

CHAPTER 16

City builds new airport near Clarkwood - Carla a near miss for Corpus Christi - O&R reopens as Army Depot - NASA tracking station monitors early space flights - City annexes Flour Bluff, but not without a fight - Three fishermen slain in a bizarre crime - Dr. Hector P. Garcia leads fight for equal rights for Mexican-Americans - Religion got a slow start in Corpus Christi - A storm named Celia wreaks havoc

If the Harbor Bridge was the most obvious symbol of a growing city, the city's new airport was not far behind. The need for a larger airport had long been evident before the city built a new facility in the Clarkwood area. Corpus Christi International Airport opened in 1960. Dignitaries were flown from the old Cliff Maus Field to the new airport. Corpus Christi had come a long way since 1911 when Oscar Brindley gave demonstration flights in his Wright machine at North Beach on July 3 and 4, 1911, eight years after Wilbur and Orville made history at Kitty Hawk, N.C. The flights conducted by the Wright Brothers Company in Corpus Christi were part of a big Fourth of July program that year. The plane was shipped in crates and assembled on North Beach. Brindley, the flier, was the manager of the Wright Brothers field and training academy near Dayton, Ohio.[1]

A crowd gathered on Monday, July 3, 1911 north of the Epworth League encampment. Admission to see the flights was 50 cents for adults, 25 cents for kids. People rode the new trolley car line from downtown to North Beach to see the flights. The first day's exhibition occurred before a crowd estimated at from 2,000 to 4,000. Brindley in his first flight flew low over the breakers off North Beach, before climbing high into the air, soaring over the sailboats on the bay. Brindley's last maneuver of the day, the *Caller* reported, was the spiral glide which had caused the deaths of so many daring pilots.[2]

"Straight down the machine came, until within 200 feet of the earth, when the horizontal rudder was given an adroit turn, and the biplane changed course, flying away in a beautiful swoop heavenward." During the second day's exhibition, on the Fourth, Brindley took up a volunteer, land promoter F.Z. Bishop, who founded the town of Bishop. A headline said that Bishop, who weighed 220 pounds, was the heaviest passenger ever carried aloft in a flying machine, but the writer was surely guessing. When asked if he had been afraid, Bishop said flying in an airplane was "as easy as sleeping on a feather bed."[3]

Another Wright plane with pontoons was shipped to Corpus Christi in the fall of 1912. It was assembled on North Beach and flown by pilot Charles de Remer. On Christmas Day, 1912, DeRemer made his first flight from the water of Corpus Christi Bay. On the last day of the year, he took up members of the Commercial Club and newsmen. That March, DeRemer was supposed to carry the mail from Corpus Christi to Port Aransas, but he lost a propeller on takeoff and the mail had to be taken across by boat. The plan to carry the mail to Port Aransas by air came five years before airmail service began nationally.[4]

Ten Army planes from the new Kelly Field in San Antonio landed on the flats on North Beach in 1917. The planes brought a baseball team for a game. The following year, 17 army planes from Kelly landed on North Beach. The old North Beach field on the sand flats served as the city's unofficial landing place for a decade, until 1928, when a new municipal airport was built on pasture land off old Brownsville Road. The first flier to land at the new field was a barnstorming pilot and former World War I aviator from San Antonio, Cliff Maus.[5]

Cliff Maus and business partner Bob Maverick moved their Texas Air Company to Corpus Christi in 1928. It was mainly a crop-dusting operation. Corpus Christi hired Maus to spray the city with mosquito insecticide. Maus and Maverick started a flight club, the Corpus Christi Aero Club, and a flight school, the Southern Academy of Aeronautics. Flying clubs were very popular at a time of record-setting flights like Lindbergh's trip across the Atlantic. Maus was named the airport manager. Passenger service began in 1929 when Southern Air Transport, with a six-seat Fokker, flew between San Antonio, Corpus Christi, and Brownsville. A round-trip flight cost $27.90.[6]

The new airport was busy in 1930 with some 250 planes landing or taking off each month. That year, an exhibition team led by Clyde "Upside Down" Pangburn gave demonstrations at the airport. People were taken up for flights over the city. On Oct. 19, 1931, Jimmy Doolittle touched down for 16 minutes during his attempt to set a speed record from Ottawa to Mexico City. On June 1, 1932, American Airways (later American Airlines) began passenger service to Corpus Christi with a 10-passenger Fairchild. It landed at Corpus Christi on a flight from Brownsville and when it took off for San Antonio the plane was carrying 360 pounds of mail, inaugurating air-mail service to the city.[7]

After Maus left in 1934 to work for Braniff, he was killed when his plane crashed in a fog outside Fort Worth. In honor of the dead pilot, the airport's name was changed to Cliff Maus Municipal Airport; in common usage, the name was shortened to Cliff Maus Field. Braniff began flying out of Corpus Christi in 1935 and Eastern in 1939. The city in 1947 gained control of Cuddihy Field, a World War II Navy training base. The need for a larger airport was realized when Corpus Christi International Airport opened on Aug. 7, 1960.[8]

The Weather Bureau warned on Friday, Sept. 8, 1961 that a slow-moving and dangerous storm, Hurricane Carla, would hit the Texas coast, probably around Corpus Christi. On Sunday, Corpus Christi residents began the familiar routine of boarding up. The downtown was evacuated after reports warned that Carla's storm surge could top the seawall. North Beach and the islands were evacuated. Some 15,000 people in Corpus Christi sought shelter at the courthouse and the schools. The National Guard was called out before the storm hit.[9]

On Monday, Sept. 11, the gods of chance spared Corpus Christi. Carla, which had been aimed straight at Port Aransas, abruptly turned right and slammed into the coast at Port Lavaca. There was damage, but much less than had been anticipated. Winds knocked down power lines, uprooted trees, and broke windows. Bridges were washed out on Ocean Drive. Old island passes were reopened. The Padre Island Causeway was damaged. The state's new million-dollar Port Aransas Causeway, from Aransas Pass to Harbor Island, was wrecked.[10] This new causeway replaced the old Aransas Harbor causeway, built in 1912 as the Aransas Harbor Terminal Railroad. The tracks were covered with asphalt and it was converted into a roadbed for cars in the 1950s.[11]

Carla was a near miss for Corpus Christi. After the storm, experts said if Carla had not veered and had struck Port Aransas as expected, with the pass funneling the force of the storm directly at Corpus Christi, it would have swamped North Beach and downtown Corpus Christi, even with the seawall, like the deadly 1919 hurricane. Vice President Lyndon Johnson flew over the storm-damaged area of the coast and a reception was held for him at Memorial Coliseum. Later that year, voters rejected a bond issue to pay for repairing the bridges on Ocean Drive.[12]

It was Lyndon Johnson's second trip to Corpus Christi that year. He led a delegation from Washington in June to inspect Padre Island as a site for a national park. The delegation was treated to a giant fish fry on Padre Island. At the time of the visit, various bills in Congress to establish a national seashore on the island were halted over questions of how large the seashore would be. After Carla struck in September, other questions were raised about the wisdom of the government investing and building structures on hurricane-vulnerable Padre Island.[13]

The Corpus Christi economy suffered a severe jolt when the Navy closed the O&R facility at the Naval Air Station. The Navy's Overhaul & Repair department, created during World War II to repair and rebuild damaged planes, was the largest employer in Corpus Christi before it was shut down in 1959. Corpus Christi exerted all of its pull and influence in Washington to prevent the closure, to no avail. In late 1960, a request for the Army to reopen the closed facility was turned down. Then, in January of 1961, after the new Democratic administration of John F. Kennedy and Lyndon Johnson took office, the request to reopen the O&R was reconsidered. On Feb. 22, Corpus Christi's Rep. John Young reported that the reopening of the O&R had been approved. On March 6, more than 1,000 job-seekers stood in line for interviews for jobs at the new Army maintenance center.[14]

Corpus Christi lost out on a NASA laboratory center, which went to Houston, but it was happy to get the Army Aeronautical Depot Maintenance Center (with the awkward acronym ARADMAC), which opened on April 21, 1961. It was the army's only complete aircraft overhaul facility. The number of employees at the depot would steadily rise during the 1960s, up to nearly 5,000, as the depot began to repair helicopters for the escalating war in Vietnam.[15]

Corpus Christi and Flour Bluff held what essentially turned out to be competing elections on Aug. 5. The voters in Corpus Christi voted to annex Flour Bluff. The voters in Flour Bluff voted to incorporate as a separate city, spurning the advances of Corpus Christi. Not to be denied, the Corpus Christi City Council, acting on the wishes of Corpus Christi voters and disregarding Flour Bluff's wishes, passed an annexation ordinance. The logic of the modern, progressive city demands expansion—that cities must expand, or wither—so used car lots replace farm fields. The suburbs—which benefit from the city without paying its taxes—will be brought in and brought along, willing or no. City police began to patrol in Flour Bluff. A suit was filed contesting whether Corpus Christi could annex Flour Bluff against its will, which would not be settled until 1964.[16] Suits filed by Flour Bluff residents against annexation were heard in the district court of Nueces County, which found the annexation legal and binding, then an appeal went to the Texas Court of Civil Appeals and, finally, the U.S. Supreme Court, which ruled that it did not have jurisdiction to act in the matter.[17]

The year 1961 was a hot year for city politics. With Mayor Ellroy King deciding not to seek re-election, three slates fought over the prize. They included Odell Ingle's Corpus Christi Party, Joe Salem's Alert Party, and Ben McDonald's Progress Party. Voters elected McDonald mayor and elected three members of his slate to the City Council: Tom Swantner, James H. Young, and M. P. Maldonado. Three other council members were elected from Ingle's Corpus Christi Party: Dr. James L. Barnard, Jose DeLeon, and W. R. Roberts.[18]

The Project Mercury tracking station, one of 17 such stations around the world, was completed at Rodd Field, the old auxiliary World War II Navy aviator training base. While many early astronauts in the space program completed flight training at the Naval Air Station, that was not why Corpus Christi was chosen for the tracking station. The site was chosen because NASA scientists determined that orbiting space capsules would pass over Corpus Christi more often than at any other location in the United States, and more frequently than any location in the world except for two sites in Australia.[19]

Astronauts Alan B. Shepard, Jr., America's first man in space, and Virgil Grissom, the second man in space, visited the Rodd Field tracking station in June. Both men had been stationed at the Naval Air Station for advanced flight training several years before. Tracking Station No. 16, at Rodd Field, built by Western Electric, began operating in 1961. The station monitored the orbits of early space flights. It was one of the few tracking stations equipped to help astronauts get back to Earth in the event of an emergency. The Rodd Field station, beginning with John Glenn's orbital mission in 1961, was one of NASA's main tracking stations throughout the Mercury, Gemini and Apollo projects.[20]

On the city's "to do" list for progress was the removal of the old bascule bridge, a squat, black, greasy symbol of frustration for many people in the city. After the bascule was removed in 1961, the port entrance was widened to allow for two-way ship traffic under the new Harbor Bridge. Not long afterwards, a tanker and barge collided in the port turning basin, spreading 10,000 barrels of volatile benzene. Two children were hospitalized after breathing benzene fumes.[21] Movie star Kathy Grant (the former Kathryn Grandstaff of Robstown) arrived in Corpus Christi to campaign for her father, Delbert Grandstaff, in his unsuccessful race for the U.S. Senate.[22] Kathy Grant married Bing Crosby in Las Vegas in 1957. She was remembered locally as the little Miss Buccaneer-Navy of 1949.[23]

Annexation, a hot topic in 1961, was still a hot topic in 1962. Voters by a narrow margin approved almost doubling the size of the city by annexing 49 square miles of land that included the Naval Air Station to the south and Clarkwood, Annaville and Calallen to the west. Those who opposed annexation were led by former mayor Farrell Smith, who argued that extending city services to the annexed areas would cost the city more than $800,000. The vote was 8,030 for with 7,252 against. With the annexed areas, the city's population was estimated to be 184,163.

Four years after legislation was first introduced, and a year after Vice President Johnson led a Washington delegation to visit Padre Island, President Kennedy signed a bill in 1962 to make an 80 ½ mile-long area on the island a National Seashore.[24]

The summer of 1962, after the fifth case of polio struck, many thousands in Nueces County took the Sabin oral polio vaccine on sugar cubes. After the first shipment of the vaccine arrived, a national controversy erupted over the Type III vaccine, which delayed the immunization drive. After the campaign began, some 500,000 doses were administered in Corpus Christi and Nueces County.[25] The year 1962 marked the end of an era that began when Uriah Lott's Tex-Mex Railroad inaugurated railroad passenger service to Laredo in 1875. The Missouri-Pacific ran its last passenger coach out of Corpus Christi on June 20, 1962.[26]

The following year, work began on constructing the Crosstown Expressway. This was high on the city's "to do" list. Also on that list was completing the second span of the Nueces Bay Causeway, which was finished in August 1963.[27]

A courtroom in the Nueces County Courthouse was packed in January 1963 when Mrs. Loraine Lambert Graning was sentenced to life in prison for murdering her husband. Court testimony revealed that she and her 16-year-old son from a previous marriage killed her husband, Melvin B. Graning, 61, head supervisor of Western Electric, which built the NASA tracking station at Rodd Field. Graning had been struck in the head, then hauled in the trunk of a car to the Nueces River near Calallen, his head held under water until he drowned.[28]

A more sensational and bizarre crime occurred on April 12, 1965 when three fishermen were shot to death. The trail of circumstances that led to a lonesome stretch of the Laguna Madre began in California. Paul Eric Krueger, 17, and John Phillip Angles, 16, were the sons of well-to-do parents in Hollywood, Calif., and San Clemente. The two met at school and talked of running away, going to South America to join a rebel movement. They stole Krueger's mother's car and headed for Mexico, then decided they would hijack a boat at Corpus Christi. They had an arsenal of weapons, including an AR-15 rifle and an M-1 carbine, both military weapons. When they arrived in Corpus Christi, they parked their car at the JFK Causeway, rented a small aluminum boat, and traveled down the Laguna Madre. They stopped at a deserted fishing shack and drank from a bottle of wine. On the way back, about six miles from the causeway, they saw three men fishing from a pier. Krueger told Angles, "I'm going to kill those people." They landed, struck up a conversation with the fishermen, then returned to their boat and picked up the AR-15 and M-1. Krueger opened fire on the three men; they all fell into the Laguna Madre. He stood above them on the pier and continued to shoot until his rifle was empty and then took the M-1 and emptied that into the lifeless bodies. They returned to their car, drove to San Antonio, then split up, with Angles hitchhiking to Kerrville and Krueger driving into Mexico.[29]

The bodies of the three men were discovered near the fishing shack, by the pier, just inside the Kleberg County line. The dead men were all from Corpus Christi: Noel Douglas Little, 51; Van Dave Carson, 40; and John David Fox, 38. All were married with children. The bodies were so riddled with bullets that an autopsy couldn't determine how many times they had been shot. Angles was picked up in Kerrville and told officers the story, which they found hard to believe. Krueger was arrested in Mexico, somewhere between Juarez and Chihuahua. Angles, a juvenile at 16, was not brought to trial. He was eventually released from the State School for Boys at Gatesville in 1968. Krueger was tried in Dallas, on a change of venue. He entered a guilty plea and was sentenced to life in prison. The widows of the three slain fishermen were all in court for the sentencing. They were stay-at-home housewives who were forced to take jobs to support their families after their husbands were killed. It was the most violent and mindless of crimes in a violent age—two runaway, homicidal kids with high-powered weapons and vague ideas of joining some revolutionary movement in Venezuela. It was one of the worst crimes in South Texas history, a crime of pure happenstance, as random as they come, without motive or reason except in the psyche of the killer.[30*]

In 1966, the Port of Corpus Christi observed its 40th anniversary. The Nueces County Navigation District retired the first bonds issued during the 1920s to build the port. In conjunction with the anniversary, the port completed a project to deepen the ship channel to 40 feet. It finished extending the channel west to the Viola Turning Basin. The Port also constructed the Richard King Terminal and dredged the Rincon Basin on the south shore of Nueces Bay to serve shallow-draft barges.[31]

An outbreak of St. Louis encephalitis claimed five lives in 1966, with 103 confirmed cases. In 1967, the public grain elevator at the port was heavily damaged by lightning; it was rebuilt and new equipment added. The JFK Causeway and the Port Aransas Ferry became toll-free in '67. Nueces County turned them over to the state to operate the following January. The second big hurricane of the decade, after Carla in 1961, was Hurricane Beulah. Corpus Christi was on the edge of the storm, which produced record rains and flooding after it made landfall near Brownsville on Sept. 20, 1967. Every hurricane, it is said, has different and distinctive features and effects. One effect from Beulah was that commodes all over Corpus Christi backed up from the increased pressure in the sewer system. Long afterwards, people would say that something with an awful odor "smelled as bad as Beulah." The year after Beulah, on April 8, 1968, Mrs. Lyndon B. Johnson officially dedicated the Padre Island National Seashore. Thousands attended the speech-making celebration on Padre Island.[32]

Dr. Hector P. Garcia returned to Texas from the battlefields of Europe after World War II. He came to Corpus Christi to practice medicine in 1946. He appraised the situation and didn't like what he saw. There were no Hispanics on the City Council. There were no Hispanics on the Nueces County Commissioners Court. There were few Hispanic doctors or lawyers in the state of Texas. In broader terms, racial and ethnic prejudice was

---

* Paul Eric Krueger was released from prison after serving 12 years. He had earned three degrees while in prison and was hired as a professor at Penn State University, without the university's knowledge that he was on parole for a triple-homicide. Krueger's past was revealed in a TV documentary and news reports in 2004.

ubiquitous. Hispanics and blacks were treated as inferiors or, at best, with friendly condescension. This state of affairs dated back more than a century, to the town's earliest years. It was Dr. Garcia, locally, and the civil rights movement nationally, that forced people to begin to reconsider their attitudes. It forced them to ask questions of themselves, questions that had been submerged for too long. The civil rights movement, here and elsewhere, engendered bitter feelings between those like Dr. Garcia who could not accept the inherent unfairness of the status quo and those who could not or would not accept the need for change.[33]

Dr. Garcia, the returning veteran, would not be satisfied with a return to the kind of society he had known before the war. From that time on, Dr. Hector P. Garcia had a cause, and he served that for the rest of his life. His great influence cannot be charted in terms of specific actions or programs, yet he was one of the figures of the 20th century, along with Martin Luther King Jr., who helped reshape America, who helped rediscover its long-lost ideals of equality. Hector P. Garcia was born in the small Mexican village of Llera on Jan. 17, 1914. After the town was attacked during the Mexican Revolution, his parents moved to Mercedes in the Valley. His father, a professor in Mexico, was strict; if he found young Hector playing baseball instead of studying, he would use his belt. Hector's mother taught him that nobody was a servant and for the rest of his life he would avoid using the Spanish "tu," often employed in speaking to a servant.[34]

In 1948, the Manon Rice Funeral Home in Three Rivers refused to host a wake in its chapel for Pvt. Felix Longoria, who was killed in action on the island of Luzon in the Philippines in World War II. Garcia brought national attention to the incident and, with the help of Lyndon Johnson, arranged for Longoria's body to be buried in Arlington National Cemetery. This incident gave impetus to the developing organization formed by Garcia, the American GI Forum, which became the nation's largest Hispanic veteran's organization. Garcia's fight for recognition for Hispanics, veterans and otherwise, continued for the rest of his life. He went on to become a member of the U.S. Civil Rights Commission and a representative of the United States at the United Nations.[35]

Dr. Garcia was not eloquent, but he was earnest and intense. He once said in an interview that he was not a revolutionary, that he was very happy to work within the system. "I am a capitalist," he said, pointing to his Cadillac. "I only wish there were more capitalists named Garcia and Gonzalez." Later, when others his age were dead or resting on their laurels, he was still working for the cause that had dominated his life since his return from Italy after World War II. He was a man who acted on his morals and he could inspire others to see the justice of his beliefs. His influence was felt in other ways: He helped persuade the Kennedy administration to reopen the closed O&R repair facility to help provide jobs for Hispanics in Corpus Christi. When the Naval Air Station was in danger of being closed in 1976, Garcia, who had often mobilized voter turnout for Democratic tickets, used his clout in Washington to help keep it open. Former *Caller-Times* publisher Edward H. Harte wrote after Garcia went to Washington to lobby in behalf of keeping the Naval Air Station open, "The doctor laid it all on the line — his 30 years of leadership among the Mexican-Americans, his efforts in behalf of Adlai Stevenson, Jack Kennedy, Lyndon Johnson, Hubert Humphrey, and George McGovern, and finally his phenomenal job in getting out the vote for Jimmy Carter. I don't think I have ever before seen a major political figure put all his chips on one square on the roulette table quite that way. Garcia has put everything he's got —which is considerable—at the service of this community. But . . . he's more likely to deserve the praise of his fellow citizens than to hear it."[36]

Dr. Garcia and other civil rights leaders wrought greater changes than people appreciated at the time. The changes have become so fundamental that we take them for granted today. Historian Joe B. Frantz said Dr. Hector P. Garcia did more for Hispanic civil rights than anyone else in the country. Dr. Pat Carroll of Texas A&M University-Corpus Christi said, "What he was able to do was to act as a broker; he could bridge the gulf between the Hispanic community and the Anglo power structure." Carroll said Garcia was unquestionably the single most important figure, as an agent of change for Hispanics, in this area in the 20th century. He died on July 26, 1996.[37]

Corpus Christi's history is intertwined with the stories of its churches. When Zachary Taylor's army camped along the shoreline, preparing for the coming war with Mexico, a Catholic priest, the Rev. Ubald Estany, arrived to preach to the troops. One officer wrote that Estany was "a native of old Spain who has become a traveling savior of souls. He resides on the San Antonio River, and makes periodical visits to villages in a circumference of 400 miles. He gave us an excellent sermon in Spanish and English."[38]

That was in 1845. After Estany came a Methodist minister, the Rev. John Hayne (sometimes spelled Haynie) who arrived in February, 1846, a month before the army left for the Rio Grande. Hayne was escorted by Texas Rangers. They crossed the reef road on horseback. Hayne didn't have a place to sleep. He bedded down on bags of shelled corn and pinto beans. He preached in the Union Theater before a congregation of officers and soldiers. In 1848, the Rev. James Giraudon celebrated mass in the home of Cornelius Cahill.[39]

Religion got a slow start in Corpus Christi, Eugenie Reynolds Briscoe wrote, because ministers didn't want to move to a "godless city."[40] No ministers were listed in the 1850 census. It was a rough frontier town more conducive to saloons with dirt floors than churches with stained-glass windows. Not until 1853, some 14 years after Henry Kinney founded the town, did the city gain its first house of worship. The First Methodist Church, at the corner of Mann and Mesquite, was made of shellcrete (an adobe made of clay and crushed shells). The church was organized by Rev.

Henderson Lafferty; charter members included 18 whites and six blacks. The church had space for 200 worshippers. In 1872, the Methodists built a frame building with a tall bell tower. The church was used as a school during the week and a meeting house on Sunday. The old adobe church built in 1853 was turned into a parsonage.

A few years later, in 1879, the Methodists lost their parson when the Rev. C.M. Rogers married wealthy ranch widow Martha Rabb and they moved to Austin. The Methodists in 1912 built a new church to replace the frame building that had served since 1872. There was no financing for the building; the money was raised as the work went on. Rev. T. F. Sessions, the pastor, would pay workers with "faith checks" on Saturday and church elders would go to the bank on Monday to sign notes to cover the checks. The 1912 Methodist church was the pride of the city. It lasted until the new First United Methodist Church was built on Shoreline in 1955.

In 1854, the Rev. Bernard O'Reilly built the first Catholic church, St. Patrick's, on Tancahua, between Antelope and Leopard. It was also built of shellcrete, described as a crude building 40 feet by 40 feet. The only adornment was a painting of the Last Supper over the altar. The building was not actually completed until 1857.[41]

The yellow fever outbreak in 1867 claimed one of the best-loved priests in the city's history, Rev. John Gonnard, who worked tirelessly caring for the sick until he collapsed himself. When he died, wrote Mary Sutherland, he was mourned by every man, woman and child in Corpus Christi. Dominic Manucy, installed as the new bishop at Brownsville in 1874, decided to move the Vicariate to Corpus Christi. The bishop's first priority was to replace the old church, built in 1854. The new St. Patrick's, built on the same block but behind the old church, was designed by Charles Carroll, father of Mary Carroll, who would become school superintendent in Corpus Christi.[42]

The second St. Patrick's was two years old in 1884 when one of the more outstanding priests in the city's history arrived. Rev. Claude Jaillet, a native of Lyons, France, came to Texas in 1866. He spent years riding the ranch circuit in South Texas. A book about him was titled *Father Jaillet, Saddlebag Priest of the Nueces* written by Sister Mary Xavier. Corpus Christi Cathedral, one of the city's most beautiful churches, was built in 1940 on Upper Broadway on land donated by the John G. Kenedy family. The old St. Patrick's was stripped down and moved to North Beach to become Our Lady Star of the Sea Catholic Church.[43]

The Presbyterians in 1859 tried to establish a church, but there was a falling out among prospective members between Union loyalists and ardent secessionists. It would be another eight years, after the war, before Presbyterians organized. Members of the new Presbyterian Church were awaiting the building of their new church on land donated by Richard King. The lumber was stacked on the bluff site when yellow fever hit in 1867. The dressed lumber was used to make coffins. The fever claimed the pastor, Rev.

William Mitchell, and many church members.[44]

Lucile White, a preacher's daughter, once recorded her memories of services in the old First Presbyterian Church. She remembered the whiff of cologne when Henrietta King took her seat. She remembered the weary sigh of Mrs. Perry Doddridge when the preacher made one point too many in a long sermon. Presbyterians in 1901 constructed a new church on the bluff made with white brick from Laredo and red brick from San Antonio, paid for by Mrs. King. It lasted almost three decades. The church in 1930 moved into a new building built on the site of the old Perry Doddridge home on South Bluff.[45]

The Episcopalians, organized in 1860, held services at the Nueces Courthouse (built in 1854) then moved to the Cahill building on Chaparral (the first Cahill building was on Water Street). The Episcopalians finally got a church in 1873. The Church of the Good Shepherd, at Chaparral and Taylor, was a landmark with its lofty steeple that could be seen far out in the bay. The Episcopalians had a church, but it was a struggle to pay the pastor.

Rev. William Brittain, who became pastor in 1871, resigned in 1872. In his letter of resignation, he reminded the Vestry that they owed him "44 and 37/100 coin dollars" in back wages. He wanted payment in silver or gold coin, not paper dollars.[46]

The problem persisted for years. Hortense Warner Ward tells of a minister who went on strike over his unpaid salary. One Sunday, Harry Heaney (the future doctor) was being taken to church by his father, Dr. A.G. Heaney. Since it was time for services to start, they were surprised to see the minister, Rev. Horace Clark, sitting on the front porch of the rectory smoking a pipe.[47]

"Aren't you going to have services?" Dr. Heaney asked.

"No," said Dr. Clark. "The children may come to Sunday school, for they cannot help what their parents do. But we will have no service for the adults until I am paid my salary."[48]

The First Baptist Church was organized in 1878. But the founding members didn't get a permanent meeting site until they bought a blacksmith shop on Mesquite Street in 1883. The church was so weak it couldn't pay the pastor; his salary was subsidized by the Baptist State Convention. The First Baptist Church moved from its converted blacksmith shop to a new brick building on Mesquite at Taylor (where the *Caller-Times* is today). The old church building was moved to South Staples, where it became the Staples Street Mission. The hurricane of 1919 flooded the basement of the new brick church, blew off part of the roof, and ruined the furnishings. In 1950, the beautiful new First Baptist Church was built on Ocean Drive.

The St. John Baptist Church was founded in 1875 as a Baptist church for blacks in Corpus Christi. The first meeting was held in Gussett's barn. The founding members came from Indianola after the disastrous hurricane of 1875. The first church, built on North Broadway, was called St. John Free

Mission Baptist Church. A group of blacks held prayer meetings in homes in 1884, which led to the creation of St. Paul United Methodist Church. Even older was the Congregational Church. During the occupation by federal troops after the Civil War, the chaplain of a black regiment, Rev. Aaron Rowe, founded a church for freed slaves. The Congregational Church, financed by the Congregational Church of New England, occupied a prized location on the bluff.[49]

The Mexican Methodist Church was organized in 1874. The name was changed in 1948 to the Kelsey Memorial Methodist Church, after Anna Kelsey donated $75,000 to build a new brick building at Comanche and Mexico. Kelsey was the adopted daughter of early Corpus Christi settlers John and Amanda Kelsey. Our Lady of Guadalupe, built on Tancahua in 1903, was the first Catholic church built expressly for Hispanics; services were conducted in Spanish. The church was moved and the name later changed to Holy Cross Church. In 1906, St. Boniface Church was constructed for the German community. As Czech settlers moved into the Kostoryz area, they also joined St. Boniface's. The church was renamed in honor of the Slavic patron saints Cyril and Methodius in 1931.[50]

Corpus Christi's early Jewish settlers, including Julius Henry and David Hirsch, were influential in the community, but their numbers were small. After the turn of the century, out-of-towners were needed to form a quorum of 10 men necessary for a Jewish service. When Sidney Wolf, a newly ordained 25-year-old rabbi, arrived in 1932, he found a congregation of 60 families using a frame building with a pot-bellied stove and "some of the most uncomfortable folding chairs" in existence. He led a campaign to build a new temple, which resulted in the construction of Temple Beth El, dedicated in 1937. Wolf came to Corpus Christi on a three-month trial basis in 1932. He died in 1982 after five decades of promoting harmony among religious and ethnic groups. His death was mourned by all who knew him.[51]

A storm began as a rain squall over Africa, a hurricane seedling, on July 23, 1970. It formed into a tropical depression, named Celia, between Swan Island and Grand Cayman eight days later. On Saturday, Aug. 1, the storm, still a tropical depression, hit western Cuba, killing five on the Guanacabibes Peninsula. On Sunday, the U.S. Weather Bureau announced a possible hurricane watch.

It was a sunny day in Corpus Christi. The approach of a storm sets off thousands of calculations. People absorb the information and calculate the odds of the storm hitting Corpus Christi, then they calculate the odds of survival if it should, they balance the pros and cons, the what-ifs and maybe-nots, then decide to stay or go. A part of that calculation is the understanding that officials always, always, exaggerate the danger. This time they didn't. The calculations were easy on Sunday. Celia was headed toward Port Lavaca, like Carla nine years before, and it was derided by the hurricane watchers as "more show than blow."[52]

People woke to the news that Celia had turned west, in the face of a high pressure area, and by 10 a.m. on Monday, winds were gusting at 90 mph and tides were running two feet above normal. The storm was moving 15 mph. Evacuation was ordered for Rockport, Port Aransas, North Beach and low areas around Flour Bluff. Police squad cars with loudspeakers patrolled North Beach, urging people to leave. Corpus Christi began to board up with a will. A line of yachts were waiting to be hoisted out of the water by two mobile cranes at the bayfront marina. As the nervous yacht owners watched, with the atmosphere tense before a storm, a yacht lifted high in the air began to spin wildly. The winds reached 112 mph and any chances of getting the waiting yachts out of the water were gone. Only 45 of the 240 boats in the marina were pulled out for safety. Pilots closed the Port of Corpus Christi.[53]

By 1 p.m. Monday, intensifying, gale-force winds lashed the coast. The wildly flapping red and black hurricane flags at the marina were ripped to shreds. By 2 p.m., the sky was black and ugly overhead, with a sickly orange cast to the east, like a bad color filter over the horizon. Patients at Spohn Hospital were moved away from the east-facing windows and placed in the hallways. The eye of the storm compacted, from 40 miles wide to 10 miles wide. This was bad news. Like an ice skater who brings in her arms to spin faster, the storm was gaining speed and intensity.[54]

By 3:30 p.m., a hurricane plane measured Celia's winds at 140 mph. The center of the storm was just south of Port Aransas. Ten minutes later, hurricane winds whipped inland, with hard, driving, horizontal rain. The winds, screeching and roaring, exceeded 100 mph. Power went out. Celia's eye was practically over Corpus Christi Bay. The winds reached 118 mph at the Reynolds plant at Gregory. At 4:30 p.m. in Corpus Christi, the winds uprooted trees, broke windows, tore off roofs, filled the air with flying debris. By 5:30, the winds reached 161 mph. Three hours later, it was just about over. The winds died down as darkness fell over a damaged and bruised city.[55]

People began to assess the damage. On Tuesday morning, 450,000 people in Corpus Christi and 12 surrounding towns were without electricity. Dazed residents found their neighborhoods in shambles, with uprooted trees, splintered fences, caved-in walls, crushed cars, downed telephone poles, and roofless houses. Checkpoints were set up to stop sightseers from coming into the city. A woman bar-owner in downtown Corpus Christi, sweeping up glass in front of her bar, yelled at the rubber-neckers, "Go home, you creeps, there's nothing to see here."[56]

Capt. Eddie Mathisen rode out Celia on his 36-foot boat in Corpus Christi harbor. "It wasn't supposed to be much of a storm, maybe winds of 75 mph, no worse than a strong norther or spring storm. But the winds came out of the northwest and pushed all the water from the boat basin. We were sitting in the mud. Leon [another boat captain] held his beer up in a toast and about that time his chart house took off, spinning 500 feet in the air. My boat rose in the air like it was on a wave. It was he wind. It came down on top of a 14-inch piling which crushed through the hull. We crawled across Shoreline Boulevard holding onto curbs."[57] As Mathisen noted, Celia did unusual things with the tides. Instead of rising, Corpus Christi Bay dropped more than four feet, causing tremendous damage to boats that were left in the marina.[58]

In the wake of the storm, people found some strange things. In San Patricio County, the storm destroyed a man's chicken houses, scattering 18,000 chickens over 20 acres.[59] A desk from a top floor of the 600 Building on the bluff was found below on the roof of the Amusu Theater on Mesquite. Confidential papers from the offices of an oil company in the Guaranty Bank Plaza were blown into the offices of a competitor in the Oil Industries Building. Attorney Charles Lyman's framed college diploma was blown from his office on the sixth floor of the Wilson Tower to the law office of Max Bennett on the fourth floor of the Wilson Building. A chair from an office in the Wilson Tower was blown out of a window, which appeared smaller, to Lower Broadway. In one office, a desk that weighed up to 500 pounds was blown halfway through a large window, like a cork in a bottle.[60] One Corpus Christi man returned to his demolished apartment. The only thing still standing was a small table on which the phone still sat. And it was working.

It was said the whole town smelled like burning charcoal. With good reason. With power out, barbecuing was the only way to cook. People across the city held barbecue parties to cook meat in the freezer before it could spoil. There was meat, but no ice for their drinks. Ice was in great demand. When a man died in Corpus Christi, people took ice instead of flowers. A man from Corpus Christi drove to Falfurrias to get a bag of crushed ice for his neighbor who was ill and he thought might die of a heart attack during the heat. An out-of-town dealer arrived with a truckload of ice, expecting to make a handsome profit. It was confiscated by police and distributed free, at the orders of the mayor. A mother from Port O'Connor met her daughter halfway to give her 200 pounds of ice. One Corpus Christi family drove to Kingsville just for a cold drink with ice in it.[61] People would always remember what it was like without power: dark nights, no TV, no airconditioning, the heat thick and still, like being in the country a long time ago.

Celia left 31 dead: five in Cuba; 14 in Florida to undertows and high waters; and 11 in Texas. Five deaths were attributed to the storm in Corpus Christi. Boyd Wilson, 66, on Lawton Street, was killed when a window blew in and struck him on the head. Cleofas Leal Gonzales, 42, on Delores Street, was killed when a wall collapsed on him. Three other deaths were attributed to heart attacks during the storm: Leonal Salinas, 46, August Emmert, 71, Noe Garcia, 48. At Sandia, Richard Gotcher, 23, was killed when the roof of his house caved in. At Port Aransas, Mrs. Michael Hughes Sr., her son Michael Jr. and daughter Melba all drowned in a ditch. At Alice, Sam Fuller was killed when he cut into a live power line felled by a broken tree limb.[62]

Almost the entire federal building on Starr Street was commandeered by the Office of Emergency Preparedness. A dozen federal agencies set up shop in the building. A radio station was installed on the first floor of the building and law offices were converted into an emergency communication center. In the days after the storm, experts tried to figure out what had happened with the storm that was supposed to be more show than blow. They agreed that Celia was a most unusual storm. Corpus Christi received more than 90 percent of its damage from the left side of the storm, normally the weak side, in an unprecedented manner. It was not a major hurricane, in every sense of the word, said Dr. Robert Simpson, director of the National Hurricane Center. They were shocked at the storm's sudden change from a moderate to a severe hurricane. Celia was "super-energized." But, by comparison, Celia was "way down on the list" with other major storms, such as the hurricane of 1919 or Hurricane Carla in 1961 or Hurricane Beulah in 1967.[63]

Simpson, who grew up in Corpus Christi and went through the 1919 storm as a youngster, told a Corpus Christi reporter that 90 percent of the damaged homes and other structures in Corpus Christi were caused by winds in the west and southwest or rear of the storm. "No hurricane has ever done this before," he said. "It is a phenomenon we don't profess to understand. I don't know what happened. We did everything science will let us do to try to explain it. And we still don't know why."[64] One lesson was clearly understood. The unpredictable Celia taught, if nothing else, that with a hurricane in the Gulf, you can never assume anything.

EPILOGUE

Corpus Christi had good years and bad in the decades after Celia. In the 1970s, Rev. Harold Branch was elected to the City Council, the first black person to sit on the council since 1889. A sensational crime of the era was the killing of sportsman-businessman-playboy Randy Farenthold, who had inherited a fortune from his grandfather, pioneer farmer Rand Morgan. Farenthold's mutilated body, with a concrete block wired around his neck, was found in the surf at Port Aransas. The motive was that he was a witness in a fraud case. Years later, Bruce Bass was convicted and sentenced to prison for the slaying; he served six years of a 16-year term, was released, then killed in Corpus Christi. That year, 1972, the Art Museum of South Texas moved into its new building at the north end of Shoreline, designed by famed architect Philip Johnson. Big news in 1975 was the suicide of George Parr, the "Duke of Duval." Parr was found dead on his ranch near Benavides after a manhunt. He was due in federal court in Corpus Christi, facing a possible prison term for tax evasion, when he killed himself. This ended the Parr family's long reign of corruption in Duval County.

On Aug. 1, 1977, the doors were locked on the 1914 county courthouse. Officials and employees moved into a new $19.6 million courthouse with its gold façade on Leopard. A top murder story that year was the slaying of Wanda Kirk and her daughter Kira, from Bastrop. Their charred bodies were found 50 miles south of Bob Hall Pier on Padre Island; no motive and no suspects were ever found for the slayings. The following year, in 1978, the polarizing Mayor Jason Luby resigned to run for Congress. He refused to leave council chambers after announcing his candidacy and was forcibly removed by policemen. He lost the race, then ran in 1982, but lost to Solomon Ortiz.

In 1979, the Ixtoc I oil rig exploded in the Bay of Campeche, spreading oil and goo on the beaches of Texas. U.S. District Judge Owen Cox ruled that the Corpus Christi school district's method of electing board members was unconstitutional because it diluted the voting power of Mexican-Americans. He accepted a plan for a mixed at-large and single-member district elections, ending a long, contentious period that began with school busing.

In the days leading up to August 10, 1980, Hurricane Allen frightened a lot of people before it weakened and stormed ashore in the remote ranch region between Brownsville and Corpus Christi. The almost nine foot storm surge was the highest along the Corpus Christi bayfront since the 1919 storm. North Beach stood under five feet of water; Bob Hall Pier and the Cole Park pier were destroyed; the lower roadway section of the Kennedy Causeway and parts of Flour Bluff were under water.

President Jimmy Carter held a town hall session at Moody High School on Sept. 15. He was the first president to visit Corpus Christi since Franklin D. Roosevelt came to visit the Naval Air Station in 1943. Ronald Reagan, running against Carter, made a brief airport stop two days later. Voters in the 14th Congressional District, which included Corpus Christi, were shocked when Rep. Joe Wyatt sought treatment for alcoholism. He decided not to seek re-election. Nueces County Judge Bob Barnes ran in the Democratic Primary for the seat, but lost to State Sen. Bill Patman.

On April 7, 1981 an explosion at the Public Grain Elevator at the port killed nine workers and injured another 30. Almost half the grain silos were destroyed. A container of pest-control pellets flashed, igniting grain dust and causing the explosion. The grain elevator was reopened two years later.

After a long battle over competing sites, the Choke Canyon Dam and reservoir were completed on June 8, 1982. The 20-year-long fight was over whether the best site was on the Frio River, between two brush-covered hills called "The Choke," or a place on the lower Nueces below the Bluntzer community called the R&M site. In 1985, Corpus Christi celebrated the Fourth of July two days early. It received word that a Navy base would be located at Ingleside. The Corpus Christi area was one of six finalists for the installation before the Navy picked Ingleside. Plans called for the base to homeport the battleship USS Wisconsin and aircraft carrier USS Lexington. When the Wisconsin was mothballed and the Lexington decommissioned, the mission of the base was changed to mine-warfare operations. Two years later, political power broker Hayden W. Head was killed in a plane crash as he tried to land at his ranch in Zavala County. His wife, Annie Blake Morgan Head, survived the crash. A ranch foreman tried to pull Head from the burning cockpit of the Cessna, but the injured Head waved him off, telling him to see to his wife first. He was 82. Head was the acknowledged kingpin of the Corpus Christi establishment, at a time when major political decisions could be decided by a small group of men and made to stand. Sen. John Tower said, "I've never heard a disparaging word about Hayden Head from anybody. That's rare in this business." That same year, after a fierce campaign, Betty Turner defeated Tony Bonilla to become Corpus Christi's first female mayor.

In 1990, after a 20-year struggle to become a reality, the Texas State Aquarium opened on North Beach. The Lexington traveled across the bay from Naval Station Ingleside to its new berth, and final resting place, off North Beach. The Navy awarded the Lexington to Corpus Christi after a national bidding contest. The aircraft carrier, which served in the Pacific in World War II, became the Lexington Museum on the Bay. It was dedicated on Nov. 14, 1992. Ten years later, the decommissioned aircraft carrier was named to the National Register of Historic Places. Corpus Christi State University, which dated back to 1971, became Texas A&M Corpus Christi in 1993. What had been an upper-level university, serving junior and senior students, was expanded to become a full four-year university. A building expansion followed, ushering in a new era of development for the city. Corpus Christi had been the largest city in the state (indeed, the largest in the country) without a four-year university.

Tejano superstar Selena was shot and killed on March 31, 1995, by the president of her fan club, Yolanda Saldivar, who was convicted later that year and sentenced to life in prison. The following year, on July 26, longtime civil rights leader and founder of the American GI Forum, Dr. Hector P. Garcia, died. In death, people began to realize what he had been able to accomplish in his fight against discrimination by the force of his personality, and of course the rightness of his cause. On June 4, 1997, former mayor Mary Rhodes died of breast cancer. She had served three terms as mayor and was seen as a strong and committed leader. Her great achievement was to push for building the 101-mile-long pipeline from Lake Texana to bolster the city's water supply. She was able to push the project through over fierce public opposition. The pipeline, completed in 1999, was named the Mary Rhodes Memorial Pipeline. Luther Jones, who served four terms as mayor, from 1979 to 1987, died in 2002. A rare snowfall covered Corpus Christi on Christmas Eve, 2004. The national weather service recorded 4.4 inches in 24 hours.

Corpus Christi received a severe blow in May, 2005, when the Base Realignment and Closure Commission recommended closing Naval Station Ingleside. As the decision to locate the base created a mood of celebration in 1985, the decision to close cast a pall over the city. Local leaders figured the base's closure would cost the area 7,015 direct and indirect jobs and a loss in annual payroll of $364 million. It was a big setback, like the Navy's closing of the Overhaul & Repair facility in 1959. That September, as Hurricane Rita threatened, the city ordered a mandatory evacuation, but when the storm turned, the order was lifted. In 2006, voters by a 55-45 margin rejected the city's plan to close a stretch of Padre Island beach to vehicular traffic to accommodate a planned $1.5 billion resort. The rejection of the vehicle ban scuttled the resort development. The beach closure plan was only one of several fierce controversies during the decade such as razing the Memorial Coliseum, made redundant by the building of the American Bank Center. This fit an old an old character trait of Corpus Christi. The city's inhabitants have always been up in arms over something. In the early years, after the town was founded in 1839, it was divided over the question of whether the land around it belonged to Texas or Mexico. In the Civil War, it was divided between Confederate and Union loyalists. In the era of the railroads, the town was divided between those who saw the railroads as progress and those who worried they would stifle the oxcart trade. It was divided over raising taxes to pay for the new port infrastructure and it was divided over building the seawall. In more recent years, it was split over whether to build a dam at Choke Canyon on the Frio or the R&M site on the Nueces; it was divided over expanding the university to four-year status, over various developments along the bayfront and on the islands, and over whether to preserve Memorial Coliseum or tear it down. In the first decade of the 21st Century, it seemed that Corpus Christi had evolved into an acrimonious, contentious, fractious, edgy, and sometimes exhausting city. That was nothing new for Corpus Christi. It was always so. As quarrelsome as the city can be, it is a vibrant, living city, a place of complexity, a place with all the stresses and strains that define modern life, a place that, for many people, will always mean home.

One day before sundown, near the completion of this work, the writer took a walk along the bayfront. The usual evening breeze was beginning to freshen the air, but it was still hot, being early September, and there were only a few pink-faced tourists about, gazing around, not sure about what they were supposed to be looking at. Short waves slapped at the bottom steps of the seawall while beyond the breakwater, the line of sky and bay was darkening into a smudge on the horizon and beginning to fade from view. Looking at the sweep of the bay, one thought back to the sweep of time. One of the last of Zachary Taylor's soldiers to leave, on March 8, 1846, was Capt. W.S. Henry. As the soldiers marched away, he took a long look back. The fields of white canvas were no longer visible, he wrote in his diary, and the campground looked like desolation itself, but the waters of the bay looked as sweet as ever.

1919 HURRICANE

PLATE 3.1 – After the 1919 hurricane, Laguna Street was a scene of massive destruction as workers remove storm debris. Despite the destruction, utility poles stand with telephone and electrical lines still attached, indicating that the damage was mostly caused by the 12-foot storm tide and not by the hurricane-force winds.

CAUSEWAY

PLATE 3.2 – After the 1919 storm demolished the Nueces Bay Causeway, a temporary structure was built in 1921 to eliminate the 40-mile trip around Nueces Bay. Remains of the old causeway are visible on the left. The temporary causeway was used for another 30 years. The railroad trestle on the right, built in 1884, survived the storm.

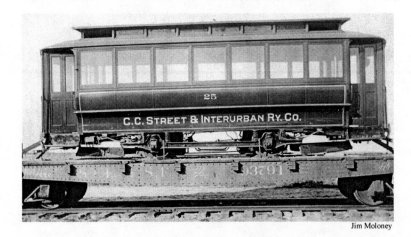

CORPUS CHRISTI STREET & INTERURBAN RY. CO.

PLATE 3.3 – New streetcars arrived in Corpus Christi in February 1910.

BAYFRONT PIER

PLATE 3.4 – After storms in 1916 and 1919 destroyed piers and wharves on the bayfront, the city built a new Pleasure Pier in 1922. The 1,000 foot long pier extended from the end of Peoples Street into the bay, where the T-head is today.

PORT OF CORPUS CHRISTI

PLATE 3.5 – Seven years to the day after the 1919 hurricane struck, the Port of Corpus Christi opened. The port became a major economic force for the Corpus region. In its early years, the port's major export was cotton. That began to change in the 1930s after oil was discovered.

Jim Moloney

NIXON BUILDING

PLATE 3.6 – Maston Nixon, a cotton farmer and entrepreneur, built Corpus Christi's first "skyscraper," the Nixon Building, in 1927 to provide offices for cotton brokers attracted to Corpus Christi by the opening of the port. The region around the city was a major cotton-producing area and the port led the nation in cotton exports.

278

The First Annual South Texas Agricultural
▼ ▼ and Industrial Exposition ▼ ▼

All Roads Lead to Corpus Christi, April 10 to 14

Jim Moloney

THE EXPOSITION

PLATE 3.7 – The South Texas Agricultural and Industrial Exposition was held in April 1934 in a warehouse on 19th Street. Expositions were held in 1935 and 1936. Programs ranged from farm and livestock exhibits to displays of industrial concerns.

Jim Moloney

NUECES COFFEE COMPANY

PLATE 3.8 – Yarborough Brothers came to Corpus Christi and the new port in 1929.

RANCH HOUSE

PLATE 3.9 – Pat Dunn's second ranch house was built a mile from Packery Channel.

DRIFTWOOD CORRAL

PLATE 3.10 – An old corral on Pat Dunn's ranch on Padre Island. Dunn used corrals and cutting chutes to eliminate roping, which he thought was cruel.

GARZA

PLATE 3.11 – Ben Garza was the driving force behind the founding of LULAC at Corpus Christi. In his push for equal rights for Mexican-American citizens, he was a man ahead of his time. He died at age 42 from tuberculosis.

SAXET FIELD

PLATE 3.12 – Oil wells dot the skyline in the Saxet Field near the port. on the west side of Corpus Christi. When the first oil well in the Saxet Field, Dunn No. 6, came in on Aug. 16, 1930, Corpus Christi expected an oil boom like that of Spindletop three decades before.

NORTH BEACH

PLATE 3.13 –A squatter's shack on North Beach made good use of 7-UP signs.

DAM COLLAPSE

PLATE 3.14 – On Nov. 26, 1930, the La Fruta Dam at Mathis gave way, allowing Lake Lovenskiold to drain into the Nueces River channel and Nueces Bay. The collapse emptied the city's water supply, forcing the city to rely on the Nueces River until a new dam could be constructed.

FRIGATE'S ARRIVAL

PLATE 3.15 – The *U.S.S. Constitution* approaches the opening to the Port of Corpus Christi. The ship scraped its side on the fender of the Bascule Bridge.

THE U.S.S. CONSTITUTION

PLATE 3.16 – Visitors crowd the deck of *Old Ironsides*.

Jim Moloney

SOUTHERN ALKALI

PLATE 3.17 – Southern Alkali Corp. was Corpus Christi's first major industry on the port channel, when it began operations in 1934, and the first alkali plant in the South. It was later known as Pittsburgh Plate Glass Co.

Jim Moloney

FISHING TRIP

PLATE 3.18 – President Franklin D. Roosevelt relaxes after a day of fishing for tarpon on his trip to Port Aransas in the first week of May, 1937.

285

Jim Moloney

BAYFRONT WORK IN PROGRESS

PLATE 3.19 –The seawall project in 1940 reached the Municipal Wharf at Cooper's Alley (far left). The light area between the seawall and buildings along Water Street is dredged sand pumped from the bay bottom to become new land.

Jim Moloney

STEP BY STEP

PLATE 3.20 – The seawall steps were cast in 40 foot sections. Builder J. DePuy designed a contraption (far right) to furnish the forms, pour the concrete and after the concrete had set could be lifted to move on to the next 40-foot section.

AMPHITHEATER ON THE BAY

PLATE 3.21 – The seawall was built to give the downtown storm protection, but it provided the unexpected benefit of giving Corpus Christi a beautiful bayfront with a unique stepped amphitheater facing Corpus Christi Bay.

DRISCOLL HOTEL

PLATE 3.25 – The Robert Driscoll Hotel was built north of the White Plaza Hotel on the site once occupied by the old First Presbyterian Church and the home of Mildred Seaton. The Driscoll Hotel structure today is the Wells Fargo Bank Building.

BUILDING THE NAS

PLATE 3.22 – A hod carrier at work on housing units for married personnel at the Corpus Christi Naval Air Station in 1940.

NAVAL AIR STATION

PLATE 3.23 – Headquarters of the new Naval Air Station on Nov. 12, 1941, almost a month before the attack on Pearl Harbor put the base on a wartime footing.

FLIGHT TIMES

PLATE 3.24 – Navy aviators check the afternoon flight board at the NAS.

U-BOATS IN GULF

PLATE 3.26 – *The Evening Sun* of Baltimore headlined a story that a German submarine was sighted on Jan 28, 1942. The article read in part: "The Navy announced today a submarine had been sighted fifteen miles southeast of Port Aransas, Texas at 9 A.M. It was not determined whether it was an enemy submarine, but it is presumed it is, said the report from the office of Commander R.R. Ferguson, Navy port director for Port Arthur."

Murphy Givens

CHRISTMAS 1945

PLATE 3.27 – It would take several years to return to normal after the war. One of the first signs was the appearance of Christmas lights and decorations on Chaparral Street in December 1945. The Nueces Hotel is on the right.

ASARCO

PLATE 3.28 – In 1942, the government built a plant on UpRiver Road to produce zinc and cadmium for defense. It was later sold and became the American Smelting and Refining Company, ASARCO. It operated until 1985.

A WOMAN OF INFLUENCE

PLATE 3.29 – Clara Driscoll, one on Texas' most politically influential persons, was known as the savior of the Alamo. She used her Democratic connections to Vice President John Nance Garner to help Corpus Christi gain the new Naval Air Station. During the wartime boom that resulted, she built the Robert Driscoll Hotel on the bluff.

Murphy Givens

SAM AND ADA WILSON

PLATE 3.30 – Sam E. Wilson, Jr., an oil lease broker in El Dorado, Ark., and his wife Ada moved to Corpus Christi and hit 44 consecutive oil wells. He bought the Nixon Building and renamed it the Wilson Building. He purchased much of Mustang Island. His wife, Ada, was flashy and flamboyant. She used some of her wealth to create a hospital for crippled children and forced reluctant state officials to buy part of her land to establish the Mustang Island State Park.

295

INCARNATE WORD

PLATE 3.31 – The Incarnate Word Academy, built in 1885, was located on church property on the bluff. The building faced Tancahua at Leopard. The Incarnate Word Academy first began operations in 1871 in a frame house.

HIGH SCHOOL

PLATE 3.32 – Corpus Christi High School, built in 1911, was called the Brick Palace. It was located on the bluff on Carancahua Street, south of Leopard. The building became a refuge during the 1919 hurricane and after the storm the school's "domestic science" kitchen was used to prepare meals for storm victims.

Jim Moloney

NEW HIGH SCHOOL

PLATE 3.33 – When W. B. Ray opened on the city's Southside in 1950, students could look out their windows and see vacant fields to the west and east of the new school.

TEXAS HIGHWAYS

OLD AND NEW BRIDGES

PLATE 3.34 – In 1959, the Harbor Bridge towers over the bascule bridge. The comparison shows what a tight squeeze the bascule opening was for large ships.

CARLA

PLATE 3.35 – While the Coastal Bend escaped severe damage from Hurricane Carla in 1961, the Horace Caldwell Pier in Port Aransas was an exception.

DR. HECTOR P. GARCIA

PLATE 3.36 – After returning from World War II, Dr. Hector P. Garcia founded the American GI Forum to address societal problems of Mexican-American Citizens. He continued to work for equality for all citizens for the rest of his life.

LBJ AND LADY BIRD JOHNSON

PLATE 3.37 – Vice President Lyndon B. Johnson and Lady Bird ride in a motorcade to Exposition Hall on Shoreline Boulevard. The vice president led a congressional delegation to visit Padre Island in June, 1961 when Congress was debating the establishment of a national park on the island. Riding with the Johnsons in the back seat is Corpus Christi Mayor Ben McDonald.

Jim Moloney

CELIA

PLATE 3.38 – Shrimp boats have been piled up on the shore of Aransas Bay after the winds of Hurricane Celia hit Aransas Pass.

MAPS

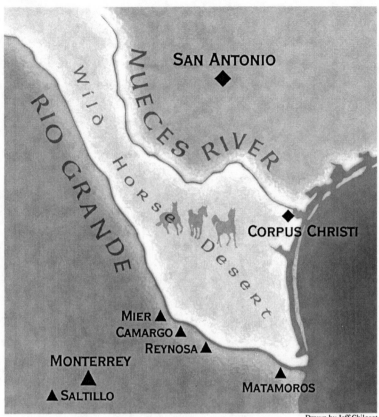

Drawn by Jeff Chilcoat

NUECES STRIP

MAP 1 - The treaty of Velasco signed by Gen. Antonio Lopez de Santa Anna after his capture at San Jacinto made the Rio Grande the border between Texas and Mexico. The Mexican government refused to ratify the treaty on the grounds that Santa Anna was coerced and he was not authorized to sign such an agreement. The contested area, the Nueces Strip, was claimed by Texas and Mexico. The only settlement in the region was Kinney's Rancho, which by 1842 was called Corpus Christi.

303

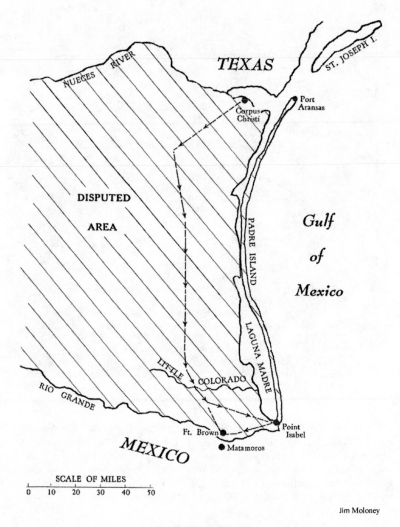

TEXAS

ST. JOSEPH I.

NUECES RIVER

Corpus
Christi

Port
Aransas

DISPUTED

AREA

PADRE ISLAND

Gulf

of

Mexico

LAGUNA MADRE

LITTLE

COLORADO

RIO GRANDE

Ft. Brown

Point
Isabel

Matamoros

MEXICO

SCALE OF MILES

0   10   20   30   40   50

Jim Moloney

TAYLOR'S TRAIL

MAP 2 – Zachary Taylor's army followed the same route to the Rio Grande that the retreating Mexican army followed after its defeat at San Jacinto. The Cotton Road during the Civil War also followed the same track to the Rio Grande.

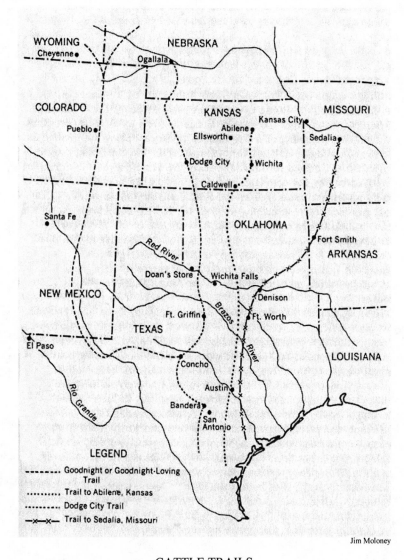

Jim Moloney

CATTLE TRAILS

MAP 3 – South Texas was the start of the cattle trails, which could diverge by up to 50 miles depending on grass conditions, drought, and flooded rivers. The great cattle drives to railhead towns in Kansas ended with the spread of barbed wire fences and the coming of railroads to Texas.

Murphy Givens

NUECES COUNTY IN 1879

MAP 4 – Today's Kleberg and Jim Wells counties were included in the Nueces County of 1879. The map shows the location of the great ranch pastures of the 1870s, including the ranches of W.W. Wright, Martha Rabb, D.C. Rachal, Richard King, Blas Maria Falcon, and Mifflin Kenedy. The map was drawn by surveyor Lafayette Caldwell for the Nueces County Commissioners.

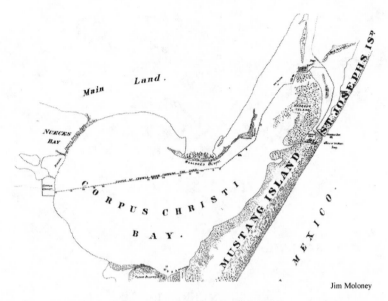

MORRIS & CUMMINGS CUT

MAP 5 – In 1872, Corpus Christi contracted to have a ship channel dredged to the Aransas Pass. By 1874, the work was completed. The cut zigzagged north of Harbor Island from the channel leading to Rockport. It then went east and south of McGloin's Bluff (today's Ingleside), then west-southwest across Corpus Christi Bay to the city.

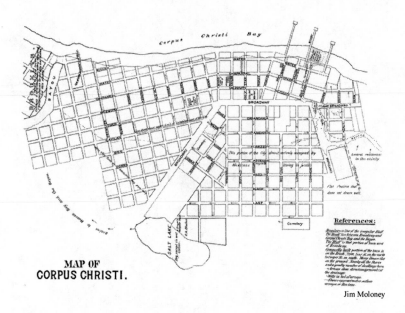

MAP OF
CORPUS CHRISTI.

Jim Moloney

CORPUS CHRISTI – 1875

MAP 6 – In 1875, the populated portion of Corpus Christi stretched from Brewster Street on the north to the arroyo (Cooper's Alley) on the south. On the bluff, houses stretched west about six blocks, with the most western occupied by "Mexicans living in jacals." North Beach, then called Brooklyn, was separated from the city by Hall's Bayou. North Beach was the site of several beef packing plants, called packeries.

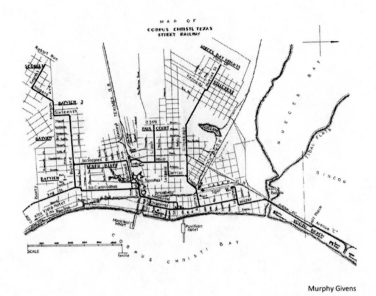

Murphy Givens

CORPUS CHRISTI STREET & INTERURBAN RY CO.

MAP 7 – In 1918, the streetcar lines covered the city from Third and Booty to North Beach. This was the heyday of the streetcar line, with Camp Scurry training thousands of soldiers for World War I in Europe.

APPENDIX

MAYORS OF CORPUS CHRISTI

Mayor	Term	Mayor	Term
Benjamin F. Neal	1852-1853	Roy Miller	1913-1919
E. H. Winfield	1853 (1)	Gordon Boone	1919-1921
C. R. Hopson	1853-1854 (2)	Dr. Perry G. Lovenskiold	1921-1931
Henry F. Berry	1854-1855	Edwin F. Flato	1931-1933
Benjamin F. Neal	1855-1856	William Shaffer	1933-1935
Henry A. Maltby	1856-1857 (1)	Dr. H. R. Giles	1935-1937
Cornelius Cahill	1857 (2)	A. C. McCaughan	1937-1945
Henry W. Berry	1857 (3)	Roy Self	1945-1946 (1)
Ruben Holbein	1857-1860	Robert T. Wilson	1946-1947 (5)
Henry W. Berry	1860-1863	Wesley Eli Seale	1947-1949
Dr. George W. Robertson	1863-1866	Leslie Wasserman	1949-1953
Weymon N. Staples	1866-1868	A. Albert Lichtenstein	1953-1954 (1)
Nelson Plato	1868-1870	Ellroy King	1954 (2)
J. B. Mitchell	1870-1872	P. C. Callaway	1954-1955
Perry Doddridge	1872-1875	Farrell D. Smith	1955-1959
Nelson Plato	1875-1876	Ellroy King	1959-1961
William Headen	1876-1877	Ben F. McDonald	1961-1963
J. C. Russell	1877	Dr. James L. Barnard	1963-1965
John M. Moore	1877-1880	Dr. McIver Furman	1965-1967
John Baptist Murphy	1880-1884	Jack R. Blackmon	1967-1971
George F. Evans	1884-1886	Ronnie Sizemore	1971-1973
Cheston C. Heath	1886-1888	Jason Luby	1973-1979
Henry Keller	1888-1892	Luther Jones	1979-1987
Oscar C. Lovenskiold	1892-1902	Betty Turner	1987-1991
H. H. Segrest	1902-1904 (4)	Mary Rhodes	1991-1997
H. H. Segrest	1904-1908	Loyd Neal	1997-2005
Dan Reid	1908-1909 (5)	Henry Garrett	2005-2009
W. H. Hull	1909-1910 (2)	Joe Adame	2009-present
Clark Pease	1910-1913		

1 Resigned
2 Pro-tem
3 Abandoned office
4 Acting Mayor
5 Died in office

POPULATION AND AREA

YEAR	POPULATION CITY	POPULATION COUNTY	AREA (SQ. MI.) COUNTY
1846			18,250
1850	533	698	4,124
1860	1,200	2,906	2,256
1870	2,140	3,975	2,256
1880	3,257	7,673	2,256
1890	4,387	8,093	2,256
1900	4,703	10,439	2,256
1910	8,222	21,955	2,256
1920	10,522	22,807	1,166
1930	27,789	51,779	1,166
1940	57,301	92,661	1,166
1950	108,287	165,471	1,166
1960	167,690	221,573	1,166
1970	204,525	237,544	1,166
1980	232,134	268,215	1,166
1990	257,453	291,145	1,166
2000	277,454	313,645	1,166
2010	305,215	340,223	1,166

END NOTES

CHAPTER 1

[1] John J. Linn, "Reminiscences of Fifty Years in Texas," p. 3-4, 10-12. (Linn established the town of Linnville on the west bank of Lavaca Bay.)

[2] Frank Wagner, Research Papers, Corpus Christi Central Library.

[3] Jack Jackson, John Wheat, "Texas by Teran," p. 5

[4] Bill Walraven, "Which came first: Kinney or the City?" *Corpus Christi Caller*, May 21, 1986.

[5] Rev. Z.N. Morrell, "Flowers and Fruits in the Wilderness," p. 98-99.

[6] Mary Sutherland, "The Story of Corpus Christi," p. 3.

[7] James T. DeShields, "Border Wars of Texas," p. 128.

[8] Columns by the author, Feb. 18, 1998; April 19, 2006; April 22, 2009; W.W. Newcomb Jr., "The Indians of Texas," p. 59-81; Mary Jourdan Atkinson, "The Texas Indians," chapter, "The Cannibal of the Coast," p. 193-207.

[9] Dr. Thomas Hester, Foreword, "The Karankawa Indians of Texas" by Robert Ricklis.

[10] Newcomb, p. 62, 65.

[11] Dr. Carlos E. Castaneda, "Our Catholic Heritage in Texas"; Augustin Padilla Davila, "*Historia de la Fundacion y Discurso de la Provinciade Santiago de Mexico*" (1596); "Documentary Sources - 1554 Fleet," the Texas Antiquities Committee report, Corpus Christi Central Library.

[12] Newcomb, p. 62-63. William C. Foster, "Spanish Expeditions Into Texas - 1689-1768," p. 43-44.

[13] Keith Guthrie, "History of San Patricio County," p. 2.

[14] Newcomb, p. 81; Herbert E. Bolton, "The Founding of Mission Rosario," Texas Historical Association Quarterly, Vol. X, p. 137-139.

[15] David G. McComb, "Galveston, A History," p. 39.

[16] "Journal of Stephen F. Austin," Texas Historical Association Quarterly, p. 305.

[17] Jack Jackson, John Wheat, "Texas by Teran," p. 33-34.

[18] Noah Smithwick, "The Evolution of a State," p. 3, 10.

[19] J.W. Willbarger, "Indian Depredations in Texas," p. 198.

[20] J.H. Kuykendall, "Reminiscences of Early Texans," Texas Historical Association Quarterly, Vol. 6, p. 253.

[21] Ibid; Roy Bedichek, "Karankaway Country," p. 14.

[22] Kuykendall, p. 253.

[23] Ibid.

[24] Kuykendall, Bedichek.

[25] Guthrie, "History of San Patricio County," p. 3.

[26] "Journal of Stephen F. Austin," Texas Historical Association Quarterly.

[27] Bedichek, p. 15-16.

[28] Ibid.

[29] Jack Jackson, Margaret Howard, Luis A. Alvarado, "History and Archeology of Lipantitlan State Historic Site, Nueces County, Texas," p. 96.

[30] Bethel Coopwood, "The Route of Cabeza de Vaca," Southwestern Historical Quarterly, Vol. 3, p. 237; Hobart Huson, "History of Refugio," Vol. 1, p. 51.

[31] Linn, "Reminiscences of Fifty Years in Texas."

[32] Paul Horgan, "Great River," p. 561.

[33] "History of Nueces County," p. 43-44.

[34] Hobart Huson, address in Corpus Christi, May 4, 1940.

[35] Lamar Papers, letter from Kinney to Lamar, Vol. IV, Part 1, p. 211-214.

[36] Charles G. Norton, "Colonel Henry L. Kinney, Founder of Corpus Christi," *Corpus Christi Times*, May 16-31, 1936.

[37] "British Correspondence Concerning Texas," *Southwestern Historical Quarterly*, Vol. XV, p. 205.

[38] Huson, pg. 445; Eugenia Reynolds Briscoe, "City by the Sea," p. 78-80; Hortense Warner Ward, "Abduction and Death of Philip Dimitt"; Keith Guthrie, "History of San Patricio County," p. 198.

[39] Travis Moorman, "Abduction of Philip Dimitt," *Caller-Times*, Jan. 18, 1959; *Austin Gazette*, August, 1841, contains an account of the trial.

[40] Guthrie, p. 198.

[41] Ibid.

[42] Lamar Papers, letters from Kinney to Lamar, Vol. IV, Part 1, p. 211-214.

[43] Ibid; Guthrie, p. 198.

[44] History of Nueces County, p. 45-46.

[45] John Hoyt Williams, "Sam Houston," p. 213; George Coalson, "The Battle of Lipantitlan, July 7, 1842," *The Journal of South Texas*, p. 18-22; Jackson-Howard-Alvarado, p. 108.

[46] Jonathan W. Jordan, "Lone Star Navy," p. 212.

[47] Coalson, p. 20.

[48] Hobart Huson, "Refugio," p. 256-257.

[49] Jackson-Howard-Alvarado, p. 110.

[50] Ibid, p. 111.

[51] Ibid, p. 112.

[52] Huson, p. 468.

[53] Jackson-Howard-Alvarado, p. 114.

[54] Ibid, p. 115.

[55] Ibid, p. 118.

[56] Ibid, p. 119.

[57] Coalson, p. 21.

[58] Ibid.

[59] Guthrie, p. 197.

[60] Ward, "Physical Courage and Moral Cowardice Found in Kinney, "*Caller-Times*, Jan. 18, 1959; Norton, *Times*, May 16-31; Lamar, Vol. 4, p. 213-214; Guthrie, p. 197.

[61] J.W. Wilbarger, "Indian Depredations in Texas," p. 66-69.

[62] Gammel, "Laws of Texas," Vol. 2, p. 1049; Walter Prescott Webb, "Texas Rangers," p. 33-34.

[63] Guthrie, "San Patricio County History," p. 177; Grady Phelps, "Old oyster reef provided passage across Nueces Bay," *Caller-Times*, May 26, 1974.

[64] W.R. Gore, "The Life of Henry Lawrence Kinney," master's thesis, 1948.

CHAPTER 2

[1] Justin H. Smith, "The War with Mexico," p. 140-145.

[2] Eugenia Reynolds Briscoe, "City by the Sea," p. 15.

[3] Ethan Allen Hitchcock, "Fifty Years in Camp and Field," p. 193.

[4] W.S. Henry, "Campaign Sketches of the War with Mexico," p. 14-15; Hitchcock, 193-194.

[5] *Daily Picayune*, Aug. 3, 1845.

[6] J. Reese Fry, "A Life of Zachary Taylor," p. 76; Alpha Kennedy Wood, "Texas Coastal Bend," p. 50-51; William Allen, Sue Hastings Taylor, "Aransas," p. 106-107.

[7] Hitchcock, p. 194.

[8] Bernard DeVoto, "The Year of Decision, 1846," p. 15.

[9] Napoleon Jackson Tecumseh Dana, "Monterrey Is Ours," p. 5.

[10] Dana, p. 2; Henry, p. 27.

[11] *Daily Picayune*, Sept. 5, 1845.

[12] Joseph Chance, "My Life in the Old Army: The Reminiscences of Abner Doubleday," p. 48; U.S. Grant, "Memoirs," p. 43.

[13] Henry, p. 27.

[14] Ibid, p. 30.

[15] Ibid, p. 28.

[16] Mexican War Correspondence, House Executive Documents, 30th Congress.

[17] Henry, p. 31.

[18] K. Jack Bauer, "Zachary Taylor," p. 117.

[19] Chance, p. 43-44.

[20] Bill Walraven, column, letter by George K. Donnelly, *Caller-Times*, Oct. 10, 1955.

[21] N.S. Jarvis, "Army Surgeon's Notes of Frontier Service - Mexican War," p. 437; Henry, p. 40-41.

[22] John James Peck, "Sign of the Eagle," p. 7. Joseph Dorst Patch, "The Concentration of Zachary Taylor's Army at Corpus Christi, Texas," p. 12; Smith, p. 143.

[23] Frank Wagner's Research Papers, Corpus Christi Central Library.

[24] Dana, p. 13.

[25] Holman Hamilton, "Zachary Taylor, Soldier of the Republic," p. 166; Hitchcock, p. 199; Jarvis, 436.

[26] Hitchcock, p. 197.

[27] Wood, p. 50-51; Allen-Taylor, p. 106-107.

[28] Grant, p. 43; Briscoe, p. 38.

[29] Henry, p. 34-37; Hitchcock, p. 200-201.

[30] *Daily Picayune,* Sept. 19, 1845.

[31] Jarvis, p. 437.

[32] Dana, p. 14.

[33] Geoffrey Perrett, "Ulysses S. Grant, Soldier and President," p. 47-49; Grant, p. 16.

[34] Henry, p. 46.

[35] Grant, p. 48-50.

[36] Lloyd Lewis, "Captain Sam Grant," p. 129.

[37] Jarvis, p. 437.

[38] Henry, p. 45.

[39] Ibid, p. 44-45; Hitchcock, p. 195; Walraven, Donnelly letter; Josiah Turner, article, *Corpus Christi Caller,* Jan. 24, 1908.

[40] Hamilton, p. 168; Patch, p. 15.

[41] *Corpus Christi Gazette*, Jan. 8, 1846.

[42] Jarvis; *Galveston News*.

[43] Eli Merriman, "Random Recollections of Nearly 90 Years," Corpus Christi Central Library.

[44] Henry, p. 50.

[45] Jarvis, p. 440.

[46] *The Telegraph*, Houston, April 1, 1846.

[47] Lewis, p. 134-135.

[48] Henry, p. 51; Charles Masland, Letters, Corpus Christi Central Library.

[49] Henry, p. 52-53; Jarvis, p. 441; Peck, p. 14-15.

[50] Dan Kilgore, "Men, Armies That Made Texas History Trod Nueces Highway," *Corpus Christi Caller-Times*, Jan. 18, 1959.

[51] Lewis, p. 135.

[52] Smith, p. 147.

[53] Richard Irving Dodge, "The Hunting Grounds of the Great West," p. 148-149.

CHAPTER 3

[1] *The Telegraph*, March 25, 1846.

[2] Charles G. Norton, "Colonel Henry L. Kinney, Founder of Corpus Christi."

[3] *The American Flag*, Matamoros, June 6, 1846.

[4] William A. McClintock, "Journal of a Trip Through Texas and Northern Mexico in 1846-1847," Southwest Historical Quarterly.

[5] Eugenia Reynolds Briscoe, "City by the Sea," p. 115.

[6] Nueces County Commissioners Court minutes, Jan. 11, 1847.

[7] *The American Flag*, Matamoros, July 17, 1846.

[8] Ibid, July 7, 1846.

[9] Ibid, July 24, 1846.

[10] Briscoe, p. 116.

[11] Ibid.

[12] *Democratic and Texas Register*, Houston, Sept. 21, 1848.

[13] J. Williamson Moses, "Texas in Other Days," as edited by M. Givens, pg. 36-37.

[14] *Democratic and Texas Register*, Houston, Oct. 12, 1848.

[15] Norton, pg. 19; Briscoe, pg. 116.

[16] *Caller-Times*, Jan. 18, 1959; Briscoe, pg. 124.

[17] Southwest Historical Quarterly, "Opening Routes Across West Texas 1848-1850," Vol. 37, pg. 130-131; Texas Handbook under "Michler."

[18] Briscoe, pg. 117; *Star*, Sept. 19, 1848.

[19] *Corpus Christi Star*, Oct. 17, 1848.

[20] *Corpus Christi Star*, editions from December-March, 1848, 1849.

[21] *The Star*, Jan. 27, 1849.

[22] Marilyn McAdams Sibley, "Lone Stars and State Gazettes," pg. 205.

[23] *The Star*, March 24, 1849.

[24] Ibid: "Letter from Mr. Peoples."

[25] Bill Walraven, "History of Press Here Begins With Republic," *Caller-Times*, Jan. 18, 1959.

[26] James H. Mundy and Earle G. Shettleworth Jr., "The Flight of the Grand Eagle," p. 96-103.

[27] Ibid, p. 117.

[28] "Indian Wars and Pioneers of Texas," p. 109; *The New York Herald*, Feb. 11, 1850. "Texas Indian Papers, 1846-1859," p. 111-113; Walter Prescott Webb, "The Texas Rangers," p. 142.

[29] Mundy and Shettleworth, p. 118.

[30] Mary Sutherland, "The Story of Corpus Christi," p. 14 (she mistakenly calls the boy Dolan); Rosalie B. Hart Priour, "The Adventures of a Family of Emmigrants Who Emmigrated to Texas in 1834" (her spelling), p. 89.

[31] John Salmon Ford, "Rip Ford's Texas," edited by Stephen B. Oates, p. 147-148.

[32] Thomas W. Cutter, "The Handbook of Texas," p. 1111; Ruth Dodson, "Fort Merrill: the Putman Shipp Ranch," p. 329; *Corpus Christi Caller-Times*, "Fort Merrill Ruins on West Bank of Nueces River Stand as Relic of Forgotten Era in South Texas," Nov. 12, 1939.

[33] Ford, p. 156.

[34] Ibid, p. 156-158.

[35] *The Nueces Valley*, editions from 1858.

[36] Webb, p. 130.

[37] Ernest Wallace, "Texas in Turmoil," p. 18.

[38] Seventh Census of the United States, Nueces County.

[39] Eugenia Reynolds Briscoe, "City by the Sea," p. 259.

[40] Ibid, p. 259; "Slave Schedules," U.S. Census, 1850, Nueces County.

[41] Neal's obituary, *Corpus Christi Weekly Gazette*, July 19, 1873.

[42] "The Fandango Ordinance," minutes of Corpus Christi City Council meetings, La Retama Library archives.

[43] Briscoe, p. 148.

[44] Ibid, p. 122-124; Sutherland, p. 16; Centennial History, p. 59; Helen Chapman, "The News from Brownsville," edited by Caleb Coker, p. 289-295.

[45] Hortense Warner Ward, "The First State Fair of Texas," Southwestern Historical Quarterly, Vol. LVII, p. 163-174; Charles G. Norton, "Colonel Henry L. Kinney, Founder of Corpus

Christi," p. 20.
[46] Bruce Cheeseman, "Maria von Blucher's Corpus Christi," p. 71-72.
[47] Ward, "The First State Fair of Texas," p. 163-174.
[48] Ibid.
[49] Dan Kilgore, "Two Six-Shooters and a Sunbonnet," the Story of Sally Skull," Texas Folklore Society Number XLIII; Bill Walraven, "Sally Skull," *Corpus Christi Caller*, Feb. 26, 1982; John Warren Hunter, "Heel-Fly Time in Texas," Frontier Times, 1936, p. 57-58.
[50] John S. Ford, "Memoirs," Vol. 4, p. 645.
[51] Ward, "The First State Fair of Texas," p. 163-174.
[52] "Centennial History of Corpus Christi," p. 59.
[53] Chapman, "The News from Brownsville," p. 289-295.
[54] Ibid.
[55] "Maria von Blucher's Corpus Christi," p. 84; Arnoldo de Leon, "They Call Them Greasers," p. 81-82.
[56] Briscoe, p. 151.
[57] Lydia Spencer Lane, "Old Days in the Old Army," p. 21-25.
[58] Frank Wagner's Research Papers, Corpus Christi Central Library.

CHAPTER 4

[1] Tom Lea, "The King Ranch," p. 2-3; Don Graham, "Kings of Texas," p. 19-20; Frank Goodwin, "Life on the King Ranch," p. 7-8; James Rowe, "Capt. King started as River Pilot, Founded Famous Ranch," *Corpus Christi Caller-Times*, July 12, 1953.
[2] Lea, p. 4-9; Rowe.
[3] Lea, p. 51-58; Graham, p. 37.
[4] Lea, p. 69.
[5] Ibid, p. 93-95 Rowe.
[6] Jack Jackson, "Texas by Teran," p. 265.
[7] Lea, p. 93-95; Rowe.
[8] Column by the author, "King Ranch absorbed older Bobedo Ranch," *Corpus Christi Caller-Times*, Dec. 20, 2006.
[9] Ibid; Lea, p. 119.
[10] John Salman Ford, "Rip Ford's Texas," edited by Stephen B. Oates, p. 144-145.
[11] Lea, p. 95-99; Rowe.
[12] Lea, p. 144-145; Graham, p. 72-73.
[13] Lea, p. 105.
[14] Graham, p. 65; Lea, 123.
[15] Lea, p. 115; Graham, 63.
[16] Lea, p. 127-128; Graham, 67; Rowe.
[17] Lea, p. 128-129.
[18] Mike Cox, "Texas Ranger Tales," p. 17-26; Graham, p57-62.
[19] A.J. Sowell, "Life of 'Big Foot' Wallace," p. 72.
[20] Graham, p. 57; obituary, *Galveston Weekly News*, April 24, 1855.
[21] Paul N. Spellman, "Forgotten Texas Leader: Hugh McLeod and the Texan Santa Fe Expedition," p. 135; Lota M. Spell, "Pioneer Printer: Samuel Bangs in Mexico and Texas," p. 129-132.
[22] Hortense Warner Ward, "The First State Fair of Texas," *Southwestern Historical Quarterly*, Vol. LVII.
[23] Marilyn McAdams Sibley, "Lone Stars and State Gazettes: Texas Newspapers Before the Civil War," p. 205; Cox, p. 23.
[24] Lea, p. 100-101.

[25] Ibid.

[26] Ibid, p. 132-134; Graham, 70-71; Cox, p. 24-26.

[27] *Galveston Weekly News*, "Capt. G.K. Lewis Killed," April 24, 1855.

[28] *Texas State Gazette*, "The Late Capt. G.K. Lewis," April 28, 1855.

[29] Lea, p. 135-139; Coker, p. 333-335.

[30] Spellman, p. 150-151; Ward, "The First State Fair of Texas; Charles G. Norton, "Colonel Henry L. Kinney, Founder of Corpus Christi," p. 21.

[31] Probate Records: "Inventory of Personal Effects of John Peter Schatzell, deceased Oct. 23, 1854."

[32] Copy of the "Nueces Valley Land & Emigration" pamphlet in the author's possession.

[33] *Corpus Christi Caller*, May 15, 1952; *Caller* Special Edition, Nov. 26, 1933; biographical files, Corpus Christi Central Library.

[34] Sharry M. Reynolds, "Joseph Almond Diary," preface; Robert Adams, "Learning by Hard Licks," interview, Corpus Christi Central Library; William Adams, "Pioneer Days in Corpus Christi and Nueces County," Corpus Christi Central Library.

[35] Robert and William Adams' interviews.

[36] Ibid.

[37] Ibid.

[38] Columns by the author: "Sheepmen of the Nueces Valley," Dec. 25, 2002; Jan. 1, 2003; Jan. 6, 2003; Jan. 13, 2003.

[39] Mary Sutherland, "The Story of Corpus Christi," p. 15; Eugenia Reynolds Briscoe, "City by the Sea," p. 154.

[40] Lydia Spencer Lane, "Old Days in the Old Army," p. 21-22.

[41] M.L. Crimmins, "W.G. Freeman's Report on the Eighth Military Department," *Southwestern Historical Quarterly*, Vol. LI, p. 353-355.

[42] Norton, p. 26.

[43] William Headen, "Historical Sketch," published in 1883, vertical files, Corpus Christi Central Library.

[44] Val W. Lehmann, "Forgotten Legions: Sheep in the Rio Grande Plain of Texas," p. 112; Paul H. Carlson, "Texas Woollybacks," p. 50-52; Lea, p. 125; Coker, p. 194.

[45] Norton, p. 31.

[46] Ibid, p. 33-34.

[47] Ibid, p. 35-36; Hortense Warner Ward, "Physical Courage, Moral Cowardice Found in Kinney," *Corpus Christi Caller-Times*, Jan. 18, 1959.

[48] Bruce Cheeseman, "Maria von Blucher's Corpus Christi," p.47, 74.

[49] Ward, "Physical Courage, Moral Cowardice Found in Kinney."

[50] *Nueces Valley*, "The Colonel's Return," and "Complimentary," July 3, 1858.

[51] Ibid, June 19, 1858.

CHAPTER 5

[1] E.T. Merriman, "Story of Old Banquete," Pathfinders of Texas, by Mrs. Frank DeGarmo, p. 171.

[2] Slave Schedules, Seventh Census of the United States, Nueces County; Eugenia Reynolds Briscoe, "City by the Sea," p. 165.

[3] Slave Schedules, Eighth Census of the United States, Nueces County.

[4] *Nueces Valley*, June 18, 1858.

[5] Ronnie C. Tyler, *The Journal of Negro History*, 1972, January.

[6] Briscoe, p. 184.

[7] *Ranchero*, June 8, 1861.

[8] Andrew Anderson, "Do You Know the Story of Corpus Christi?" biographical files, Corpus Christi Central Library.

[9] *Ranchero*, April 21, 1861.

[10] Briscoe, p. 192; *Ranchero,* March 2, 1861.

[11] Carlton Savage, "Policy of the United States Toward Maritime Commerce in War," p. 415-420.

[12] *Ranchero,* July 13, 1861; Briscoe, p 202.

[13] Ibid, June 15, 1861.

[14] "The History of Nueces County," p. 63.

[15] Muster Rolls of Military Companies Organized in Nueces County During the Civil War, compiled by Dan Kilgore.

[16] *Ranchero*, July 21, 1861.

[17] War of the Rebellion, Official Records of the Union and Confederate Armies, Series I, XV, p. 102-103.

[18] Briscoe, p. 379; "The History of Nueces County," p. 71.

[19] Robert W. Delaney, "Matamoros, Port for Texas During the Civil War," *Southwestern Historical Quarterly,* April, 1955, p. 473-487. Ronnie C. Tyler, "Cotton on the Border, 1861-1865," *Southwestern Historical Quarterly.*

[20] Dan Kilgore, "Men, Armies That Made Texas History Trod Nueces Highway," *Corpus Christi Caller-Times*, Jan. 18, 1959.

[21] Robert Adams, "Learning by Hard Licks," interview, Corpus Christi Central Library; William Adams, "Pioneer Days in Corpus Christi and Nueces County," Corpus Christi Central Library.

[22] John Warren Hunter, "Heel-Fly Time in Texas," *Frontier Times,* 1936, p. 57-58.

[23] Briscoe, 203-207; Merriman, "Story of Old Banquete," Pathfinders of Texas, p. 169-171.

[24] Hunter, p. 57-58; Kilgore, "Two Six-shooters and a Sunbonnet, the Story of Sally Skull."

[25] Tom Lea, "The King Ranch," p. 184.

[26] Rosalie B. Hart Priour, "The Adventures of a Family of Emmigrants Who Emmigrated to Texas in 1834" (her spelling), p. 116, Corpus Christi Central Library.

[27] Ibid; Briscoe, p. 213.

[28] Rosalie B. Hart Priour.

[29] James Arthur Lyon Fremantle, "The Fremantle Diary," p. 6-7.

[30] Hortense Warner Ward, "Physical Courage, Moral Cowardice Found in Kinney," *Corpus Christi Caller-Times,* Jan. 18, 1959.

[31] John B. Dunn, "Miscellaneous Recollections," p. 2, Corpus Christi Central Library.

[32] Briscoe, p. 206-207.

[33] Ibid.

[34] Ernest Morgan, "South Texas and the Civil War," *Corpus Christi Caller-Times*, Feb. 5, 1961.

[35] Briscoe, p. 209.

[36] Ibid.

[37] War of the Rebellion: Reports of Maj. Hobby, C.S. Army, to Maj. E.F. Gray, San Antonio and Kittredge's report to Gideon Wells; *Ranchero Extra,* Aug. 19, 1862; Briscoe, p. 210-211.

[38] Priour, p. 103-105.

[39] Anderson, "Do You Know the Story of Corpus Christi?" biographical files, p. 7; Bruce Cheeseman, "Maria von Blucher's Corpus Christi," p. 131.

[40] Cheeseman, p. 130.

[41] Anna Moore Schwien, "When Corpus Christi Was Young," biographical files, Corpus Christi Central Library.

[42] Corrie Fitzsimmons, interview note, Oct. 17, 1940, Corpus Christi Central Library.

[43] War of the Rebellion: Reports of Maj. Hobby, C.S. Army, to Maj. E.F. Gray, San Antonio; Briscoe, p. 211.

[44] William Adams, "The Bombardment of Corpus Christi in 1862," biographical files, Corpus Christi Central Library; War of the Rebellion: Reports of Maj. Hobby, C.S. Army, to Maj. E.F. Gray.

[45] War of the Rebellion, Official Records of the Union and Confederate Armies; Operations in Texas, N. Mexico, and Arizona, Chapter XXL, P. 618-624; Report of Acting Volunteer Lt.

Kittredge, U.S. Navy, to Gideon Wells, Secretary of the Navy; Reports of Maj. Hobby, C.S. Army, to Maj. E.F. Gray, San Antonio.

[46] Briscoe, p. 213; Mary Sutherland, "The Story of Corpus Christi," p. 25-27; Ernest Morgan, "Corpus Christians Beat Off Yankee Ships," *Corpus Christi Caller-Times*, March 12, 1961; "Nueces County History," p. 67-70.

[47] Joseph Fitzsimmons, deposition, March 3, 1871, in behalf of a claim for war reparations from Margaret Meuly, National Archives, copy at the Corpus Christi Central Library.

[48] Ibid.

[49] Andrew Anderson, "Do You Know the Story of Corpus Christi?"

[50] Margaret Meuly depositions.

[51] Columns by the author, "Town bitterly divided during the Civil War," Jan. 11, 2006, and "Unionists leave city after two hangings," Jan. 18, 2006, *Corpus Christi Caller-Times*.

[52] Individual biographical files at the Corpus Christi Central Library; J.B. Dunn, "Perilous Trails of Texas," p. 4.

[53] War of the Rebellion: Report of Capt. John Ireland, C.S. Army to Maj. E.F. Gray, San Antonio, Sept. 15, 1862, Series I, XXL, p. 626; Andrew Anderson, "Do You Know the Story of Corpus Christi?"

[54] Office of Naval Records and Library, letter to Marie V. Blucher, La Retama Library, Jan. 25, 1939; extract from the Navy Gazette, General Order 23, Oct. 27, 1863.

[55] War of the Rebellion: Report of Capt. H. Willke, C.S. Army, Dec. 7, 1862, Series I, XXVII, p. 190-191; Ernest Morgan, "Kittredge's Successor Meets Bloody Resistance on Island," *Corpus Christi Caller-Times*, April 23, 1961; Briscoe, p. 215-216; Hobart Huson, "History of Refugio," Vol. 1, p.58-59.

[56] Ibid.

[57] Ibid.

[58] Ibid.

[59] Ibid.

[60] Andrew Anderson, "Do You Know the Story of Corpus Christi?"

[61] Bruce Cheeseman, "Maria von Blucher's Corpus Christi," p. 134.

[62] *Ranchero*, Dec. 18, 1862.

[63] Bruce Cheeseman, "Maria von Blucher's Corpus Christi," p. 132-133.

[64] *Ranchero,* "Salt From Laguna Madre," July 13, 1861.

[65] Robert Adams, "Learning by Hard Licks," interview, Corpus Christi Central Library.

[66] Sister Mary Ann Roddy, thesis, "Rancho Perdido," July, 1954, p. 16-17.

[67] Dee Woods, "Island Was Salt Trading Center in Civil War Days," *Corpus Christi Caller*, July 24, 1939.

[68] Robert Adams, "Learning by Hard Licks."

[69] "Padre Island," p. 55.

[70] T.R. Fehrenbach, "Lone Star," p. 356.

[71] Bruce Cheeseman, "Maria von Blucher's Corpus Christi," p. 139.

[72] Thomas Noakes diaries, Corpus Christi Central Library; Robert Adams, "Learning by Hard Licks."

[73] Bruce Cheeseman, "Maria von Blucher's Corpus Christi," p. 141.

CHAPTER 6

[1] Edwin Lufkin, "History of the 13th Maine Regiment," Chapter 5, p. 51-52.

[2] Shelby Foote, "The Civil War," Vol. 1, p. 427; James G. Hollandsworth, "Pretense of Glory: The Life of Nathaniel P. Banks," p. 68; Geoffrey Perrett, "Ulysses S. Grant, Soldier and President," p. 302; the Handbook of Texas.

[3] Lufkin, p. 52. Dudley G. Wooten, "A Comprehensive History of Texas: Military Events and Operations in Texas and Along the Coasts and Border, 1861-1865," p. 537-538.

[4] Lufkin, p. 51.

[5] War of the Rebellion: N.P. Banks to Gen. H.W. Halleck, Chap. XXXVIII, p. 409-411.

[6] Lufkin, p. 52-53.

[7] Wooten, P. 540; Lufkin, p. 57; Ernest Morgan, "North Recaptures Coast Easily," *Corpus Christi Caller-Times*, May 28, 1961.

[8] Lufkin, p. 54-56; Wooten, p. 541; War of the Rebellion: The Rio Grande Expedition, Chap. XXXVIII, p. 409-410.

[9] Wooten, P. 540; Ernest Morgan, "North Recaptures Coast Easily," *Corpus Christi Caller-Times*, May 28, 1961; War of the Rebellion, Report of N.P. Banks to H.W. Halleck, XXXVIII, p. 409-411; Lufkin, p. 57.

[10] Lufkin, p. 58.

[11] Ibid.

[12] Ibid.

[13] Ibid; Eugenia Reynolds Briscoe, "City by the Sea," p. 540; War of the Rebellion, The Rio Grande Expedition, Chap. XXXVIII, p. 409-411.

[14] Lufkin, p. 58-59.

[15] Briscoe, p. 430.

[16] Depositions for a claim for war reparations from Margaret Meuly, National Archives; copy, Corpus Christi Central Library.

[17] Briscoe, p. 430; Morgan, "North Recaptures Coast Easily," *Corpus Christi Caller-Times*, May 28, 1961.

[18] War of the Rebellion, Bee's report: Chap. XXXVIII, p. 442-444.

[19] War of the Rebellion, Series I, Vol. 53, p. 914-915.

[20] Dee Woods, "Yankee Cannon Ball That Hit Lighthouse Is Saved," *Caller-Times,* Aug. 19, 1939.

[21] *Ranchero*, Dec. 23, 1863.

[22] Author's Note: The *Ranchero* was later moved to Brownsville and after the war to Matamoros.

[23] Briscoe, p. 430; author's note: "In Vacation" is inscribed in both the Corpus Christi City Council minutes and the Nueces County Commissioners Court minutes for this period of the war.

[24] Lufkin, p. 59; Ernest Morgan, "Bad Times Brought Hunger, Fear, Disunity," *Caller-Times*, July 9, 1961.

[25] Letter by Maj. William C. Thompson, commander of the 20th Iowa, to his wife, Thompson Letters, Corpus Christi Central Library.

[26] Ibid.

[27] Capt. C. Barney, "Recollections of Field Service With the Twentieth Iowa Infantry Volunteers: What I Saw in the Army," p. 258, 262.

[28] Thompson letter of Dec. 26, 1863.

[29] Bruce Cheeseman, "Maria von Blucher's Corpus Christi," p. 149.

[30] Thomas Noakes diaries, 1864, pg. 48, Corpus Christi Central Library.

[31] Briscoe, p. 235.

[32] Morgan, "Bad Times Brought Hunger, Fear, Disunity," *Caller-Times*, July 9, 1961; Thompson Letters.

[33] Lufkin, p. 59; War of the Rebellion, Chap. XXXVIII, p. 426-427, Brig. Gen. Ransom's report of Nov. 18, 1863.

[34] Ibid. War of the Rebellion: Gen. C.C. Washburn's report to Gen. Banks, dated Nov. 25; Wooten, "A Comprehensive History of Texas," p. 541-542.

[35] Author's note: The "Columbiad" was a large gun designed to fire shells at high elevations.

[36] Lufkin, p. 60-61.

[37] Ibid.

[38] Briscoe, 236; Lufkin, p. 69-70.

[39] Hobart Huson, "District Judges of Refugio County," p. 81-84; Vernon Smylie, "A Noose for Chipita"; Keith Guthrie, "History of San Patricio County," p. 267-270.

[40] Alwyn Barr, "Texas Coastal Defense: 1861-1865," Southwestern Historical Quarterly, Vol. 65, p. 6.

[41] Morgan, "Blockaders Lose Knack for Raiding," *Caller-Times*, May 14, 1961.

[42] Smylie, "A Noose for Chipita"; Guthrie, "History of San Patricio County"; Travis Moorman, articles, *Caller-Times*, Jan. 18, 1959; Nov. 13, 1959; March 24, 1963; Nov. 13, 1970; columns by the author: "The day they hanged Chipita," *Caller-Times*, April 22, 1998; "The man who had Chipita executed," *Caller-Times*, Nov. 7, 2007.

[43] Ibid.

[44] *Ranchero*, Oct. 29, 1863.

[45] Smylie, "A Noose for Chipita"; Guthrie, "History of San Patricio County"; Moorman, articles, *Caller-Times;* columns by the author.

[46] Thomas Noakes diaries, 1864, Corpus Christi Central Library.

[47] Ibid.

[48] Ibid.

[49] Ibid.

[50] Ibid.

[51] Ibid.

[52] Ibid.

[53] Ibid.

[54] John Salman Ford, "Rip Ford's Texas," edited by Stephen B. Oates, p. 154-157; 318-320; columns by the author, Aug. 23, Aug. 30, Sept. 6, 2000.

[55] Guthrie, "History of San Patricio County," p. 22.

[56] Ford, p. 354-355; Frank Wagner, Cecilio Balerio, Wagner Research Papers, the Corpus Christi Central Library; Wooten, "A Comprehensive History of Texas," p. 545-546; Mat Nolan's report, dated March 15, 1864, War of the Rebellion, Vol. XXXIV, Pt. 1, p. 638-639.

[57] *Caller-Times* article, "Mat Nolan, a fighting man, lived - and died - by the gun," Jan. 23, 1983; Frank Wagner, "The shooting of Sheriff Mat Nolan," Wagner Research Papers, the Corpus Christi Central Library; Bill Walraven, "City's most famous rebel deserved more dignified death," *Caller*, Feb. 19, 1982; Ernest Morgan, "The Century-Old Mystery: Why Was Mat Nolan Killed?" John Salman Ford, "Rip Ford's Texas," p. 384-385.

[58] E.T. Merriman, "Reminiscences of Civil War Days In and Around Corpus Christi," *Corpus Christi Caller,* June 2, 1929.

[59] Briscoe, p. 246.

[60] Ironclad oath copy signed by Thomas Fitzpatrick, Corpus Christi Central Library.

[61] Briscoe, p. 240; J. Williamson Moses, "Texas in Other Days" memoirs edited and reprinted by the author, p. 107.

CHAPTER 7

[1] V.V. Daniels, "Affairs of Nueces County In Civil Wars Days Practically at Standstill, Record Shows," *Caller-Times*; column by the author, "City in shambles at Civil War's End," *Caller-Times,* Nov. 4, 1998; Eugenia Reynolds Briscoe, "City by the Sea," p. 249.

[2] Ibid.

[3] Tom Lea, "King Ranch," Vol. 1, p. 243.

[4] Briscoe, p. 480.

[5] Daniel.

[6] Briscoe, p. 251.

[7] Andrew Anderson, "Do You Know the Story of Corpus Christi?" biographical files, Corpus Christi Central Library.

[8] Deposition, March 3, 1871, in behalf of a claim for war reparations from Margaret Meuly, National Archives, copy at the Corpus Christi Central Library.

[9] Helen Chapman diary, 1866, May 21, 1866 (transcribed and copyrighted by Caleb Coker, Anne F. Dunn).

[10] J.B. (Red) Dunn, "Perilous Trails of Texas," p. 10.

[11] Ibid.

[12] Ibid, p. 11.

[13] Merriman, "Reminiscences of Civil War Days In and Around Corpus Christi."

[14] Briscoe, p. 250, 268.

[15] Rosalie B. Hart Priour, "The Adventures of a Family of Emmigrants Who Emmigrated to Texas in 1834" (her spelling), Corpus Christi Central Library; Bill Walraven, "Civil War was brief for city," Corpus Christi *Caller-Times*.

[16] E.T. Merriman, "Reminiscences of Civil War Days In and Around Corpus Christi"; Andrew Anderson, "Do You Know the Story of Corpus Christi?"; Chapman diary, May 15, 1866; Dee Woods, "Mesquite Tree Justice Prevailed Over Jurors' Deliberations," *Caller-Times*, July 5, 1940.

[17] Ibid.

[18] Coleman McCampbell, "Saga of a Frontier Seaport," p. 27; Author's columns, May 17 and May 24, 2006; Briscoe, p. 257. [Note: Briscoe writes that the outbreak started with the arrival of a Mexican fruit vessel; this is usually attributed to the origin of the 1854 fever outbreak in Corpus Christi; in 1867, most accounts attribute the outbreak to the arrival of a sick traveler from the yellow-fever-stricken town of Indianola.]

[19] *Corpus Christi Advertiser*, July 16, 1867.

[20] Brownson Malsch, "Indianola: The Mother of Western Texas," p. 192.

[21] Mary A. Sutherland, "The Story of Corpus Christi," p. 15-16.

[22] Joseph Almond Diary, 1861-1875, text transcribed by Sharry M. Reynolds, p. 44.

[23] Helen Chapman diary, 1867, from July 2 to Sept. 17.

[24] Dee Woods, "Yellow Fever Killed Many Early Settlers," *Caller*, July 7, 1939; "Ernest G. Fischer, article on Pat Dunn, "Padre Island Ranching Never Like That of the Films, But It Isn't Altogether Prosaic," one of a series of articles in the *Caller*, July, 1927.

[25] Anna Moore Schwien, "When Corpus Christi Was Young," memoirs, p. 22; "Fever Outbreak Delayed Work on First Presbyterian Church," *Caller-Times* article, April 27, 1952.

[26] "On This Bluff, Centennial History, 1867-1967, First Presbyterian Church, p. 16.

[27] Briscoe, p. 485.

[28] Sister Mary Xavier, "Father Jaillet, Saddlebag Priest of the Nueces," p. 31; Schwien, p. 21; Andrew Anderson, "Do You Know the Story of Corpus Christi?" biographical files, Corpus Christi Central Library.

[29] Schwien, p. 21-22.

[30] Ibid.

[31] *Corpus Christi Advertiser*, Aug. 14, 1867.

[32] Helen Chapman diary, 1867, p. 22.

[33] Xavier, p. 30.

[34] Sister Mary Xavier, "Father Jaillet, Saddlebag Priest of the Nueces," p. 30.

[35] The Handbook of Texas; David G. McComb, "Galveston: A History," p. 96.

[36] Anderson, "Do You Know the Story of Corpus Christi?" p. 26-27.

[37] Ibid.

[38] Dee Woods, "Yellow Fever Killed Many Early Settlers," *Caller*, July 7, 1939.

[39] Chapman, Almond diaries.

[40] Corpus Christi Cathedral, "Celebrating 150 Years," p. 5-7.

[41] Almond diary, p. 44-47.

[42] Columns by the author: July 9, 16, 23, 2003, Jan. 9, 2008; Bill Walraven, "Texans hated first Republican governor," *Caller-Times*, Nov. 9, 1978; Dave Allred, "Ex-Corpus Christi Law Student Was Stormy Governor," *Caller-Times*, April 15, 1956.

[43] John Salman Ford, "Rip Ford's Texas," edited by Stephen B. Oates, note, p. 427.

[44] Columns by the author; Walraven; Allred.

[45] *Nueces Valley*, April, 1858.

[46] Marie v. Blucher, "E.J. Davis House," vertical files, Corpus Christi Central Library.

[47] *Ranchero*, April 21, 1861; see Chapter 6.

[48] Muster Rolls of Military Companies Organized in Nueces County During the Civil War, compiled by Dan Kilgore, p. 4.

[49] Edna May Tubbs, "E.J. Davis, Only Republican To Ever Govern Texas Came From Corpus Christi," *Caller*, Aug. 27, 1939; Ernest Wallace, "Texas in Turmoil, The Saga of Texas: 1849-1875," p. 133; Tom Lea, "King Ranch," p. 203.

[50] E.T. Merriman, "Random Recollections of Nearly Ninety Years," Corpus Christi Central Library.

[51] Helen Chapman diary, 1866-67.

[52] "History of Nueces County," p. 78.

[53] Bill Walraven, "History of Press Here Begins With Republic," *Caller-Times,* Jan. 18, 1959.

[54] Anna Moore Schwien, "When Corpus Christi Was Young," p. 21-22, vertical files, Corpus Christi Central Library.

[55] Mary Sutherland, "The Story of Corpus Christi," p. 38.

[56] Wallace, p. 207-209.

[57] Tubbs, *Caller,* Aug. 27, 1939.

[58] Wallace, p. 212.

[59] Ibid, p. 218; John Salman Ford, p. 419.

[60] Sutherland, p. 39.

[61] John Salman Ford, p. 427; T.R. Fehrenbach, "Lone Star," p. 432.

[62] Merriman, "Random Recollections of Nearly Ninety Years."

[63] Garth Jones, "A Hated Texan: His Monument Towers Highest in State Cemetery," *Caller-Times,* Feb. 20, 1958.

[64] Grady Stiles, "South Texas: Home Range of American Cattle Industry," *Caller-Times,* Jan. 18, 1959; Hobart Huson, "Refugio," p. 223; Jimmy M. Skaggs, "The Cattle Trailing Industry."

[65] "Bryden Took Cattle To Kansas Market," *Corpus Christi Caller*, May 8, 1952.

[66] C.C. Cox, "Reminiscences," Texas Historical Association Quarterly, Vol. 6, p. 113-138.

[67] Dobie, "Vaquero of the Brush Country," p. 23.

[68] *Nueces Valley*, April, 1872.

[69] Keith Guthrie, "Raw Frontier," Volume One, p. 91.

[70] Guthrie, p. 90.

[71] Walter Prescott Webb, "The Great Plains," p. 211; Ernest Staples Osgood, "The Day of the Cattlemen," p. 27-28; J. Frank Dobie, "The Longhorns," p. 9.

[72] Ibid, 212.

[73] "Stompede" was the old Texian word; see J. Frank Dobie, "The Longhorns," p. 87.

[74] First-hand accounts of trail-driving can be found in "Trail Drivers of Texas," edited by J. Marvin Hunter.

[75] Dobie, "The Longhorns," p. 309-310.

[76] Ibid.

[77] Amanda Burks, "Trail Drivers," p. 295-305.

[78] "Trail Drivers of Texas."

[79] W.F. Fielder, "Trail Drivers," p. 689.

[80] Thomas Welder, "Trail Drivers," p. 294.

[81] M.A. Withers, "Trail Drivers," p. 102.

[82] W.T. (Bill) Jackman, "Trail Drivers," p. 861.

[83] Fielder, "Trail Drivers," p. 690.

[84] J. B. Pumphrey, "Trail Drivers," p. 28.

[85] Column by the author, Nov. 21, 2001; *Nueces Valley*, July, 1871.

[86] *Nueces Valley*, Aug. 10, 1871.

[87] Column by the author, Nov. 21, 2001; *Nueces Valley*, July, 1871.

[88] Andrew Anderson, "More About Corpus Christi, Further Recollections," biographical files, Corpus Christi Central Library.

[89] Ibid.

[90] Jim Greenwood, "69-Year-Old Ledger Reflects Early Days in City," *Caller-Times*, Sept. 24, 1950.

[91] *Nueces Valley*, June 1, 1872, and editions in August, 1872.

[92] Dee Woods, "Firemen Were Socialites in Volunteer Days," *Corpus Christi Caller*, July 14, 1939; Coleman McCampbell, "Saga of a Frontier Seaport," p. 40-41.

CHAPTER 8

[1] Walter Prescott Webb, "The Great Plains," p. 208-209.

[2] J. Frank Dobie, "The Longhorns," p. 11.

[3] O. Henry, "A Call Loan."

[4] Alpha Kennedy Wood, "Texas Coastal Bend: People and Places," p. 51.

[5] Tom Lea, "The King Ranch," p. 104-105.

[6] Dobie, "A Vaquero of the Brush Country," p. 27-28; George W. Saunders, "The Trail Drivers of Texas," edited by J. Marvin Hunter, p. 923-924.

[7] Lea, p. 8.

[8] Ibid, p. 172.

[9] Ibid, p. 182-187; John Salmon Ford, "Rip Ford's Texas," edited by Stephen B. Oates, p. 457-470.

[10] "John and Martha Rabb, Nueces County cattle barons," *Caller-Times*, Jan. 23, 1983; column by the author, "The cattle queen of Texas," *Caller-Times*, May 10, 2000; Dan Kilgore, "Mrs. Rabb's Pasture."

[11] Kilgore.

[12] Ibid.

[13] Ibid; Mrs. Howell Ward, "Mrs. John Rabb Was a Colorful Pioneer Woman," *Caller-Times*, March 10, 1946.

[14] John Dunn, "Perilous Trails of Texas," p. 141.

[15] Ibid.

[16] Dobie, "A Vaquero of the Brush Country," p. 119.

[17] David J. Weber, "Foreigners In Their Native Land," p. 153.

[18] Kilgore.

[19] Mrs. P.A. Hunter, daughter of D.C. Rachal, quoted by Kilgore.

[20] Andrew Anderson, "Do You Know the Story of Corpus Christi?" biographical files, Corpus Christi Central Library, p. 13.

[21] Rachel B. Hebert, "The Rachals of White Point."

[22] Ibid.

[23] A.P. Rachal, "The Trail Drivers of Texas," edited by J. Marvin Hunter, p. 809-810.

[24] Columns by the author: "The old barons of beef and bone," Dec. 13, 2000, and "Longhorn barons, a vanished breed," Dec. 20, 2000, *Caller-Times*.

[25] Paul H. Carlson, "Texas Woolly Backs," p. 50-51; Lea, p. 125.

[26] Lea, p. 125.

[27] Ibid, p. 122.

[28] Carlson, p. 54-56.

[29] William Headen, "Historical Sketch," published in 1883, vertical files, Corpus Christi Central Library.

[30] *Ranchero*, April 28, 1860.

[31] Coleman McCampbell, "Era of Wool and Sheep in Nueces Valley," *Frontier Times*; Grady Stiles, "Sheepmen's Heyday Here Short-Lived," *Caller-Times*.

[32] Bruce Cheeseman, "Maria von Blucher's Corpus Christi," p. 127.

[33] Ibid, p. 161.

[34] Carlson, p. 50.

[35] Wayne Slater, "Buckley patriarch helped change Texas politics," *Caller-Times*, Sept. 27, 1987; New Handbook of Texas, p. 804.

[36] Val W. Lehmann, "Forgotten Legions, Sheep in the Rio Grande Plain of Texas," p. 113.

[37] Diary of Oscar M. Edgerley, "Sheep Rancher, 1861," copy in the author's possession.

[38] Robert Adams, "Learning by Hard Licks," interview, Corpus Christi Central Library, p. 10-12.

[39] W.G. Sutherland, "Sandy McNubbin Tells Of Vanished Herds of Sheep in South Texas," *Corpus Christi Caller*, July 19, 1925.

[40] Ibid; McCampbell, *Frontier Times*.

[41] *Nueces Valley*, May, 1871.

[42] Mary Sutherland, "The Story of Corpus Christi," p. 48-49.

[43] Carlson, "Texas Woolly Backs," p. 61-62; column by the author, "Woolly times in South Texas," *Caller-Times*, Dec. 22, 1999; W.G. Sutherland, article, *Caller*, Nov. 30, 1930.

[44] Frank Wagner, Research Papers, Corpus Christi Central Library.

[45] Column by the author, "Rise and fall of the sheep and wool era in South Texas," *Caller-Times*, Sept. 2, 2009.

[46] T.R. Fehrenbach, "Lone Star," p. 574.

[47] *Ranchero*, Oct. 13, 1860.

[48] Eugenia Reynolds Briscoe, "City by the Sea," p. 182.

[49] *Galveston Daily News*, May, 1873.

[50] *Nueces Valley*, 1871.

[51] Ibid.

[52] *Nueces Valley*, March 16, 1872.

[53] Lea, p. 277.

[54] Ibid, p. 273-274.

[55] Bill Walraven, "Weakness of Reconstruction Texas Invited Border Bandits," *Caller-Times*, Jan. 18, 1959.

[56] *Nueces Valley*, September, 1872.

[57] J.B. (Red) Dunn, "Perilous Trails of Texas," p. 71.

[58] *Nueces Valley*, September, 1872.

[59] Bruce Cheeseman, "Maria von Blucher's Corpus Christi," p. 218.

[60] Bill Walraven, "City of bad guys burned to ground," *Caller-Times*, Aug. 29, 1975; Corpus Christi Gazette, May 16, 1874; Dunn, "Perilous Trails of Texas," p. 59; Jim Davis, "A Hole in a Sack of Sugar Traced a Sweet Trail to the Gallows," *Frontier Times*, Nov. 1970.

[61] Dunn, "Perilous Trails of Texas," p. 48-55; Dunn, "The Capture of Hypolita Tapia and Andres Davila," *Caller-Times*, May 3, 1931.

[62] Ibid.

[63] Ibid.

[64] Ibid.

[65] Davis, *Frontier Times*, Nov. 1970.

[66] John Young and J. Frank Dobie, "A Vaquero of the Brush Country," p. 69.

[67] Ibid.

[68] Ibid.

[69] Ibid.

[70] Hobart Huson, "Refugio County History."

[71] Kenneth W. Howell, "The Untold Story of Reconstruction in South Texas, 1865-1876," South Texas Studies - Victoria College.

[72] Fehrenbach, "Lone Star," p. 575.

[73] *Corpus Christi Caller*, "Ship channel: It didn't come easy," Sept. 22, 1974.

[74] *Corpus Christi Star*, Sept. 19, 1848; Dr. Carl Helmecke, "The Seaport of the South, Corpus Christi," manuscript, Corpus Christi Central Library, p. 16.

[75] Helmecke, p. 30-31.

[76] *Corpus Christi Caller,* "Ship channel: It didn't come easy," Sept. 22, 1974.

[77] Robert Adams, "Learning by Hard Licks," interview, vertical file, Corpus Christi Central Library.

[78] Riddle letter, July 23, 1859, Corpus Christi Central Library, the John M. Moore collection.

[79] E.H. Caldwell, memoirs, edited by Robert J. Caldwell.

[80] Spencer Pearson, "Morgan Lines Monopolized Gulf Shipping for Decades," *Caller-Times,* Jan. 18, 1959.

[81] Helmecke, p. 17; Coleman McCampbell, "Saga of a Frontier Seaport," p. 29.

[82] *Corpus Christi Gazette,* June 6, 1874.

[83] Laws of the state of Texas, June 2, 1873.

[84] E.T. Merriman, "Random Recollections of Nearly 90 Years," p. 5-6; Caldwell, memoirs, p. 88.

[85] E.T. Merriman, "Supplement to the History of Corpus Christi," Corpus Christi Central Library.

CHAPTER 9

[1] John Young and J. Frank Dobie, "A Vaquero of the Brush Country," p. 24.

[2] Ibid, p. 25.

[3] Ibid.

[4] E.H. Caldwell, memoirs, edited by Robert J. Caldwell, p. 76; Hobart Huson, "History of Refugio," p. 222-223.

[5] Hobart Huson, "History of Refugio," p. 222-223.

[6] Tom Lea, "The King Ranch," p. 265.

[7] Young/Dobie, p. 24.

[8] J. Frank Dobie, "The Longhorns," p. 240-241.

[9] Huson, p. 222-223.

[10] John Dunn, "Perilous Trails of Texas," p. 62.

[11] Young/Dobie, p. 58.

[12] Lea, p. 269.

[13] Huson, p. 223.

[14] Young/Dobie, p. 24.

[15] Walter Prescott Webb, "The Great Plains," p. 231.

[16] Young/Dobie, p. 24-29.

[17] Caldwell, memoirs, p. 76.

[18] Hortense Warner Ward, "Great Slaughter Made Coast A Boneyard," *Caller-Times,* Jan. 18, 1959.

[19] William Allen and Sue Hastings Taylor, "Aransas: The Life of a Texas Coastal County," p. 158-164; Hortense Warner Ward, "Hide and Tallow Factories," Manuscript for a History of Nueces County.

[20] Young/Dobie, p. 26-27.

[21] Ibid.

[22] Alpha Kennedy Wood, "Texas Coastal Bend: People and Places," p. 111.

[23] Dunn, p. 19.

[24] Ibid.

[25] Ibid.

[26] *Corpus Christi Advertiser,* July 26, 1872.

[27] Dobie, "The Longhorns," p. 240.

[28] Ward.

[29] Eugenia Reynolds Briscoe, "City by the Sea," p. 526.

[30] Ward.

[31] Young/Dobie, p. 29.

[32] *The Weekly Gazette,* Sept. 12, 1874; the *Nueces Valley,* Sept. 12, 1874.

[33] Ibid.

[34] Ibid.

[35] Bert C. West, "Storm-Leveled Indianola Was Once Texas' Leading Seaport," *Caller-Times*, Sept. 15, 1957.

[36] Brownson Malsch, "Indianola, The Mother of Western Texas," p. 228-251; Hobart Huson, "History of Refugio," p. 246-248.

[37] Andrew Anderson, "Do You Know the Story of Corpus Christi?" biographical files, Corpus Christi Central Library, p. 19.

[38] Malsch; West; Huson.

[39] Leopold Morris, "The Mexican Raid of 1875 on Corpus Christi," Texas Historical Association Quarterly, October, 1900, p. 128-139; Handbook of Texas, "Nuecestown Raid of 1875," p. 1055.

[40] John Dunn, "When Mexican Raiders Swooped Down on Corpus," *Corpus Christi Caller*, April, 1920.

[41] Ruth Dodson, "The Noakes Raid," Frontier Times, July 1946, p. 175-187.

[42] Ibid, p. 179; Morris, p. 129.

[43] Dee Woods, "Stories of Noakes Raid . . ." *Corpus Christi Caller*, Aug. 24, 1939.

[44] Dunn, "When Mexican Raiders Swooped Down on Corpus."

[45] Ibid; Dodson, p. 177.

[46] Morris, p. 129; Dunn.

[47] Morris.

[48] Ibid.

[49] Ibid.

[50] Dunn, "Perilous Trails of Texas," p. 75.

[51] Andrew Anderson, "Do You Know the Story of Corpus Christi?" biographical files, Corpus Christi Central Library, p. 10.

[52] Caldwell, memoirs.

[53] Ibid, p. 92-100.

[54] Ibid.

[55] Dodson, p. 185-186; Dee Woods, "Difficulties Encountered In Finding Hanging Site," *Caller*, Aug. 26, 1939.

[56] Morris, p. 139; Lois Felder, "Nueces River Village Raided 75 Years Ago," *Corpus Christi Times*, March 28, 1950; Dodson, p. 187.

[57] Tom Lea, "The King Ranch," p. 280.

[58] George Durham/Clyde Wantland, "Taming the Nueces Strip," p. 23-24.

[59] Ibid, p. 57-66.

[60] Ibid, p. 85.

[61] Walter Prescott Webb, "The Texas Rangers," p. 265; Charles M. Robinson III, "The Men Who Wear The Star," p. 201.

[62] Webb, p. 252.

[63] Writers Roundtable, "Padre Island," p. 192.

[64] Columns by the author: Oct. 4,, 11, 18, 2000; Feb. 5, 2008; July 29, 2009; Dee Woods, "Mercer Family One of Best Known in South Texas," *Corpus Christi Caller*, Aug. 23, 1939; Phyllis Coffee, "Logs Reveal Texas Gulf Coast History, 1866-1900," Southwestern Historical Quarterly; Coffee, "After 90 Years, 5 Old Diaries Make News Again," *Corpus Christi Times*, Aug. 5, 1957; Cyril Matthew Kuehne, "Hurricane Junction: A History of Port Aransas."

[65] Mercer log entry, March 19, 1875, Corpus Christi Central Library.

[66] Mercer log entry, May 1, 1876, Corpus Christi Central Library.

[67] Columns by the author; Woods, *Caller*, June 11 and Aug. 23, 1939; Coffee, Southwestern Historical Quarterly; Coffee, *Corpus Christi Times*, Aug. 5, 1957; Kuehne, "Hurricane Junction: A History of Port Aransas."

[68] Mercer log entry, March 30, 1866, Corpus Christi Central Library.

[69] Mercer log entry, Sept. 16, 1866, Corpus Christi Central Library.

[70] Mercer log entry, March 30, 1866, Corpus Christi Central Library.

[71] Mercer log entry, August, 1870, Corpus Christi Central Library.

[72] Mercer log entry, Dec. 18, 1872, Corpus Christi Central Library.
[73] Mercer log entry, Sept. 12, 1870, Corpus Christi Central Library.
[74] Mercer log entry, Jan. 9, 1872, Corpus Christi Central Library.
[75] Mercer log entry, Sept. 16, 1875, Corpus Christi Central Library.
[76] Mercer log entry, Dec. 22, 1878, Corpus Christi Central Library.
[77] charges for pilot fees.
[78] Mercer log entry, Jan. 4, 1872, Corpus Christi Central Library.
[79] Mercer log entry, Jan., 1879, Corpus Christi Central Library.
[80] Mercer log entry, Nov. 24, 1873, Corpus Christi Central Library.
[81] Mercer log entry, Nov. 30, 1876, Corpus Christi Central Library.
[82] Mrs. S.G. Miller, "Sixty Years In The Nueces Valley," p. 25.
[83] Ibid, p. 26-27.
[84] Ibid, p. 28.
[85] Ibid, p. 29.
[86] *Corpus Christi Gazette*, Dec., 1876.
[87] Dee Woods, "Wreck of Steamer Mary Was Event Back in 1876," *Corpus Christi Caller*, July 19, 1939.
[88] Ibid.
[89] Eli T. Merriman, "Opposition Plentiful in 60-Year Fight For Deep Water," Oct., 1936.
[90] Coffee, "Mercer Logs: The Story of an Ill-Fated Vessel," *Corpus Christi Times*, Aug. 6, 1957.
[91] Mercer log entry, Dec. 19, 1872, Corpus Christi Central Library.
[92] *Corpus Christi Gazette*, June 26, 1875.
[93] Ibid.
[94] Ibid.
[95] Margaret Ramage, "Jasper Blucher Recalls Days of Early Ice Plant," *Times,* July 29, 1971.

CHAPTER 10

[1] W.G. Sutherland, "Century of Education In South Texas Reviewed by the Sage From Bluntzer, *"Corpus Christi Caller.*
[2] Mary Mahoney, "Miss Kelsey Will Get Special Church Medal," *Corpus Christi Times*, April 29, 1948.
[3] *Corpus Christi Star*, Sept. 19, 1848; "History of Nueces County," p. 115.
[4] *Corpus Christi Star*, Nov. 28, 1848.
[5] Sue Fahlgren, "Education history dotted with false starts," *Corpus Christi Caller-Times*, Centennial Journey, Jan. 23, 1983.
[6] Ibid.
[7] Fahlgren.
[8] Mary Sutherland, "The Story of Corpus Christi," p. 80.
[9] Mrs. Willie Hoffman, interview, June 10, 1940, vertical files, Corpus Christi Central Library.
[10] Ibid.
[11] "History of Nueces County," p. 117.
[12] Rosalie B. Hart Priour, "The Adventures of a Family of Emmigrants Who Emmigrated to Texas in 1834" (her spelling), Corpus Christi Central Library.
[13] E.T. Merriman, "Random Recollections of Nearly Ninety Years," Corpus Christi Central Library, p. 4-5.
[14] Fahlgren; Gladys Gibbon, "Education in Corpus Christi, 1856-1900."
[15] Ibid.
[16] E.T. Merriman, article, "More Early History of City Schools."
[17] Ibid.
[18] E.T. Merriman, "Random Recollections of Nearly Ninety Years," Corpus Christi Central

Library.

[19] "History of Nueces County," p. 118.

[20] "History of Nueces County," p. 117.

[21] *Nueces Valley*, August, 1872.

[22] Fahlgren.

[23] Medeleine Greene, article, *Caller-Times*, Sept. 27, 1959.

[24] "History of Nueces County," p. 118.

[25] Corpus Christi Gazette, "Meeting of the school directors," June 14, 1873.

[26] Ibid; W.G. Sutherland.

[27] "History of Nueces County," p. 119.

[28] Ibid.

[29] Fahlgren.

[30] Anne Dodson, "Solomon Coles, First Negro Principal, Was Born Slave," *Corpus Christi Caller-Times*, Jan. 18, 1959; Edna Jordan, "Black Tracks to Texas," Nueces County Historical Commission Bulletin, Nov., 1989.

[31] Ibid.

[32] Ibid.

[33] "History of Nueces County," p. 112.

[34] Roy Terrell, Reminiscences, (As told to Marguerite Terrell, April 1967), a copy in the author's possession.

[35] Ibid.

[36] Fahlgren.

[37] Ibid; Mrs. Howell Ward, "First Public School Commencement Was Conducted at Old Market Hall in 1893," *Caller-Times*, May 27, 1945.

[38] J.L. Allhands, "The Gringo Builder"; E.T. Merriman, "Random Recollections of Nearly Ninety Years," Corpus Christi Central Library, p. 8-9.

[39] Ibid; Bill Walraven, "Uriah Lott, Railroad Builder," Jan. 18, 1959.

[40] *Caller-Times*, "Tex-Mex Railroad Boosted Early Development of Area," April 27, 1952.

[41] Walraven, "A guy could lose his pants doing business in 1877," *Corpus Christi Caller*.

[42] Bruce S. Cheeseman, "Perfectly Exhausted with Pleasure: The 1881 King-Kenedy Excursion Train to Laredo," booklet published in 1992, p. 11, 29.

[43] Texas-Mexican Railway, Symbol of International Friendship," publication, 1982.

[44] *Corpus Christi Crony*, March 8, 1902.

[45] *Corpus Christi Caller*, article, June 16, 1940.

[46] *Corpus Christi Caller*, Jan. 21, 1883; Centennial Journey, *Corpus Christi Caller*, Jan. 23, 1983, p. 2.

[47] Coleman McCampbell, "Era of Wool and Sheep in Nueces Valley," *Frontier Times*; Grady Stiles, "Sheepmen's Heyday Here Short-Lived," *Caller-Times*, Jan. 18, 1959.

[48] Ibid.

[49] Ibid.

[50] Column by the author, "Woolly times in South Texas," Dec. 22, 1999; *Corpus Christi Caller*, 1896.

[51] Tom Lea, "The King Ranch," p. 368-371; *Corpus Christi Caller*, 1925, "Captain King's Body Interred at Kingsville."

[52] J.L. Allhands, "The Gringo Builder"; Walraven, "Uriah Lott, Railroad Builder," Jan. 18, 1959.

[53] E. T. Merriman, "Opposition Plentiful in 60-Year Fight for Deep Water," *Corpus Christi Caller-Times*, Oct., 1936; Thelma Peterson Walton, thesis, 1949; E.H. Caldwell, memoirs, edited by Robert J. Caldwell, p. 72.

[54] John C. Rayburn, "First Rainmaking: 1891; Ranchmen Exploded Balloons, Dynamite, and Showers Fell," *Caller-Times*, Jan. 18, 1959.

[55] Ibid.

[56] Roy Terrell, Reminiscences.

[57] Ibid.

[58] *Corpus Christi Times*, article, May 24, 1948.

[59] *Corpus Christi Caller*, "Angry Flames: Corpus Christi Visited by the Most Destructive Fire In Its History," July 15, 1892; Ann Dodson, "Fire of 1890s Razed One Block of Chaparral," *Caller-Times*, Nov. 20, 1955.

[60] Dee Woods, "Caller Shouted the 'Glad News' When Water Was Piped Over City Residential Section in 1892," *Caller,* July 13, 1939; John S. McCampbell, "A History of Corpus Christi's Municipal Water Supply," Corpus Christi Central Library.

[61] Sue Harwood, "Ropes' Premature Dream," *Caller-Times*, Jan. 18, 1959; Centennial History of Corpus Christi, *Caller-Times,* 1952.

[62] Ibid.

[63] Ibid.

[64] Ibid.

[65] *Corpus Christi Caller*, Letter to the editor, March 6, 1956.

[66] Harwood, "Ropes' Premature Dream," *Caller-Times*, Jan. 18, 1959; Centennial History of Corpus Christi, *Caller-Times*, 1952.

[67] Centennial History of Corpus Christi, *Caller-Times*; Mary Sutherland, "The Story of Corpus Christi," p. 59; Bill Walraven, "Recalling the days when North Beach had some class," *Caller,* Sept. 29, 1978; *Caller-Times,* "Varied History Preceded Development of North Beach as Resort," Jan. 1, 1950.

[68] Ibid.

[69] Columns by the author, *Caller-Times*, Feb. 18, 1998, and April 5, April 12, 2006; *Corpus Christi Caller*, editions of February-May, 1898.

[70] Ibid.

[71] Letter from T.P. "Tobe" Fitzsimmons, *Corpus Christi Caller*, Jan. 13, 1899.

[72] Ibid.

[73] Letter from Robert Hall, *Corpus Christi Caller*, Jan. 8, 1899.

[74] Letter from Sam Tinney, *Corpus Christi Caller*, Jan. 27, 1899.

[75] Ibid.

[76] Ibid.

[77] *Corpus Christi Caller*, March 31 and April 21, 1899.

[78] Ibid.

[79] *Corpus Christi Caller,* Feb. 17, 1899.

[80] Ibid.

[81] Andrew Anderson, "The Terrible Freeze of 1899," biographical files, Corpus Christi Central Library.

[82] *Corpus Christi Caller*, Feb. 17, 1899.

[83] Ibid -- Advertisement by the George L. Caldwell Co.

[84] Travis Moorman, "Skaters Once Used Corpus Christi Bay," Feb. 12, 1960.

[85] *Corpus Christi Caller*, Feb. 17, 1899.

CHAPTER 11

[1] *Caller-Times*, "Old Salt Mill On Water Street Recalled," Jan. 25, 1939; Andrew Anderson, "Do You Know the Story of Corpus Christi?" biographical files, Corpus Christi Central Library.

[2] Mrs. Roy Anderson Crossley, "The Anderson Family History: The Life and Times of Capt. John Anderson," biographical files, Corpus Christi Central Library.

[3] *Caller-Times*, "Old Salt Mill On Water Street Recalled," Jan. 25, 1939; Andrew Anderson, "Do You Know the Story of Corpus Christi?" biographical files, Corpus Christi Central Library.

[4] E.H. Caldwell, Memoirs, "Corpus Christi and South Texas," p. 16, biographical files, Corpus Christi Central Library.

[5] Mary Sutherland, "The Story of Corpus Christi," p. 57; Dee Woods, article, *Corpus Christi Caller*, Sept. 21, 1939.

[6] Ibid.

[7] *Corpus Christi Caller*, Jan. 20, 1905.

[8] *Corpus Christi Caller*, Feb. 17, 1905.

[9] Sutherland.

[10] Roy Terrell, Reminiscences, (As told to Marguerite Terrell, April 1967), a copy in the author's possession.

[11] *Corpus Christi Caller*, Feb. 10, 1905.

[12] *Corpus Christi Caller*, Aug. 25, 1905.

[13] *Corpus Christi Caller*, March 9, 1905.

[14] *Corpus Christi Caller*, June 2, 1905.

[15] *Corpus Christi Caller* articles: March 9, April 14, April 28, 1905.

[16] *Corpus Christi Caller*, Jan. 13 and Jan. 27, 1905.

[17] *Corpus Christi Caller*, Jan. 20, 1905.

[18] *Corpus Christi Caller*, "Lone Star Margaret," April 14, 1905; Katheryn Pate, "Capt. Anderson, 89 Today, Wants To Go Back To Boats," *Corpus Christi Times*, Nov. 27, 1941.

[19] *Corpus Christi Caller*, May 12, 1905.

[20] *Corpus Christi Caller*, March 24, 1905.

[21] *Corpus Christi Caller*, Jan. 6, 1905.

[22] *Corpus Christi Caller*, Jan. 13 and Oct. 20, 1905.

[23] *Corpus Christi Caller*, Dec. 15, 1905.

[24] *Corpus Christi Herald*, March 17, 1905; James V. Allred and David Allred, "Imprints in Sidewalk Recall Tenure of Colorful Sheriff," *Corpus Christi Caller-Times*, July 15, 1956.

[25] *Corpus Christi Caller*, May, 1905.

[26] Ibid, Dec. 11, 1905 and Dec. 14, 1906.

[27] Dan Kilgore, Corpus Christi: A Quarter Century of Development, 1900-1925," Southwestern Historical Quarterly, Vol. 75, p. 434-443.

[28] Ibid.

[29] Stephens, "1886 Drought Forced Land Sale to Farmers."

[30] Grady Stiles, "Agriculture Has Been Basis For Coastal Bend Prosperity," *Caller-Times*, April 27, 1952.

[31] T.R. Fehrenbach, "Lone Star," p. 605-606.

[32] A. Ray Stephens, "1886 Drought Forced Land Sale to Farmers," *Caller-Times*, Aug. 5, 1964.

[33] Dan Kilgore, Corpus Christi: A Quarter Century of Development, 1900-1925," *Southwestern Historical Quarterly*, Vol. 75, p. 436.

[34] *Corpus Christi Caller*, "Big Bohemian Colony; The Grim Ranch of 7,000 Acres Sold for Colonization Purposes," Aug. 1904.

[35] *Corpus Christi Caller*, "Busy Clearing Farms," Jan. 31, 1908.

[36] A. Ray Stephens, "Taft; The Taft Ranch," p. 156; *Caller-Times*, "Developer of Bishop Opened 80,000 Acres," Jan. 18, 1959.

[37] Dee Woods, "Small Farms Signaled Breakup of Large Ranches," *Caller-Times*, July 23, 1939.

[38] George H. Paul, "City's Founder Traces Establishment of Robstown in 1907," *Robstown Record*, Oct. 31, 1957.

[39] Ibid.

[40] Stephens, "Taft Ranch," p. 156.

[41] George H. Paul.

[42] J.L. Allhands, "Uriah Lott," p. 167.

[43] E.T. Merriman, "Reminiscences of Early Days in Texas"; Hoyt Hager, "Ranching, farming have different look from the early days," *Caller-Times*, Jan. 23, 1983.

[44] Roy Bedichek, "Karankaway Country," p. 92, 105-107.

[45] *Corpus Christi Caller*, "Steam Plowing," Dec. 21, 1900.

[46] W.D. Doughty, "Homeseekers Found Area Undeveloped," *Robstown Record*, Oct. 31, 1957.

[47] Keith Guthrie, "History of San Patricio County," p. 69;

[48] Ramon Adams, "Cowboy Words," p. 170.

[49] Sutherland.

[50] E.T. Merriman, article, "From Cattle Ranges to Extensive Farms."

[51] Margaret Ramage, "Jasper Blucher Recalls Days of Early Ice Plant," *Caller-Times*, July 29, 1971.

[52] *Corpus Christi Caller*, Sept. 12, 1902.

[53] Anne Dodson, "Peter McBrides Recall Long-Ago Scenes of City," *Caller-Times*, Aug. 21, 1955.

[54] Roy Terrell, Reminiscences, (As told to Marguerite Terrell, April 1967), a copy in the author's possession.

[55] *Corpus Christi Caller*, Dec. 21, 1906.

[56] *Corpus Christi Caller*, July 6, 1906.

[57] *Corpus Christi Caller*, March 27, May 22, 1908.

[58] Carlyle Leonard, "It Wasn't So Very Long Ago That C.C. Was Just a Village," *Caller-Times*, April 21, 1952.

[59] Sue Smith, "I Remember: Buggy Was Must in Grocery Business," *Caller-Times*, June 2, 1963.

[60] Harriet Tillman, "The Poenisch Family History," p. 80, a copy in the author's possession.

[61] A. Ray Stephens, "Taft Ranch," p. 163.

[62] Bernard Brister, "Taft Visited City 30 Years Ago Today," *Caller-Times*, Oct. 22, 1939; column by the author, "President Taft's visit was big event for Corpus Christi," Oct. 21, 2009; Coleman McCampbell, "Saga of a Frontier Seaport," p. 30.

[63] Ibid.

[64] Roy Terrell, Reminiscences (As told to Marguerite Terrell, April 1967), a copy in the author's possession.

[65] Bernard Brister, "Taft Visited City 30 Years Ago Today," *Caller-Times*, Oct. 22, 1939; column by the author, "President Taft's visit was big event for Corpus Christi," Oct. 21, 2009.

[66] Sutherland, p. 63.

[67] Stephens, "Taft Ranch," p. 164-165.

[68] E.T. Merriman, article, *Corpus Christi Caller,* Sept. 14, 1927.

[69] *Corpus Christi Caller*, Jan. 25, 1916.

[70] A. Ray Stephens, "Taft Ranch," p. 175; Keith Guthrie, "History of San Patricio County," p. 74; Bill and Marjorie Walraven, "Wooden Rigs - Iron Men," p. 51-52.

[71] Eugenia Reynolds Briscoe, "City by the Sea," p. 471.

[72] Ibid.

[73] V.V. Daniels, "Affairs of Nueces County In Civil Wars Days Practically at Standstill, Record Shows," *Caller-Times*.

[74] *Corpus Christi Caller*, article, May 5, 1939.

[75] *Nueces Valley*, June, 1872.

[76] Sutherland, "The Story of Corpus Christi," p. 74.

[77] Conrad Casler, article, *Corpus Christi Times*, Sept. 14, 1954.

[78] Sue Smith, "I Remember: Buggy Was Must in Grocery Business," *Caller-Times*, June 2, 1963.

[79] Jim Greenwood, "Oyster Shell Helped City Improve Early Day Streets," *Caller-Times*, 1952.

[80] Jan Jackson, "Mrs. Westbrook Recalls Hard Life Here in 1900s," *Caller-Times*, Jan. 22, 1961.

[81] *Caller-Times*, "Bluff's Concrete Balustrade Was First Major Improvement."

[82] Ernest Morgan, "Fiery Talks Spiced City's 1916 Prohibition Campaign," *Caller-Times*, March 11, 1962; various *Corpus Christi Caller and Daily Herald* newspaper articles from February, March and April, 1916.

[83] Ibid.

[84] Ibid.

[85] Ibid.

[86] Ibid.

[87] Ibid.

[88] *Corpus Christi Caller and Daily Herald*, March 24.

[89] Stephen Sharpe, "Moonshining and bootlegging were family affairs," *Caller-Times* Centennial Journal, p. 43, Jan. 23, 1983.

[90] *Corpus Christi Caller*, "Character of Forgotten Era Passes With Death Wednesday of 'Old

Dan', Sept. 25, 1936.

[91] Stephen Sharpe, "Moonshining and bootlegging were family affairs," *Caller-Times* Centennial Journal, p. 43, Jan. 23, 1983.

[92] *Corpus Christi Caller*, Jan. 10, and June 12, 1908; Sept. 2, Dec.9, 1915; *Corpus Christi Times*, Sept. 22, 1929.

[93] Michael J. Ellis, "The Hurricane Almanac," p. 106.

[94] Ibid.

[95] Ibid.

[96] Guthrie, "History of San Patricio County," p. 274.

[97] Mrs. Lee Dickinson, "Riviera founded several years before Kleberg County came into being," *Kingsville Record,* Oct. 16, 1963.

[98] Guthrie, "History of San Patricio County," p. 274.

[99] A. Ray Stephens, "Taft Ranch," p. 185.

[100] Guthrie, "Texas' Forgotten Ports," p. 100.

[101] Stephens, "Taft Ranch," p. 224.

[102] Guthrie, "Texas' Forgotten Ports," p. 88.

[103] Guthrie, "History of San Patricio County," p. 274.

[104] *Caller-Times,* "Centennial History," p. 114.

[105] Column by the author, April 4, 2001.

[106] Ibid.

[107] Ibid.

[108] Ibid.

[109] Column by the author, "Soldiers trained here for 'Over There', *Caller-Times*, Nov. 11, 1998; Bill Walraven, "Corpus Christi Was Host To Army Long Before Navy," *Caller-Times,* Dec. 28, 1956; Cliff Russell, "Despite Looks, Camp Had A Fighting Spirit," Nov. 20, 1957; Dan Kilgore, Corpus Christi: A Quarter Century of Development, 1900-1925," Southwestern Historical Quarterly, Vol. 75, p. 439.

[110] Jim Moloney, "Camp Scurry: Corpus Christi and the Mexican Border Incidents," Nueces County Historical Commission Bulletin, Nov., 2006.

[111] Column by the author, "Soldiers trained here for 'Over There', *Caller-Times*, Nov. 11, 1998; Bill Walraven, "Corpus Christi Was Host To Army Long Before Navy," *Caller-Times,* Dec. 28, 1956; Cliff Russell, "Despite Looks, Camp Had A Fighting Spirit," Nov. 20, 1957; Dan Kilgore, Corpus Christi: A Quarter Century of Development, 1900-1925," Southwestern Historical Quarterly, Vol. 75, p. 439.

[112] Grady Phelps, "Ex-Soldier Finds City Grew Much Since 1918," *Corpus Christi Times*, Nov. 15, 1963.

[113] *Corpus Christi Caller-Times*, "Legendary Football Team," Jan. 15, 1959.

[114] Column by the author, "Diary records the flu times of 1918," *Caller-Times*, Feb. 4, 2004, and "Events in 1918 flu year captured in girl's diary," *Caller-Times*, May 6, 2009; various editions of the *Corpus Christi Caller* from August through November, 1918.

[115] Roy Terrell, Reminiscences (As told to Marguerite Terrell, April 1967), a copy in the author's possession.

[116] *Corpus Christi Caller,* Oct. 18, 1918.

[117] *Corpus Christi Caller,* Oct. 26, 1918

[118] Anita Lovenskiold's diary for September-November, 1919, a copy in the author's possession.

[119] Ibid.

[120] *Corpus Christi Caller,* Nov. 16, 1918.

CHAPTER 12

[1] Columns by the author, June 1-16, 2004; book by the author and Jim Moloney, "1919 The Storm," p. 11; Georgia Nelson, "40th Anniversary of City's Blackest Day," *Caller-Times*, Sept.

13, 1959; *Caller-Times*, "Greatest Disaster Struck City on Sept. 14, 1919," April 27, 1952.

[2] Ibid; Lucy Caldwell, "Letter of Disaster," *Caller-Times*, Sept. 20, 1970.

[3] Keith Guthrie, "History of San Patricio County History," p. 275.

[4] Dan Kilgore, "Hurricane of 1919 was awesome," *Caller-Times*, Sept. 14, 1980.

[5] Writers Roundtable, "Padre Island," p. 143-144.

[6] Alpha Kennedy Wood, "Texas Coastal Bend," p. 132-133.

[7] *Corpus Christi Caller*, "Dog Saves the Life of Mrs. Percy Reid," Sept. 24, 1919.

[8] Caldwell, "Letter of Disaster," *Caller-Times*, Sept. 20, 1970.

[9] Nelson, "40th Anniversary of City's Blackest Day," *Caller-Times*, Sept. 13, 1959.

[10] *Corpus Christi Caller*, "Dog Saves the Life of Mrs. Percy Reid," Sept. 24, 1919.

[11] Barbara Isbell, article on Marion Clemmer, *Caller-Times*, Feb. 12, 1958.

[12] Mary Gene Kelly, "Pellegrino Remembers City As Fishing Village," July 13, 1948.

[13] Caldwell, "Letter of Disaster," *Caller-Times*, Sept. 20, 1970.

[14] Ibid.

[15] Columns by the author, June 1-16, 2004; book by the author and Jim Moloney, "1919 The Storm"; Nelson, "40th Anniversary of City's Blackest Day," *Caller-Times*, Sept. 13, 1959; *Caller-Times*, "Greatest Disaster Struck City on Sept. 14, 1919," April 27, 1952.

[16] Theodore A. Fuller, "When the Century and I Were Young," Corpus Christi Central Library.

[17] Interview by the author, "Survivor recalls great storm," April 17, 1998.

[18] "Company I Back At Fort Brown, Wet, Cheerful," *Brownsville Daily Herald*, Sept. 22, 1919.

[19] *Corpus Christi Caller*, "Captain and Mrs. Egeland Perish on Raft Together," Sept. 25, 1919.

[20] *Corpus Christi Caller*, Sept. 15, 1919.

[21] *Corpus Christi Caller*, "The Sisters of the Incarnate Word Fought Bravely Through Raging Storm To Save Lives," Sept., 1919; Florence Patton, "Visiting Nun Recalls Storm in Old Spohn," *Caller-Times*, Oct. 18, 1955.

[22] Lois Felder, "30 Years After Tragic Storm Finds City Greater Than Ever," Caller-Times, Sept. 11, 1949.

[23] *Corpus Christi Caller*, "Dog Saves the Life of Mrs. Percy Reid, " Sept. 24, 1919.

[24] *Corpus Christi Caller*, Oct. 2, 1919.

[25] Fuller, "When the Century and I Were Young," Corpus Christi Central Library.

[26] Ibid.

[27] Ibid.

[28] Caldwell, "Letter of Disaster," *Caller-Times*, Sept. 20, 1970.

[29] Interview by the author, "Survivor recalls great storm," April 17, 1998.

[30] Conrad Casler, "Detective Recalls Storm Washed 108 Dead to Ranch," *Caller-Times*, Jan. 18, 1959.

[31] News stories from the *Corpus Christi Caller*, Sept., 1919; *Caller-Times*, "Centennial Journey," p. 14, Jan. 23, 1983.

[32] Fuller, "When the Century and I Were Young," Corpus Christi Central Library.

[33] Columns by the author, June 1-16, 2004; book by the author and Jim Moloney, "1919 The Storm," p. 11; Georgia Nelson, "40th Anniversary of City's Blackest Day," *Caller-Times*, Sept. 13, 1959; *Caller-Times*, "Greatest Disaster Struck City on Sept. 14, 1919," April 27, 1952.

[34] *Caller-Times*, Nueces Bay Causeway 25 Years Old Today," Oct. 8, 1946.

[35] Ibid; *Corpus Christi Caller*, Oct. 8, 1921.

[36] *Caller-Times*, "Railway destroyed by storm," Aug. 19, 1973; Columns by the author, Jan., 2001.

[37] *Caller-Times*, "Clang, Clang, Clang . . . And the Trolley Went," June 13, 1965; *Caller-Times*, "A Sometimes Trolley," Jan. 1, 1950; *Corpus Christi Caller* editions from March 29, 1890 to Sept. 20, 1890.

[38] Peter Stambaugh, "Bumpy, Slow And Awkward, But Fun," *Caller-Times*, Nov. 10, 1963; Margaret Ramage, "Those were the days of streetcars and bells," *Caller-Times*, Aug. 19, 1973.

[39] Ibid.

[40] *Caller-Times*, "Many changes came about after 1919," Aug. 19, 1973.

[41] *Corpus Christi Caller*, Nov. 20, 1921.

[42] *Corpus Christi Caller*, Nov. 21, 1921.

[43] *Corpus Christi Caller*, Golden Anniversary Edition, 1933.

[44] Ibid.

[45] Louis Rawalt, "Island of Reprieve," p. 13-14, a copy in the possession of the author.

[46] Bill Walraven, column, April 20, 1980.

[47] C.W. Carpenter, "Klan activities fostered gun-toting, cross burnings," *Caller-Times* Centennial Edition, Jan. 23, 1983; *Corpus Christi Caller*, Oct. 15-17, 1922.

[48] Ibid.

[49] Column by the author, *Caller-Times*, March 11, 2009; *Corpus Christi Caller*, July 6-8, 1925.

[50] *Corpus Christi Caller*, Golden Anniversary Edition, 1933.

[51] *Corpus Christi Caller*, April 2, 1952; Robstown Record, Diamond Anniversary edition, Nov. 18, 1982.

[52] Joe Carmichael, "Fight for Deep Water Port Began Over a Century Ago," *Caller-Times*, April 27, 1952.

[53] Dr. Carl Helmecke, "The Seaport of the South: Corpus Christi," Corpus Christi Central Library, p. 38; "Centennial History of Corpus Christi," p. 117.

[54] Carmichael; "Centennial History," p. 118.

[55] "Centennial History," p. 44; "History of Nueces County," p. 54, 162.

[56] U.S. Grant, "Memoirs," p. 42-43.

[57] "History of Nueces County," p. 59; Helmecke.

[58] Ibid.

[59] Helmecke, p. 30-31; "Centennial History," p. 59.

[60] J. Frank Dobie, "Tales of Old-Time Texas: A Ranch on the Nueces," p. 157.

[61] Richard A. Laune, "The Political Struggle for the Port of Corpus Christi, 1900-1926," *Journal of South Texas*, p.91.

[62] Brownson Malsch, "Indianola, The Mother of Western Texas," p. 228-251; Texas Writers Project," p. 71; Guthrie, "History of San Patricio County History," p. 273; *Caller-Times*, article, May 20, 1956.

[63] Column by the author, Nov. 24, 1999; Eli T. Merriman, "Opposition Plentiful in 60-Year Fight For Deep Water, "Oct., 1936.

[64] E.T. Merriman, "Random Recollections of Nearly Ninety Years," p. 10; Laune, p. 92; Helmecke, p. 33-34.

[65] *Caller*, March 1, 1907; Laune; Helmecke, p. 33; "History of Nueces County," p. 166; John W. Johnson, "Establishment of Deep Water Port Here Climaxed Long Fight," *Caller-Times*, Jan, 1, 1950; Joe Carmichael, "Fight for Deep Water Port Began Over a Century Ago," *Caller-Times*, April 27, 1952.

[66] Carmichael.

[67] Jim Greenwood, "The Roy Miller Story," July 22, 1955, *Victoria Advocate*; Carmichael, "Fight for Deep Water Port Began Over a Century Ago," *Caller-Times*, April 27, 1952.

[68] Helmecke, p. 32; "History of Nueces County," p. 166.

[69] Laune, p. 105; "History of Nueces County," p. 167.

[70] William Allen, Sue Hastings Taylor, "Aransas," p. 268.

[71] Carmichael; Helmecke, p. 41.

[72] Laune; Guthrie, "History of San Patricio County History," p. 197.

[73] M. Harvey Weil, "A Brief History of the Port of Corpus Christi," manuscript, Corpus Christi Central Library; Laune, p. 103.

[74] Laune, p. 104; Helmecke, p. 43.

[75] Laune, p. 105.

[76] Ibid.

[77] Ibid.

[78] *Caller*, various articles, Sept. 15, 1926; Helmecke, p. 45-46; "History of Nueces County," p. 168; *Caller-Times*, "Port Dedication Was Celebrated In High Style," Sept. 9, 1951.

[79] Merriman, "Opposition Plentiful in 60-Year Fight For Deep Water, "Oct., 1936.

[80] *Caller-Times*, "Corpus Christi's Bluff Area: Now and Then," Jan. 20, 1963.

[81] Maston Nixon, "The Conception of the Multi-Story Nixon Building at the Corner of Broadway and Leopard," Dec., 1962, vertical files, Corpus Christi Central Library.

[82] Ibid; *Corpus Christi Times*, "Plaza Hotel Opened Here Last Spring," Sept. 22, 1929.

[83] Ibid; Edward H. Harte, "White Plaza Pioneered Development On the Bluff," *Caller*, Oct. 11, 1961.

[84] "Maston Nixon, Oil Man," the *Independent Petroleum Monthly*, March, 1961.

CHAPTER 13

[1] Ernest G. Fischer, "Padre Island Mecca of Many Motor Parties," *Corpus Christi Caller*, July 31, 1927.

[2] Pauline Reese, "History of Padre Island," thesis, 1938, Texas College of Arts and Industries, p. 5, 20.

[3] Dee Woods, "Texas Rangers Went to the Sea Horseback . . .," Corpus Christi *Caller*, Aug. 9, 1939.

[4] Ibid.

[5] Writers' Round Table, "Padre Island," p. 163-164.

[6] Jerry Needham, "Road named after local legend," *Caller-Times*, Oct. 19, 1978; "Padre Island," p. 179.

[7] Fischer, *Corpus Christi Caller*, July 31, 1927; Grace Dunn Vetters, "Pat Dunn's Padre Island Ranch House," vertical files, (application for a state historical marker), Corpus Christi Central Library.

[8] Writers' Round Table, "Padre Island."

[9] Ibid.

[10] Bill Duncan, "The Long, White Island - Padre," *Caller-Times*, April 24, 1966.

[11] Reese, p. 5; Vetters, p. 9.

[12] Fischer, Aug. 14; "Padre Island," p. 176.

[13] "Padre Island," p. 177.

[14] Ibid, p. 20; Fischer, *Corpus Christi Caller*, July 31, 1927.

[15] Vetters, p. 4.

[16] Vetters, p. 5.

[17] Ibid.

[18] Vetters, p. 9.

[19] Ibid.

[20] Fischer, *Corpus Christi Caller*, Aug. 14, 1927; "Padre Island," p. 183.

[21] *Corpus Christi Caller*, "Patrick F. Dunn, Pioneer Corpus Christian," March 26, 1937.

[22] *Caller-Times*, "Latin-American Organizations Consolidated at Meeting Here," vertical files, Corpus Christi Central Library; Bill Walraven, "Corpus Christi: The History of a Texas Seaport," p. 85.

[23] David J. Weber, "Foreigners in Their Native Land," p. 216.

[24] Ibid.

[25] Juan Cardenas, "Equality of races foremost goal of Ben Garza," *Caller-Times* Centennial Edition, Jan. 23, 1983.

[26] *Caller Times*, "Both LULAC and GI Forum Were Born in Corpus Christi," Jan. 18, 1959.

[27] *Caller-Times*, "Ben Garza Goes to Washington To Aid in Fight on Immigration Bills," vertical files, Corpus Christi Central Library.

[28] Cardenas.

[29] Column by the author, Feb. 28, 2001; Frederick Lewis Allen, "Only Yesterday," p. 266-281.

[30] *Corpus Christi Caller*, "Prosperity Days Will Be Observed on Nov. 13, 14, 15," vertical files, Corpus Christi Central Library.

[31] *Corpus Christi Caller*, Feb. 21, 1930.

[32] *Corpus Christi Caller,* Jan. 12, 1930; *Caller-Times* Centennial Edition, 1983, p. 22.

[33] *Corpus Christi Caller,* editions from July 24 through Aug. 25, 1930; *Caller-Times* Centennial Edition, 1983, p. 22; Marshall Anderson, "Local marathon broke the record in 1930," *Caller-Times,* June 2, 1988.

[34] Column by the author, Feb. 28, 2001; *Corpus Christi Caller,* various editions in 1930; *Caller-Times* Centennial Edition, 1983, p. 24.

[35] *Caller-Times* Centennial Edition, 1983, p. 92.

[36] Bill Hester, "City has had full share of disasters," *Caller,* July 4, 1976.

[37] *Caller-Times* Centennial Edition, "Corpus Christi Entered the Petroleum Age in 1930," p. 22, 89.

[38] *Caller-Times,* articles, Oct. 20, Oct. 21, 1931.

[39] Tom Lea, "King Ranch," p. 624-626.

[40] Atlee M. Cunningham, "Corpus Christi Water Supply Documented History," Corpus Christi Central Library, p. 5; Bill Walraven, column, June 2, 1983; Vertical files, street names, Corpus Christi Central Library; John S. McCampbell, "A History of Corpus Christi's Municipal Water Supply," vertical files, Corpus Christi Central Library.

[41] Cunningham, p. 4.

[42] Cunningham; "History of Nueces County," p. 54.

[43] Cunningham, p. 4.

[44] *Corpus Christi Advertiser,* July 6, 1867.

[45] Andrew Anderson, "Do You Know the Story of Corpus Christi?" biographical files, Corpus Christi Central Library.

[46] Cunningham, p. 6; *Caller-Times,* "Four Aged Residents See Village Grow Into a City," Jan. 10, 1937; McCampbell.

[47] Cunningham, p. 8.

[48] Cunningham, p. 6.

[49] Ibid.

[50] Corpus Christi *Caller-Times,* "Idea of Water Supply From Bay Tried in 1913," Centennial Edition, 1952.

[51] Jo Russell, "Work on Municipal Dam Near Mathis Completed Late in August," *Corpus Christi Times,* Sept. 22, 1929; Al McCullough, "City's Plaint for Last Century Can Be Silenced by New Lake," *Caller-Times,* Nov. 19, 1955.

[52] Ibid, Russell and McCullough.

[53] Cunningham, p. 72-73.

[54] *Caller-Times,* article, Nov. 1, 1957.

[55] Ibid, p. 74.

[56] Cunningham, p. 74-76.

[57] McCampbell, p. 20.

[58] McCullough.

[59] *Corpus Christi Caller,* Feb. 15, 1932.

[60] *Corpus Christi Caller,* Feb. 23, 1932.

[61] *Caller-Times,* "Visit of Historic Frigate 'Old Ironsides' Was Big Event in 30s," Jan. 1, 1950.

[62] *Corpus Christi Caller,* editions from Feb. 15 through Feb. 23, 1932.

[63] Juliet Knight Wenger, "Visit by 'Old Ironsides' in '32 touched off air of excitement," *Caller-Times* Centennial Edition, Jan. 23, 1983.

[64] Ibid.

[65] *Corpus Christi Caller,* Feb. 23, 1932.

[66] *Caller-Times,* "Excellent Progress Being Made on Intracoastal Canal, Miller Asserts," Oct. 20, 1931.

[67] *Caller-Times* Centennial Edition, 1983, p. 22; Column by the author, "Hard times," Corpus Christi *Caller-Times,* Feb. 28, 2001.

[68] Ibid.

[69] Ibid; *Caller-Times,* "Nueces Farmer Opened New Era by Accepting U.S. Check," *Caller-Times* Centennial Edition.

[70] Juliet Knight, "Mrs. Shaw, Resigning as Cheston Heath Principal After 42 Years in System, Fears She Has Become 'Landmark', *Corpus Christi Caller,* April 16, 1943.

[71] Diane Solether Smith, "The Armstrong Chronicle, A Ranching History," p. 206; Column by the author, Feb. 28, 2001.

[72] Ibid, Smith.

[73]Column by the author, "Hard times," Corpus Christi *Caller-Times*, Feb. 28, 2001; *Caller-Times*, "Free Meat Aided Needy During 1930s," Jan. 18, 1959.

[74] Column by the author, Corpus Christi *Caller-Times*, Dec. 24, 2008 based on a letter from L. Frank Kollaja, White Point Oil & Gas Co.

[75] Column by the author, Feb. 28, 2001.

[76] *Caller-Times*, "Trade Checks, Of $1 Denomination, To Be Accepted At Full Value," March 4, 1933; *Caller-Times* Centennial Edition, 1983, p. 22, 24; Grady Phelps, "40 Years Ago, This Was a Near Cashless City," *Caller-Times*, March 2, 1973.

[77] Marshall Anderson, "Year of the Storms," *Caller-Times,* Oct. 6, 1988.

[78] Ibid; *Corpus Christi Times*, Sept. 5, 1933.

[79] Column by the author, "Hard times," Feb. 28, 2001.

[80] Ibid; *Caller-Times*, "South Texas Fair Held Here In 1930s," Jan. 18, 1959.

[81] *Caller-Times* Centennial Edition, 1983, p. 89.

[82] Maston Nixon, "The Coming of Southern Alkali Corporation to Corpus Christi," paper written in 1964, vertical files, Corpus Christi Central Library.

[83] *Caller-Times* Centennial Edition, 1983, p. 89.

[84] Nixon.

[85] *Corpus Christi Times*, April 28, 1931.

[86] *Caller-Times*, Jan. 18, 1959.

[87] Column by the author, Feb. 28, 2001.

[88] *Caller-Times* Centennial Edition, 1983, p. 89; Nixon; *Caller-Times*, "Combination of Gas, Shell Gave Industry Start," Sept. 26, 1954; *Caller-Times*, "City's First Big Industry 30 Years Old," Sept. 10, 1964.

[89] Centennial History, p. 125-126.

[90] Column by the author, "Hard years for Corpus Christi," *Caller-Times*, Oct. 28, 2009; Caller-Times, "WPA Sewing Room Gives Work to 75 Women and Girls."

[91] Columns by the author, Feb. 28, 2001, Oct. 28, 2001.

[92] Kay McCracken, "Del Mar Serves Community In Ever Growing Numbers," *Caller-Times*; "Del Mar College Shows Steady 17-Year Growth," *Caller-Times,* April 27, 1952.

[93] Ibid.

[94] Georgia Nelson, "Cotton Field Grocery Store Now Strangled By Traffic," *Caller-Times,* April 23, 1959.

[95] Column by the author, *Caller-Times*, Aug. 2, 2006; *Corpus Christi Times*, "St. James Hotel Will Be Razed In Few Weeks," Jan. 4, 1937.

[96] Ibid.

[97] *Caller-Times* articles, Jan. 18, 1959, Dec. 9, 1965; "Fabulous Port Aransas," p.29.

[98] Ibid; Spencer Pearson, "Roosevelt's visit caused quite a stir in Port Aransas," *Caller-Times*, April 21, 1985.

[99] Columns by the author, June 9, 16, 1999; *Caller-Times'* coverage of the trial; Ike Elliff's account of the case in Mrs. Frank DeGarmo's "Pathfinders of Texas," Corpus Christi Central Library.

[100] Ibid.

[101] *Caller-Times*, June 22, 23, 1935; Sheriff William Shely, "The Flat Iron Murder," *Corpus Christi on Parade,* June, 1936, Corpus Christi Central Library.

[102] Shely.

[103] *Caller-Times,* Feb. 20, 1948; Bill Walraven, "Joe's Place, highway joint had alligators in back," *Caller*, Sept. 11, 1980.

[104] Centennial Journey, p. 106.

[105] Ibid, p. 103.

[106] *Caller-Times* articles, May, 1939.

[107] Ibid.

[108] Centennial Journey, p. 82.

[109] *Corpus Christi Times*, "A.C. McCaughan, Mayor Four Times, Dies at 94," Feb. 10, 1964.

[110] Centennial Journey, p. 102.

[111] Columns by the author, Oct. 27, 1999, July 11, 2007; *Caller-Times,* "City's Seawall, Bayfront Are Major Attractions," April 27, 1952; *Caller-Times,* "The Sea Wall Was a Mammoth Face-Lifting Project," Jan. 18, 1959.

[112] Ibid.

[113] Ibid.

[114] Ibid.

[115] *Corpus Christi Caller,* "Bayfront Bond Issue Approved," Nov. 15, 1939.

[116] Columns by the author, Oct. 27, 1999, July 11, 2007; *Corpus Christi Times,* "Seawall Bill Passes Senate," May 23, 1939.

[117] Columns by the author, Oct. 27, 1999, July 11, 2007.

[118] Columns by the author, Oct. 27, 1999, July 11, 2007; *Caller-Times,* "Seawall Built to Hold Off Mightiest Upheaval of Ocean," Nov. 11, 1941.

[119] Columns by the author, Oct. 27, 1999, July 11, 2007; Kay Bynum, "Meet Edward N. Noyes," *Corpus Christi Times*, Feb. 22, 1956; *Corpus Christi Caller*, "Bayfront Engineer Edward Noyes Dies," Aug. 4, 1961.

[120] Don Rodman, "Seawall construction gave city sparkle," *Corpus Christi Caller*, July 4, 1976.

CHAPTER 14

[1] Bruce Patton, *Caller-Times*, Sept. 9, 1951.

[2] *Corpus Christi Caller,* "War Affecting Local Shipping," Sept. 6, 1939.

[3] *Corpus Christi Caller,* "Aluminum Drive To End Tuesday," vertical files, Corpus Christi Central Library.

[4] *Caller-Times,* "It's Bundles for Britain Day," vertical files, Corpus Christi Central Library.

[5] *Caller-Times,* "Great Wool Reserve for Britain Being Stored Here," vertical files, Corpus Christi Central Library.

[6] *Caller-Times* "Centennial Journey," p. 26.

[7] Biographical files, Corpus Christi Central Library

[8] Ibid; *Caller-Times*, "Mrs. Driscoll active politically," Oct. 6, 1940.

[9] Bill Walraven, "Corpus Christi, A History of a Texas Seaport," p. 86.

[10] *Caller-Times* "Centennial Journey," p. 79.

[11] Centennial Journey," p. 79.

[12] Ibid.

[13] Ibid.

[14] Ibid.

[15] Ibid.

[16] *Caller-Times,* "Mrs. Clara Driscoll Will Match -- Two for One -- Any Donation for Plane Base," *Caller-Times,* May 21, 1939. *Caller-Times* Centennial Edition, 1983, p. 78;

[17] "History of Nueces County," p. 158-159.

[18] *Caller-Times* Centennial Edition, 1983, p. 79.

[19] Ibid.

[20] Mary Cowles Woebler, "Corpus Christi Is Suffering Growing Pains," *Corpus Christi Times*, Dec. 16, 1940.

[21] Juliet K. Wenger, "News To Me," p. 41-42; Centennial Journey, p. 69, 80.

[22] *Caller-Times,* "NAS Dedication in 1941 Was a Day to Remember," Jan. 18, 1959.

[23] *Caller-Times,* Centennial History, p. 127.

[24] Ibid.

[25] *Caller-Times*, "NAS Dedication Was a Day to Remember," Jan. 18, 1959.

[26] "History of Nueces County," p. 159.

[27] Ibid.

[28] Ibid.

[29] Willis H. Carrier, "City's past predicts future," *Corpus Christi Caller*, Corpus Christi Central Library.

[30] Centennial History, p. 128.

Caller-Times Centennial Edition, 1983, p. 79.

[31] *Corpus Christi Times*, "City Stretches Its Facilities To Meet Population Gains," vertical files, Corpus Christi Central Library.

[32] J.E. Bell, manager of Chamber of Commerce, in an article in 1942, "Corpus Christi . . . At the dawn of '42," vertical files, Corpus Christi Central Library.

[33] Morgan.

[34] Bell.

[35] *Caller-Times*, "Corpus Christi men grumble in their beards . . . ," vertical files, Corpus Christi Central Library.

[36] Bill Walraven, "Two *Caller* columnists get together to talk Shoop," *Caller*, Dec. 2, 1981.

[37] Ernest Morgan, "A Quiet Week Became Chaotic in a Flash," *Caller*, Dec. 7, 1961.

[38] *Corpus Christi Caller*, "Living costs up because of 'boom'," vertical files, Corpus Christi Central Library.

[39] Morgan.

[40] Centennial Journey, p. 102.

[41] *Corpus Christi Caller*, Aug. 1, 1941.

[42] Ibid.

[43] Morgan.

[44] Eleanor Mortensen, "It was a calm Sunday until . . .," *Caller*, Dec. 7, 1976.

[45] *Caller-Times* Centennial Edition, 1983, p. 26.

[46] Bill Walraven, "Words of former Del Mar teacher paved way for World War II," *Caller*, Feb. 16, 1983.

[47] *Caller-Times*, "Once Upon a Time," Jan. 25, 1966.

[48] *Caller*, article, Dec. 9, 1941; Book by the author, "Old Corpus Christi," p. 115.

[49] *Caller-Times* Centennial Edition, 1983, p. 27.

[50] *Caller-Times*, "Sirens Spotted in Strategic Locations To Sound Alert . . ." March 15, 1942.

[51] *Caller-Times*, "Instructions for Blackout Drill," Jan. 16, 1942.

[52] Doc McGregor, photo layout, "City Blacks Out," *Caller-Times*, Jan. 20, 1942.

[53] Louis Anderson, "Corpus Christians Saw History In the Making During Blackout," *Caller-Times*, March 15, 1942.

[54] *Corpus Christi Caller, Corpus Christi Times*, "Blackout Brings Local Business To Standstill," and "Towns on Coast Are Blacked Out," vertical files, Corpus Christi Central Library.

[55] Anderson.

[56] Columns by the author, Sept. 30, 2009, and Sept. 29, 1999; *Corpus Christi Caller*, "Navy for First Time Describes 42-43 Nazi Sub Activity in Gulf," Aug. 23, 1945.

[57] Anderson.

[58] Wenger, p. 41.

[59] *Corpus Christi Caller*, John C. Ward Named Island," May 18, 1953; Grady Phelps, article, *Times*, Oct. 9, 1978.

[60] *Corpus Christi Caller*, "Vulnerable South Texas Spots Protected Against Sabotage," Dec. 9, 1941.

[61] *Corpus Christi Caller, "Navy To Confiscate Cameras Found on Gulf Isle Visitors,"* vertical files, Corpus Christi Central Library.

[62] Restricted Area Map "For Aerial Bombing and Gunnery Range," Corpus Christi Central Library.

[63] *Caller-Times*, "46,729 Sign Up For Ration Books," vertical files, Corpus Christi Central Library.
[64] *Caller-Times*, "6,000 Car and Motorcycle Owners Register for Gas," Nov. 20, 1942.
[65] *Caller-Times*, "Teachers Solve Transportation Problems," Sept. 24, 1942.
[66] Columns by the author on the war years, *Caller-Times,* Dec. 7, 14, 21, 2005.
[67] *Corpus Christi Times*, "Food Establishments in City Divided On Question of 'Meatless Tuesday'," Oct. 5, 1943.
[68] Column by the author, *Caller-Times*, Dec. 14, 2005.
[69] *Caller-Times*, "Robert Driscoll Hotel, Biggest Private Construction Project, Will Be Opened Monday," May 24, 1942.
[70] Juliet Knight (Wenger), "Corpus Christians Jam Agnes Street To Get Brief Glimpse of President and First Lady," *Caller-Times*, April 22, 1943.
[71] Column by the author, Dec. 14, 2005; Book by the author, "Old Corpus Christi," p. 123-125; Bill Walraven, "Corpus Christi, A History of a Texas Seaport," p. 86.
[72] Book by the author, "Old Corpus Christi," p. 120-122.
[73] *Caller-Times*, "Arrogantly Silent, Nazi Pilots Await Return to Mexia," Feb. 11, 1944.
[74] Ibid.
[75] Bob McCracken, "The Crow's Nest," "Captive Nazis," *Caller-Times*, Feb. 11, 1944.
[76] Grady Phelps, "POWs Left Nameless Mark at Naval Air Station," *Caller-Times*, March 16, 1966.
[77] Tom Mulvany, "Corpus Christians Still Stunned by News of Sudden Death of President," *Times*, April 13, 1945; *Times,* "Flags at Half Mast as City Pays Its Respects to Memory of Roosevelt." Jeanne Cameron, "City in Mourning for Roosevelt," *Caller,* April 14, 1945.
[78] *Caller-Times*, "James Burney, Atomic Bomb Researcher, Due Home Soon," vertical files, Corpus Christi Central Library.
[79] *Caller-Times,* "Victory Celebration on Chaparral," and "City Quiet Today After Big Victory Celebration," vertical files, Corpus Christi Central Library.
[80] *Caller-Times* Centennial Edition, 1983, p. 28.
[81] Wenger, p. 44.
[82] Mulvany, "Johnnie Comes Marching Home . . ." *Caller-Times,* Sept. 2, 1945.
[83] Column by the author, Dec. 21, 2005.

CHAPTER 15

[1] *Caller-Times,* Dec. 20, 1945.
[2] *Caller-Times,* "City Faces Meat Famine as Only Local Packing Houses Are Shut Down," vertical files, Corpus Christi Central Library.
[3] Mary Mahoney, "Loaves Disappear Here After Rush," *Caller-Times*, April 30, 1946.
[4] Centennial Journey, p. 62.
[5] *Corpus Christi Times*, "Boats Which Served In Coast Guard Returned To Owners," Feb. 1, 1946.
[6] *Caller-Times*, June 17, 18, 1946.
[7] Handbook of Texas, p. 637; Centennial Journey, p. 79.
[8] Ernest Morgan, "1950s Found City Moving and Growing," *Caller-Times*, Jan. 1, 1960.
[9] Ibid.
[10] Column by the author, *Caller-Times,* March 7, 2001; *Caller-Times*, "Promoters Planned Gigantic Playground on Padre in 1929," Sept. 26, 1954; Writers Roundtable, "Padre Island," p. 200, 201.
[11] Jim Greenwood, "First Visitor Shows at Five," *Corpus Christi Times*, June 17, 1950; *Caller-Times,* "Causeway to Padre Opened New Resort," Jan. 18, 1959.
[12] Book by the author, "Old Corpus Christi," p. 140.

[13] William Manchester, "The Glory and the Dream," p. 650.
[14] Ibid; Centennial Journey, p. 29.
[15] *Corpus Christi Caller,* "No Question At All About It, The United States Is At War," July 3, 1950.
[16] John W. Johnson, "Tears and Pride Mixed As Local Marines Leave," *Caller-Times,* vertical files, Corpus Christi Central Library.
[17] Ibid.
[18] Book by the author, "Old South Texas," p. 111.
[19] Centennial Journey, p. 29.
[20] *Corpus Christi Caller, Corpus Christi Times,* Jan. 30 through Feb. 1, 1951.
[21] Bruce Patton, article, *Caller-Times,* Sept. 9, 1951.
[22] Ibid.
[23] Ibid; *Caller-Times* Centennial Edition, 1983, p. 89, p. 125-126; Maston Nixon; *Caller-Times,* "Combination of Gas, Shell Gave Industry Start," Sept. 26, 1954; *Caller-Times,* "City's First Big Industry 30 Years Old," Sept. 10, 1964.
[24] Keith Guthrie, "History of San Patricio County," p. 161.
[25] Patton; Centennial History, p. 128.
[26] Bill Walraven, "The History of a Texas Seaport," p. 123.
[27] Patton.
[28] Ibid; *Caller-Times,* "Big Industry Alters City's Complexion," vertical files, Corpus Christi Central Library; Guthrie, p. 38, 86.
[29] Centennial Journey, p. 29.
[30] Patton.
[31] Bill, Marjorie K. Walraven, "Wooden Rigs - Iron Men," p. 159.
[32] Ibid.
[33] Morgan, "1950s Found City Moving and Growing," *Caller-Times,* Jan. 1, 1960.
[34] Bill Hester, "City has had full share of disasters," *Caller,* July 4, 1976.
[35] Charles Branning, "1953 remembered as miserably dry year," *Caller-Times,* Nov. 10, 1988.
[36] Columns by the author, May 16 and 17, 2001, and Sept. 23, 2009.
[37] Ibid.
[38] Ibid.
[39] Grady Phelps, "Driscoll Hospital: A Dream Come True," *Caller-Times,* Feb. 24, 1963; *Caller-Times,* "Clara Driscoll's Patriotism Led To Establishing Hospital," vertical files, Corpus Christi Central Library; Rosemary Barnes, "Clara Driscoll remembered for philanthropy," *Caller-Times,* Jan. 23, 1983.
[40] *Corpus Christi Times,* article, Feb. 15, 1966.
[41] Mary Alice Davis, "Wilson, Driscoll: Parallel of 2 queens," *Corpus Christi Times,* Feb. 9, 1976.
[42] *Caller-Times,* obituary, Feb. 17, 1977
[43] Edward H. Harte, "Ada's fight for Mustang park," *Caller-Times,* Feb. 22, 1976.
[44] Sister Jeanne Francis Minner, thesis, "The Early Development of Education in Corpus Christi, Texas, 1848-1909," p. 37.
[45] Ibid.
[46] Ibid.
[47] Bill Barnard, article, *Caller-Times,* May 30, 1937.
[48] Neely.
[49] Juliet Knight, article, *Caller,* April 16, 1943.
[50] Hoyt Hager, article, *Caller-Times,* 1946, vertical file, Corpus Christi Central Library.
[51] Margaret Ramage, article, *Caller-Times,* Aug. 1, 1965.
[52] Neely.
[53] Anne Dodson, article, *Caller-Times,* June 24, 1954.
[54] Minner.
[55] Dodson.
[56] Ramage.

[57] Ibid.

[58] Ibid.

[59] Ibid.

[60] *Caller-Times*, article, Sept. 26, 1954.

[61] *Caller-Times*, article, October, 1936, vertical files, Corpus Christi Central Library.

[62] *Caller-Times*, article1939, vertical files, Corpus Christi Central Library.

[63] Sue Fahlgren, "Education history dotted with series of false starts," Centennial Journey, p. 83-84.

[64] History of Nueces County, p. 121.

[65] Ibid, p. 121-122.

[66] Fahlgren.

[67] Ibid.

[68] Ibid.

[69] Kay Bynum, "New W.B. Ray High School Combines Function, Beauty," *Caller-Times*, Aug. 27, 1950.

[70] *Caller-Times*, "New School To Be Called Carroll High," Sept. 28, 1954.

[71] Morgan; *Caller-Times* articles, Sept. 28 and Dec. 16, 1954; Feb. 22, 1957.

[72] Centennial Journey, p. 92.

[73] Lynn Pentony, article, *Times,* Feb. 22, 1982.

[74] Bill Walraven, column, *Caller,* April 16, 1975.

[75] Centennial Journey, p. 92; *Caller-Times*, June 19, 20, 1954.

[76] Juliet K. Wenger, "News To Me," p. 90.

[77] *Caller-Times,* articles, Dec. 7, 1963; Jan. 9, 15, 1964;

[78] Morgan.

[79] Morgan; Centennial History, p. 79.

[80] Ibid.

[81] *Corpus Christi Caller,* "Federal Judge Allred Dies of Heart Attack," Sept. 25, 1959.

[82] *Corpus Christi Caller,* "Garza Praises Judge Allred," Caller, April 5, 1961.

[83] Columns by the author, April 12, 2000; Nov. 22, 2006; Feb. 3, 2010.

[84] Ibid.

[85] Ibid.

[86] Ibid.

[87] Ibid; *Caller-Times,* "Bridge vs. Tunnel Was Great Debate For Three Years," Oct. 23, 1959.

[88] Ibid.

[89] Ibid; *Caller-Times,* "Bridge Edition," Oct. 23, 1959; Caller-Times, "Harbor Bridge" in "Light Of Other Days," July 18, 1999.

[90] Bill Walraven, "El Rincon: A History of Corpus Christi Beach," p. 15.

[91] Ibid.

[92] Column by the author, May 24, 2000.

[93] Centennial History, p. 105.

[94] Ibid.

[95] *Caller-Times,* "Spohn Hospital's History Covers Span of 56 Years," Dec. 3, 1961.

[96] *Caller-Times,* "Country Club Once on North Beach," Jan. 18, 1959.

[97] Book by the author and Jim Moloney, "1919 The Storm."

[98] Ibid.

[99] *Caller-Times,* article, Jan. 1, 1950.

[100] Marshall Anderson, "Local marathon broke the record in 1930," *Caller-Times,* June 2, 1988.

[101] Walraven, p. 63.

[102] Ibid, p. 65.

[103] Beach History Time Line, vertical file, Corpus Christi Central Library.

[104] *Caller-Times*, "City Losing Bayside Playground," Sept. 15, 1957.

[105] *Corpus Christi Caller*, "Council Changes Name of Beach," Feb. 26, 1959.

[106] *Corpus Christi Caller*, "Old 'North Beach' Spans 125 Years Of Varied History," Dec. 8, 1969.

CHAPTER 16

[1] *Caller-Times*, Aug. 6, 1960; columns by the author, Feb. 13, Feb. 20, 2002.
[2] Ibid.
[3] Ibid.
[4] Ibid.
[5] Ibid.
[6] Ibid.
[7] Ibid.
[8] Ibid.
[9] *Caller-Times*, articles, Sept. 14, 1961; Sept. 9, 1962; Hurricane Almanac, p. 117; Centennial Journey, p. 30.
[10] *Caller-Times*, article, Jan. 1, 1970.
[11] Ibid; Keith Guthrie, "History of San Patricio County," p. 198-199.
[12] Cliff Lawhorne, article, *Caller-Times,* Dec. 31, 1961.
[13] Ibid.
[14] Ibid; Centennial Journey, p. 91.
[15] Ibid.
[16] Lawhorne.
[17] *Corpus Christi Caller*, "City Winner On Annexation," Jan. 14, 1964.
[18] Ibid.
[19] Ibid; Ron George, article, May 8, 1991.
[20] Ibid.
[21] Lawhorne.
[22] Ibid.
[23] *Caller-Times*, article, Oct. 24, 1957.
[24] *Caller-Times*, article, Dec. 30, 1962.
[25] Ibid.
[26] Ibid.
[27] *Caller-Times*, article, Jan. 1, 1970.
[28] Ibid.
[29] Ed Deswysen, "Krueger Receives Life Sentences Following Surprise Pleas of Guilty," *Caller*, May 12, 1966; John De Pue, article, *Corpus Christi Times,* Aug. 9, 1969.
[30] Ibid.
[31] *Caller-Times*, article, Jan. 1, 1970.
[32] Ibid.
[33] Article by the author, "11 individuals who made a difference in Corpus Christi," Jan. 2, 2000; Mary Alice Davis, "Dr. Hector Garcia leader in Mexican-American fight," *Caller,* May 24, 1971; Ernest Morgan, "A Man of Controversy," *Caller-Times,* Dec. 18, 1966.
[34] Ibid.
[35] Ibid; Patrick J. Carroll, "Felix Longoria's Wake," p. 1-2.
[36] Edward H. Harte, "Dr. Garcia laid it on line for NAS," *Caller-Times,* Dec. 19, 1978.
[37] Article by the author, Jan. 2, 2000.
[38] Columns by the author, Aug. 8, Aug. 15, 2001.
[39] Ibid.
[40] Eugenia Reynolds Briscoe, "City by the Sea."
[41] Columns by the author, Aug. 8, Aug. 15, 2001.
[42] Ibid.
[43] Ibid.
[44] Ibid.
[45] Ibid.
[46] Ibid; Hortense Warner Ward, "A Century of Missionary Effort: The Church of the Good Shepherd, 1860-1960."

[47] Ibid; Ward.
[48] Ibid.
[49] Columns by the author, Aug. 8, Aug. 15, 2001.
[50] Ibid.
[51] Ibid.
[52] *Caller-Times*, "Celia . . . Then and Now," Aug. 3, 1971; *Caller-Time* editions from Aug. 3 to Aug. 11, 1970; Michael J. Ellis, "The Hurricane Almanac," p. 120-121.
[53] Ibid.
[54] Ibid.
[55] Ibid.
[56] Ibid.
[57] Ellis, quoting Bill Walraven, p. 121.
[58] *Caller-Times,* "Celia, Fury on an August Afternoon," Aug. 11, 1970.
[59] Keith Guthrie, "History of San Patricio," p. 339.
[60] Paul Slater, "A Bear Storm for Businesses," *Caller,* Aug. 3, 1971.
[61] Grady Phelps, "Oh, For a Tall Cold One," *Caller,* Aug. 11, 1970.
[62] *Caller,* "Confirmed Storm Dead Set at 11," Aug. 5, 1970.
[63] Grady Phelps, "Hurricane's Left Hook Knocked Out City," *Caller,* Aug. 6, 1970.
[64] Ibid.

INDEX

Abbott, E. W. , 31
Abilene, Kansas, 98
Acebo, Joe, 198
Adams, L. M., 202
Adams, Robert Jr., 44, 51, 59, 106, 108, 115
Adams, Robert Sr., 44, 45
Adams, Virginia, 228
Adams, William, 44, 51, 106, 108
Ada Wilson Hospital, 242
Agnew, Letha, 244
Agua Dulce, 57, 108, 110, 140
Aguilar, Juan, 174
Alabama, 34
Alamo, 241
Alcove Chili Parlor, 244
Aldrete, Capt. Rafael, 4
Aldridge, Earl and Billy, 246
Alice, Texas, 149, 186, 241
Allen, Henry Davis, 138
Allen, Laura, 125
Allende Hall, 207
Allred, James A., 216, 247
Almond, Joseph, 44, 92, 95, 106
Almonte, Gen. Juan Nupomuceno, 1, 2
Alta Vista Hotel, 145-146, 152, 153, 182, 195
Alvarado, Francisco, 40
Alvarez de Pineda, Alonso, 6
American Airways, 256
American Bank Center, 271
American Flag, 26, 27
American G. I. Forum, 262
American Smelting & Refining Company, 239, 291
Ampudia, Gen. Pedro, 7
Amusu Theater, 244, 268
Anderson, Capt. Andrew, 50, 94, 101, 121, 123, 127, 149, 153, 210
Anderson, Capt. John, 55-57, 123, 151, 183
Anderson, Louis, 229-230
Anderson, Sam, 158
Anderson's Windmill, 151, 183
Angles, John Phillip, 260-2611
Annaville, 259
Annexation Ball, 21
Anthony, Texas, 145
Aransas City, Texas, 5, 33
Aransas Harbor Terminal Railroad, 257

Aransas on St. Joseph's, 130
Aransas Pass channel, 14, 35, 51, 54, 58, 116, 130, 179, 201, 230
Aransas Pass city, 195, 202, 229, 301
Aransas River, 67
Aranzazu, 5
Arcadia Village, 215
Arista, Gen. Mariano, 7
Armistice Day, 169
Armstrong, Ann (Millard), 34
Armstrong, Charles M. Sr. (Charlie), 213
Armstrong Ranch, 213
Army Depot (ARADMAC), 247, 258
Army Hospital #15, 168, 191, 192, 194, 251
Arroyo Colorado, 23, 216
Art Museum of South Texas, 271
Artesian Park, 17, 36, 210
Aubrey, William P., 5, 7, 21, 25, 174
Austin, Stephen F., 3
Avery Point, 214
Ayers, Bert, 134
Aztec Building, 215

Bagdad, Tamaulipas, 53, 96
Balerio, Cecilio, 70
Balerio, Jose, 70
Ball, Henry, 122
Ball, Joe, 218
Ball, William, 128
Balli, Padre Nicolas, 206
Bangor, Maine, 32
Bangs, Samuel, 26, 41
Banks, Gen. Nathaniel P., 61, 66, 90
Banquete, Texas, 35, 52, 63, 99, 104, 128, 185
Banquete Creek, 52, 69
Barnard, Bill, 225
Barnard, James R., 31, 90
Barnard, Dr. James L., 258
Barnard, John D., 158
Barnes, Robert N. (Bob), 272
Barnhard, Capt. Alva D., 225
Barry, John M., 168
Bascule Bridge, 203, 212, 247-249, 259, 297
Baskin, J.A., 34
Basquez, Tomas, 112-113
Bass, Bruce, 271
Baxter, Peter, 58
Bayside, Texas, 32
Bayside Park and Ballroom, 252

Bay View College, 165
Bayview Cemetery (Old), 58, 86, 170
Beach Hotel, 191, 251-252
Bean, Roy, 146
Beck, Nels, 235
Bedichek, Roy, 5
Beeville, Texas, 70
Bee, Gen. Hamilton P., 62-65, 72, 96
Belden, Frederick, 1, 16, 21, 108, 174
Belden, Mauricio (Arocha), 16, 21
Ben Bolt, Texas, 37
Bennett, Max, 268
Benton Pasture, 155
Beranger, Jean, 3
Berry, Henry W., 10, 56-57, 71, 89-90, 123
Besancon, Capt. L.A., 27-28
Beynon, Rosa, 137
Biel, Irma Kathryn, 233
Big Sands, 23
Big Wharf (Rockport), 122
Biggio, William, 143, 216
Bisbee, C.M., 199
Bishop, Texas, 157, 256
Bishop, F.Z., 155, 256
Black Hill (Padre Island), 206
Blackland Special, 199-200, 203
Blackout, World War II, 229-230
Bledsoe, R. R., 199
Bliss, W. W. (Perfect), 19
Blizzard, 1899, 148-150, 238
Blizzard, 1951, 238
Blossman Grocery, 101
Blucher, Felix, 40, 55, 58, 60, 72
Blucher, George, 134, 157, 197
Blucher, Maria, 35, 55, 58-60, 66, 107, 111
Blucher, Marie, 153
Blucher Park, 143, 209
Bluff Balustrade, 162
Bob Hall Pier, 271-272
Bobedo Creek, 23
Bobedo Ranch, 40
Boca del Rio, 53
Boerum, Janet, 244
Bohemian Colony, 155
Bonham, Gladys, 215
Bonilla, Tony, 270
Bonnie View Ranch, 103
Borden, Gail, 35

Borden, Sidney, 125-128
Borden's Ferry, 125
Borglum, Gutzon, 220
Borjas Ranch, 128
Bragg, Braxton, 18, 24
Branch, Rev. Harold, 271
Brazos River, 99, 123
Brazos Santiago, 206
Brazos Santiago Island, 61-62, 91
Brazos Santiago Pass, 62
Breakers, The, 252
Breakwater, 203,
Brennan, Ed, 186
Brennan, Mike, 124
Bridge-Tunnel Fight, 247-249
Bridges, Alice, 2
Brindley, Oscar, 255-256
Briscoe, Eugenia Reynolds, 263
Brittain, Rev. William, 265
Britton, Anne Elizabeth (Lizzie), 96
Britton, Edward S., 96
Britton, Forbes, 27, 34, 43, 50, 56
Britton Ranch, 96
Britton, Rebecca (Millard), 34
Brooklyn (North Beach), 250, 307
Brooks County, 26, 220
Brooks, Mrs. Terrell, 192
Brownlee, Billy Jack, 229
Brownsville, 26, 40, 51-52, 62, 71, 87, 90-91, 96, 103, 111, 120, 129, 140, 152-153, 194, 214
Brundrett, Ancel, 217
Brundrette, Tom, 133
Brunwinkel, Bill, 122
Bryant, Charles J., 21, 32
Bryden, James, 90, 97, 106-107
Buccaneer Stadium, 226
Buckley, Ed, 108, 112
Buckley, John, 107
Buckley, William F. Jr., 107
Buckley, William F. Sr., 107
Buena Vista Hotel, 165
"Buffalo Hunters," 27
Bundles for Britain, 224
Burke, Rhoda, 137
Burkett, Nathan Boone, 9
Burks, Amanda, 99
Burnett, Lemmawayne, 194
Burney, Cecil, 233

Burney, James, 233
Byington Hotel, 52
Byington house, 21

Cabaniss Field, 225-226, 232, 236
Cabe, Paul, 161
Cabeza de Vaca (Alvar Nunez), 3
Cahill, Catherine, 95
Cahill, Cornelius, 27, 95, 263
Cairns, W. J., 8
Calallen, 144, 259-260
Caldwell, Edward H., 121, 128, 144
Caldwell, Lafayette, 306
Caldwell, Lucy, 189-194
Callahan, Charles, 30-31
Camerena, Don, 35
Camargo, Tamaulipas, 1, 39
Cameron County, 26
Cameron, Ewen, 9, 41
Camino Real, 52
Camp Funston (Fort Riley, Kansas), 168
Camp Mabry, 147
Camp Onward, 147
Camp Scurry, 167-168, 188, 196, 309
Campbell, Joseph, 125-126
Campbell, L. E., 153
Campion, W. S., 137
Campo Borrego (Padre Island), 206
Campo Bueno (Padre Island), 206
Canales, Gen. Antonio, 5, 6, 9
Cannibal Creek, 5
Cape Horn, 29
Carlis, V. Don, 217
Carmel Ranch, 108
Carroll, Charles, 264
Carroll, Mary, 243-246, 264
Carroll, Pat, 263
Carruth, W. E., 158
Carson Association, 30
Carson, Van Dave, 260-261
Carter, Ella B. (Wheeler), 244
Carter, President Jimmy, 262
Casa Blanca, 29
Castro, Culegas de (Lipan Apache chief), 17-18
Cazneau, Gen. William, 28-29
Cedar Bayou, 66
Celanese, 239
Census 1850, 33, 49, 78-79

Central Power & Light, 197
Central School, 243
Central Wharf, 116, 142, 150, 165, 177, 189, 199
Cerro Gordo, 109
Chagres, Panama, 29, 31
Chandler, D. T., 14
Chapman, Helen, 30, 43, 90-91, 93-94, 96, 107
Chapman Ranch, 213
Chapman, William W., 36, 43, 46, 106-107
Chase Field, 225-226, 232
Chatham's Ravine, 209
Cheston L. Heath School, 213, 244-245
Chihuahua State, 28-31
Chihuahua trade, 28-29, 34, 124, 140
Child, Gerald F., 232
Choke Canyon Dam, 272, 274
Christmas Snow, 271
City Hall, 233-234, 240
City National Bank, 213
Chocolate Bayou, 32
Church of the Good Shepherd, 212, 265
Clara Ranch, 241
Clark, Ellen C., 137
Clark, Rev. Horace, 265
Clark, Jasper, 120
Clarkwood, Texas, 255, 259
Clemmer, Almyr and Marion, 191
Cleveland, President Grover, 141
Cliff Maus Field, 255-257
Club Reciproco, 207
Clubb, Thomas, 54
Coahuila, 27
Coakley, F. M., 112
Cochrane, R. E., 21
Cody, Judge Matthew, 55, 90
Coffee, Mrs. Guy T., 228
Coke, Gov. Richard, 97
Cole Park, 215, 272
Coleman, Thomas, 105
Coleman-Fulton Pasture Company (Taft Ranch), 106, 121, 155
Coles, Solomon, 138
Collins, Bruce, 251-253
Collins, N. G., Ranch, 155
Comanche Indians, 10-11, 26, 33, 250
Commercial Club, 164
Committees of Public Safety (Posses), 110, 115, 129
Company B, 15th Marines, 237-238
Confederate Memorial Fountain, 162

Congregational Church, 91, 138, 264
Conklin, Hannah M., 137
Conley, J. B., 50
Connally, Sen. Tom, 224, 228
Constitution, U.S. Frigate, 212-213, 252, 284
Cooke, Louis P., 10, 17
Copano, 10
Copano Bay Causeway, 5
Copley, J. J., 153
Coppini, Pompeo, 162
Corbett, "Gentleman" Jim, 146, 251
Corn Products, 239
Corpus Christi Academy, 135
Corpus Christi Advertiser, 93-94, 210
Corpus Christi Aero Club, 254
Corpus Christi Bank & Trust, 204
Corpus Christi Bay, 200-201
Corpus Christi Bayou, 54
Corpus Christi Beach (North Beach), 252-253
Corpus Christi Caller, 141, 144, 146, 150, 158, 163, 168-169, 194, 196, 216, 220, 237, 248, 255-256
Corpus Christi Cathedral, 104, 262
Corpus Christi Electric & Ice Company, 197
Corpus Christi Gazette, 21-22, 26, 41, 116, 133, 139
Corpus Christi High School (the Brick Palace), 244, 296
Corpus Christi Hotel, 30
Corpus Christi International Airport, 255-257
Corpus Christi Pass, 58, 62, 206-207
Corpus Christi Railway & Light Company, 196-197
Corpus Christi, San Diego & Rio Grande Railroad, 139-140
Corpus Christi Star, 27-31
Corpus Christi Street & Interurban Railway, 276, 309
Corpus Christi Union Record, 96
Corpus Christi Yacht Club, 212
Cortina, Juan Nepomuceno (Cheno), 125, 129
Cosby, Lt. Blake, 37
Cotton Road, 51-53, 60, 104, 301
Cox, Owen, 271
Crescent Hotel, 109
Crittenden, Dr., 19
Crixell, Jose, 148
Crockett Elementary, 245
Crosby, Bing, 257
Crossley, C. W., 139
Crosstown Expressway, 260
Cruillas, Tamaulipas, 40
Crystal Beach Park Ballroom, 209, 252
Cuevas Ranch, Las, 125

Cuddihy Field, 225-226, 232, 257
Culver, Martin, 105, 121, 128
Culver's Packery, 110, 121
Cummings, James, 116
Curtis, A. B., 237
Curry Settlement, 93, 207, 236

Dana, Napoleon Jackson Tecumseh, 15, 19, 62
Dance on the Ship, 251-252
Daniels, Lincoln, 164
Darby, Dan, 158
Daugherty, Pat, 87
David Hirsch Elementary, 244
Davila, Andres, 112-113
Davis, Anne Elizabeth (Britton), 96-97
Davis, A. M., 109
Davis, Gov. Edmund J., 50, 57, 93, 95-97, 171
Davis, James, 9
Davis, President Jefferson, 53, 67
Dayton Steamboat Accident, 18
De Alba, Jose, 21
DeAvalon, Alonzo A., 50, 122
DeBerry, Adele, 125
DeLeon, Jose, 258
DeLeon, Martin, 4, 98
De Luna, A., 207
De Meza, Madame, 135
Del Mar College, 215, 228
Dent, Margaret, 153
De Planque, Louis, 143
De Puy, J., 220-221, 286
DeRemer, Charles, 256
De Solis, Fray Gaspar Jose, 3, 4
Desert of the Dead, 23, 39
Diaz Ordaz, 129
Dickinson, John, 251
Diezmero Ranch, 52
Dimmitt, Philip, 7
Dittmer, Albert E., 219
Dix, John J., 56-57, 89, 136-137, 161
Dix, Mary Eliza (Hayes), 136
Doan's Store, 98
Dobbins, Lt., 17
Dobie, J. Frank, 114, 119
Doddridge Building, 201
Doddridge home, 263
Doddridge, Lott & Davis, 108, 161
Doddridge, Perry, 109, 116-117, 137

Doddridge, Mrs. Perry, 263
Don Patricio Causeway, 205, 207, 214, 236
Donelson, Andrew, 13
Donigan, V. M., 153
Donnelly, George K., 17, 21
Doolittle, James H., 209, 256
Doran, Father Paulinus, 169
Doubleday, Abner, 16-17
Dougherty, Robert, 137
Doughty, James M., 121
Doyle, James, 32
Doyle's Watering Hole, 32
Dragon Grill, 234
Driscoll, Texas, 157
Driscoll Children's Hospital, 140-242
Driscoll, Clara, 105, 204, 224, 231, 241-242, 294
Driscoll Foundation, 241-242
Driscoll, Jeremiah, 97, 105, 241
Driscoll, Julia (Fox), 241
Driscoll, Robert Sr., 97, 105, 155, 174, 241
Driscoll, Robert Jr., 105, 158, 204, 241
Drought, 119, 142, 143
Dugan, Mrs., 160
Dunn, Clara (Jones), 207
Dunn, Jim, 126
Dunn, John, 91, 126-127
Dunn, John B. (Red John), 26, 34, 91, 95, 110-112, 120, 122, 126-127
Dunn, George, 126
Dunn, Lalla, 207
Dunn, Matt, 91, 217
Dunn, Matthew, 27
Dunn, Mike, 127
Dunn, Patrick F. (Don Patricio), 190, 205-207, 230, 278
Dunn, Thomas and Catherine, 44
Dunne, Geraldine, 243
Durham, George, 154
Durst, James H., 49, 52
Duval County, 26, 107, 120, 220, 241, 269

Edgerley, Oscar M., 107-108
Edroy, Texas, 157
Egeland, Mr. and Mrs. B. M., 192
Edward Furman Elementary, 244
El Caney, 147
El Mar Ranch, 130-131
El Paso, Texas, 29
Elliff, Josiah (Si), 105
Elliff Ranch, 155

356

Emmert, August, 266
Emmert, Mrs. Pauline, 190
Encinal Peninsula, 224
Epworth League, 152
Epworth Revival, 152, 183, 251
Escovar, Padre Joseph, 3
Essex Mining Company, 30
Estany, Rev. Ubald, 261
Evans, Annabelle, 218
Evans, George F., 123
Exposition Hall, 240, 298

Fairview School, 245
Falcon, Blas, 36
Falcon, Blas Maria, 306
Falcon, Blas Maria de la Garza, 40
Falcon, Cesario, 54
Fandango Ordinance, 34
Farenthold, Randy, 271
Farley, Barney, 217
Farley, C. C., 135
Federal Building, 164, 219, 269
Fehr Baking Company, 209
Fehrenbach, T. R., 110, 115
Fifth Engineers, 167
Filisola, Vicente, 5, 23
First Baptist Church, 265
First Methodist Church, 263
First Presbyterian Church, 264-265, 290
First United Methodist Church, 264
Fitch, W. A., 153
Fitzsimmons, "Blacksmith" Bob, 146, 250-251
Fitzsimmons, Joseph, 56-57, 89-90
Fitzsimmons, Tobe, 147
Flat Iron Murder, 217-218
Flato, Edwin, 212, 214
Flintoff, Thomas, 80
Flores, Juan, 114
Flour Bluff, 7, 48, 55, 57, 121, 123, 145, 155, 206, 224-225, 236-237, 258, 267, 272
Flu Epidemic, 1918, 168-169
Fogg, John, 92, 123
Ford, John S. (Rip), 32-33, 35, 70, 71
Fort Brown, 36
Fort Duncan, 36
Fort Esperanza, 64, 66
Fort Inge, 29, 45
Fort Jesup, 13-14
Fort Lipantitlan, 5-6, 9

Fort Marcy, 16-17
Fort Merrill, 33, 37
Fort Semmes, 62-63, 66-67
Fort St. Louis, 3
Fort Sumter, 50
Fort Worth, 98
Fortress Monroe, Va., 107
Fourth Field Artillery, 167
Fourth Ward School, 243
Fox, John David, 260-261
Fox, Monroe, 198
Foy Moody High School, 245, 272
Frank & Weil, 108
Frank, George, 49, 125
Franks, Fred, 125-126
Frantz, Joe B., 261
Freedman's School, 91
Freeman, W. G., 46
Fremantle, James Arthur Lyon, 53
Frio River, 29, 272, 274
Fuller, Esther, 193-194
Fuller, Sam, 266
Fuller, Theodore (Ted), 191-194
Funston, Frederick, 167

Gallagher Ranch, 217
Gallagher, Richard, 124
Galveston, Texas, 30, 32, 43, 51, 60, 90, 99, 194, 200-202
Galveston Coast Guards, 8
Galveston Island, 2-3
Galveston Ranch, 155
Galveston Weekly News, 28
Galvez, Bernardo de, 98
Gambel, D. R., 85
Gamble, John, 176
Garcia, Alejandro, 2
Garcia, Dr. Hector P., 261-263, 273, 299
Garcia, Jesus, 110
Garcia, Juan Saenz, 49
Garcia, Mathias, 104
Garcia, Noe, 268
Garcitas Creek, 3
Garner, James Marion, 127-128
Garner, Jim, 92
Garner, John Nance, 159, 164, 201, 203, 216, 224, 294
Garza, Adelaida, 208
Garza, Alberto (Segundo), 120
Garza, Ben, 207-208, 215, 281

Garza, Reynaldo, 247
Gatschet, Albert S., 2
George Evans Elementary, 233, 244
Gerhardt, Minnie, 218
Germany, 34, 60
Giles, Dr. H. R., 218-219
Gilpin, Henry A., 1, 54, 108, 125, 174
Giraudon, Rev. James, 263
Givens, Royal, 143-144
Glasscock, C. G. (Gus), 247
Gleason, George, 10
Goliad, Texas, 3, 11, 32, 52, 69, 90, 114, 136
Gonnard, Father John, 71, 94, 136-137, 264
Gonzales, Texas, 91
Gonzales, Cleofas Leal, 268
Gonzales Inquirer, 42
Gonzalez, M. C., 207
Goodwin, Jim, 213
Gotcher, Richard, 268
Gourley, James Jr., 7
Graham, Lt., 18
Graham, P. A., 195-196
Grande, Francisco, 243
Grandstaff, Delbert, 259
Graning, Mrs. Loraine (Lambert), 260
Graning, Melvin B., 260
Grant, James (Daddy), 91
Grant, Julia (Dent), 153
Grant, Kathy (Kathryn Grandstaff), 259
Grant, Ulysses S., 16, 18-19, 23-24, 76, 97, 200
Grant, William, 134
Gravis, Charles and Frank, 71
Gravis, John A. F., 17
Gray, Mabry B. (Mustang), 26
Great Chihuahua Train, 28-29
Great Depression, 208-215, 236
Great Exhibition, London, 34, 36
Great Western, the (Sarah Bourjett), 22
Green Flag, 214-215
Green Hill (Padre Island), 190, 206
Greer, John, 134
Grice, Capt., 14
Griffin, W. H., 154
Grigg's Pig Stand, 214
Grim Ranch, 155
Grimm, Heinz Joachim, 232
Grissom, Virgil, 259
Grumbles, Capt. John, 32

Guffey, James M., 160
Gulliver, Louis J., 212
Gum Hollow, 32
Gussett, Norwick, 27, 97, 108-109, 116, 146, 176, 195

Hall, Bob, 192
Hall, John, 122, 250
Hall, John (tinner), 124
Hall, Lee, 154
Hall, Robert (Robby), 147
Hall, William, 121
Halliburton Portland Cement, 261
Hall's Bayou, 75, 122-123, 247, 250, 252, 308
Hall's Packery, 250
Ham, Rev. Mordecai, 162-163
Hamer, Frank, 198
Hamilton, Andrew Jackson, 97
Hamlin's Wizard Oil, 101
Hanna, William N., 137
Harbor Bridge, 249-250, 255, 259, 297
Harbor Island, 201, 216, 307
Hardin, John Wesley, 216
Harding, President Warren G., 202
Harney, Gen. William S., 46, 145
Hart, Elizabeth, 44
Hart, Gertrude, 20
Harte, Edward H., 242, 263
Harvey, H. V., 211
Hastings, John, 236
Hatch, George, 111
Hatch, James, 52
Hayne, Rev. John, 263
Hays, Capt. John Coffee, 19
Head, Annie Blake Morgan, 272
Head, Hayden W. Sr., 272
Headen, William, 46, 107-109, 137
Heaney, Dr. Alfred G., 158, 197, 251, 265
Heaney, Harry, 265
Heap O' Cream, 214
Heath & Son, 101
Heath, Cheston C., 243
Heath, Cheston L., 243
Heinly, Earl, 196
Heinly, Vinton Sweet, 196
Helena, Texas, 70
Helscher, W. P., 192
Henderson, Gov. J. Pinckney, 25
Henry, Julius, 54, 264

Henry, Capt. W. S., 16, 18-20, 22-23, 274
Herdic, Peter, 195
Hewett, Daniel, 196
Hickey, Thomas, 187
Hickok, "Wild Bill," 216
Hidalgo County, 26
Hidalgo Seminary, 71, 136
Higgins, Lt., 18
Hight, George, 235
Hill, Maj. Charles, 66
Hillcrest subdivision, 219
Hinojosa, Martin, 54
Hirsch, David, 109, 145, 266
Hirsch, Joseph, 153
Hitchcock, Ethan Allen, 14-16, 18
Hobby, Alfred M., 54-55
Hoffman, Prokop, 136, 144
Hoffman, Willie, 136
Hogg, Gov. Jim, 216
Holbein, John, 43-44
Holbein, Reuben, 44
Holmes County Mining Company, 30
Holmes, Neptune, 104
Homeseeker Era, 154-157, 184
Hood's Brigade, 105
Hopkins County, 52
Hopson, C. R., 121
Horace Caldwell Pier, 298
Houston, President Sam, 8-11
Houston Telegraph & Texas Register, 9, 25, 27-28
Howard Association, 94
Howard, D. S., 115
Howell, Joe, 125
Hughes, Mrs. Michael Sr., family, 266
Humble Oil Refinery, 230, 239
Humphrey, Vice President Hubert, 263
Hunter, James M., 126
Hunter, John Warren, 51-52
Hurricane, 1874, 123-124
Hurricane, 1875, 124
Hurricane, 1916, 165, 187, 202
Hurricane, 1919, 189-194, 197, 200-203, 220-221, 244, 251, 269, 275-276, 296
Hurricane, 1933, 213-214
Hurricane, 1961 (Carla), 257, 261, 266, 298
Hurricane, 1967 (Beulah), 261
Hurricane, 1970 (Celia), 266-269, 271, 301
Hurricane, 1980 (Allen), 272
Hurricane, 2005 (Rita), 273

Hutchinson, Judge A., 7

Ice, 134, 268
Incarnate Word Academy, 296
Incarnate Word Convent, 136
Indian Point, 111, 113, 150, 250
Indianola, Texas, 90-93, 99, 115, 124-125, 132, 200-201
Ingle, Odell, 258
Ingleside, Texas, 218, 229-230, 239, 272, 307
Intracoastal Canal, 213
Ireland, 34
Ireland, Capt. John, 57-58
Ixtoc I oil spill, 271

Jackson, Stonewall, 61
Jaillet, Rev. Claude, 94, 113, 262
James, J. T. (Jim), 121, 216
Jenson, E. R., 154
JFK Causeway (originally Padre Island Causeway), 236-237, 260-261, 272
Jim Hogg County, 26, 220
Jim Wells County, 26, 199, 220, 305
Joe, an American named, 112-113
Johnson, Chandler, 94
Johnson, Dan, 94
Johnson, Lady Bird, 300
Johnson, Lyndon B., 224, 257, 261-263, 300
Jones, Dr. Levi, 9
Jones, Mayor Luther, 273
Jones, Simon, 50
Jones, W. W., mansion, 240
Jordan, Richard, 100
Jordan, S. W., 6
Juan Saenz community, 49, 125, 127

Kansas trail drives, 97-100, 105, 109, 154, 205, 303
Karankawa Indians, 2-5, 10, 236
Katherine, Texas (Armstrong), 153
Kat's Meow bar, 218
Kearney, Dr. Thomas, 93-94, 96
Kelly, Dennis, 71
Kelly, Martin, 71, 95
Kelsey, Amanda (Brooks), 135
Kelsey, John Peter, 6, 21, 135
Kelsey Memorial Methodist Church, 266
Kenedy County, 26
Kenedy, John G., 104, 153, 158, 186, 197, 264
Kenedy, Mifflin, 39, 41, 53, 77, 89, 97, 100, 103-104, 121, 123, 139-141, 148, 175, 204, 206, 236, 306

Kenedy Rifles (Spanish-American War), 146-148
Kennedy, President John F., 258-259, 263
Kennedy, Vann, 246
Kennedy, William, 7
Key Allegro, 121-122
KEYS, 229
Kibbe Wild West Show, 214
Kieberger, Mr. and Mrs. W. A., 190
KIII, 246
King, Ellroy, 258
King, Henrietta (Chamberlain), 40-41, 141, 160, 174, 204, 265
King, John, 206
King Ranch, 40, 81, 103, 106-107, 137, 160, 167, 174, 202, 209, 213
King, Richard, 35-36, 39-43, 45, 52-53, 81, 89, 97, 100, 103-104, 106-107, 111, 116,
        121, 123, 134, 137, 139-142, 174-175, 206, 236, 264, 306
King, Richard III, 214, 240
King, Robert E. Lee, 142
Kingsville, Texas, 186, 194,
Kingsville Naval Air Station, 225-226, 232
Kinney, Henry Lawrence, 5-17, 25-28, 33-36, 41-44, 46-47, 53-54, 67, 73, 77, 82, 108,
        115, 121, 136, 166, 174, 200, 250, 263
Kinney house, 30
Kinney, Mary B. (Herbert), 47
Kinney's ranches, 43
Kinney's Rancho, 1, 6-8, 54, 73, 200, 303
Kinney Rangers, 30
Kirk, Wanda and Kira, 271
Kittredge, Lt. J. W., 54-57, 84
KGFI, 209
Kleberg County, 26, 199, 220, 260, 306
Kleberg, Rep. Richard M., 224
Kleberg, Robert J. Jr., 202, 213
Kline, Pat, 246
Knight, George, 100
Knight, Juliet (Wenger), 212, 233
Knights of America, 207
Knox, Mrs. D. O., 237
Knox, Frank, 225
Koch, Augustus, 142, 178
Koch, Theodore, 157
Kokernut, H.L., 204
Kostoryz School District, 245
Kostoryz, Stanley, 155
KRIS, 229, 246
Krueger, Paul Eric, 260-261
KSIX, 246
Kurz, Eugene, 232
Kuykendall, J. H., 3-4

KVDO, 245-246
KZTV, 246

L-Head, 220
Lacey, Tom, 133
Lacy, W. B., 137
Ladies Pavilion, 54, 152-153, 165
Laffite, Jean, 3
Lagarto, Texas, 120
La Fruta Dam, 211, 214, 240, 283
Lafferty, Henderson, 264
La Gloria Ranch, 241
Laguna Madre, 7, 59, 62, 124, 149, 151, 205-206, 230, 260
Laguna Madre monster, 47-48
Lake Corpus Christi, 211
Lake Lovenskiold, 211, 283
Lake Texana, 273
Lake Trinidad, 37
Lamar, Texas, 64
Lamar, President Mirabeau B., 6-8, 17
Lane, Lydia Spencer, 36-37, 45
La Parra, 8, 111, 129
La Quinta, 159-160, 165
Laredo, Texas, 14, 25-26, 31, 103, 106, 114, 136, 140-141, 198
La Retama Library, 240
La Salle, Sieur de (Robert Cavalier), 3
Laureles Ranch, 124, 141
League of United Latin-American Citizens (LULAC), 207-208, 215, 281
Lee, Ben, 218
Lee, Newton, 237
Lee, Robert E., 24, 40, 53, 71, 105, 142
Leona River, 29
Lerick, Billy and family, 191, 193
Lewis, Gideon K. (Legs), 40-43, 46, 77
Lexington Museum on the Bay, 272-273
Lichtenstein, Albert, 240, 249
Lichtenstein's Department Store, 226-227
Limerick, Pat, 215-216
Lincoln, President Abraham, 50-53, 61-62, 71
Linn, John J., 1
Linnville, Texas, 1
Lipan Apache Indians, 2, 10, 17, 32
"Little Mexico," 36
Little, Noel Douglas, 260-261
Littles, Hattie, 138
Live Oak County, 26, 121
Live Oak Peninsula, 5
Live Oak Point, 14, 67

Lone Star Fair, 35-43, 77, 80, 203
Lone Star Hook & Ladder Company, 102
Longoria, Felix, 262
Longstreet, James, 20, 24
Looper, Gene, 246
Los Machos Ranch, 241
Los Patricios, 71
Lott, Uriah, 109, 116-117, 123, 139-140, 142, 154, 156, 175, 181, 260
Lovenskiold, Anita, 168
Lovenskiold, Charles, 54, 71-72, 89, 135-136
Lovenskiold, Perry G., 137, 168, 198, 211
Lowman, George, 227
Loyd's Pavilion & Pleasure Pier, 165, 189, 244
Luby, James O., 143
Luby, Jason, 271
Luckett, Col. P. N., 72
Luther, Mr. and Mrs. Max, 190
Lyman, Charles, 268

McAllister, Paul, 199
McBride, Peter, 158
McCabe, Bridget, 138
McCall, George A., 24
McCampbell, John, 110
McCarty, Dan, 134
McCaughan, A.C., 219-220, 226-227
McClane, John, 90, 107, 113, 126-127, 129
McClintock, William, 25
McCracken, Bob, 232
McDonald, Ben, 256, 300
McDonald, Judge Henry, 159
McDonald, Judge Henry, home, 251
McGloin, Ameta, 219
McGloin, Gilbert, 218-219
McGloin, Margaret, 212
McGloin's Bluff, 18, 307
McGovern, George, 263
McGregor, "Doc," 215, 217, 229
McLeod, Gen. Hugh, 43
McMahon, Margaret, 70
McManigle, Pat, 127
McMurray, Rufus, 199
McNelly, Capt. Leander, 129-130, 154
Magnolia Mansion, 104
Magruder, John B., 21
Maher, Peter, 146
Maldonado, M. P., 258
Maltby's Circus, 35

Maltby, Henry, 51, 64, 67, 72, 83
Maltby, Gen. Jasper, 63
Maltby, Mary Grace (Swift), 94
Maltby, William, 63, 67, 72, 87, 94
Manhattan Café, 214
Mann, Lt. Walter, 63
Mann, William, 21, 28-29, 33, 57
Mann's red house, 124
Manon Rice Funeral Home, 262
Manucy, Bishop Dominic, 264
Marcy, William, 13
Market Hall, 100-102, 111, 148-149, 152, 173, 243
Marriott, Neal, 235
Marsh, Jane, 136-137, 219
Mary Carroll High School, 245
Masland, Sgt. Charles, 22
Matagorda Bay, 1-3, 50, 200-201
Matamoros, Tamaulipas, 7, 14, 25-26, 40, 53-54, 87, 120
Matamoros Road, 22, 51
Mathews, Teddy, 217
Mathis Dam, 211, 283
Mathis, Thomas Henry, 174
Mathisen, Eddie, 267-268
Matthews, Tommy, 233
Maus, Cliff, 254-256
Maverick, Bob, 256
Maximilian, Emperor, 61
Maxwell P. Dunne Funeral Home, 191, 217-218
Mayors of Corpus Christi, 312
Mazatlan Rangers, 30-31
Meade, George G., 17, 24
Means, Col. William, 112
Meansville, Texas, 112
Meehan, Dermot M., 167
Memorial Coliseum, 240, 257, 273
Mendiola, Juan, 40
Menger House, 141
Menger, Moses, 139
Mercer diaries, 131-134
Mercer, Agnes, 131
Mercer, Edward (Ned), 131, 133, 190
Mercer, Emma (Scott), 131
Mercer, Emma (Thompson), 131
Mercer house, 180
Mercer, John, 131, 133
Mercer, Robert A., 54, 130-131
Merriman, Eli, 71, 136, 160, 164, 191, 203
Merriman, Dr. E. T., 71-72, 93, 170

366

Metropolitan Café, 207-208
Meuly, Conrad, 56-57, 63
Meuly, Margaret, 90, 92
Mexican Central School, 243
Mexican Methodist Church, 266
Mexican National Railway (Tex-Mex), 139-140, 142, 154-155, 260
Mexico, 1, 5-10, 13, 21, 25, 27, 29, 49, 61, 75
Mexico City, 5, 21
Michler, Lt. Nathaniel, 29
Mier y Teran, Manuel de, 1-5, 39
Miller, Bessie, 198-199, 217
Miller, Jim, 119
Miller, Maude, 158
Miller, Roy, 162-163, 165, 167-168, 201-203, 211
Miller, Samuel R., 33
Miller, Mrs. S. G., 133
Miller's Hotel, 39
Minutemen (posse riders), 112-115, 129
Miramar Hotel, 145, 153, 250-251
Missouri-Pacific Railroad, 260
Mitchell, John B., 90, 143
Mitchell, William, 265
Moffett, B. G., 235
Montgomery, W. W., 96
Montero, Cayetano, 9
Monterrey, Nuevo Leon, 6
Moore, John M., 57, 115
Moore, Malvina (Britton), 55
Morfi, Padre Juan Agustin, 4
Morgan, Charles, 117
Morgan, Rand, 271
Morrell, Rev. Z. N., 2
Mosser, John, 251
Morris, Augustus T., 116
Morris & Cummings Cut, 115, 177, 200, 307
Morris, Frank, 237
Morris, W. E., 213
Morro Castle, 147
Morton, John, 111-112
Morton, Michael, 112
Moses, J. Williamson, 17, 28, 33, 72
Mosquito Coast filibuster, 46-47
Mounted Coast Guard, 54
Mote, Pvt. Henry, 56
Moya family, 114
Municipal Wharf, 286
Murdock, William, 71, 111
Murphy, John B., 95, 124, 161

Mussett, "Wash," 127
Mustang Island, 16, 43, 54, 58-59, 62, 65, 90, 121, 123-124, 130-132, 144, 179, 216, 236, 242
Mustang Island State Park, 242, 295
Mustang Point, 90
Myers & Noyes, 221

Natatorium, The, 165
Natchez, Miss., 98
Natchitoches, La., 13
National Youth Administration, 231-232
Naval Air Station, 224-233, 236, 245, 247, 257, 259, 262, 272, 288-289, 294
Naval Station Ingleside, 272-273
Neal, Benjamin F., 34, 51, 63, 67-68, 87
Neff, Pat, 203
New Braunfels, 70
New Orleans, 14, 20, 61, 98-100, 103, 122
New Orleans Daily Picayune, 14-15, 19
New Orleans Delta, 27
New York Herald, 84
Newcomb, W. W. Jr., 2, 4
Niles National Register, 23
Nimitz, Adm. Chester W., 236
Nixon Building, 203-204, 215, 278
Nixon, Maston, 200, 203-204, 214, 224, 240, 278
Noakes Brothers, 158
Noakes, Maria (Ludwig), 127
Noakes, Thomas, 66, 68-69, 88, 126-129
Noessels, 57
Noessel, Felix, 92
Nolan, Mat, 33, 52, 66, 70-71, 86
Nolan, Tom, 70, 86
Nolls, Henry, 134
Norris, 44
North Beach (Rincon, Brooklyn), 10, 15, 75, 101, 121-123, 145-146, 150, 152, 160, 167-168, 183, 190-194, 209, 214-215, 218, 225, 249, 256-257, 267, 272, 282, 308-309
North Beach Amusement Park, 252
North Beach Bath House, 251
North Beach Pleasure Park, 251
Northside Junior High, 244
Noyes, Edward, 221
Nueces Bay, 11, 32, 149-150, 193-194, 203, 206, 210, 221, 261
Nueces Bay Causeway, 11, 165, 195, 214, 252, 260, 276
Nueces Coffee Company, 279
Nueces County, 11, 25-26, 89-90, 108, 120-121, 156, 166, 199, 213, 220, 250, 6
Nueces County Commissioners, 11, 64, 89-90, 161, 261, 306
Nueces County Courthouse, 2, 50, 113, 165-166, 191, 194, 260, 271

Nueces County Navigation District, 203, 261
Nueces Hotel, 151, 161, 165, 189, 190-191, 193-194, 207, 214, 225, 290
Nueces River, 5-6, 13, 15, 17-18, 20, 26, 29, 33, 52, 64, 71, 110, 119, 125-126, 135, 143-144, 151, 166, 194, 210, 233, 260
Nueces Strip, 6, 98, 104, 129, 154, 302
Nuecestown, Texas, 31, 43, 55, 66, 82, 110, 126-128, 137, 149
Nuecestown Raid (also known as Noakes Raid), 49, 88, 113, 125-129
Nueces Valley, newspaper, 31, 41, 49, 98, 101, 110, 120, 124
Nueces Valley Land & Emigration, 43, 82
Nueces Valley, region, 103-104, 106-107, 238
Nuevo Leon, 27

Oak Park, 219
Obreros Hall, 207
Odem State Bank, 213
O'Daniel, W. Lee, 214
O. Henry (William Sydney Porter), 103
Ohler, Edward, 30, 47, 50, 56-57
Ohler, Matilda, 47, 50, 59
Ohler's Wharf, 44, 54
"Old Sam," 160
Oliphant, Jessie, 211
Oliver, E. R., 158
Olmos Creek, 23
Olympia Confectionary, 227
Orange Grove, 29, 107, 157
O'Reilly, Rev. Bernard, 264
Ornsby, James, 8
Ortiz, Rep. Solomon P. Sr., 271
Oso, 125, 129
Our Lady of Guadalupe (Holy Cross), 266
Our Lady of Pilar, 104
Our Lady Star of the Sea, 264
Overhaul & Repair Department, 247, 257-258, 262, 273
Owl's Mott, 206

Packery Channel, 123, 206-207, 236, 280
Packing houses, 121-123
Padre Island, 3, 6, 22, 93, 121-124, 190, 197, 205, 214, 230, 233, 236-237, 257, 271, 273, 300
Padre Island Causeway (renamed JFK Causeway), 236-237, 249, 252, 257
Padre Island National Seashore, 257, 259, 261, 300
Page, Joseph W., 145
Page, S. H., 125
Palo Alto, battle, 22
Palo Alto (near the border), 129
Palo Alto Ranch, 57, 104, 241
Pangburn, Clyde (Upside-Down), 256

Parker, Edith, 228
Parr Drug Store, 216
Parr, George, 271
Parrilla, Diego Ortiz, 6
Pass Cavallo, 66-67
Patman, Bill, 272
Paul, George H., 155-157, 184-185
Paxton's Crystal Palace, 34
Pea Ridge, Ark., 65
Pease, Clark, 197
Pelegrino, Matt, 191
Pena, Col. Enrique de la, 1
Pena, Julia, 243
Peñascal , 111-113
Pendleton, Susanna, 124
Pennsylvania, 34
Peoples, John H., 30-31
Peoples Light Company, 196-197
Peoples Street T-Head, 54
Perez, Genoveva, 53
Perfecto de Cos, Martin, 10
Perkins Brothers, 204, 212
Perote Castle, Mexico, 41
Peters, Josh, 153-154
Peters, Maj. Stephen, 50
Petronila, Texas, 105, 110
Petzel, Mrs. John Ernest, 56
Pfeuffer, George, 50, 54
Phillips, Edith, 227
Pierce, Abel Head (Shanghai), 100, 103-104
Pinetas Creek, 29
Pioneer Fire Company, 101, 126
Pita Island, 206
Pitts Livery, 158
Plato, Nelson, 123
Plaza Hotel (later the White Plaza), 204, 214, 226, 229, 290
Pleasure Pier, 199, 277
Plomarity, George, 214
Plummer, Capt. S. M., 33
Poenisch, Ernest, 205
Poenisch, Herman, 159
Point Isabel, 26, 236
Polk, Milas, 90
Polley, Hub, 205
Port Aransas, 63, 130-131, 149, 165, 190, 195, 201-202, 216, 229, 257, 267, 271, 298
Port Aransas Causeway, 257
Port Aransas Ferry, 261
Portland, Texas, 150, 192, 230

Port Lavaca, Texas, 257, 266
Port of Corpus Christi, 200-203, 223-224, 226, 230, 238, 244, 247-248, 261, 272, 277
Post Aransas, 65
Potter, Alexander, 162, 210
POW camp, 232-233, 236
Power, James, 5, 14
Premont, Texas, 157
Presidio del Norte, 29, 31
Prewett, V. William, 219
Priour farm, 60
Priour, Julian, 53
Priour, Rosalie Bridget (Hart), 52, 55, 71, 91, 136
Prohibition, 162-164, 197
Prosperity Days, 208
Public Grain Elevator, 272
Purl, D. S., 217

Quinn, Pat, 120
Quintanilla-Perez, Selena, 273

Rabb, Dock and Frank, 104
Rabb, John, 97, 104, 174
Rabb, Lee, 104-105
Rabb, Matha (Regan), 104-105, 127, 139, 153, 174, 204, 264, 306
Rachal, Darius C., 97, 105, 206, 252, 305
Rachal, E. R. (Nute), 105
Rachal Ranch, 194
Rachel, Ohler slave, 50
Rambo, Raymond, 235
Ramirez, Manuel Elizondo, 40
Ramsay, Benjamin, 162-163
Ramsay, Jeanne, 246
Ranahan, James, 44
Ranahan, James Jr., 55
Ranchero, The, 50-51, 64, 68, 83
Rancho Grande, 103
Rancho Seco, 125
Rangers, 10, 19, 28, 32-33, 42, 120, 129-130, 198, 205, 263
Rankin, James Agnes, 44
Rankin, W. S., 57, 92, 101
Ransom, Gen. T. E. G., 62-63, 65
Rationing, 230-231
Rawalt, Louis, 197
Ray High School, 245, 297
Ray, W. B., 245
Rea, Judge W. L., 120
Reagan, Ronald, 272
Reconstruction, 109-115

Red River, 98
Redmond, Dr. Henry, house, 204
Reed, R. K., 250
Reef road, 11, 20, 111, 250, 263
Refugio, Texas, 8, 11, 90, 113, 114
Reid, Mr. and Mrs. Percy, 190, 192
Republic of the Rio Grande, 5-6
Resaca de la Palma, 22
Reveille, The, 41
Reynolds, Alfred, 58
Reynolds, George, 106-107, 125, 128
Reynolds Metals, 239, 267
Rhodes, Mary, 273
Richard King High School, 245
Riddle, Capt. J. C., 115
Riggan Hotel, 209
Riggs, John, 90
Rincon Basin, 259
Rincon de la Boveda, 40
Rincon de Grulla (Flour Bluff), 57
Rincon del Oso, 10
Rincon (North Beach), 250
Rincon Point, 250
Ring, F. E., 251
Ring Villa Tourist Courts, 251
Rio Grande, 6, 13-14, 22-23, 26, 31-32, 49, 53, 81, 105, 109-111, 114, 120, 130, 135
Rio Grande City, Texas, 26, 125, 135
Ritter, F. R. (Robert), 90
Ritter Pier, 115
Rivera, T. P., 197
Riviera, Texas, 157
Riviera Beach, Texas, 157, 165
Robert Driscoll Hotel, 204, 224, 226, 230-231, 234, 241, 290, 294
Robert Driscoll Junior High, 228, 245
Roberts, Alfred, 217
Roberts, Fred, 198, 217
Roberts, W. R., 258
Robertson, Dr. George, 93
Robertson, Sam, 205, 207, 236
Robinson, Frank G., 198
Robinson, Randolph, 160
Robstown, Texas, 139, 184, 199, 203
Rockport, Texas, 32, 115, 121-123, 194-195, 202, 208, 267
Rodd Field, 225-226, 232
Rodd Field Tracking Station, 258-260
Rodriguez, Chipita, 63, 67-68
Rogers, Rev. C. M., 105, 262
Rogers, Will, 209

Rogers, William Long (Billy), 100, 102, 216
Roll-A-Coaster, 252
Roosevelt, Elliott, 216
Roosevelt, President Franklin D., 213, 216-217, 223-225, 228, 231, 233, 247, 272
Ropes, Elihu Harrison, 144-146, 151-152, 182, 250
Ropes Pass, 144
Ropesville (Port Aransas), 130
Ross, Reuben, 6
Rough Riders, 147
Rowe, Rev. Aaron, 266
Roy Miller High School, 244
Roy Murray Ford, 209
Rudd, W. L., 154
Russell, Gen. Charles S., 90
Russell, Judge R.C. home, 72, 90
Ryder, George, 199

Sabine Pass, 61-62, 66
St. Boniface (Cyril and Methodius), 264
St. James Hotel, 121, 195, 216, 227
St. John, Charlie, 246
St. John Baptist Church, 265
St. John Free Mission Baptist Church, 264
St. Joseph's Island (San Jose), 14-16, 27, 54, 64, 130-132, 179, 190, 201
St. Louis, Brownsville & Mexico Railroad (Brownie), 142, 152-155
St. Mary's, Texas, 32, 113
St. Mary's Cathedral, 32
St. Patrick's, 262
St. Paul, Texas, 157, 185
St. Paul United Methodist Church, 266
Salado Creek, 9
Saldivar, Yolanda, 273
Salem, Joe, 258
Salinas, Leonal, 268
Salt Lagoon (Baffin Bay), 59, 69
Salt Lake, 60, 243
Saltillo, Coahuila, 129
Saltwater Pool, 251-252
Saluria, Texas, 64
San Antonio, Texas, 8, 19, 26, 46-47, 103, 107, 124, 140, 143, 146
San Antonio & Aransas Pass Railroad (SAAP), 142, 148, 152, 154, 157, 165
San Antonio, Uvalde & Gulf Railroad, 142
San Antonio Herald, 42
San Diego, Calif., 31
San Diego, Texas, 94, 113, 120, 137, 140-143
San Fernando Creek, 107
San Jacinto, 5
San Patricio, Texas, 2, 5-6, 8, 11, 18, 20, 26, 28, 34, 52, 68, 121, 137, 199

San Rosario (Mission Rosario), 3
Sandia, Texas, 29
Sandoval, Chipito, 18
Sandoval, Jesus, 129-130
Santa Anna, Antonio Lopez, 41, 300
Santa Cruz Ranch (Padre Island), 206
Santa Gertrudis, 137
Santa Gertrudis Creek, 22, 36, 40, 46, 106-107
Santa Gertrudis grant, 104
Santa Margarita, Texas, 5, 26, 52, 64-65, 71, 89, 166
Santa Rita, 26
Savage, Mrs. R. R., 128
Savage, Alice Borden, 245
Savage homestead, 204
Saxet Field, 209, 282
Scarritt, Jeremiah, 20
Scheur, Emanuel, 92
Scheid, Father John, 169
Schwein, Anna (Moore), 93, 96
"Scotch," 192
Scott, Capt. Henry, 114
Scott, James F., 120, 153
Scott, Gen. Winfield, 21, 37
Scott, V. A., 134
Scull, George H., 35
Seaside Hotel, 136, 153, 155
Seaside Pavilion Hotel, 165, 187
Seawall, 219-221, 225-226, 286-287
Second Texas Infantry, 167
Seguin, Texas, 70
Seguira, Jesus, 127
Self, Roy, 235
Sena, Juan, 125
Sessions, Rev. T. F., 264
Sharpsburg, Texas, 125, 127
Shaw, Rose (Dunne), 213, 243
Shellbank Island, 200
Shely, Sheriff William, 218
Shepard, Alan B. Jr., 259
Sheridan, Phil, 36, 90
Sherrill, Warren Joseph, 229
Shoemaker, Libby, 59
Shoop's Grill, 226
Sidbury, E. D., 100
Sidbury, Mrs. E. D., 125, 128
Sidbury Wharf, 142
Sierra Madre Expedition, 27-28
Silva, Francisco, 10

Simpson, C. R., 161
Simpson, Robert, 269
Sinclair, Fred, 217
Singer, John, 206
Singer Ranch, 65
Sinton, Texas, 194
Sinton State Bank, 213
Sisters of the Incarnate Word, 192
Six Points, 215-216
Skinning War, 119-120
Skull, Sally (Sarah Jane Newman), 35, 52, 104
Smith, E. Kirby, 24
Smith, Farrell, 259
Smith, Frank, 134
Smith, John (Lying John), 126-127
Smith, Gen. Persifor, 34, 36, 46
Smith, Sonny, 129
Smithwick, Noah, 3
Snyder, J. S., 92-93
Sociedad Beneficencia, 207
Sociedad Ignacio Allende, 207
Sociedad Ignacio Zaragoza, 207
Sodville, Texas, 157
Soldiers Seashore Club, 169
Sonora, Mexico, 30-31
Sons of America, Order of, 207-208
South Texas Exposition, 214, 279
Southern Academy of Aeronautics, 256
Southern Air Transport, 256
Southern Alkali, 214, 239
Southern Minerals Building, 204
Sowell, A. J., 26
Specht, Franz, 111
Spindletop, 160
Spohn, Dr. Arthur, 158, 251
Spohn Hospital, 167
Spohn Sanitarium, 153, 192, 251
Spoonts, Lorine (Jones), 205
Staples, Wayman N., 90, 116, 206
Starr County, 26
State National Bank, 191
State Police, 97
Stayton, J. W., 197
Steinbach, Alfred, 217
Stevenson, Adlai, 263
Stillman, Charles, 30, 39
Stone, D. A., 156
Stutz, Alma, 101

Sullivan, butcher, 110
Sullivan, Eliza Ann, 97
Suntide Refinery, 239
Sutherland, Hugh R., 198, 201
Sutherland, John, 7
Sutherland, Mary, 2, 96, 108, 264
Sutherland, W. G., 138
Sutton, Capt. J. S., 28
Swank, George, 127
Swantner, Tom, 258
Swift, Thad, 113-114

T-Heads, 220
Taft, Charles, 159-160, 186
Taft Ranch, 159, 165, 186
Taft, William Howard, 159-160, 186-187, 251
Talley, George, 153-154
Tapia, Hypolita, 112-113
Tarpon (Port Aransas), 130, 149
Tarrant, Eleanor, 249
Taylor, Albert, 101
Taylor, Hannah, 219
Taylor, Horace, 137
Taylor, Ned, 69
Taylor, Gen. Zachary, 13-25, 39, 49, 62, 73-74, 151, 167, 205, 210, 250, 263, 274, 304
Telfener, Giuseppe, 142
Temple Beth El, 264
Templeton, Fay, 101
Terrell, Roy, 138, 143, 158-159, 168
Terrell, Stewart Blackburn, 159-160, 186
Texas Air Company, 256
Texas Café, 214
Texas Land & Cattle Company, 155
Texas Military Board, 54
Texas State Aquarium, 272
Texas State Gazette, 42
Thais, Sister M. (Lea Desroache), 192
Third Texas Infantry, 167
Thomas, George H., 24
Thompson, Ben, 216
Thompson, (Little Bob), 49
Thompson, Maj. William G., 65-66
Three-Mile Point, 145, 182
Tilgner, Herman, 11-112
Timon, Walter, 146, 163, 220
Tinney, Bill, 57
Tinney, Sam, 147
Tonkawa Indians, 3-4

Tower, Sen. John, 272
Trails to Kansas, 97-100, 105, 109, 254, 154, 205, 305
Treaty of Guadalupe Hidalgo, 27-29
Tres Palacios Creek, 103
Trinity River, 99
Tule Lake, 125
Turner, Betty, 270
Turner, Josiah, 20-21
Turtle Cove, 130, 201
Twelve-Mile Motts (Nuecestown), 31
Twenty-Five-Mile Hotel, 231

U-boats, 223, 229-230, 291
Uehlinger, John, 101
Uehlinger, Marion, 198
Union Theater, 21, 32, 263
Uribe, Praxides, 40
Uvalde County, 29

Vaky's Café, 209
Valere, 19
Ventana Ranch, 106, 128
Vetters, Clem, 127
Vicksburg, Miss., 61
Victoria, Texas, 1, 3-4, 7-8, 90, 98, 136, 146
Villa, Pancho, 166
Villarreal, Andreas, 174
Villarreal, Capt. Enrique, 5, 10
Villarreal, Refugio, 174
Viola Turning Basin, 261
Violet, Texas, 157

Waldron Field, 225-226, 232
Walker, William, 47
Wallace, William Alexander Anderson (Bigfoot), 41
Wallace, Warren W., 110
Ward, Hortense Warner, 265
Ward Island, 7, 230
Ware, James A., 52
Warren, Mr. and Mrs., G. E., 198
Washington, Iowa, 155
Washington-on-the-Brazos, Texas, 11
Wasserman, Leslie, 240
Watson, C. O., 219
Watson, O. S., 154, 156
Webb County, 26
Webb, Walter Prescott, 103, 129
Weidenmueller, Charles, 56, 71

Weil, M. Harvey, 202
Welch, Georgia, 219
Welch, Stanley, 137
Welder Ranch, 155, 185
Welder, Thomas, 99
Wells, James B. (Jim), 154, 201
Welton, Mrs. L. M., 142
Wesley Seal Dam, 240
Westbrook, Angie, 162
West Sinton, Texas, 157
Wheeler, Charles, 169
Whelan, Pat, 127
White, Frank and Edward, 105
Whitaker, H. T., 218
White, Jack, 204
White, Lucile, 263
White Point, 105, 160, 194, 206
Whiting, Daniel P., 15, 75
Whitley, W. W., 135
Whitlock, Joe, 94
Wilbarger, J. W., 3
Wild Horse Desert, 8, 40
Willacy County, 26, 220
Willke, Capt. H., 57-58
Wilson, Ada, 242, 295
Wilson, Boyd, 268
Wilson Building, 204, 242, 295
Wilson, Lt. Richard H., 16
Wilson, Robert T., 236
Wilson, Sam, 204, 242, 295
Wilson Tower, 204
Winerich Motors, 209
Wisconsin Bridge & Iron Company, 247
Woessner, John, 108
Woessner, Mary, 51
Wolf, Rabbi Sidney, 266
Woll, Gen. Adrian, 9
Woman's Monday Club, 152
Wonder Bar, 214
Wood, John Howland, 18, 32, 103
Wood, Richard, 190
Woodsboro, Texas, 103
Wool Reserve, 224
Works Progress Administration, 215
Wrather, William B., 51
Wright, 1
Wright, Frank Eddie, 211
Wright, Harry, 154

Wright, Mike, 153-154
Wyatt, Joe, 272
Wynn Seale School, 214, 227, 244

Xavier, Sister Mary, 264
Yarrington, Anna Maria (Perlee), 42, 43
Yarrington, Dr. Jacob T., 42-43
Yeargen, Mrs. A. R., 159, 161
Yellow fever, 45, 92-95, 264
Yerby, John, 8
Young, James H., 256
Young, John, 114, 119
Young, Rep. John, 258

Zackies Drive-In, 225
Zapata County, 26
Ziegler's Hotel, 92-93
Ziegler, Jacob, 50

Murphy D. Givens, the retired Viewpoints Editor of the *Corpus Christi Caller-Times,* has written more than 750 columns on Corpus Christi and South Texas history. He edited *"Texas in Other Days"* based on the writings of Texas Ranger and mustanger J. Williamson Moses and he is the author of two photo histories, *"Old Corpus Christi"* and *"Old South Texas".*

Jim Moloney is a businessman with an interest in the history of the Corpus Christi area. He is known for his presentations on local history illustrated by his extensive collection of postcards and other ephemera. He is the co-author of *"1919-The Storm"* with Murphy Givens.

Nueces Press published *"Corpus Christi – A History"* and *"1919-The Storm".* More books on Corpus Christi, South Texas and the Mexican War are in various stages of writing and publication. Please refer to the Nueces Press website, www.nuecespress.com for information on future publications.